"I'm proud to be part of the Baptist World Alliance; one hundred million men and women around the world who never let political values separate us from one another. We see ourselves as brothers and sisters, regardless of our ethnic or racial differences or our political philosophies. We are joined together in a common faith, and I'm proud to be part of it. It's very reassuring to me as I travel around the world doing the work of The Carter Center to have this feeling of comradeship and mutual support in the name of our humble Savior. I commend the Centennial History of the Baptist World Alliance."
   Jimmy Carter, President of the United States, 1977-1981

"Our history demonstrates that Baptist World Alliance unites Baptists – in gratitude for the past, in anticipation for the future – following in the footsteps of our founders to fulfill the Great Commission."
   Billy J. H. Kim, President, Baptist World Alliance, 2000–05;
   Pastor Emeritus, Suwon Baptist Church, Seoul, Korea

"To celebrate the Baptist World Alliance Centennial History is to experience again and again the joy that has filled the hearts of Baptists around the world . . . at the sight of God's personal movement in our history."
   Fausto A. Vasconcelos, Vice President, Baptist World Alliance, 2005–;
   President, Brazilian Baptist Convention; Pastor, First Baptist Church, Rio de Janeiro, Brazil

"As Baptists, we belong to a great family with an exciting history. This new family album is certainly welcome!"
   Knud Wümpelmann, President, Baptist World Alliance, 1990–1995, Denmark

"The worldwide fellowship of Baptists has always been for me personally a source of inspiration and encouragement for which I am grateful."
   Karl Heinz Walter, Associate Secretary for Europe and the Middle East, Baptist World Alliance,
   1989–1998; General Secretary, European Baptist Federation, Germany

"Thank God for the Baptist World Alliance Centennial. In spite of race, language, culture and history, we are together with the mission of taking the Gospel to every corner of the world."
   Raoul Scialabba, Vice President, Baptist World Alliance, 2000–05, Argentina

"The publication of this new volume of the history of Baptist World Alliance reminds us how rich, extensive and important are the contributions of Baptists worldwide to the cause of Christ and how our cooperation strengthens and encourages each of us. We celebrate what God has done through the Baptist World Alliance."
   A. Roy Medley, General Secretary, American Baptist Churches, U.S.A.

"Baptists have linked their arms for a century to lift the world toward freedom, justice, and abundant life. God reached down and turned this human effort into a 'must read' history of how we got here, the work we sought to do, and did begin. . . ."
   Duke K. McCall, President, Baptist World Alliance, 1980–85, U.S.A.

"The Baptist World Alliance has a richly textured history. This book is a gift of glimpses into a meaningful past that encourages us to live into a hopeful future."
   David Emmanuel Goatley, Executive Secretary-Treasurer, Lott Carey Mission Society, U.S.A.

"This book is a wonderful compendium of what the Holy Spirit has done through Baptists in the past hundred years. This is essential reading for anyone who is serious about the Great Commission. While all our opportunities are in the future, all the lessons are in the past, and we cannot afford to ignore those lessons."
    Rick Warren, Pastor, Saddleback Church, Lake Forest, California, U.S.A.;
        ***Author,* The Purpose-Driven Life**

"Australian Baptists have always been grateful to share in the remarkable story of the Baptist World Alliance. Read the Centennial History and take part in its future with the first president's clarion call, "In the name of Christ," "In the power of the Spirit.""
    G. Noel Vose, President, Baptist World Alliance, 1985–90, Australia

"The history of Baptists at the world level is important, not just to Baptists, but to Christians of all traditions who take their ecumenical calling seriously. This volume will contribute immensely to a deeper awareness of the significance and contribution of what is arguably the most widespread and versatile of all Protestant world families."
    Keith Clements, General Secretary, Conference of European Churches, Switzerland

"The history of the Baptist World Alliance has played a unique role in the lives of the African Baptist Community. The ministry of Baptist World Alliance has produced effective Christian leaders in Africa who inspire and instill confidence in the people and lead them to do great things. Surely God is calling the Baptists in Africa to rediscover our identity, dignity, and dynamism. Baptist World Alliance has motivated African Baptists to be a catalyst for change in Africa."
    Frank Adams, General Secretary, All Africa Baptist Fellowship, Fraternité Baptiste de toute l'Afrique, Ghana

"I am delighted that this Centennial History is now available and records the great things God is doing around the world through our Baptist churches."
    Nilson do Amaral Fanini, President, Baptist World Alliance, 1995–2000, Brazil

"This centenary history is an inspiring story depicting the growth of the Baptist World Alliance and the vitality of its witness on five continents. I am confident it will strengthen our fellowship and clarify our global Baptist identity."
    David Coffey, General Secretary, Baptist Union of Great Britain

"I celebrate the hundred years of the Baptist World Alliance and its constant effort to keep the unity of the Baptist people in the midst of their diversities, its evangelistic vision, its presence among the needy of the world, especially in cases of natural disasters. I applaud its constant fight for religious freedom and its belief that both men and women have the privilege and the responsibility of working together in order to extend the kingdom of God."
    Amparo de Medina, Vice President, Baptist World Alliance, 2000–05; former President of Latin American Women, Colombia

"The Baptist World Alliance is the global forum for all members of the World Baptist family not only to fellowship but also to pool our resources together for witnessing to the saving knowledge of Jesus Christ, our Lord."
    Osadolor Imasogie, Vice President, Baptist World Alliance, 1995–2000; President Emeritus, Nigerian Baptist Theological Seminary, Ogbomoso, Nigeria.

Publication of the Baptist World Alliance Centennial History by Samford University Press is made possible by friends of Samford University in appreciation of the worldwide fellowship of Baptists and their commitment to Jesus Christ.

BAPTISTS TOGETHER IN CHRIST
1905–2005

A HUNDRED-YEAR HISTORY
OF THE BAPTIST WORLD ALLIANCE

BAPTISTS TOGETHER IN CHRIST
1905–2005
A HUNDRED-YEAR HISTORY OF THE BAPTIST WORLD ALLIANCE

Richard V. Pierard, General Editor
Elna Jean Young Bentley and Gerald L. Borchert, Associate Editors

Baptist World Alliance
Falls Church, Virginia
U.S.A.

Copyright © 2005 by Baptist World Alliance

All rights reserved. No part of this publication may be reproduced or distributed in any form or by any means, or stored in a database or retrieval system, without prior written permission of the publisher.

ISBN 1-931985-13-8

Baptist World Alliance
405 North Washington Street
Falls Church, Virginia 22046, U.S.A.
www.bwanet.org

Published by Samford University Press
Samford University
800 Lakeshore Drive
Birmingham, Alabama 35229, U.S.A.
www.samford.edu

General Editor: Richard V. Pierard
Associate Editors: Elna Jean Young Bentley and Gerald L. Borchert
Cover Design: Scott E. Camp

Cover Photo Credit: President of Liberia visits United Nations Headquarters, United Nations, M. Grant
Back Cover Photo: Ninth Baptist World Congress, London (Golden Jubilee Congress) 1955

Printed and bound in the United States by BookMasters, Inc., Mansfield, Ohio

CONTENTS

Foreword	xi
Acknowledgments	xiii
Introduction	xv
1 Early Moves in the Direction of Greater Cooperation, *Horace O. Russell*	1
2 From 1905 to the End of the First World War, *John H. Y. Briggs*	20
3 Coming of Age: The Post-War Era and the 1920s, *Robert S. Wilson*	47
4 The Years of Anxiety and World War II, *Erich Geldbach*	74
5 Recovery from the War and the Advance to Maturity, *W. Morgan Patterson and Richard V. Pierard*	100
6 The Internationalization of the Alliance, 1960–70, *James Leo Garrett, Jr.*	128
7 New Structures for a Growing Family: The Baptist World Alliance in the 1970s, *Faith Bowers*	169
8 Pro-Existence Not Co-Existence: The Baptist World Alliance in the 1980s, *Ian M. Randall*	194
9 The New World, 1988–95, *Albert W. Wardin, Jr. and Richard V. Pierard*	235
10 Forward into the New Century, 1995–2005, *Ken R. Manley*	275
Afterword, *Denton Lotz*	300
Appendices	319
Abbreviations	329
Bibliography	331
Contributors	337
Index	339

Baptist World Alliance

FOREWORD

On the occasion of the one hundredth anniversary of the Baptist World Alliance, it gives me great joy to send congratulations and greetings to our brothers and sisters around the world. This centennial history will be a wonderful way for Baptists in 211 conventions and unions worldwide to remember their great history from 1905 to the present.

Baptists have always been an enthusiastic and evangelistic people. Baptists all over the world have been a great encouragement to me in all my evangelistic activity, and I could always count on Baptist leaders and people to support and encourage our efforts at world evangelization. The one thing that has always united Baptists has been their desire to make the gospel of Jesus Christ known to the world.

The motto of the Baptist World Alliance, "One Lord, One Faith, One Baptism" from Ephesians 4:5, is a call for Christians all over the world to realize that our unity is indeed found only in Jesus Christ. May all of us keep our eyes fixed on Christ and the salvation that He offers to the whole world. May we also continue to accept the challenge of evangelizing the world in this generation.

May God bless you as you read this book and discover again the inspiring history of the Baptist World Alliance and the leaders who committed themselves to the faith once delivered to the saints.

My wife, Ruth, joins me in sending you our warmest greetings on the occasion of the one hundredth birthday of the Baptist World Alliance. May the peace, joy, and love of Christ be with each one of you!

March 18, 2005 *Billy Graham*

ACKNOWLEDGMENTS

I wish to express appreciation to the many people who have helped to make this project a success. The seven members of the Core Committee were all closely involved in the venture. Four of the seven, Horace Russell, John Briggs, James Leo Garrett, and Denton Lotz, actually wrote chapters as well as advised the general editor along the way; associate editors Eljee Bentley and Gerald Borchert carefully read and improved the texts of each chapter; and General Secretary Lotz and Tony Cupit commented on chapters and smoothed the way for the final publication. Samford University President Thomas E. Corts graciously provided the support for printing the book. Sandra L. O'Brien of Samford University ably prepared the manuscript and photographs for the publication. Ruby J. Burke at the Baptist World Alliance office in Falls Church, Virginia, rendered invaluable service in helping gather and organize materials. I am grateful for the encouragement and information given by other members of the Baptist World Alliance staff as well.

On behalf of the writers and editors of this centennial history, I want to express our indebtedness to the many librarians and archivists who aided us in finding the necessary sources for telling the story of the Baptist World Alliance. Deborah B. Van Broekhoven, executive director of the American Baptist Historical Society, and assistants Betty Layton, archivist, and Ferron Okewole, project archivist, opened to us the rich Baptist World Alliance archival collection at the American Baptist Archives Center in Valley Forge, Pennsylvania. Equally indispensable was the help received from Susan J. Mills, librarian of Angus Library, Regent's Park College, Oxford, England. Sharon Taylor, director of the Franklin Trask Library, Andover Newton Theological School, made her resources available, as did the librarians of the James P. Boyce Centennial Library, Southern Baptist Theological Seminary, and of the A. Webb Roberts Library of the Southwestern Baptist Theological Seminary. Of assistance to us as well were Amy Cook at the Alma Hunt Library, Woman's Missionary Union, Birmingham, Alabama, and Elizabeth C. Wells, special collections coordinator and librarian, Samford University Library.

Finally, I owe a great debt of appreciation to two distinguished Baptist historians who encouraged me personally at crucial points in my professional life: Kenneth Scott Latourette (1884–1968) of Yale University, and William R. Estep, Jr. (1920–2000) of Southwestern Baptist Theological Seminary. Their irenic spirit and global vision are reflected in the pages of this volume.

March 18, 2005   *Richard V. Pierard, General Editor*

INTRODUCTION
Richard V. Pierard, General Editor

Who are the Baptists? What distinguishes them from other confessional or denominational groups in the larger world Christian community? Baptists are commonly identified as Christians who emphasize the authority of Scripture; salvation through faith in Christ; believers' baptism by immersion; congregational church government; and religious liberty. But the diversity within the Baptist world is breathtaking: Calvinistic versus Arminian theology; sharp differences in worship forms and personal lifestyles; contrasting approaches to interpreting the Bible; and varying attitudes toward relationships with other Christians in the world at large. In fact, they can't even agree on their own history. Some see the movement as beginning in 1609 when John Smyth and Thomas Helwys baptized themselves and a small group of followers and organized the first recognizably modern Baptist church. Others regard Baptists as the spiritual progeny of the Radical Reformation—the Anabaptists or Mennonites. Still others insist on Baptist "successionism," beginning with the "First Baptist Church of Jerusalem", and tracing the path of faithful witness to the truth of Christ through the early church, the various dissenting or "heretical" sects in the Middle Ages, the Anabaptists of Reformation times, and finally the emergence of the clearly defined Baptist congregations in seventeenth-century England.

Baptist Identity and the Baptist World Alliance

In a helpful book entitled *The Baptist Identity*, historian Walter Shurden of Mercer University analyzes the factors that make Baptists unique. Drawing upon eight twentieth-century statements on Baptist identity, he singles out four distinctive and essential "freedoms": *Bible freedom* (the freedom and obligation of Christians to study and obey the Scriptures, which are central in the life of the individual and the church); *soul freedom* (the responsibility of every person to deal with God without the imposition of creed, interference of clergy, or intervention of civil government); *church freedom* (the autonomy of local churches, which are free to determine their membership and leadership, order their worship, ordain those whom they perceive as gifted for ministry, and participate in the life of the larger body of Christ); and *religious freedom* (the freedom of the individual to hold and practice his or her religious beliefs without government interference).

Another excellent formulation of Baptist identity was developed by the Baptist World Alliance (BWA) Study Commission on Baptist Heritage and adopted at its meeting in Zagreb, Yugoslavia, in July 1989. That statement discusses the Scriptures, the gospel, the church, and discipleship, and concludes that Baptists are the following:

> Members of the whole Christian family who stress the experience of personal salvation through faith in Jesus, symbolized both in baptism and the Lord's Supper
> Those who under the Lordship of Jesus Christ have bonded together in free local congregations, together seeking to obey Christ in faith and in life
> Those who follow the authority of Scripture in all matters of faith and practice
> Those who have claimed religious liberty for themselves and all people
> Those who believe that the Great Commission to take the Gospel to the whole world is the responsibility of the whole membership

These two statements demonstrate that although Baptists are extraordinarily fractious, more binds them together than divides them. The BWA was formed to affirm these commonalities, and for a hundred years it has affirmed the principle that Baptists working together can—paraphrasing the great hero William Carey—accomplish great things for God. Given the diversity among Baptists, it was a foregone conclusion that the BWA would suffer tensions, but the most inspiring aspect of the story is how often and in how many creative ways Baptist leaders were able to overcome these differences and labor harmoniously in communicating the gospel and building dynamic church fellowships around the globe. The centenary provides the occasion to reflect on what God has accomplished through the faithful labors of his servants in the BWA.

The authors who have contributed to this volume will explain what the Alliance is and assess what it has attempted to do. They will review the personalities of the Alliance, as well as the structures these Baptists created and the tasks they undertook. The BWA's scope of concern has ranged across the entire spectrum of Baptist life. Its activities include: working to secure religious liberty everywhere; encouraging evangelism and missions; promoting peace, justice, and human rights; providing relief and development aid; carrying on dialogues and building relationships with other Christian bodies; fostering ministries among Baptist women, men, and youths; engaging in research and sharing of information in the areas of Baptist theology, ethics, doctrine, history, ecclesiology, and worship; and advancing Baptist theological education around the world. These themes serve to tie the book together and give coherence to the narrative.

Nature of the Project

Preparing a historical account of such a complex organization engaged in manifold endeavors was a daunting task. The possibility of a commemorative history had been discussed for some years, and in 1996 the Baptist Heritage Study Commission formally recommended that the BWA General Council authorize the preparation of such a volume. The motion was referred to the executive committee of the Division of Study and Research, and in March 1997, the committee endorsed the project and proposed the creation of an editorial board. A Study and Research subcommittee, meeting in Dallas on June 17, 1997, decided to form a Core Committee to carry out the project, laid out time lines, and conceptualized the nature of the work. It was considered essential that the project be a multiauthored, international enterprise. Making up the Core Committee were General Secretary Denton Lotz; Study and Research Director L. A. (Tony) Cupit; Study and Research Co-chairs James Leo Garrett, Jr. (Southern Baptist Convention [SBC]) and Gerald L. Borchert (SBC and American Baptist Churches); Baptist Heritage Study Commission Chair Elna Jean (Eljee) Bentley (SBC); and Heritage Commission members John H. Y. Briggs of the United Kingdom and Horace O. Russell of Jamaica, who is also an American Baptist. BWA Executive Assistant Ruby J. Burke would act as secretary.

Discussed at subsequent meetings of the Core Committee in 1997, 1998, and 1999 were the structure of the book, securing a general editor, identification of potential writers, and the role of the committee as consultants in writing and editing. The book was to be scholarly in character, provide an integrated account of the BWA, be written in a readable style, and be kept to a reasonable length in order to make it attractive to the constituency. The intention was to inform and edify the people who make up the Alliance. The committee recognized that a delicate balance would exist between the two objectives of scholarly integrity and readability for the ordinary person in the pew. Richard V. Pierard, at the time a vice-chair of the Baptist Heritage Commission, a professor of history at Indiana State University, and member of an American Baptist church in Terre Haute, Indiana, was asked to assume the position of general editor. Eljee Bentley and Gerald Borchert were appointed associate editors.

The Core Committee and general editor agreed that the choice of writers would be based on three considerations: (1) Involved in their local churches, they would not be detached academics but individuals who understood and practiced their faith as Baptists; (2) they must have scholarly expertise as demonstrated by writing and publication in Baptist history and/or the larger realm of Christian history; (3) writers should be from a variety of denominations and geographical areas. Such diversity would ensure that the book was genuinely representative of the BWA and not just an American enterprise.

The basic structure would be chronological rather than thematic, and the various aspects in the life of the BWA would be developed within the separate chapters. The editors would engage in rigorous editing to ensure that a consistent narrative gave a good overview of the history of the BWA. Because of the rich resources in the archival and published works of the Alliance, the writers and editors would have to make hard choices concerning what to include and exclude in order to keep the narrative to a readable length. The book would also include sidebars giving brief biographies of the BWA Presidents and General Secretaries.

An editorial decision was made to use American English spelling and punctuation throughout the book and to adopt a consistent style in the annotations. Although half of the contributors regularly use other forms of the English language, consistency would make reading easier. The editors also decided to mention women by their first names whenever possible; however, discovery of their first names was not always possible, particularly in the early sections of the book because women in those years often took their public names from their husbands. Not included are such titles as Rev., Dr., Mr., Mrs., Miss, and Ms., as they add unnecessarily to the length of the text and often changed over time. The first time they are mentioned, Baptists from the United States are generally identified by their convention or conference; other Baptists are identified only by country. Another and perhaps more controversial decision was to capitalize the titles of BWA office holders (such as President, Vice President, General Secretary, etc.) The purpose was to link the person with his or her BWA post. These individuals and so many people mentioned often held positions with the same titles in their respective conventions and unions, and the capitalization helped to distinguish BWA posts from denominational ones.

The team who labored on this volume hopes that this history will help readers to appreciate the remarkable achievements of the BWA in its first hundred years. Only the divine power that has been present in the Alliance made this effort possible. May the next century of endeavor in God's kingdom be as inspiring and fruitful as this first century has been.

1
EARLY MOVES IN THE DIRECTION OF GREATER COOPERATION
Horace O. Russell

Over the years following the formation of the first generally acknowledged modern Baptist congregation in 1609, the people called Baptists—with their distinctive emphases on believers' baptism, congregational self-government, the freedom of each person led by the Holy Spirit to interpret the Scriptures, and a separation of church and state that would guarantee religious liberty—developed into a socially diverse and geographically widespread movement. Gradually, more and more Baptists became aware of the need for some sort of greater unity that would enable them to more effectively carry out the divine mandate to preach the gospel of Jesus Christ. As they came to know each other better and learned to work together, the foundations were laid for what would become the Baptist World Alliance (BWA).

Early Moves Toward Cooperation
The first recorded expression of the desire to cooperate was a statement in 1678 by Thomas Grantham, the leader of the General Baptists in England: "I could wish that all congregations of Christians of the world that are baptized according to the appointment of Christ would make one consistory, at least sometimes, to consider the matters of difference among them."[1] However, more than a century was to pass before united Baptist action was to come to the fore. John Rippon, who published the first major collection of Baptist hymns in 1787 and from 1775 to 1836 pastored the Carter Lane Church in Southwark, London, inaugurated *The Baptist Annual Register* in 1790. This periodical was designed to introduce Baptists to one another. It contained details about the English associations, as well as the Welsh, Scottish, and Irish churches, some information about free churches on the continent, and news of Baptist life in North America. "An interchange of kind offices between the English and American Brethren, since the last war," Rippon argued, "has produced a pretty general wish on both sides [of] the Atlantic, of enjoying a more comprehensive knowledge

of each others' circumstances," and he concluded this would stimulate mutual assistance and prayer.² In the next issue he included a listing of ministers and professors among the Baptists in continental Europe who in reality were Mennonites, but he still regarded them as part of a larger Baptistic family. More importantly, *The Baptist Annual Register* carried a dedication on the page following the title page "to all the baptized ministers and people in America, England, Ireland, Scotland, Wales, the United Netherlands, France, Switzerland, Poland, Russia, Prussia and Elsewhere" and expressed the expectation that within a few years representatives from all these areas would meet "probably in London to consult the ecclesiastical good to the whole."[3]

Rippon's hope was fulfilled at least partially by the formation of the Baptist Missionary Society (BMS) in 1792 and the departure of the first missionaries soon afterward. The origins of this landmark development lay in the decision of the ministers of the Northamptonshire Association to begin meeting regularly for prayer. This was a response to the teaching of the American theologian Jonathan Edwards about the importance of God's people uniting in prayer for revival and the advancement of Christ's kingdom on earth. From this humble beginning emerged the BMS, with its vision for universality and unity in the endeavor to win the world for Christ.[4]

Such preachers as Andrew Fuller and John Sutcliff had begun to question the extreme Calvinism prevalent in Baptist circles that placed exclusive emphasis on the sovereignty of God and divine election and thereby rendered any engagement in missions problematic. Instead they placed ideas of moral obligation and human responsibility in the foreground and held that Christian missionaries could play a role in the carrying out of God's plan of salvation and evangelize the world. Energized by this idea, the youthful William Carey wrote a tract entitled *An Enquiry into the Obligation of Christians to Use Means for the Conversion of the Heathen* that affirmed the church's need to engage in worldwide missionary outreach. German pietists had already set the process in motion earlier in the century, and Carey's achievement was to awaken the English Baptists (and soon other Protestants as well) to the mandate of the Great Commission. Later that year, as a result of his sermon that ended with the immortal lines "Expect great things—attempt great things," a group of Carey's associates decided to form a society "to evangelize the poor, dark, idolatrous Heathen" by publishing the glorious gospel of Christ and preaching "the glad tiding of salvation by the blood of the Lamb," as Fuller put it.[5] Carey left for India in 1793, and when additional missionaries joined him over the next few years, a flourishing ministry was established at

Serampore, near Calcutta (Kolkata). They cooperated with the other mission societies that soon came into existence, and their work quickly proved to be an inspiration to Baptists and other denominations in various parts of Europe and North America.

Carey became convinced of the need for a coordinated strategy to carry out world evangelism, and in 1806 he made the bold proposal in a letter to Fuller that "a general association of all denominations of Christians, from the four quarters of the earth," should meet decennially, possibly as early as 1810 or 1812, at the Cape of Good Hope where the individuals "could understand one another better, and more entirely enter into one another's views by two hours' conversation than by two or three years of epistolary correspondence." Fuller called this a "pleasing dream" but discouraged pursuing it further as it might be a seedbed for dissension.[6] Although Count Nicholas von Zinzendorf, the leader of the Moravian church until his death in 1760, engaged in some practices that foreshadowed ecumenism, Carey's was the first specific ecumenical proposal as such. It would eventually come to fruition in the great international missionary conferences of 1888 (London), 1900 (New York), and especially 1910 (Edinburgh) and for his own denomination, in the formation of the BWA.

Although critics accused missionaries of being the handmaidens of European imperialism, in actuality they did much to advance the cause of human rights throughout the world by providing education and medical care in those areas where such was lacking and by combating infanticide, the burning of widows in India, foot-binding in China, the exploitation of women and children, and slavery. The witness and struggle of the BMS against the institution of slavery in the West Indies and its eventual abolition in the British colonies were a source of pride and encouragement to peoples of African descent. (Interestingly, the congress at which the BWA was founded took place in London's Exeter Hall, a prominent venue for missionary conventions and assemblies of evangelical Christians to oppose slavery.)

In fact the successful missionary initiatives in Asia, Africa, and the Caribbean would be a major reason why Baptists came to see the need to develop a world organization. The cooperative efforts that occurred on the mission fields soon led to church cooperation back in the sending countries and inspired the formation of not only ecumenical but also confessional bodies that linked denominations across international boundaries. A reflection of the missionary endeavor's success was that the newer believers overseas united in autonomous churches and expressed their desire to relate to other Baptists as churches rather than have their local ministries directed by mission boards in Britain and North America.

An important step in international Baptist cooperation was taken by African-Americans who had originally come to the New World in the bonds of slavery. George Liele began ministering among blacks in Savannah, Georgia, during the American Revolution and, after the war, moved to Jamaica where he preached, organized churches, and started schools. David George, who had worked with Liele, fled to Nova Scotia in 1782 and organized seven churches in nine years before leading a group of his followers, many of them former Jamaican slaves, to Sierra Leone in Africa. The BMS engaged in missionary work among the Jamaican blacks as well as played an important role in bringing an end to slavery there and the odious apprentice system that replaced it. The ties between Britain, Jamaica, and West Africa grew steadily, and the Jamaican blacks engaged in missionary work in their ancestral homeland.[7] The Jamaican Baptists even sent a representative, C. S. Bullock, to the Ecumenical Missionary Conference in New York in 1900.

International Organization

The first appeal for an international organization of Baptists as such came in a series of letters in the *American Baptist Magazine and Missionary Intelligencer* in 1824 by a young Boston pastor using the pseudonym Backus. The author was actually Francis Wayland, who later became the most important American Baptist theologian of the first half of the nineteenth century. These articles assessed the role of the association in Baptist life, and in one of them Wayland called for changes in the local structure whereby the associations would send delegates to a state convention that "would embody all the information, and concentrate the energies of a state." The state groups in turn would send delegates to a national general convention that would bring about "concentrated and united action" by the "whole denomination." He hoped that eventually there could even be some sort of a British-American Baptist connection whereby "the Baptists on both sides of the Atlantic" would be united in a "solid phalanx."[8] In 1843 an anonymous writer called Hanno issued a call in the Virginia Baptist *Religious Herald* for an international Baptist association.[9]

Various individuals in continental Europe, Britain, and the United States advocated an international Evangelical Alliance (EA), and some prominent British Baptists were involved in its founding meeting in London in 1846 that attracted some eight hundred luminaries from various countries on both sides of the Atlantic. But the unity that the new group hoped to offer was immediately threatened by the slavery issue.

John Howard Hinton, secretary of the Baptist Union (BU), proposed the exclusion of slave-owners from EA membership, but such a move would put in jeopardy the international character of the organization. Finally, a compromise was reached whereby slavery was listed as "a sin and a social evil," with the international EA becoming a federation of national alliances, each with its own constitution. This left the way open for the British EA to deny membership to slaveholders, but it meant the international EA per se was nothing more than a voluntary convention of interested individuals from various denominations.[10] However, the larger EA continued to hold conferences every few years in various cities (including Berlin in 1857), where the speakers surveyed developments in religious life around the world. The group strongly advocated missions, defended religious liberty, and disseminated information about the churches and religious conditions in various countries.

In 1835, shortly after the abolition of slavery in the British Empire, the BU sent a delegation to the Triennial Convention, the national organization of Baptists in the United States that carried out foreign missionary work, to make "friendly expostulation" against churches allowing slave owners within their membership.[11] Because the American Baptist body was rapidly becoming polarized over the slavery issue, the plea from abroad apparently had no impact. In 1847, Americans did try to launch the EA in their country but the effort failed. In 1867, only after the Civil War had laid the slavery issue to rest, was an American EA founded, and the sixth general conference of the World Evangelical Alliance took place in New York in 1873. The American Baptists were not enthusiastic about the EA, since its communion services included those who had not been baptized as believers. Although such leaders as William F. Dodge, Philip Schaff, and Josiah Strong breathed some life into the American EA, its influence soon waned as the evangelical ecumenical impulse increasingly shifted to the international missionary movement. It was moribund after 1900 but existed on paper until 1944.

Factors Enabling Closer Ties

Baptists were scattered throughout those areas originally colonized by Great Britain: North America (the United States) and the "white" Dominions of Canada, Australia, New Zealand, and South Africa. These communities had ties of kinship with the United Kingdom as well as with the other European countries that were sources of immigrants. Thus, mutual relations between Baptists in the mother country and the Atlantic seaboard colonies were a feature of the eighteenth century, and these ties continued and expanded in the nineteenth century. British and American mission agencies also fostered evangelism on the European continent, thereby helping to connect people there to the Anglo-Saxon Baptist community.

Two developments in the later nineteenth century opened the way for Baptists in various parts of the world to come in closer contact: One was the revolution in transportation and communications. The great expansion of the railroad network after 1870 enabled rapid travel within Britain, much of continental Europe, and North America. The steamship facilitated international travel, and religious leaders now began to cross the Atlantic on a regular basis and even journeyed to such distant places as Australia and New Zealand. Improved transportation also enabled sending out a much greater number of missionaries than earlier in the century. The development of mass literacy in the western lands and advances in printing technology resulted in the production of vast quantities of religious books and periodicals, and in the leading thinkers and preachers being widely read and quoted in churches throughout the world. Telegraph lines and submarine cables fostered virtually instant communications within the developed countries and with the overseas world. New inventions—such as the telephone, phonograph, lantern-slide projectors, and motion pictures—further enhanced the ease of interpersonal contacts and spreading the gospel.

The second development was the appearance of international denominational or confessional organizations.[12] These organizations were preceded by the founding in Britain of the Young Men's Christian Association (1844) and the Young Women's Christian Association (1854), both groups that were wholeheartedly evangelistic and missionary in their character. They quickly formed branches in various countries, and other youth organizations, such as Christian Endeavor (1881) and the Student Volunteer Movement for Foreign Missions (1888), promoted evangelism and missions as well. The world confessional fellowships themselves arose out of international conferences held at intervals ranging from four to ten years. They sought to strengthen the weak churches and heal the divisions within their respective confessional traditions. Although on the surface they seemed to be antiecumenical because of their affirmation of denominationalism, in fact they helped lay the groundwork for the twentieth-century ecumenical movement.

The first of the world confessional fellowships was the decennial assembly of Anglican and Episcopal bishops from around the world at London's Lambeth Palace that began in 1867. (The initial pan-Anglican Conference, involving clergy and laity as well as bishops, was held at

Lambeth in 1908.) The Alliance of Reformed Churches throughout the World Holding the Presbyterian System met for the first time in London in 1875 and functioned mainly as a fraternal gathering. At a meeting in London in 1881 attended by delegates from twenty-eight Methodist bodies in twenty countries, the Ecumenical Methodist Conference (later to be called the World Methodist Council) was formed; the International Congregational Council was founded at a gathering in London in 1891. The Baptists had been invited to participate, and John Clifford did attend as a representative of the BU; but the hope that the "other great branch of the Congregational family" would unite with the Council went unfulfilled.[13] Even the liberal churches took part in the movement for closer ties and in 1900 formed the International Council of Unitarian and Other Liberal Religious Thinkers and Workers.

Movements in the Direction of Baptist Unity
Craig Sherouse, in a paper presented in 1999 to the BWA's Baptist Heritage Study Commission, maintained that three factors contributed to greater unity in American Baptist work in the late nineteenth and early twentieth centuries.[14] The first was the effort of Baptists in the north to improve relations with their southern counterparts. The southerners had adopted a more connectional-type convention structure in 1845, while Baptists in the north and west continued to function through their local associations and state conventions and autonomous national societies. They included the foreign mission board (founded as the Triennial Convention in 1814 and renamed the American Baptist Missionary Union in 1846 and American Baptist Foreign Mission Society in 1910); the American Baptist Publication Society (1824); the American Baptist Home Mission Society (ABHMS) (1832); the American Baptist Historical Society (1853); the Woman's American Baptist Foreign Mission Society (1874/1883); three women's home mission societies (united in 1909 as the Woman's American Baptist Home Mission Society); and the American Baptist Education Society (1868/1888).

After the Civil War the northern societies were much better funded than their southern counterparts. The ABHMS directed most of its efforts to the South by distributing Christian literature and establishing schools to educate the freed slaves, including some twenty-eight institutions of higher education. It also made overtures for reunion that the southerners flatly rejected. As the South recovered from the devastation of the war and developed its own territorial consciousness, tensions between northern missionaries and the indigenous white Baptists increased steadily. In 1882, a Southern Baptist Home Mission Board executive complained that the northern society was now spending three times as much as the southern one on home mission work in his region. Finally, at the Fortress Monroe Conference in Virginia in 1894, the two agencies agreed to coordinate their missionary activities in the South. The northerners would scale back their involvement there and redirect their efforts to ministries elsewhere in the country. The issue of funding and control of the African-American educational institutions was discussed, but the solutions offered by the southerners were much too paternalistic to satisfy the black participants at the gathering. The agreements reached in 1894 for establishing geographical boundaries for the work of the northern and southern Baptists were reinforced by "Principles of Comity" adopted at meetings in 1911 and 1912. These did much to ease tensions between the two and guide their regional ministries for the next thirty years.[15]

Meanwhile, the two groups sought to foster cooperation in a little-known and now forgotten venture known as the General Convention of the Baptists of North America. Formed with great fanfare at a meeting of nearly six thousand "representatives" at the Third Baptist Church in St. Louis on May 16, 1905, it aspired to unite the Baptist denomination "in spirit, in motives, and determination." Chosen as president was E. W. Stephens of Columbia, Missouri, who had just been elected president of the Southern Baptist Convention at its meeting a few days earlier. George W. Truett of Texas gave the keynote address entitled "The Unity of the Baptist Spirit." A second meeting, attended by representatives from the Canadian and National Baptists (the black Baptist groups had united into one convention in 1895) as well as the northern and southern bodies, took place in the neighboring cities of Norfolk and Hampton Roads, Virginia, in May 1907. Those present elected Northern Baptist Augustus H. Strong as president and issued a joint invitation for the next Baptist World Congress to be held in the United States.

A third gathering in Baltimore, slated for 1910, was postponed until 1911 to coordinate with the BWA Congress in Philadelphia. Named president at this time was A. L. McCrimmon of Canada. The conventions were largely inspirational gatherings and encouraged cooperation among the missionary agencies, but nothing concrete was achieved. Both the growth of denominationalism in the North and South and the success of the BWA as an international body diverted attention from the North American Convention. No further meetings took place, although an executive committee continued to meet until 1917 and the two denominations appointed representatives to this "paper committee" until 1931.[16]

For Baptists in the North, the society system was becoming too cumbersome, and as the new century approached, various moves took place to improve cooperation among these independent bodies. Finally, the executive secretaries of the foreign and home missions and publications societies acceded to grassroots demands to form a national denomination and, in May 1907, created a provisional organization to draft a constitution and bylaws. The following year the Northern Baptist Convention (NBC) was established "to give expression to the sentiment of its constituency upon matters of denominational importance and general religious and moral interest, to develop denominational unity, and to give increasing efficiency to efforts for the evangelization of America and the world." As Baptist historian Bill Leonard put it in *Baptist Ways: A History*, the new denomination enabled greater connectionalism among the societies and their supporters and made the structures more manageable, productive, and businesslike. It was a compromise that linked elements of both the convention and society methods, a "loose federation of societies and churches."[17] The northerners now were united and could—more or less—speak with one voice.

The Baptist Congresses

The move for greater Baptist unity that probably most directly affected the eventual formation of the BWA was the Baptist Congresses in America. They reflected the various forces at work in the late nineteenth-century United States. Many Protestants, particularly in the northern metropolitan areas, were apprehensive about Roman Catholic influence because of the heavy immigration from Ireland and Central and Southern Europe. They were concerned that the flood of newcomers from countries that did not operate under democratic governments would compromise the political institutions of the country, especially since some of these were places from which earlier migrants had themselves fled to escape religious persecution.

On the other hand the social and political needs of the new arrivals evoked genuine sympathy and concern and required remedies, and the Baptists of New York began working together to tackle current issues facing the church and society. Church figures, such as Baptist Walter Rauschenbusch, provided leadership in developing a theological basis for social action.

In November 1881 a group of Baptist ministers in New York City decided to organize a "forum for the discussion of current questions—religious, social, political, or philosophic," subjects that were uppermost in public thought. Rather than defend or advocate specific Baptist principles or take concrete actions per se, an "exchange of views" would take place that could help ordinary people grapple with current problems. It would be patterned after the various world congresses of other denominations and the Convention of Baptist Social Unions that had met in Brooklyn, New York, in 1874 and would function in a manner similar to the fall meetings of the British BU at which no business as such was transacted but pertinent topics were discussed at length. A General Committee was formed to draw up a "Plan of Organization" and "Rules for Discussion" for an "Autumnal Baptist Conference." They agreed that any person would be allowed to address the subject under consideration but that "no resolution or motion shall be entertained at the public conference." Any member of a Baptist congregation could become a member of the Congress by paying two dollars annual dues. The stated purpose of the Baptist Congress was "to promote a healthful sentiment among Baptists through free and courteous discussion of current questions by suitable persons."[18]

The first "Baptist Congress for the Discussion of Current Questions" was convened in Brooklyn in 1882, and over the next three decades subsequent gatherings took place annually in various cities. The last Congress was held in 1914, but no volume of papers appeared. Although the Congresses received little press coverage, their proceedings were published each year, and the volumes offer valuable insights into contemporary Baptist thought. A wide range of issues dealing with Baptist polity, theology, social action, and history were discussed, but no resolutions or statements were ever adopted. The participants were largely from urban churches and Baptist institutions of higher education. It began as a northern enterprise but soon took on a national and even international character, as it attracted southerners, Canadians, and even a few British Baptists. It was inclusive as well, in that it embraced the black Baptist constituency on equal terms and placed on the agenda matters of concern to African-American Baptists and the National Baptist Convention.

Sherouse maintained that the (American) Baptist Congress was a forerunner of the BWA in several ways: Its modest international character prefigured the larger association that would be formed in 1905, while its organizational structure was analogous to the BWA's—a broadly representative General Committee and a local Executive Committee. Nearly all of the Southern Baptists who were influential in the formation of the BWA had participated in the Congresses, and their dissatisfaction with the church unionist direction that the Congress seemed to be taking was a motivating factor in their support of a more loosely structured body. The precedent of a discussion format was continued in the BWA, and it reflected the aversion of the organizers of the American Congresses to functioning as a legislative body. At various BWA gatherings over the years, conversations occurred about what kind of unity might be possible, but no sympathy was expressed for an organic union.

At the 1903 Congress the question of "how can Baptists secure for themselves a more practical working union" was aired, and opinion seemed to favor some kind of a stronger, international organization. Russell H. Conwell, the popular Philadelphia preacher whose published sermon *Acres of Diamonds* had become a classic, proposed the formation of a national or international Baptist association on the model of the other world denominational fellowships. He also argued that it was the duty of the Congress to instigate such an effort. A. J. Rowland, secretary of the American Baptist Publication Society, suggested the idea of an international congress that would gather at stated intervals, like the councils of the early church.[19]

The BWA in fact became what many of the speakers had wanted, and it should be no surprise that the Baptist Congress folded once the BWA was up and running. Other difficulties also plagued the Congress: Being essentially a U.S. institution, it had little international support. The annual meeting format discouraged regular attendance because of the time and costs involved in travel. The academic character of the addresses and discussion did not appeal to those who were primarily interested in a fellowship-oriented organization. Financial problems beset the Congress after the death in 1897 of its principal benefactor, soap manufacturer Samuel Colgate. Many northerners viewed the new NBC as the logical successor to the Congress and shifted their support to it. Finally, conservatives labeled it as theologically liberal when such people as Rauschenbusch (Rochester Seminary) and Shailer Mathews (University of Chicago) appeared on the program. Southern Landmarkers, who concentrated exclusively on the local church, were suspicious of all denominational-type bodies, especially if they held "open" views on baptism and communion. After the meetings in 1907 and 1908, when the matter of organic union with the Disciples of Christ and Free Will Baptists was discussed, the Congresses lost most of their southern participants. Once the BWA had supplanted the Baptist Congress, it no longer had any reason for existence.[20]

Developments in Britain

The start of a new century found British Baptists in a healthy state. The General Baptists had united with the BU in 1891, the work of the Baptist Missionary Society was prospering, and the doctrinal crisis known as the

Down Grade Controversy had receded. British Baptists also possessed well-developed relationships with their fellow believers abroad. Overseas visitors were welcomed to sessions of the BU Council, to London pulpits, and to the columns of Baptist periodicals, while college principals spent considerable effort finding suitable men for overseas pastorates. For example, in 1900 the BU Council devoted several sessions to identifying a suitable person for a position in Dunedin, New Zealand.[21] Also that year, the Council received a sensitive report about a meeting of the Evangelical Alliance during which the situation of the Russian Stundists, a quasi-Baptist group, had been reviewed and strategies discussed as to how they might be assisted. It was agreed that in the context of Russian law it would be best that the BU be the lead organization in negotiating with the Russian authorities. If need be, an approach could be made to the Tsar. In addition, BU President Charles Williams was directed to raise the matter with the secretary of the American Baptist Missionary Union (ABMU) during his forthcoming visit to the United States.[22]

In January 1901, a small committee was appointed to consider what might be done "to promote a closer union between the Baptists of the colonies and ourselves, and especially to consider the present condition and future prospects of our brethren in South Africa." Thus, while the South African War (also called the Boer War) was still in progress, the Baptist South African and Colonial Missionary Society was formed to promote church extension there in anticipation of an expected influx of immigrants and to initiate work among the indigenous peoples.[23] Then in April 1901, Silas Mead presented a memorial from the seven Australasian unions, representing some twenty thousand Baptists in Australia and New Zealand, that thanked the British Baptists for their diligence in pursuing issues of religious freedom: "We long for a closer intimacy between the parent Union at home and our Colonial Unions." They were thankful for the visits of such distinguished preachers as Alexander Maclaren and John Clifford and expressed a desire for a continuing interchange of visitors.[24] The Council also acted on a request from Pastor Reuben Saillens of France that the BU liaise with the ABMU to provide English-language preachers for the great Paris Exhibition.[25]

At its spring 1901 meeting in Leicester, the BU Assembly resolved to introduce an "Ecumenical Session" at its October meeting in Edinburgh. At the time the term "ecumenical" was used in the sense of international relations among Baptists. This was done in "recognition of the oneness of the English-speaking Baptists and with a view to provide among them yet more of brotherly sympathy and mutual happiness."[26] Baptists in the

British colonies and the United States were invited to send delegates to this gathering of English-speaking brethren. Continentals heard of this initiative and expanded an English-speaking occasion to embrace themselves. As a result, seventeen people from the United States, Canada, Jamaica, Australia, South Africa, and five European countries attended; in the evening session, twelve of them were asked to give five-minute talks outlining their home situations. Maclaren thanked them for their contributions in "sharing like precious faith with ourselves." *The Baptist Magazine* opined, "It is to be hoped that one result of this unique session will be to tighten the bonds which bind Baptists together in whatever part of the world they are found."[27] This process of networking patently demonstrated the need for some overarching umbrella organization.

The American Impulse

As in England, the soil for closer cooperation had become fertile in the United States. By improving their relationships with the southerners, the northern Baptists had opened the way to closer cooperation. Southern Baptists, however, took the crucial steps that led to the formation of the BWA. Now that the denomination had returned to a solid financial footing and was able to contain the pressures of Landmarkism, it was in a position to promote the idea of a broader Baptist fellowship.

The controversy over what actually happened was never fully resolved, and it continued to stir feelings for three decades. The initial action appears to have been that of William Warren Landrum, then pastor of the Second Baptist Church in Richmond, Virginia. He was impressed by the growing strength of the Presbyterian alliance and did not wish to see the Baptists left behind when other denominations were planning world gatherings. From his pulpit he began advocating a "Pan-Baptist Conference," a vision that he communicated to R. H. (Robert Healy) Pitt, editor of the *Religious Herald,* published in Richmond. Landrum urged Pitt to float the idea of such a conference. Pitt responded with an editorial in the April 5, 1895, issue: "Why might not we have at some early day a Pan-Baptist Council—representative gathering of Baptists from all parts of the globe for mutual acquaintance and the discussion of matters of common interest?"[28] His idea attracted some attention from other Baptist papers, and a year later he reiterated it when reporting on a meeting of the Presbyterian alliance. When this second appeal received little response, Pitt issued another call in December 1900 for a "Baptist World Council," either at the BU meeting in Edinburgh in 1901 (he was obviously aware of the discussions occurring in England) or in St. Louis in May 1903, an

> **Robert Healy Pitt**
>
> *In April 1895* Religious Herald *editor Robert Healy Pitt urged Baptists to unite in a world organization, a "Pan-Baptist Union." Pitt, who was born in Virginia in 1853, served the Baptist World Alliance as Western Secretary from 1913 until the Congress in Stockholm in 1923.*
>
> *He had attended the Virginia Baptist College of Richmond and then traveled to Georgia to study at its Baptist college, Mercer. Returning to Virginia, he pastored several churches.*
>
> *While serving the congregation at Venable Street in Richmond, he began contributing articles to the Virginia Baptist paper,* Religious Herald. *In 1888 Pitt was named associate editor of the paper and in a short time became its owner and editor. Not only his paper's readers but also editors of other papers enjoyed his clear, concise, and vigorous editorials. They were frequently reprinted, and a wider Baptist public became acquainted with his views.*
>
> *He promoted temperance, missions, and education. While serving as president of the Southern Baptist Education Commission, he encouraged opening a school of higher education for women. Pitt fought for separation of church and state. When the Virginia legislature proposed employing a chaplain for the state prison, he argued against it both in his paper and at the legislature. He opposed required Bible reading in public schools. Pitt died in 1937.*

occasion when both the Southern Baptist Convention and the various northern Baptist societies would be holding their annual meetings in the city as part of the Louisiana Purchase centennial celebration and world's fair.[29] Pitt's appeals then stopped, and he turned his attention to a more likely enterprise to achieve unity: the General Convention of the Baptists of North America.

According to Sherouse, the reason for this distraction was the fallout from the "Whitsitt controversy." In 1895, church historian William H. Whitsitt was named president of the Southern Baptist Theological Seminary in Louisville, Kentucky. He had studied baptismal practices among seventeenth-century Baptists and discovered that immersion had only been instituted around 1641. He published his findings in *A Question in Baptist History* (1896), a book that evoked a firestorm of criticism because it challenged the prevailing Landmark belief that an unbroken succession of Baptist churches existed from the time of Jesus's baptism until today. When some powerful trustees urged the Southern Baptist Convention (SBC) to cut off funding for the seminary, Whitsitt concluded it would be in the school's best interests for him to resign. He spent the remainder of his career at the University of Richmond. The incident revealed the vulnerability of SBC theological schools to the power of Landmarkism and its populist constituency.[30]

Pitt was one of only four Southern Baptist state newspaper editors who supported Whitsitt. The controversy helped to create an atmosphere in which suggestions for greater cooperation could be ignored. On the other hand, it did produce an interest among southern scholars to delve into the history of their English forebears and thus helped to encourage dialogue between English and American Baptists. In 1897, however, a new, more progressive paper known as *The Baptist Argus* (renamed *The Baptist World* in 1908) was launched in Louisville. Its editor, J. N. (John Newton) Prestridge, was a strong supporter of Whitsitt, and his organ was intended to be an alternative to the *Western Recorder,* the Kentucky paper edited by T. T. Eaton, a strident foe of the controversial professor.

A member of the *Argus* staff was the respected Southern Seminary Greek professor A. (Archibald) T. Robertson. In 1902 he persuaded Prestridge to include a "World Outlook" supplement in the first issue of each year that reported on Baptist work in other countries, and this stimulated awareness on Prestridge's part of the global dimensions of Baptist life. Then, in the January 14, 1904, Robertson contributed, on "my own initiative" he claimed,[31] an unsigned editorial renewing the Pitt-Landrum vision. He proposed that "the Baptists of the world send some of its [*sic*] mission and education leaders for a conference on Baptist world problems." If this could lead to a "Pan-Baptist Conference on a larger scale as to attendance, well and good." His hope was that it could take place in London later in 1904.[32]

Although Robertson said he was merely throwing out the suggestion, Prestridge promptly took up the idea as his own and, supported by the seminary professor, worked indefatigably to promote the idea of a meeting. The response was enthusiastic, and endorsements came from the SBC,

John Newton Prestridge

The first Western Secretary, John Newton Prestridge, promoted a world organization for Baptists in his newspaper, **The Baptist Argus.** *Prestridge, born in Selma, Alabama, and educated at Alabama Baptists' Howard College (now Samford University), had pastored one church in his home state before moving to Kentucky. There he continued as a pastor and served as president of Williamsburg Institute 1894–98.*

In 1897 Prestridge began publishing the Argus. Some professors who taught at the Southern Baptist Theological Seminary were angry because the established Kentucky Baptist newspaper, the **Western Recorder,** *was attacking the views of the seminary president, William H. Whitsitt. They sponsored Prestridge's* **Argus.** *In January 1904 one of those professors, A. T. Robertson, contributed an article encouraging Baptists of the world to unite.*

Prestridge published the article and made the idea his own. He mailed copies of that issue of the Argus to Baptist leaders around the world. He helped plan the 1905 Congress, eagerly attended, and was coconvener of the committee that drew up the plan of organization before accepting the post of Western Secretary.

Back home in Kentucky, he changed the name of his paper to **The Baptist World** *and used it to promote the young Baptist World Alliance to his fellow Baptists in the United States. He assisted with the 1911 Congress and soon after it published* **Modern Baptist Heroes and Martyrs.** *This book retells the stories that he had heard in Philadelphia of Baptists who persevered despite persecution. One of these heroes was John Clifford, the first President of the Baptist World Alliance.*

ABMU, BU of Great Britain and Ireland, and Baptists in other countries. Pitt's *Religious Herald* quickly jumped on the bandwagon, while objections were to be found only in the Landmark papers. In England pastor-historian (and former president of the Baptist College of Victoria in Australia) William T. Whitley reminded his colleagues that Rippon had already suggested a pan-Baptist conference, but BU secretary J. H. (John Howard) Shakespeare was somewhat more hesitant. He wrote to Prestridge that he was "in general sympathy with the proposal" but did not feel it could be carried out in 1904. It would require at least twelve months to arrange a Baptist Congress. Shakespeare also suggested that a resolution of support from the SBC and the various northern Baptist societies for a "Pan-Baptist Conference in 1905" would be needed to secure British support for the endeavor.[33]

Over the next few months, the Council of the BU became aware of the high level of support in the United States for an international Baptist meeting. It took up the organizational initiative and on October 4, 1904, adopted a formal resolution inviting representatives of the worldwide Baptist family to meet in London the following July. The SBC named a twenty-three member Pan-Baptist Conference Committee that included both Pitt and Prestridge, and the group met with a similar body of northern Baptists to form a joint American Committee. To plan the Congress, the Americans worked with the sixty-member British Committee, a body that included eight women and represented both the BU and the Baptist Missionary Society.[34]

Inspiration was to be provided by distinguished British personalities Maclaren and Clifford. Shakespeare was responsible for organizing and administering the Congress, assisted by Whitley, who was released from his pastorate in Preston to help. The global vision was about to be translated into reality.

To Whom Belongs the Credit?
Unfortunately, the issue of claiming credit for the idea of the first Congress dogged BWA discussions for some years. Did it belong to the English, who became aware of the need for closer ties with other Baptists and were already involved in developing connections? Or, did the initiative come from the United States? And if the latter were true, which American deserved the credit? As the second World Congress approached, Pitt renewed his claim to primacy in various *Religious Herald* editorials in 1910, but the rivalry between him and Prestridge apparently subsided.[35]

But then in a speech, "The Baptist World Alliance in Retrospect and Prospect," at the 1928 Toronto Congress, BWA General Secretary

J. H. (James Henry) Rushbrooke gave the credit to Pitt and Landrum.[36] This upset Robertson, who told Rushbrooke that Prestridge was actually responsible and that he should correct his statement in the official report. The General Secretary said he would, but it did not happen. Robertson then placed an article in the *Watchman-Examiner* (reprinted in the *Review and Expositor*) setting the record straight as to Prestridge's and his own role in the process. In his opinion, the effort of Pitt "had nothing whatsoever to do" with the origin of the Congress "except as it may have prepared people's minds for it."[37]

Robertson even had the Southern Baptist Seminary librarian Thomas A. Johnson check the *Baptist World/Argus* archive housed there and unearth Shakespeare's response to Prestridge's letter that had contained the marked copy of the 1904 editorial. After he had seen this evidence, Rushbrooke admitted that he had erred at Toronto as to the origins of the Baptist Congress and sent an apologetic letter to the editor of the *Review and Expositor* corroborating Robertson's contentions.[38] This apology was "thoroughly satisfactory and gratifying" to Robertson, but apparently Rushbrooke did not issue a formal public correction. The question has long since ceased to arouse any concern among Baptist historians.

---

1. Richard Knight, *History of the General or Six Principle Baptists in Europe* (Providence: Smith and Parmentor, 1827), pp. 120–121. Also quoted in John H. Y. Briggs, "British Baptists and the Beginnings of the Baptist World Alliance," *Baptist Quarterly* 42 (January 2005), p. 2. Both the Briggs essay and Craig A. Sherouse, "The Formation of the Baptist World Alliance" in *Baptist Faith and Witness, Book 2: The Papers of the Study and Research Division of the Baptist World Alliance 1995–2000*, ed. L. A. (Tony) Cupit (McLean, VA: BWA, 1999), pp. 150–168, are useful treatments of the historical background of the organization.

2. *The Baptist Annual Register for 1790*, p. 4. On Rippon's action see Ken R. Manley, *'Redeeming Love Proclaim': John Rippon and the Baptists* (Carlisle, United Kingdom: Paternoster, 2004), pp. 272–273.

3. William T. Whitley, *A History of British Baptists* (London: Charles Griffin, 1923), p. 242.

4. On the formation and development of the BMS see Brian Stanley, *The History of the Baptist Missionary Society, 1792–1992* (Edinburgh: T. & T. Clark, 1992).

5. Andrew Fuller, *An Account of the Particular Baptist Society for Propagating the Gospel among the Heathen* (London: 1793), pp. 1–2.

6. Timothy George, *Faithful Witness: The Life and Mission of William Carey* (Birmingham, AL: New Hope, 1991), p. 162.

7. See Horace O. Russell, *The Missionary Outreach of the West Indian Church: Jamaican Baptist Missions to West Africa in the Nineteenth Century* (New York: Peter Lang, 2000), and Grant Gordon, *From Slavery to Freedom: The Life of David George, Pioneer Black Baptist Minister* (Hantsport, N.S.: Lancelot Press, 1992).

8. *American Baptist Magazine and Missionary Intelligencer* 4 (May 1824), pp. 324–328 (quote on 327). According to William W. Barnes, the pseudonymous author went beyond missionary leader Luther Rice's vision of a national organization of Baptists. "The New Hampshire Confession of Faith: Its Origin and Use," *Review and Expositor* 39 (January 1942), p. 5.

9. Sherouse, "Formation of the Baptist World Alliance," p. 152.

10. Ian Randall and David Hilborn, *One Body in Christ: The History and Significance of the Evangelical Alliance* (Carlisle, United Kingdom: Paternoster, 2001), pp. 62–69.

11. J. H. Y. Briggs, *The English Baptists of the Nineteenth Century* (Oxford: Baptist Historical Society, 1994), pp. 232, 214. Francis A. Cox and James Hoby, *The Baptists in America: A Narrative of the Deputation form the Baptist Union in England to the United States and Canada* (New York: Leavitt, Lord, 1836).

12. See Richard V. Pierard, "The Christian World Communions: Denominational Ecumenism on a Global Scale," in *Ecumenism and History: Studies in Honour of John H. Y. Briggs*, ed. Anthony R. Cross (Carlisle, United Kingdom: Paternoster, 2002), pp. 106–107.

13. Sherouse, "Formation of the Baptist World Alliance," p. 154.

14. Ibid., pp. 154–158.

15. Bill J. Leonard, *Baptist Ways: A History* (Valley Forge, PA: Judson Press, 2003), pp. 203–204, 269, 394–395.

16. Sherouse, "Formation of the Baptist World Alliance," p. 155; Carl W. Tiller, *The Twentieth Century Baptist: Chronicles of Baptists in the First Seventy-five Years of the Baptist World Alliance* (Valley Forge, PA: Judson Press, 1980), pp. 1–6, 2–3, 3–6.

17. Leonard, *Baptist Ways*, pp. 391–392.

18. Norman Fox, "The Baptist Congress," in A. H. Newman, *A Century of Baptist Achievement* (Philadelphia: American Baptist Publication Society, 1901), pp. 288–293, describes the formation and work of the congress. The only significant scholarly assessment of the endeavor is William H. Brackney, "The Frontier of Free Exchange of Ideas: The Baptist Congress as a Forum for Baptist Concerns, 1881–1913," *Baptist History and Heritage* 38 (Summer/Fall 2003), pp. 8–27.

19. Sherouse, "Formation of the Baptist World Alliance," pp. 156–157.

20. Ibid., pp. 157–158.

21. *BU Council Minutes,* July and October 1900, p. 16.

22. Ibid., April 1900, pp. 5–8.

23. *Baptist Magazine,* 1901, pp. 488–489.

24. *BU Council Minutes,* January 1901, pp. 2–3.

25. Ibid., April 1900, p. 19.

26. *Baptist Union Handbook,* 1901.

27. *The Baptist Magazine,* 1901, p. 519.

28. *Religious Herald*, April 4, 1895, p. 2.

29. Ibid., July 30, 1896, p. 2; Dec. 20, 1900, p. 8.

30. Sherouse, "Formation of the Baptist World Alliance," pp. 160–161; Leonard, *Baptist Ways*, pp. 215–216.

31. A. T. Robertson, "Memories of the Toronto World Congress," *Watchman-Examiner* 16 (July 19, 1928), pp. 920–921. The steps leading to the formation of the BWA were detailed in a handwritten memorandum prepared by Southern Baptist Theological Seminary Librarian Thomas A. Johnson for J. H. Rushbrooke to use in writing a history of the organization. Mimeographed text, c. 1930, contained in BWA I. 1. 1. F.

32. Text in Tiller, *Twentieth Century Baptist*, p. 1–2.

33. BWA I. l. l. F. J. H. Shakespeare to J. N. Prestridge, March 2, 1904. Robertson's biographer claims that Shakespeare at first "had no sympathy" for the idea of such a meeting in London and considered it "rather foolish." But when he saw "how the entire Baptist world was enthusiastic over the plan," he dropped his objections and worked to make it a success. Everett Gill, *A. T. Robertson: A Biography* (New York: Macmillan, 1943), p. 97. On the other hand, Peter Shepherd in his biography of the BU secretary, *The Making of a Modern Denomination: John Howard Shakespeare and the English Baptists* (Carlisle, United Kingdom: Paternoster, 2001), does not indicate that he had such reservations about the meeting.

34. Sherouse, "Formation of the Baptist World Alliance," pp. 162–163; F. Townley Lord, *Baptist World Fellowship: A Short History of the Baptist World Alliance* (London: Carey Kingsgate Press, 1955), pp. 3–4. The BWA Minute Book details the actions of the planning committee. BWA IX 1 .1.

35. Gill, *A. T. Robertson*, pp. 97–99.

36. *BWA Congress*, 1928, p. 64. The speech was reprinted in the *Watchman-Examiner* (July 12, 1928) and the *Review and Expositor* (July 1928).

37. Robertson, "Memories of the Toronto World Congress," *Review and Expositor* 25 (October 1928), pp. 469–472. The article was originally published in the July 19, 1928 *Watchman-Examiner* (note 31).

38. BWA I.1.1.F. Mrs. J. N. Prestridge later published a brief essay, *The Baptist World Alliance: Its Beginning* (Nashville: Broadman, 1939), that defended her husband's leading role in the founding. It added nothing of substance to the discussion.

2

FROM 1905 TO THE END OF THE FIRST WORLD WAR

John H. Y. Briggs

Baptists were on the threshold of experiencing the fulfillment of their long-held dream of greater unity. With a more unified witness, they could better represent the unique Baptist principles within the larger Christian community and carry out more effectively the divine mandate to evangelize the nations. The Baptist World Congress thus marked a crucial turning point in Baptist history. The Baptist groups scattered across the globe could now begin coordinating their efforts in evangelism and promoting religious freedom and have an impact far beyond what they had had prior to that time.

Translating the Global Vision into Reality

In accordance with the Baptist Union (BU) Council's decision to convene the Congress in 1905, an organizational structure was created that included twelve preliminary "district meetings" in London churches on the eve of the gathering; large plenary sessions in Exeter Hall with papers on a wide range of topics; and numerous luncheons, receptions, and other social events. Named as president of the Congress was the revered seventy-nine-year-old Scottish-born preacher and expositor and long-time pastor of Union Chapel, Manchester, Alexander Maclaren;[1] John Clifford, the indefatigable advocate of Free Church causes, was made vice chairman.[2] The administrative duties were handled by J. H. (John Howard) Shakespeare, secretary of the BU, with the assistance of William T. Whitley, whose congregation in Preston had given him leave to work full-time for the Congress, and Harold Knott, the secretary of Maclaren's church. Shakespeare described Maclaren as possessing "features, stern and ascetic, sometimes melting into tenderness, or irradiated with a playful kindliness," while Clifford, an energetic activist in matters of religious liberty, was "the hero of the world battle against priestly aggression, superstition and tyranny in every form."³ Assisting Maclaren in presiding over the sessions of the Congress were ten vice presidents, six of whom came from the United Kingdom, including the future prime minister David Lloyd George, and one each from Germany, the United States, Australia, and Canada. Significantly, seven of the ten were laymen.

Under Shakespeare's leadership, a British committee collaborated with the Americans to plan the Congress. It had sixty members, including eight women, and embraced the interests of both the BU and the Baptist Missionary Society (BMS). By contrast the committee appointed during the Congress to design the structure for a continuation body was composed of eight from the United States, two from Canada, four from the United Kingdom, and one each from Australia and continental Europe. It included no women but did have one black member, E. C. Morris from the National Baptist Convention. Some women did, however, address the Congress, including the redoubtable Nannie Helen Burroughs, secretary of the Women's Auxiliary of the National Baptist Convention, who also spoke at a Sunday open-air gathering in Hyde Park. Another female speaker was Lucy Peabody (listed in the program as Mrs. Norman Mather Waterbury), a missionary to India who returned

John Clifford

The first President of the Baptist World Alliance, John Clifford, was born into a working-class Baptist family in the English Midlands in 1836. At the age of eleven he had to leave school to work at a lace factory. He educated himself through reading and, in 1855, was accepted by the Baptist Academy at Leicester as a candidate for the ministry. Three years later he became pastor of Praed Street Church in London.

The church was small, but Clifford had many innovative ideas. He created the Mutual Benefit Society, whereby church funds could help members in times of need; began Wednesday evening free lectures and study classes for the community. Clifford was also an able preacher. The congregation outgrew its premises twice and, in 1877, built an imposing structure in Westbourne Park.

Clifford continued his education by earning a series of degrees at the University of London. He attracted attention in Baptist circles, was invited to the address the assembly of London Baptists at their annual meeting. From 1870–74 he was editor of the **General Baptist Magazine**. *He became president of the General Baptist Union in 1872, of the London Baptist Association in 1879, and of the Baptist Union in 1888.*

When Baptists gathered in 1905, Clifford was the natural choice for President. He entered into the work of the Baptist World Alliance wholeheartedly, both behind the scenes and at its public gatherings. He died in 1923 while discussing evangelism with members of the Baptist Union Council.

home after her husband's death, served as home secretary of the Woman's Baptist Foreign Missionary Society of the East, and was a major figure in American Baptist missions. Two women's organizations were formally represented—the Woman's Baptist Foreign Missionary Society and Woman's Home Missionary Society from the United States—and 290 women were listed among the "foreign delegates" at the Congress.[4]

Lacking denominational membership lists—or for that matter even specific criteria for membership—it was impossible to know ahead of time who from among the greater Baptist family would attend; and thus, it was difficult to predict what shape the Congress would have. Since deep divisions existed among Baptists in North America and the British Isles caused by such things as Landmarkism, the Down Grade Controversy, and the new "modernist" theology, it seemed unlikely that conservative groups would have any interest in a body as broad as the Baptist World Alliance (BWA) promised to be, but positions were not as yet firmly defined. As will be shown below, the new BWA itself imposed no creedal tests on membership; the preamble to the constitution simply referred to "Churches of the Baptist order and faith."

Discovering One Another

Twenty-six countries, from Finland in the North to New Zealand in the South, were represented at the Congress. The roll call of the nations at the opening session was a colorful celebratory event. Of the three thousand delegates registered, some twenty-five hundred came from the four United Kingdom nations (England, Scotland, Wales, and Ireland). An analysis of the roll-call responses, the names mentioned at the Congress, delegation claims, and identified speakers reveals that more than three hundred delegates came from North America, more than a hundred represented continental Europe, some twenty—mainly laypeople—came from Australia and New Zealand, fourteen were from South Africa,and seven were from the Caribbean and Central America; but China, India, Japan, and Africa were, with only two exceptions, represented by expatriate missionaries. There were Americans from the North, the South, and two black conventions (the large National Baptist and the smaller Lott Carey). In fact, fifty blacks from the United States attended the meeting. A large percentage of the overseas delegates were accommodated in the homes of London Baptists, while the BU raised sufficient funds to cover the Congress's costs and help with subsidizing those from particularly needy parts of the world.

A challenging discovery was the extent of Baptist persecution. In the

United States separation of church and state and the accompanying ban on religious establishments had enabled the growth of strong denominations, but such was not the case in many other areas. The Danish delegation paid tribute to the support they had received from British Baptists when they were suffering under the heavy hand of the state. Unfortunately, persecution still persisted in Europe, as was exemplified by the harsh treatment experienced by Baptists and other evangelical groups in Romania.[5]

Particular attention was drawn to the situation in the Russian Empire. Gospodin Pavlov, who was working in Georgia, reported that he had been exiled to Siberia because he refused to assure the police that he would stop preaching. Baron Waldemar Uixkiull of Estonia, who had been converted through the preaching of Swedish missionaries in the Baltic provinces, spoke of the persecution of Stundists in southern Russia and the sufferings of various preachers in Poland. Another evangelical baptistic advance, initiated by the Plymouth Brethren luminary Lord Radstock (Granville Waldegrave, Third Baron Radstock) among aristocrats in St. Petersburg, seemed to be faring a little better. In April 1905 the Tsar had issued a decree promising religious freedom in Russia, but it did not include evangelistic work by any group other than the Orthodox. The Baptists and Mennonites were granted a degree of recognition but they were not allowed to work among ethnic Russians. They were living in great poverty though they did receive some help from British and American Baptist sources. The Russian Baptist leadership disapproved of the war with Japan in East Asia, recognizing "the justice of God in using the heroic and wonderful Japanese people as His instruments to destroy the bureaucracy of Russia."[6]

A Pentecostal Experience?

In his welcoming address, BU President Judge William Willis declared the Congress to be "a Pentecostal gathering," representing that same strength of numbers and diversity of race and language as was present at the first Pentecost.[7] Doctrinal difficulties of past years were put to one side. Widespread respect for the legacy of Charles H. Spurgeon, described by Willis as "the greatest Evangelical preacher,"[8] permeated the celebrations, which included the unveiling of a statue of this giant of the pulpit that was to stand in the foyer of the new Baptist Church House.

Clifford insisted that Christ was being exalted at the meeting: "His place is supreme in the life of the individual, supreme in the life of the Christian Church, and supreme also and ultimately in the life of the world." This was a testimony to "soul liberty," in that Christ was the "one absolute Authority" in the religious life, with the believer "free from everybody else," noting that soul liberty naturally led to political liberty.⁹ The published proceedings of the Congress incontrovertibly revealed the Baptists to be evangelical in faith, when speaker after speaker affirmed the central doctrines of the Christian faith. As Augustus H. Strong of Rochester Seminary (U.S.) put it, the Pentecostal spirit was captured in Christ's two crucial imperatives: "Know me" and "Make me known." It is these essentials that made the church "into an institution inclusive of all mankind."¹⁰

To put aside any doubt that Baptists stood in the tradition of the historic orthodox Christian faith and of the "Holy Catholic Church," Maclaren invited all present to affirm their faith by repeating the Apostles' Creed, line by line. Such an act, he suggested, would rid the world of considerable misunderstanding about the Baptists and stop a good deal of slander. He went on to say in his presidential speech that a relationship with the living Christ and possession of the indwelling Spirit was imperative. Without these two reference points, everything else was of no advantage, "however orthodox or earnest or eloquent or learned or up-to-date or wise our methods." His prayer was that the Congress might help to direct all to come "nearer to the only Source of life and power and peace and ability of character—the touch of the fiery Spirit, the Spirit of burning, and the Spirit of Holiness." There was a great need for revival, which "must begin with each of us by ourselves . . . . Your revival, Christian minister, must begin in your study and on your knees. Your revival must be for yourselves . . . . Congresses may be multiplied a million-fold, and all our instruments may be in perfect order, but unless the fire comes the sacrifice will be unconsumed."¹¹ An interesting commentary on Maclaren's affirmation came from Principal Edwards of Cardiff, who told the Congress that Welsh church membership had quite remarkably risen from 117,000 to 157,000, that is, by rather more than a third in the last six months, as Baptists harvested the fruit of the Welsh Revival.¹²

The conferees were anything but cautiously optimistic about the global impact of the Baptist witness. They believed it was advancing on almost every front. Shakespeare rapturously labeled the assembly "an achievement of faith which must be added to the eleventh chapter of the Epistle to the Hebrews." He said the delegates represented a family of some six million baptized believers worldwide, although he exaggerated by suggesting "almost every land upon earth is represented by members of the Baptist community." He then went beyond John Rippon's inclusion of Mennonites in the Baptist numbers to claim an additional one million Disciples of Christ "who correspond with us in faith and practice."¹³ By adding Sunday School children, nonbaptized adherents, and others who associated with

> ## John Howard Shakespeare
>
>
>
> The organizer of the first Baptist World Congress, who became the Baptist World Alliance's first European Secretary, was John Howard Shakespeare. Born in Malton, England, in 1857, educated at Regent's Park College and London University, he pastored in Norwich before being chosen in 1898, as secretary of the Baptist Union, a position in which he served until 1924.
>
> A man of considerable administrative ability and a fertile brain, Shakespeare gathered around him able men and women who, with him, generated a spirit of enthusiasm as British Baptists entered the twentieth century. He led the Baptist Union to play a more active role, strengthened ties between churches, and raised money for new buildings and to help poorer pastors. He and his brother established **The Baptist Times**, and for many years he was its editor.
>
> In June 1904 Shakespeare urged the Baptist Union general purposes committee to plan a Pan-Baptist Conference in London in the summer of 1905. After receiving a copy of the article from Prestridge's paper, he had decided to take on the project. His work behind the scenes ensured a successful Congress and made him the obvious choice as Secretary.
>
> Shakespeare believed in bringing people together. He worked hard to see that the Congress was not a one-time event but resulted in an organization. He wanted to cement ties between European Baptists and led in organizing European Congresses. He became interested in uniting all Christians, a dream that his fellow Baptists did not share. He died in 1928.

the Baptist cause, he came up with a worldwide strength of at least twenty million. Then, he grew even more expansive by insisting we "are the greatest Protestant evangelical community on earth, as we certainly are in the influence we have on Christian thought and activity."[14]

Approaching Baptist identity from a more theological perspective, J. D. Freeman of Bloor Street Church in Toronto argued in his keynote address entitled "The Place of Baptists in the Christian Church" that "the Baptist denomination is not an accident or an incident, nor an experiment; it is the normal development and permanent embodiment of a great Christian principle." He defined this as "an acute and vivid consciousness of the sovereignty of Christ, accompanied by a steadfast determination to secure the complete and consistent recognition of His personal, direct, and undelegated authority over the souls of men." This "is the spinal column of our theology. It is the bed-rock of our church polity. It is the mainspring of our missionary activity."[15]

Modern Thought and the Congress

The strong affirmation of evangelical faith was necessary to provide a biblical and theological foundation for the discussion of major issues. One issue was the matter of contemporary biblical scholarship. Principal

J. T. Marshall of Manchester College (U.K.) affirmed the positive contributions that the critical methods made in understanding the story of Abraham: "What has been disclosed suffices abundantly to show that we are not dealing with romance, or myth, but with substantial historical traditions."[16] Professor Milton Evans from Crozer Theological Seminary in Pennsylvania (U.S.) was equally confident that New Testament criticism moved the reader away from the bare form of Scripture and the familiar and hallowed language found there to engagement with the search for truth and meaning: "Protestant Christianity must take modern criticism seriously and joyously, both for what it is in itself, and for what it has done. It has given us a better interpretation, a better appreciation of early Christianity, a better apologetic. It has rendered signal service by insisting that the Scriptures must be judged by their purpose to disclose God's redemptive plan . . . . The net result of modern criticism is that the Bible is conceived to be a truly human book and therefore intelligible . . . . As modern historical inquiry more vividly presents to the imagination the truly human nature of the incarnate Word of God, without shaking confidence in his true Deity, so modern Higher and Lower Criticism make the written Word of God truly human literature, without destroying its inspirational character. Research has not destroyed a single fact upon which Christian faith rests; it has only destroyed the error of conjectures concerning the method of our Father in giving us a Bible and has modified methods of interpretation."[17]

Others were less enthusiastic about indiscriminately embracing the new scholarship. John Thomas of Liverpool (U.K.) challenged the criticism of the Pentateuch on its own critical canons. A. T. Robertson of Louisville (U.S.) said the problem was not so much with the critical method itself as with the underlying philosophy of critics that was every bit as prejudicial as the alleged prejudices of believing scholars. Strong complained that all too many critics lacked the literary sense of being able to appreciate the presence of the spiritual and the supernatural element in the Word of God. Criticism that was "animated by the Spirit of Christ and recognizes Christ's mastery" was of a wholly different order.[18]

Southern Baptist Theological Seminary President E. Y. (Edgar Young) Mullins gained enormous stature through his address that critiqued both modern and traditional theology. As J. H. Rushbrooke later remarked: "He arose to speak, a man practically unknown east of the Atlantic, and sat down with a world reputation."[19] Mullins insisted that the newer thought was "tentative and unauthoritative because it is simply a protest against the old . . . . Much of the old is also inadequate because it ignores aspects of truth which are essential to a complete Scriptural representation . . . .

Both theologies are simplified too much."[20] To be adequate, theology had to answer great moral questions, not just provide rational satisfaction. Rejecting the kind of criticism that was the tool of philosophical doubt, Mullins said it could play a positive role: "Sober, sane and reverent criticism has rendered a mighty service in creating a sense of perspective in the progressive revelation of the Bible, in fostering the method of careful historical exegesis, and in other ways." When it recognized its limitations and did not make assertions unless they had a basis of fact, criticism was a valuable department of theological science. "No man is a true Baptist who is unwilling to accept all the light and truth which criticism may bring."[21] Then he dealt with some of the failings of recent scholarship and suggested that while God was sovereign over his creatures, doctrinal statements always needed to be based on the authority of Scripture and informed by the facts of Christian experience. Pastor John G. Raws of Australia took the argument further and insisted that conduct rather than creed would be the effective test of commitment in an age when correct action was more important than correct belief.[22]

Mullins concluded by offering the Congress six axioms as the basis for a new Baptist apologetic and a platform for universal adoption. He called them "the predestined goals of man's religious thinking" because they sprang out of Scripture teaching, met a deep response in Christian experience, and were universal, necessary, self-evident forms of religious life:

1. The theological axiom: *The holy and loving God has a right to be Sovereign.*
2. The religious axiom: *All men have an equal right to direct access to God*
3. The ecclesiastical axiom: *All believers have equal privileges in the Church.*
4. The moral axiom: *To be responsible man must be free.*
5. The social axiom: *Love your neighbor as yourself.*
6. The religio-civic axiom: *A free Church in a free State.*[23]

To explore both biblical criticism and modern theology in the context of a three thousand–delegate Congress was far from easy, given the size of the meeting and the range of views held by those present. But because the subjects were approached within the warm confidence of an evangelical commitment, they were tackled without rancor or accusations of heresy. Nothing revealed this more poignantly than the nearly universal admiration expressed for Clifford who in his own person combined openness to modern thought with commitment to personal evangelism. Such tolerance said something profound about the ties that bound the Baptist family together.

John Clifford and Social Issues

John Clifford, the sixty-eight-year-old pastor of Westbourne Park Chapel in London's Paddington district, was one of the foremost Baptists in England. His social activism and more open theological views, particularly on the Bible, made him a controversial figure, but still he played a prominent role in the Congress. At the time a bitter conflict was raging between Free Churchmen and the Church of England over the funding of church schools. Thus, in his opening remarks at the Congress session on education that he chaired, Liberal Party Member of Parliament David Lloyd George denounced the Tory government's policy and insisted that the Anglican Church controlled over two-thirds of the schools and three-fifths of the teacher training colleges. Clifford then praised the legislator, a leader in the struggle for secular public education, as "a good Baptist."[24] Judge Willis had earlier pointed out that under the Education Act of 1902 public funds were directed to Anglican and Roman Catholic schools, and in his opinion this was "the most afflictive action of the Legislature which the brethren of the Baptist Churches have ever known." The "Catechism of the Church of England substitutes infant sprinkling for regeneration," a doctrine Baptists could not accept without "betraying the teaching of their Lord."[25]

After providing a lengthy explanation of the education situation, Clifford expressed gratitude for the support he had received in the Passive Resistance Movement (PRM). Although George White, a Member of Parliament and 1903 president of the BU, had launched the PRM, Clifford was its popular leader. Those involved in the protest refused to pay the tax that might go to support church schools, and many of them suffered confiscation of their property and were even jailed.[26] In the ensuing discussion period F. B. McGowan of Godstone, a village near London, declared that he had been sent to prison three times for noncompliance with the Education Act. He saw no reason to pay for an Anglican priest to contradict on Monday the teaching he had given in Sunday School the previous day. Those who had been imprisoned were invited to stand up; a few did, while others reported that their property had been seized to pay the tax.[27] Persecution was neither just a historical experience, nor something only experienced in Eastern Europe.

A lengthy debate took place on the Baptist attitude toward the working classes and ethics in business. The speakers made it clear that a "no politics" rule must not be used selectively to avoid dealing with such questions as temperance, housing, poverty, and misuse of wealth and power. Mullins pointed out that the function of the church and the gospel is spiritual, yet we must not "divorce the gospel from social reform." One speaker claimed that "a very large percentage of the business done in London is done dishonestly," and this provoked a robust defense by others from the business community. The vigorous debate finally had to cease because time had run out.[28]

Missiological Questions

As Baptists were one of the most missions-minded denominations in Protestantism, it was no surprise that missiological matters were aired at length. In a session on the world faiths, the emphasis was that the greatest need of the nations was for the gospel and the Christian's duty was to convey it. Richard Glover of Bristol, speaking on "The Inadequacy of Non-Christian Religions to Meet the Needs of the World," strongly affirmed that only the religion of the Bible provided a worthy conception of God and spoke of a Savior accessible to all people. However, while maintaining that it was not for the church to limit the embrace of the Holy One of Israel, he was bold enough to say that "the title of my subject must not be held to imply a belief on my part that the salvation of God is limited to those exclusively who know the Gospel story."[29]

Another speaker urged Baptists to discontinue using the word "heathen" and to inform themselves as much as possible about the other faiths. They should master the culture of those to whom they witnessed, recognize whatever truth their religion might contain, and make it the basis for the larger and fuller revelation that Christianity brought.[30] A third contributor argued that they should refrain from wounding others' feelings by denouncing their superstitions and instead preach Christ.[31] As for mission strategy, it was better that it be determined on the field than back in the homeland, and comity agreements with other agencies to carry out work more efficiently should be considered. W. O. Carver of Southern Baptist Seminary warned of the unhealthy trend in some circles in his country to restrict missionary work solely to preaching, thereby rejecting any outlay of money and effort in medical relief, education, and training an indigenous ministry. Indeed, one state convention had all but committed itself to the view that "nothing is missions except the preaching of the Gospel from the pulpit." Such an extreme position was happily not widespread. In the past Southern Baptist methods had been "scriptural and loyal, but not always broad and liberal," and, therefore, Carver confessed, "our part has been too small in the world's redemption."[32]

Papers on the mission of the church in specific areas—China, Japan, India, Africa, and Europe—were delivered, while others looked at mission support, the contribution of women in missionary work, and the self-propagation of indigenous churches. In the most radical of these addresses, Timothy Richard, the veteran BMS worker stationed in Shanghai, questioned current missionary practice and used China's failure to deal with the intrusion of the Western powers as a parable to challenge the churches.[33] After surveying the virtual partition of China and the ineffectiveness of the Peking government's response, he urged Christian missions to seize their opportunities. The strategy Richard proposed was one of holistic mission that met the needs of "the whole man, body and soul," saving him "from hell in this world as well as in the next" rather than pietistically focusing on salvation for the soul only. His proposal included a general educational program that challenged the whole nation on issues of religion and ethics, deploying indigenous agents rather than expatriate missionaries, targeting those elites who had the most influential positions in society, utilizing the indigenous press rather than the foreign pulpit to reach people, and pursuing the prospect of universal peace rather than maintaining expensive standing armies. For his strategies he claimed the blessing of the Spirit, while designating the methods he criticized as ones that had "failed in the past."[34]

He also pleaded for ecumenical action and urged Baptists to move beyond denominational boundaries to united Protestant effort. He envisioned a federation of the six major denominations at work in China—Episcopalians, Methodists, Presbyterians, Congregationalists, Lutherans, and Baptists—into one cooperating force because "God will not judge us by our creeds so much as by our fruit."[35] Unless this was done, Confucianism, Buddhism, and Taoism—notwithstanding divine elements in each—would through ignorance continue to oppress the people of China. The divine call was to establish the Kingdom of God in all the earth in this generation, but "where are the volunteers?"[36]

A Vehicle for Baptist Togetherness

The delegates did not envision this meeting as a one-time event at which Baptists could exult in their distinctives and achievements and then return to business as usual. As Shakespeare commented, "We have travelled far when it has become possible to federate the great Baptist community for common purposes, and as a demonstration of the fact that there is now in existence, and to be reckoned with, a Baptist world consciousness."[37] Thus, it was a foregone conclusion that the Congress would set up a vehicle to give permanent expression to Baptist worldwide fellowship. On the first morning, July 12, a motion was adopted authorizing the president to appoint a Committee on Future Congresses, with J. N. (John Newton) Prestridge (U.S.) and Shakespeare as conveners. The committee was directed to report on July 17.[38] Its duties included proposing a plan of organization and developing a constitution and bylaws. When the report was submitted, Clifford moved its adoption. It was carried "unanimously, and with great enthusiasm." A nine-person nominating committee was then appointed to choose the officers and Executive Committee, and the session ended with the singing of the "Doxology."[39]

The principal features of the constitution of the new body, to be known as the Baptist World Alliance, were as follows: The preamble expressed the feeling of the need to manifest "the essential oneness in the Lord Jesus Christ as their God and Saviour of the Churches of the Baptist order and faith throughout the service and cooperation among them." At the same time the Alliance, extending to every part of the world, was not a confederation as such. It recognized the independence of each particular church and would not assume the functions of any existing organization. Membership, however, was to be corporate in nature, not individual persons or congregations. It would be open to any "general union, convention, or association of Baptist Churches." The officers would be a President, a Vice President from each country represented in the Alliance, a Treasurer, a British secretary, and an American Secretary. The president, treasurer, two secretaries, and twenty-one other members apportioned according to a geographical quota would comprise the Executive Committee and would be elected at each general meeting of the Alliance. The Alliance would meet in general assembly every five years unless otherwise determined by the Executive Committee.

The next morning the nominating committee presented a slate of officers that also was accepted by acclamation. The President was Clifford; the two Secretaries were Prestridge and Shakespeare; and the Treasurer was Henry Kirke Porter of Pittsburgh, Pennsylvania. Twenty-four Vice Presidents, one for each country joining as charter members, were named, as well as the twenty-one members-at-large of the Executive Committee.[40]

Thus the Baptist World Alliance was born. It did not aspire to be a superchurch, but rather it was intended to be a forum for fellowship, an agency of compassion, a voice for liberty, an instrument for evangelism, and a channel of communication.[41] The founders regarded the strength of the fellowship achieved across so many boundaries as so important that they had little apparent consciousness that members of the Baptist family existed who had no desire to be part of the fellowship here defined.

Deepening Fellowship with European Baptists: The Commission to Hungary

Clifford was now installed as President of the Alliance, and an office was opened in the London headquarters of the BU. He had hoped to follow up the Congress with a pastoral visit to the scattered and sometimes persecuted Baptist groups in Europe, but his duties at Westbourne Park Chapel and involvement in the Passive Resistance campaign in Britain precluded him from doing so at the moment. He delegated the task to the thirty-five-year-old Newton H. Marshall, pastor of Heath Street Baptist Church in Hampstead, London. As a youth, Marshall belonged to Westbourne Park and participated in the Preachers' Institute that Clifford had formed to train young men for leadership in the church. After studying at Midland Baptist College in Nottingham, he went on for further study in Germany and subsequently entered the ministry. Supported by the BU's Continental Committee, Marshall undertook a lengthy visit that provided him with a wide range of information about European Baptist life.[42]

Another person whom Clifford mentored through his Preachers' Institute was Rushbrooke. A year older than Marshall, he too studied at Midland and in Germany at Halle and Berlin, and in 1902 assumed a pastorate in Derby. In January 1907 he relocated in London as pastor of the Archway Road Baptist Church in Highgate, where Shakespeare was a member. Having married Dorothea Weber, whom he had met in Berlin, Rushbrooke could move with ease between Germany and England. He was recruited for service in the new BWA and would play a key role in its work, both in Europe and on the world scene.[43]

The Executive Committee agreed at its first meeting in London on February 16, 1906, to sponsor a World Congress every five years in alternate hemispheres. The group also decided to hold a European Baptist Congress in Berlin in 1908. A principal objective would be to promote freedom of worship for Baptists in lands where they did not enjoy it.[44]

In November 1907 Clifford, along with Shakespeare and Marshall, journeyed to Hungary to reconcile the feuding Baptist groups there. The dictatorial Heinrich Meyer (he regarded himself as "pastor of the Baptists of Hungary") in 1873 had formed a primarily German-speaking denomination, but it could not get along with a newer Hungarian-speaking body (founded 1893) that in frustration had accepted state recognition. The three-man arbitration commission criticized the behavior of both groups, faulting Meyer for paying inadequate attention to congregational self-government and the other faction for compromising the Baptist principle of separation from state authority. It assisted the Hungarians in drawing up a constitution for a centralized national Union, with the country divided into geographical areas and the churches in each region to work together in a sort of presbyterial system.[45]

Unfortunately, the venture came to naught as the solution proved unacceptable to either side. Rushbrooke went to Budapest in January 1908 to chair the Hungarian Union's assembly that was intended to resolve the conflict, but his effort was fruitless.[46] Indeed, when Hungarian Pastor L. Balogh made a presentation at the Berlin Congress in 1908, German Baptist Johann G. Lehmann noted "that many influential and well-informed delegates dissented from certain portions of the paper, but there was not time for discussion." However, he assured those present that the Congress Committee was fully aware of the difference of opinion.[47] Unity would only come in 1920, when the post-war boundary changes imposed on the Hungarian state totally altered the dynamics between the two churches.

First European Congress, Berlin 1908

Before the next general congress, now set for Philadelphia 1911, European Baptists had the opportunity to deepen relationships at the continental meeting in Berlin August 29–September 3, 1908. The host was Lehmann, the son of Gottfried Wilhelm Lehmann, one of German Baptist founder Johann Gerhard Oncken's closest coworkers.[48] The venue paid tribute to the vital contribution of Oncken in establishing Baptist life and work across Central and Eastern Europe. Berlin, with some ten churches and four thousand church members, represented the vitality of German Baptists. Shakespeare, assisted by Marshall and Rushbrooke, was once more busy with the practicalities—generating interest in Britain and raising money to enable poor preachers to attend. Rushbrooke wrote the congress report. With all the presentations in both German and English, it was a time of rich fellowship. The face-to-face encounters deepened the ties of friendship and mutual confidence and reflected that the brotherhood of European Baptists was becoming a reality. Of the approximately twelve hundred delegates, between five and six hundred were from Great Britain, while a hundred came from the Nordic countries (including Sweden whose Baptist union now exceeded the German in size) and sixty from Hungary. From the Latin South there were twenty-five delegates. The Russian union, which no longer was linked with the German organization, sent some one hundred people who spoke glowingly of growing Baptist influence. Guests came from most other European countries as well. The delegations represented a total of six hundred thousand Baptists. Only one American came in an official capacity, church historian Albert H. Newman of Texas.

A person from each country represented gave a brief address, after which his countrymen in the hall stood up and sang a verse of a hymn. The congress's motto—"One Lord, One Faith, One Baptism"—reflected its theme of unity. President Clifford spoke twice—at the beginning and the end. He affirmed the new world of European Baptist brotherhood and looked back on the passing world of separations and antagonisms with no regret. He rejoiced that "its bitterness and hatred, oppression and cruelty, war and woe" were slowly giving way to a new world of hope and respect, in which international consciousness resulted in the development of alliances and mutual encounter through exchange visits. As he put it, "Everywhere Baptists are growing together in a holy brotherhood in the Lord." To an inherited individualism and respect for the independence of the local church, new dimensions of witness were being added. Now "we organize for worldwide co-operation and complete abandonment to the spirit and purpose of the catholicity of the Gospel of Christ." But this coming together had to be for a purpose: "We seek to revive the passion for souls: the missionary ardor of the men who counted all things but loss that they might win Christ for themselves and the world, and win themselves and their fellows for Christ . . . . God has sent us to preach the gospel, not to baptize men in platoons or in their unwitting infancy . . . . With one hand on the cross, we reach out with the other to the circumference of the human race. We are therefore missionary."[49]

Another speaker, J. W. Ewing of London, referred to "Christ the centre of our Confession." He argued that creeds and confessions were inefficient mechanisms for perpetuating religious belief. The only faithful depository was not what was "written with ink, but on the fleshly tables of the heart." Baptists came together "untrammeled by creeds" but confident of holding a common body of truth. He affirmed Christ as the center of Christian faith. If Baptists kept their attention focused on Christ and tolerated "divergency at the circumference," they could not be defeated.[50]

The enthusiastic delegates at the Berlin conference formulated several resolutions, a few of which threatened to lead the BWA into difficult waters. There was no controversy over the resolutions declaring war as "contrary to the will of the Lord Jesus Christ and opposed to the spirit and genius of Christianity" and affirming religious liberty. However, one that urged the Alliance to view Europe as a mission field was problematic. Forming a missionary society would violate the constitution, and other agencies already existed for that purpose. Resolutions also called for assistance in the building of chapels, the establishment of an international European Baptist Seminary, and the creation of a European Baptist "intelligence

>
> ### Robert Stuart MacArthur
>
> *Robert Stuart MacArthur, the second President of the Baptist World Alliance, served as pastor in only one Baptist church, Calvary of New York City. He was born in Dalesville, Quebec (Canada), July 31, 1841, and studied at the Canadian Literary Institute before emigrating to the United States. He was awarded a B.A. degree by the University of Rochester and completed the course of study at Rochester Theological Seminary in 1870.*
>
> *That same year MacArthur was ordained and became pastor of Calvary. Over the years he welcomed more than five thousand new members into its fellowship and led it to contribute more than two million dollars for benevolent and missionary causes. When elected to Baptist World Alliance office in 1911, he resigned his pastorate in order to devote full time to the Alliance.*
>
> *MacArthur was editor of* The Calvary Hymnal *and author of* The Attractive Christ, Current Questions for the Thinking Man, *and* Due West to the Far East. *He was the exponent of the proposal to create a genderless pronoun in the English language to replace "he" or "she." He suggested "thon," an abbreviated form of "that one." He died in 1923.*

agency" to share news of what was happening on the continent.[51] Although the BWA acknowledged that it could not act directly to fulfill the latter concerns, over the course of the century various members of the Baptist family eventually did undertake these tasks.

Second Baptist World Congress, Philadelphia 1911

The growing movement toward greater Baptist unity on the other side of the Atlantic, as reflected in the formation of the Northern Baptist Convention and the meetings of the General Convention of the Baptists of North America (discussed in Chapter One), as well as the Americans' close involvement in the London conference, assured that the United States would be the venue of the next Baptist World Congress. In his role as Secretary of the BWA, Shakespeare journeyed there in spring 1910 for a planning session, and according to Marshall, he did most of the work to organize the meeting. In fact, "the whole Alliance project" was facing disaster, and it was only rescued by Shakespeare's "patience, resource, and indomitable will."[52]

Around seven thousand people, a larger number than in London, attended the Second Congress that met in Philadelphia June 19–25, 1911, at the spacious Grace Baptist Temple, whose pastor was Russell H. Conwell. A nearby church provided overflow accommodations. Baptist unions and conventions from over thirty countries were represented. The most notable delegation was that from the Russian

Empire. Shakespeare had personally arranged the funding and necessary travel papers for over twenty people from Russia, as well as several others from Eastern Europe. Like today, language problems plagued the BWA, and those delegates not well versed in English (or German in the early years) were handicapped. As noted at the time, the Russians had little command of English, but they did understand the language of the heart.

In his presidential address Clifford spoke on "The Baptist World Alliance: Its Origin and Character, Meaning and Work." He noted how remarkable a creation the Alliance was, emerging among "a people, delivered over, body and soul, to individualism, and in mortal terror of the slightest invasion of their personal and ecclesiastical independence." On the other hand, some who grasped "the intrinsic catholicity of our fundamental principles" were astonished that Baptists had delayed so long in devising for themselves an instrument for world consultation. They had lived in isolation from one another.[53]

The "ecumenical character" of the Alliance existed in "its central and formative ideas; not from one or two in their separateness; but from the whole body judged as a coherent and compact whole." Together these principles "clothe the Alliance with the attributes and functions of a universal Council." Following this line, Clifford claimed the Alliance was "catholic," with a wider catholicism than that of Rome, and "orthodox" with an orthodoxy more spiritual and biblical than that of the Eastern Church, since the Baptists were meeting as "a Pentecostal fellowship based on spiritual ideas and principles more truly universal than any of those of older times." His denial of any effective grace within sacramental practice, though expressed in strong language, represented the view of most Baptists. The emphasis on believer's baptism "is entirely due to our antagonism to the view that sacraments have any saving efficacy."[54]

The Christianization of the World

The main theme of the Congress was "The Christianization of the World," and more than twenty papers were presented on this topic. The imperative for such concern was provided by presentations on "The Sufficiency of the Gospel" and "Vital Experience of God." Many speakers confirmed with considerable passion the priority of traditional patterns of evangelism; others condemned the work of liberal theologians—and Adolf Harnack in particular—for working from the wrong philosophical presuppositions. Some, however, were content to admit the methodology of the critics but expressed confidence, as English pastor J. Moffat Logan put it, "that fair enquiry will but make more evident the great rock-facts, that the Bible is the centre of God's revelation, and that the gospel is the centre of the Bible, and that the centre of the gospel is the Cross of Christ."[55]

Important as was the testing of Scripture, of greater importance was the application of its message: "Men whose experience of God is vital enough to keep them loyal to the least of Christ's commandments can be trusted with the largest liberty." Since the great rank of Baptists was orthodox, there was no need for subscribing to creeds. "When it comes to giving an assent to aged symbols," Logan argued in an attack on creedalism, "we declare that such should never be required from living, honest men . . . . The authoritative creeds of bygone times have all been instruments of cruelty . . . . The reunion of Christendom will never even grow into a possibility until the great authoritative creeds have been reduced to the level of provisional hypotheses."[56]

Martha Hilliard (Mrs. Andrew) MacLeish, formerly principal of Rockford Seminary (a women's school) and president of the Woman's Baptist Foreign Missionary Society of the West, gave a noteworthy address on "Woman's Part" in the Christianizing of the world. She detailed the extraordinary contributions of women, both as individuals and through their various autonomous societies, in foreign and home missionary service, education, medical work, and fund-raising, and forcefully argued "the woman's point of view is just as necessary in this great work as the man's."[57]

In the midst of so many lectures were some truly memorable sermons. Even as Strong's 1905 address on "Know Me and Make Me Known" had set a tone for the first Congress, Thomas Phillips's sermon on the theme of "Grace and Glory" from Psalm 84:11 served a similar function. He was the forty-three-year-old pastor of Bloomsbury Central Baptist Church in London; later he would be principal of Cardiff Baptist College.[58] It was a very positive, thought-provoking oration, full of well-crafted symbols and language. He affirmed many good things but insistently pressed on beyond the good and the useful to the best: "Grace saves the incarnation from being commonplace and preserves its dignity and wonder." Today, no doctrine is more popular than the incarnation of Christ and the humanity of God. "But it has been almost monopolized for the purpose of transfiguring ordinary life and inspiring social reform. We say and say rightly that our Lord by becoming man revealed the worth of life and the sacredness of time. He sanctifies the home and the cradle, He dignified labor and the workshop, He hallowed friendship, He honored marriage . . . . All this is true and it means much for the burdens of humanity . . . . But that is only an aspect of the truth." What happened here was more than the enrichment of man; it was also the impoverishment of God. "Grace then is the downward stoop and reach of

God . . . . Grace is the Christlikeness of God."[59]

Similarly he wanted the highest for the church, for it was "easy for the church to degenerate to be merely a secular society, a club, an institute, or an academy. While it has a sacred right to guide and transfigure all the manifold activities of human life, first of all it is the banqueting house of divine grace." Grace puts a value on human life even though camouflaged in the most hopeless wretchedness. "Every day of my life," testified Phillips, "I come into touch with the submerged men and women of London. If the whole crowd were sunk into the depths of the sea no art nor science, no industry nor form of service would suffer one whit. The State would not miss them, but God would . . . . If the Saviour died for all men then manhood is sacred and democracy is guaranteed."[60]

The demands of the city, according to J. E. Roberts—Maclaren's successor at Union Chapel, Manchester—posed the need for ecumenical working: "The evangelization of cities is impossible so long as different denominations hold aloof from one another and work on independent lines. The divided state of Christendom is one chief cause of our lost influence over the masses." He criticized the absorption in the quest for denominational success, saying that it "quenches the passion for the kingdom." A church that will "lose its own denominational life in the search for the shining city will discover its own fitness and will possess its own truth. The church of Christ will wake up one fine morning to find that it has gained denominationalism and has lost the cities."[61]

Not all the delegates were so convinced. For example, Charles Holman of Canada reported: "We in Canada have not been much enamored with the blandishments of Christian union." He was much more interested in Baptist advance. "When our principles are fully understood then will the time be ripe for union—union not based upon weak compromise with error but upon loyalty to truth and obedience to the Master."[62] Clifford was more measured and warned against perpetuating separation when opportunities for unity existed: "We should hold ourselves guilty if we created or upheld any ecclesiastical division on mere technicalities of the faith or on insignificant details of the practice of churches." But "a visible, formal, and mechanical unity has no charm for us whatever . . . . Unity of life and love, and of governing ideas and ideals let us have by all means but unity of 'order,' of 'machinery,' or of 'creed' is not in keeping with 'unity in diversity' either of Nature or of Grace."[63]

The Christianization of Society

Social concerns were very much in the minds of church leaders. The sufficiency of God had to be effective not only for the individual but also for society. Frank Goodchild of New York addressed the problems of labor, while Walter Rauschenbusch (Rochester) and Shailer Mathews (Chicago) spoke on the social crises of the day. Clifford was a towering icon of how successfully social Christianity and a commitment to personal evangelism could be combined. His vision was never narrow but always holistic, and he made a strong appeal for churches with a full spiritual life, a large ministry—a brotherly spirit, and a broad sweep of service; churches meeting the needs of the whole life of man with a whole gospel; churches that hold that the soul to be saved is the self, all the self, and all its relations; churches that are "social settlements," communities of brothers and sisters of Jesus, willing to go into an uninteresting obscurity for the sake of men lost in the dark regions of Slumdom, or to ascend into the highest realms of culture for the sake of spiritualizing the entire life through the intellect.[64]

Mathews challenged those who believed that the fabric of this world was so hopelessly corrupt that it was pointless to seek to transform it. "The real evangelization of the world is something more than the preaching of an escape from punishment to come; it is rather such a transfusion of the forces of civilization with the ideals of the gospel as to bring justice into the economic order." Noting that the high proportion of the capitalist classes, people who could "determine the distribution of economic surpluses," were church members, he insisted that he would be an evil counselor if he "did not warn the churches that the spectacle of their quarrels over doctrinal and practical details on the one side, and their unwillingness to urge more distinctly upon their members the need of democratizing privilege, will serve to decrease confidence that the gospel they profess to embody is sufficient for social regeneration." The crisis of the times called for cooperation to bring the ideals of Christ into social life. Moreover, the gospel sets forth in its eschatology "the inevitableness of that social order in which the Heavenly Father is to be supreme and which is to be composed of those who are ready to treat one another as brothers." As a mere message, the gospel was impotent, except as it moved men and women to action in accordance with its ideals. Yet, "a gospel without the cross is a gospel without truth and without power. Only the cross must not be simply the cross of Jesus but that which everyone of His disciples takes as he attempts to follow Him."[65]

Other Events at the Congress

Many different things took place at this complex conference. There were sectional meetings for various language groups. Two black leaders—National Baptist Convention President E. C. Morris and the renowned educator Booker T. Washington—gave plenary addresses. An afternoon was dedicated to women's concerns, where Marie C. Kerry, the Home Secretary of the Baptist Zenana Mission; Isabel (Mrs. Russell) James, representing the Baptist Women's League, a home missionary agency that expanded opportunities for women in British Baptist life; Nannie Helen Burroughs, in 1911 the head of the National Training School for Women and Girls in Washington, D.C.; and Fannie E. S. Heck of the Southern Baptist Woman's Missionary Union spoke to an audience of three thousand about women's ministry. Their addresses were followed by shorter reports by women from Scotland, Russia, Bulgaria, New Zealand, and Canada.[66]

Another session was dedicated to young people's work. On "Baptist Day" Sunday, June 25, 1911, a catechism designed for use by Sunday School children throughout the world was introduced.[67] Charles T. Byford, European Commissioner for the BWA, and Marshall reported on the travels they made in eastern Europe to encourage churches there, and speakers from some of these countries supplemented their remarks. Rushbrooke delivered an impassioned plea for religious liberty, while Latin American delegates told of the difficulties of Roman Catholic oppression.

Actions Taken at the Congress

On June 21 the Congress adopted a resolution endorsing governmental actions taken to promote world peace and calling on the churches to pray and work for peace. A committee was named to further the idea.[68] Establishing a Baptist seminary in Russia was discussed, and in a quick canvass of the audience, F. B. Meyer (U.K.) obtained sixty-six thousand dollars in pledges. The matter was pursued in the next two years, but nothing concrete resulted. Also supported was a Southern Baptist proposal to establish a theological seminary to train pastors and evangelists in southern Europe.[69] Other resolutions called for the formation of a committee on social progress to study concerted action on social evil, a second to prepare a plan for closer cooperation by all Baptist boards on unoccupied foreign mission fields, and a third to devise plans to organize Baptist young people worldwide.[70] World War I disrupted these efforts, although the missions committee did lay some groundwork for post-war cooperation in Europe. An important action was the formation of the Women's Committee, designed to draw together leaders of Baptist women's organizations throughout the world. The secretary was Edith Campbell Crane of Baltimore, Maryland. She engaged in a vigorous program of correspondence with women's groups but was unable to get a projected newsletter off the ground.[71]

Some changes were made to the BWA constitution: One change was the creation of a Deputy President, who would be from the hemisphere in which the President did not reside. The two Secretaries would continue, with the American Secretary responsible for the Western Hemisphere and the European Secretary for the Eastern Hemisphere. The Treasurer's post was divided in two: a European and an American Treasurer. Membership eligibility was expanded to include any "Conference of Native churches and missionaries or general Foreign Missionary Society."[72]

Elected as the new President was Robert Stuart MacArthur, pastor of Calvary Baptist Church in New York City. John Clifford became Deputy President for the Eastern Hemisphere. Named Treasurer for Europe was the BU treasurer Herbert Marnham of London, while Canadian Ezekiel M. Sipprell, of St. John, New Brunswick, was named the American Treasurer. Shakespeare and Prestridge were re-elected Secretaries, and when the latter died in 1913, R. H. Pitt succeeded him. The Congress closed with Shakespeare announcing that they would meet again in five years in Berlin.[73] Unfortunately, that never happened, as Europe would be locked in the life-and-death struggle of World War I.

Second European Congress, Stockholm 1913
Only a year before the outbreak of the Great War, one thousand European Baptists gathered in Stockholm, Sweden. Two-thirds were from the home country. The congress, which Rushbrooke helped to organize, took place July 19–24, 1913, and recognized the growth of Swedish Baptists from less than five hundred to fifty-three thousand in half a century. Byford, who had frequently intervened on behalf of Baptist prisoners of conscience, gave an upbeat report of Baptist advance, and others presented papers on the witness in the East. One of the notable features of the eastern Baptists was the fervency of their prayer meetings where restrictions of language did not prevail. The religion of the heart was allowed its proper place, and Stockholm reinforced this by giving considerable time to the spiritual resources underpinning the contemporary witness: the Scriptures, fellowship with God, the certainly of redemption, and the potency of the Holy Spirit.

Foreign missions were a focal point of discussion, with attention given to an awakening Islam, and a Committee on Unoccupied Mission Fields (better known as the Continental Committee) was chosen to coordinate British and American missionary efforts in Europe. Resolutions were adopted on peace, white slavery, temperance, the Judson centenary and John Hus quincentenary, and the campaign for liberty of conscience. An open letter to the churches urged them to renew their endeavors in evangelism, not forgetting "the need of conversion and the power of the Grace that make all things new."

The magnetism of Clifford's personality dominated the meeting, and in his presidential address he gave voice to openness and a social engagement that on other lips might have been seen as unevangelical. He introduced issues of criticism, ecumenical relations, and injustice in stirring evangelistic terms. He argued that "no interpretation of the Bible is barred against revision and reconstruction according to the fuller light shed upon the Scripture by the Spirit. No confession is final. No church order is infallible or beyond improvement." Christians must be sensitive to the Spirit's guiding, which for Baptists was a basic principle. Clifford appealed to the churches "to take the lead in the recovery and advocacy of the true social ideals of Jesus." As the inequalities in social relations were increasingly revealed, the church had to become committed to the quest for God's kingdom by addressing the issues of injustice that caused unrest and rebellion. At the same time people were eager to know Christ as Savior and to experience his saving power. Baptists were "pioneers in the religious, social, and moral work of the world," and the conference itself was a sign that the Kingdom of God was moving swiftly.[74]

Peace was much on the mind of the Baptists, and both Rushbrooke and Marshall were members of the delegation of English churchmen who went to Germany in 1909 to foster friendship between the two countries. Resulting from this visit was the establishment of the "Associated Council of the Churches of the British and German Empires for Promoting Friendly Relations," and Clifford, Shakespeare, and Ewing were among its vice presidents. Philanthropist Andrew Carnegie endowed the Church Peace Union to promote closer cooperation by churches in peace efforts, and the council held its first meeting in Constance, Germany, August 1–3, 1914. Clifford and Rushbrooke traveled together to the gathering, which adjourned prematurely because of the outbreak of hostilities. However, from it emerged the World Alliance for Promoting International Friendship through the Churches, a body that contributed significantly to the modern ecumenical movement. Clifford returned to England. Rushbrooke was stranded in Germany with his wife who was visiting there; three months later he was repatriated. Rushbrooke remained active in the peace society and edited its journal, *Goodwill,* from 1915 to 1920.[75]

BWA activities came to a complete standstill. The Continental Committee did meet five times in the next four years but dealt only with eastern European concerns; the American Committee met only twice.[76]

Like other churchmen, British Baptists loyally supported the Allied cause (as did the Americans following 1917).[77] Russian Baptists who were receiving ministerial training in Germany were forced to return home, where they were accused of being unpatriotic. The Allied forces interned and repatriated the German Baptist missionaries in Cameroon; only an American citizen, Carl Bender, was allowed to remain and keep the mission going. Outside funding for Baptist projects on the continent ceased, and some churches in Belgium and France lay in the combat zone. The Great War had shattered the dream of Baptist unity.

1. For biographical details see J. H. Y. Briggs, "MacLaren, Alexander," in *Biographical Dictionary of Evangelicals*, ed. Timothy Larson (Downers Grove, IL: InterVarsity Press, 2003), pp. 397–399.

2. J. H. Y. Briggs, "Clifford, John," Ibid., pp. 148–150. (See also Lewis A. Drummond, "A Brief Biography of Dr. John Clifford," paper presented to the Baptist Heritage Study Commission, 1997.)

3. *BWA Congress*, 1905, pp. vi–vii.

4. Ibid., pp. xvi–xxviii.

5. Ibid., p. 5. Pastor J. A. Ohrn of Norway also spoke of persecution and imprisonments in the past in his land but it lay behind the vitality of lay witness in the present. Ibid., p. 7.

6. Ibid., pp. 183–184.

7. Ibid., p. 2.

8. Ibid., p. 4.

9. Ibid., pp. 8–9.

10. Ibid., pp. 52, 58.

11. Ibid., pp. 20–21.

12. Ibid., p. 30.

13. Ibid., p. 1. To add Mennonite numbers to the Baptist figures was no longer feasible because of the presence of mainstream Baptist churches in Europe. However, the Dutch Mennonite Missionary Union was placed in the section on Denominational Statistics, as was the Missionary and Tract Committee of the German Baptist Brethren [Dunkards], now the Church of the Brethren (U.S.). Also, 1.25 million Disciples of Christ were included in the list of "Baptized Believers," pp. 340, 342, 343. See also Chapter One.

14. Ibid., p. 1.

15. Ibid., p. 22.

16. Ibid., p. 132.

17. Ibid., p. 137.

18. Ibid., pp. 139, 142.

19. Quoted in William R. Estep, Jr., "E. Y. Mullins: The Third President of the Baptist World Alliance, 1923–1928," paper presented to the Baptist Heritage Study Commission, 1997, p. 9.

20. *BWA Congress,* 1905, p. 150.

21. Ibid., p. 148.

22. Ibid., pp. 152–153.

23. Ibid., pp. 151–152.

24. Ibid., pp. 38, 43. At the Philadelphia Congress Clifford waxed eloquently about the Welsh Baptist Lloyd George, by then Chancellor of the Exchequer, calling him a "working Baptist" and a "prophet statesman" whose program of social legislation was "simply the application of Baptist ideas to social life," that is, "the great principles for which our fathers fought more than three centuries ago." *BWA Congress,* 1911, p. 19.

25. *BWA Congress,* 1905, p. 3.

26. Ernest A. Payne, *The Baptist Union: A Short History* (London: Carey Kingsgate, 1958), p. 172. Clifford's role in the PRM is described in Paul Dekar, *For the Healing of the Nations: Baptist Peacemakers* (Macon, GA: Smyth & Helwys, 1993), pp. 69–70.

27. *BWA Congress,* 1905, pp. 43–49, 51.

28. Ibid., pp. 264–280.

29. Ibid., pp. 65–67.

30. Ibid., pp. 86, 92.

31. Ibid., p. 92.

32. Ibid., p. 108.

33. Ibid., pp. 110–116.

34. Ibid., p. 115.

35. Ibid.

36. Ibid., p. 116.

37. Ibid., p. ix.

38. Ibid., p. 36.

39. Ibid., pp. 241–242.

40. Ibid., pp. 280–281.

41. Walter B. Shurden, *The Life of the Baptists in the Life of the World: 80 Years of the BWA* (Nashville: Broadman, 1981), pp. 13–14.

42. F. Townley Lord, *Baptist World Fellowship: A Short History of the Baptist World Alliance*

(London: Carey Kingsgate Press, 1955), p. 16. Marshall was well received in Europe during these early years, but his untimely death of typhoid fever in January 1914 was a severe blow to the Alliance. Historian Ernest A. Payne felt Marshall was so brilliant that had he lived, he might have been the person whom the BWA chose after the war to be its representative in Europe instead of J. H. Rushbrooke. Payne, *James Henry Rushbrooke 1870–1947: A Baptist Greatheart* (London: Carey Kingsgate, 1954), p. 3

43. See Bernard Green, *Tomorrow's Man: A Biography of James Henry Rushbrooke* (Oxford: Baptist Historical Society, 1997).

44. BWA IX. 1. 1. Minute Book, Feb. 16, 1906.

45. Peter Shepherd, *The Making of a Modern Denomination: John Howard Shakespeare and the English Baptists* (Carlisle, United Kingdom: Paternoster, 2001), p. 40; BWA I. 1. 1. F.

46. Shepherd, *Making of a Modern Denomination*, p. 67; Tiller, *Twentieth Century Baptist*, pp. 2–4; BWA I. 1. 1 F. Rushbrooke History (ms.).

47. *Baptist World Alliance: First European Baptist Congress, held in Berlin, 1908* (August 29th to September 3rd), introduced and edited by J. H. Rushbrooke with E. C. Pike (London: Baptist Union, 1908), p. 165

48. The most recent works on Oncken are by Günter Balders: "Johann Gerhard Oncken—Aspects of His Life and Work" paper presented to the Baptist Heritage Study Commission, 1999, and a biography *Theurer Bruder Oncken* (Wuppertal and Kassel: Oncken Verlag, 1984).

49. BWA, *First European Baptist Congress*, pp. 45–59.

50. Ibid. pp. 57–62.

51. Ibid., pp. 234–239.

52. Marshall's statement in the *Baptist Times*, July 21, 1911, quoted in Shepherd, *Making of a Modern Denomination*, p. 89.

53. *BWA Congress*, 1911, pp. 54–55.

54. Ibid., pp. 56–57, 62.

55. Ibid., p. 116.

56. Ibid., pp. 116–117.

57. Ibid., pp. 270–276.

58. See Faith Bowers, *A Bold Experiment: The Story of Bloomsbury Chapel and Bloomsbury Central Baptist Church 1848–1999* (London: Bloomsbury Central Baptist Church, 1999). pp. 238–260. The sermon was widely reprinted and gained for him the reputation of "Grace and Glory Phillips."

59. *BWA Congress*, 1911, pp. 153–154.

60. Ibid., pp. 156, 158.

61. Ibid., p. 198.

62. Ibid., pp. 31–32.

63. Ibid., pp. 62–63.

64. Ibid., p. 69.

65. Ibid., pp. 82, 84, 86–88.

66. An important discussion of the role of women's work in the early years of the BWA is Karen E. Smith, "British Women and the Baptist World Alliance: Honored Partners and Fellow Workers," *Baptist Quarterly* 42 (January 2005), pp. 25–46.

67. *BWA Congress,* 1911, pp. 450–452.

68. Ibid., p.149.

69. Ibid., pp. 264–265.

70. Ibid., pp. 333–334, 302–306, 89. The appointees to the committees are listed on p. xvi.

71. Ibid., p. 358. See also Ferne Levy, *God's Command–Our Response: A History of the Women's Department of the Baptist World Alliance* (McLean, VA: BWA, [1985]), p. 5. The relationship of the committee to the BWA was unclear, and its functioning ceased during the war. A similar committee was appointed at Stockholm in 1923 but again with no specific arrangements for coordination. In 1928 women were specifically appointed to the Executive Committee. BWA I. 1. 1. F. Rushbrooke's notes.

72. *BWA Congress,* 1911, pp. 332–333.

73. Ibid. p. 434.

74. Lord, *Baptist World Fellowship,* pp. 35–37; *Baptist Times,* July 25, 1913, p. 565.

75. Dekar, *Healing of the Nations,* pp. 80–82.

76. BWA IX.1. 1. Minute Book.

77. Payne, *The Baptist Union,* pp. 179–181.

3

COMING OF AGE:
THE POST-WAR ERA AND THE 1920s
Robert S. Wilson

The First World War shattered monarchies, nations, and empires. Large parts of Europe were physically devastated or experiencing economic distress, new states formed out of the rubble of old empires, Russia was torn by revolution, and Germany was prostrate and embittered by the lost war and imposed peace settlement. Baptists were on both sides of the lines, and many of them had suffered greatly. The Baptist World Alliance (BWA) leaders sought to bring together the remnants of the international unity and the ministries they had worked so hard to implement. Had the nascent movement been fractured beyond repair?

The Reconstruction Effort

The Baptists had to confront the issues of the post-war era and find their way through the maze of new conditions. European reconstruction, surging nationalism, freedom of trade for some and protectionism for others, new political movements such as Communism and Fascism, the intensification of racism, pressures from state churches, and revitalizing the global missionary movement all presented challenges. Could the BWA with its roots among the English-speaking peoples of the British Empire and the United States regain the momentum of the pre-war years?

The BWA structure remained the same as before 1914, Robert Stuart MacArthur as President, octogenarian John Clifford as Deputy President, R. H. Pitt as Western Secretary looking after American matters, J. H. Shakespeare serving as the Eastern Secretary, an Executive Committee based in London and the Continental Committee, whose concern was European missions. The immediate task was reconstructing and renewing the Baptist witness in Europe and organizing a common advance. The Executive sought to reestablish contacts with European Baptists and anticipated that greater religious freedom would exist in the new countries formed out of the Russian and Austrian empires. It began planning a third Baptist World Congress in a European city, since the one slated for Berlin in 1916 never took place. The Hague and then Prague seemed to be possibilities, but eventually Stockholm won out.[1]

The Southern Baptist Convention (SBC) had people in England prepared to enter Europe. The corresponding secretary of its Foreign Mission Board, J. Franklin Love, led a survey team in 1919, but the difficult conditions limited its efforts. The foreign secretary of the American Baptist Foreign Mission Society (ABFMS), James H. Franklin, made a six-week trip to the continent in March 1919 and opened several relief centers in France and Belgium. The ABFMS then sent Charles Alvin Brooks, secretary for the foreign-speaking work of the American Baptist Home Mission Society, to Europe to study the situation more closely. He took up residence in Switzerland and made numerous contacts in Western and Central Europe.[2] His visits found that the European Baptists, though devastated by the war, were resilient and ready to rebuild.

Those who attended the meeting of the Executive Committee on October 23, 1919—the first since the war's end—discussed sending a survey commission to the continent. On March 31, 1920, its British members (along with the Continental Committee) authorized Brooks and J. H. Rushbrooke to travel to Central and Eastern Europe. Their specific instructions were to do the following:

1. Renewal of contact with continental Baptists as they greeted them with resolutions of support;
2. Exploration of the needs of the lands and of the immediate needs of Baptist Communities in preparation to meet the larger needs, such as trained teachers for churches, literature, organization for missionary outreach, etc.;
3. Preparation for a London Conference with representatives from various lands to formulate a final report for the BWA.[3]

As both men had extensive personal connections on the continent, they were ideally qualified to undertake the survey. They carried with them a letter of introduction from Prime Minister David Lloyd George, which Shakespeare's son Geoffrey, a secretary for Lloyd George, obtained for them. This opened a number of official doors in the new states.[4]

The journey was anything but easy. They visited many of the hard-hit areas but could not gain admittance to Russia. In spite of "closed borders and disease as well as difficulties of travel," they covered sixty-four hundred miles in nine weeks (May 10–July 8, 1920) with over twenty-seven border crossings and innumerable baggage and passport inspections. They documented the woeful conditions of poverty, death of leaders, and scattering of congregations, and this data enabled various Baptist agencies to begin sending aid. They also sought information about religious oppression. Baptists, like most evangelicals, were "frequently denied legal recognition" and thus lacked protection under the law. The appeals for religious liberty, however, were made on behalf of all religious groups, not just the Baptists. The two men experienced a wide range of situations, both distressing and hopeful, that left deep impressions on them.[5]

The commissioners were favorably impressed with Czechoslovakia, which had begun its new existence with a democratic regime and felt that Prague was a good possibility for a future BWA Congress. They recognized the need for training preachers, teachers, and evangelists to assist in reconstructing Baptist work on the continent and saw Prague as the potential site for a pan-European Baptist seminary. They even envisioned that the University of Prague would allow Baptist professors and tutors to serve on its Protestant theological faculty. The high point of their visit was a meeting with President Thomas G. Masaryk to discuss relief and religious liberty matters.[6]

Much more discouraging was the situation in Romania. The established Romanian Orthodox Church used the turbulent situation to maintain religious control in the country and to suppress the Baptists. Through the peace settlement the country had acquired large chunks of territory from the former Austro-Hungarian and Russian Empires, but the regime prevented the non-Romanian-speaking peoples there from evangelizing. Services were disrupted or forbidden, church properties were seized, and believers were violently mistreated. Brooks and Rushbrooke personally asked the diplomatic representatives of their governments in Bucharest to intervene in the matter and tried in vain to meet with the Romanian authorities. They could not secure any resolution of the religious liberty problem in the country, and the quest for this became a long-term project for the BWA. Rushbrooke campaigned up to his death in 1947 on behalf of freedom for the Romanian Baptists, but harassment by the political and religious authorities continued unabated. An end to oppression only came in the last decade of the twentieth century.[7]

Another thing that impressed the commissioners was the German Baptists' evangelistic work among Russian prisoners of war. More than two thousand such converts had been baptized, and they returned home as evangelists. Some of these former prisoners sparked a revival among Russians living in Bessarabia, an area annexed by Romania. While in Germany, the two men worked to reestablish the ties that had been broken by the war. They discussed the future of German missionary work in Cameroon (it eventually was resumed in the portion under the British League of Nations mandate in 1927[8]) and persuaded the Germans to send representatives to the upcoming Conference on Post-War Needs. This was to take place July 19–23, 1920, in conjunction with the Executive Committee meeting.[9]

London Conference, 1920

Upon their return, the commissioners submitted a report that described the trip, argued that Baptists could make a difference in Europe, and suggested how to turn the disaster of the war into opportunities for ministry. As Townley Lord later observed, "[T]he problems created by war both widened and deepened the scope of Alliance work."[10] Their report provided the focus for BWA activities during the next few years.

Seventy-two delegates from the Baptist Unions (BU) and conventions in Britain, the United States, Canada, Australia, and eighteen continental European countries assembled at Baptist Church House in London to review the report and to draft recommendations for action by their member bodies. As the rigors of an Atlantic voyage were too much for the seventy-nine-year old President MacArthur, Deputy President Clifford occupied the chair. Such key figures as Shakespeare, William T. Whitley, and Rushbrooke from Great Britain, and Franklin, James B. Gambrell, E. Y. Mullins, and George W. Truett from the United States were in attendance.[11] The delegates were optimistic that by working together they could make a difference. The conference provided a unique opportunity for Baptists to organize aid for their brothers and sisters and to play a part in the reconstruction of Europe.

Commissioners Brooks and Rushbrooke spent two days presenting their report and describing the European scene. The delegates also had Love's SBC survey from the previous year, and they heard speakers from twelve European countries. The "Governing Ideas of the Commission" that formed the core of the agenda and shaped BWA policy directions for the future were as follows:

First, "the material distress of the members of our communities in the war-torn regions impose on those more happily situated, e.g., in the United States, Britain and Sweden, a heavy and immediate burden of Christian obligation." If the needs were not met, the work would be impoverished for many years to come. There were open doors for outreach.

Second, Baptists in the new states as well as the old ones should "as far as possible be treated as unities." Following the principle of "one land, one union," factions within national Baptist communities were expected to work together to receive BWA recognition and aid. The commissioners put pressure on the Polish Baptists, then divided by people groups, to form one union. They told the local leaders the BWA "would regard the unity of Poland as a presupposition in all its dealings with the situation there, and that the London Conference in July would probably register a formal decision upon the matter as it affects Poland and other lands."[12]

Third, while emphasizing the "super-national" and "super-racial" unity of Christians, due account would have to be taken of ethnic individuality and self-consciousness—not as a divisive but as an enriching element in human life.

Finally, it was essential to take "long views" even though "Christian Education" efforts would not be reflected for some time in denominational statistics. This call for long-range planning and emphasis on the principles of Baptist unity and support would place the BWA in good stead during the turbulent days of the early 1920s.

Working groups were then chosen to prepare concrete plans for consideration at the closing plenary session. On the last day five proposals were adopted and forwarded to the parent bodies in Great Britain, Sweden, the British Empire, and the United States of the various Baptist agencies for their action. The principal idea behind the proposals was to provide immediate aid and a new direction for Baptist energies.[13]

First, the BWA would give material assistance to the "feeble Baptist groups" in the stricken areas but would move beyond denominational boundaries in meeting needs when and where it was possible: "We would go in the spirit of Christ with relief for all who suffer, regardless of religious or racial difference."[14] The American mission agencies were to assume responsibility for relief efforts for at least a three-year period. In accordance with this recommendation, the SBC Foreign Mission Board appointed Everett Gill, Sr. and the Northern Baptists' American Baptist Foreign Mission Society chose Walter O. Lewis as their European representatives. Within two years both men were on the field coordinating their respective agencies' endeavors.

Second, the BWA would address "the urgent need for trained ministry in Eastern Europe" by supporting schools in Romania, Finland, Hungary, Estonia, and Latvia and by providing a central college in Prague for "the Slav peoples" of Czechoslovakia, Russia, Bulgaria, Yugoslavia, Ruthenia (then an eastern province of Czechoslovakia, now in Ukraine), and hopefully Poland. The British and Americans assumed responsibility for these initiatives, while the Swedish Baptists would aid Finland. The schools would supplement the well-established seminaries in Hamburg and

Stockholm and would focus on training pastors and leaders for work in their own countries. Schools were also foreseen for Spain and Portugal. By 1923 seven schools were actually up and running.

Third, to meet the continuing missionary needs of Baptists on the continent and to avoid costly duplication of efforts, one Baptist union in each country would be in partnership with a stronger Baptist group from the west. The assignments were made with the proviso that the parties involved would consult with one another to determine the form and extent of the cooperation that would be provided.[15] The tasks were divided as follows:

> Portugal—Brazilian Baptists
> France, French-speaking areas of Belgium, and Switzerland—Northern Baptists, with Breton work under the British
> Norway, Denmark, and Poland—Northern Baptists
> Netherlands—British and Australian Baptists
> Spain, Italy, Yugoslavia, Romania, and Ukraine—Southern Baptists
> Czechoslovakia—British and Northern Baptists
> The new Baltic States—British, Canadian, and Northern Baptists
> Austria and Bulgaria—German Baptists
> Finland—Swedish and British Baptists

Fourth, religious persecution, particularly in Romania, was strongly condemned. The conferees called upon the British and American governments to bring pressure on the local authorities to allow religious liberty and directed an appeal to the Romanians to bring an end to persecution. They also adopted a resolution supporting the creation of the League of Nations.

Finally, to coordinate the relief efforts and other European initiatives of the BWA, the Continental Committee reconstituted itself as a "commission," created the position of Baptist Commissioner for Europe, and offered the post to Rushbrooke. He was to be essentially a Baptist ambassador, a person who could approach national rulers and governments and speak authoritatively "with the weight of Baptist world opinion behind him."[16] Financing for the relief program came from the missionary societies; they also funded his salary and travel.

A particularly noteworthy event occurred at the conference. One of the three German delegates, Friedrich Wilhelm Simoleit, rose to speak and asked Rushbrooke to translate. He expressed his appreciation for the generous help his people had received and the brotherly spirit shown to them. Tears flowed as the former combatants saw the harmony of the gospel overcome the hostility of war. This was one of the first demonstrations of reconciliation between western Christians and their German brethren. Bernard Green observed that in retrospect delegates at the London meeting thought it had achieved more than all four Baptist gatherings in 1905, 1908, 1911, and 1913 put together to make the Alliance a living reality. "In a strange way the war, which must have seemed catastrophic to the infant Alliance, created conditions in which through the London Conference the Alliance found its raison d'être."[17] In his 1923 account of the continental Baptists, Rushbrooke subtitled the chapter on the London conference: "A turning point in Baptist history."

With his broad knowledge of and experience in Europe, Rushbrooke was the logical choice as Commissioner. He accepted the assignment even though it meant he would have to give up his pastorate as well as his ecumenical peace work in the World Alliance for Promoting International Friendship through the Churches. He feared that if he did not accept, cooperative work on the continent would cease. For the next four years the Continental Commission, which managed the relief fund raised to meet European needs, was the most active arm of the BWA.

Rushbrooke as European Commissioner
A significant part of Rushbrooke's task was raising funds for relief and reconstruction in Europe. He was effective at telling stories of deprivation that touched Baptist hearts and resulted in shiploads of material and aid being sent to continental Europe. In spring 1921 he went to North America to shore up support from the Baptists there. He attended the denominational conventions, built personal friendships, and even met with U.S. President Warren G. Harding and Secretary of State Charles Evans Hughes, both of whom were Baptists. He had to allay suspicions that Baptists in England wanted closer union with the Anglicans and convince doubters of the necessity of aid for Europe.

He also traveled widely in Europe, where he engaged the problem of religious oppression in Romania, developed strategies for getting aid to stricken areas, and fostered the establishment of preacher-training institutes. In 1922 a "Baptist Relief Train" carried enough food, grain, medicines, and clothing from Poland into Russia to keep an estimated twelve thousand people alive until the next harvest.[18] While there were no strings attached to the aid, it became a means of witness and large numbers were baptized. Rushbrooke managed to travel to Russia several times, met with high-ranking Soviet officials, and offered encouragement to the churches there.

Holding the diverse Baptist grouping together was not easy. Writing to Shakespeare from Nashville on November 3, 1922, Rushbrooke raised several touchy issues that he feared might derail the efforts for a successful Baptist World Congress, now set for Stockholm in 1923.[19] There was concern whether sufficient space on the program would be available for prominent Americans who desired to speak. I. J. Van Ness of the SBC Sunday School Board wanted more room on the agenda for youth rallies and Christian education matters. Rushbrooke added: "[T]he SBC is enduring a great deal of strain in preserving its relations with the BWA and consideration of one of its most important departments (which will in any case be represented at the Congress) would assist in securing smooth sailing." Another issue was a controversial sermon by Harry Emerson Fosdick of New York that some interpreted as "repudiating the Virgin Birth." The possibility of his preaching at Stockholm might create an outcry, and Rushbrooke said he hoped Fosdick would be too busy to attend (he did not come).

The final and most significant issue was one on which Shakespeare and Rushbrooke strongly disagreed: namely, the possibility that British Baptists might establish a formal relationship with the Anglican Church. The 1920 Lambeth Appeal had encouraged the various Free Churches to engage in discussions with the established Church of England about closer ties, and the Baptist Union (BU) Secretary had written in support of church union. In fact, Shakespeare's biographer Peter Shepherd insisted that his "pursuit of church unity during and after the war became an obsession."[20] In the letter to Shakespeare, Rushbrooke pointed out: "The best friends of the Alliance are most resolutely opposed to the lines of union suggested by Lambeth and are anxious to see the issue disposed of." He had questioned all sorts of people—"liberals" and "orthodox," northerners, southerners, and Canadians—and found that not one Baptist on this side of the Atlantic favored BU acceptance of the Lambeth proposals: "The lack of a definite pronouncement plays into the hands of adverse critics of the Alliance in both the American Conventions, and I feel you ought to know this."

As the ecumenical movement gained momentum in the 1920s, Baptists were divided as to whether to follow the interdenominational model or opt for an international Baptist organization. C. E. Benander of Sweden made a strong case for the latter approach in 1922 when he called upon his fellows to support the European Baptist churches because: "They organize their churches after the apostolic pattern, and insist on maintaining the New Testament principle of regenerate church membership." They also support religious liberty, freedom of conscience, competency of the soul, and the need for evangelism to be done locally as well as in other parts of the world. He commended Rushbrooke for working with national leaders and praised the BWA as the proper form of ecumenical organization because it united Baptist bodies of the various countries, brought them into contact with each other, gave them occasions to learn to know each other and awakened a consciousness of solidarity that was unknown before. The unions that are strong have reviewed the worldwide mission fields together and have become inspired with a growing zeal for a victorious extension of the evangelizing movement they represent. The small and weak sister organizations are encouraged to feel that they may count on support from their more favorably situated brethren. They are enabled to go forward with their work in the sure hope that, some day, they too would be numerous and strong.[21]

The fundamentalist-modernist controversies of the 1920s helped undermine support for broad ecumenism. Amzi C. Dixon—a southerner who served several northern churches, preached at Spurgeon's Metropolitan Tabernacle in London from 1911 to 1919, and then returned home to pastor a church in Baltimore—was a central figure in the fundamentalist movement. In his personal newspaper Dixon criticized Shakespeare for talking about church union and accused him of theological liberalism. Dixon did much to raise suspicions about the British Baptists in the United States. Shakespeare, however, had no backing in his own denomination. The BU firmly supported closer Baptist connections and evangelism, and Rushbrooke himself articulated the "essentially anti-ecumenical" feeling of most English Baptists.[22] While the BWA might be seen as part of the broad movement in the early part of the century to form unions, Baptists chose to do it in their own way.

Historians Samuel S. Hill and Robert G. Torbet's assessment of ecumenism among Baptists was essentially this: "At the very least, the total Baptist communion has no instrument of unity intrinsic in its structure. It is easier for the Baptist fellowship to splinter than for most other denominational groups . . . . This tendency has been reinforced by the Biblicism and individualism of Baptists." They go on to say: "Where there is unity among Baptists, it is an achievement, motivated by a specific desire among some to practice the given spiritual unity of the Body of Christ. Baptists have not drifted into unity as a result of organizational structures, but have realized it on some occasions through deliberate efforts."[23] Those groups seeking doctrinal purity withdrew from the main Baptist bodies in the 1920s and had little interest in the BWA. At the same time, in this era of theological controversy, the BWA offered a place where Baptists could cooperate around the common themes of fellowship, evangelism, and social action. The Congresses provided an atmosphere of trust where such a movement could grow.

Third Baptist World Congress, Stockholm 1923

As planning went forward for the first post-war Congress, consideration was briefly given to Prague, but travel problems made this venue impracticable. Stockholm, which had experienced a century and a half of peace and was untouched by the recent war, became the city to welcome Baptists from around the world. Between July 21 and 27, 1923, some 2,384 delegates—480 from Britain, 768 from North America, 656 from Sweden, 55 from Germany, 37 from Russia, and the remainder from elsewhere in Europe, Canada, South America, Africa, India, China, and Japan—gathered in the Baptist Immanuelskyrkan to celebrate the work that was being accomplished, particularly in Europe.[24] Most British and American representatives came on chartered ships, and travel funds were raised to bring two hundred delegates from continental Europe.

In the twelve years since the Congress in Philadelphia, personnel changes had occurred. President MacArthur had died on February 23, 1923. Deputy President Clifford was unable to come because of his advanced age and sent a message to be read. New leaders emerged to chair the meetings and make presentations. Inspiring sermons, progress reports, position papers, and music from various choirs (some choirs, such as the Russians and Latvians, wore native costumes), added to the international flavor of the event. As in the two earlier Congresses, African-Americans took part as speakers and providers of musical inspiration.

The delegates talked of Baptist work in many countries, and small groups met for discussion of matters of mutual interest. Based upon the reports and information shared at the meetings, they formulated plans for relief, propaganda, seminary instruction, and assisting the continental Baptists to survive. As Shakespeare said: "This is the true method and the work of the World Alliance and its Congresses, not academic discussions which divide, but eager and thoughtful service which unites."[25] It also was the first Congress with a "Baptist World Exhibition," with contributions from Baptists in many parts of the world.

An invigorating optimism pervaded the Congress reports about Baptist endeavors, even though attendees did not sidestep current problems resulting from nationalism, communism, and moral laxity. There was a belief that Baptists working together could make a difference. Whether the goal was world peace, industrial relations, religious liberty, Christian education, race relations, or national issues, the delegates passed resolutions and planned for progress. In a show of ecumenical solidarity, Archbishop Nathan Söderblom of Sweden's established Lutheran Church invited Secretary Shakespeare to preach in Uppsala Cathedral.

Social issues were energetically discussed. Since Baptists were primarily from the working classes, they tended to be sympathetic to the interests of labor, and the ideas of social gospel advocate Walter Rauschenbusch inspired many of them. Nevertheless, they disavowed radicalism and were averse to socialism because they saw it as threat to the freedom of the individual. Baptists generally subordinated their social concern to evangelism.[26]

An illustration of Baptist social thought was the paper, "Christianity and Industrial Relations," by pro-labor political activist J. C. Carlisle. After lauding the advances of modern industry, he said that industrialism was not "an invention of the devil and a means of human slavery. Industrialism had, however, with its mass production and specialized work . . . made the worker a hand, a cog in the wheel." He argued that professing Christians needed to bring their faith "to the employment of labor, and the rendering of honest service in return for wages paid." He lamented the open war between capital and labor and expressed concern about communism, insisting instead that Baptists were "advocates of peace between nations and classes . . . and the only way to prevent revolution is to give full and equal liberty, religious, civil and industrial." Christian Socialism is not the answer. A kind of social change that represents the Christian conscience is the program of national health insurance, unemployment insurance, and old-age pensions in Britain that was "largely the product of that great Baptist, David Lloyd George."[27]

Women were quite visible at the Congress. In her plenary address entitled, "The New Opportunity for Baptist Women," Helen Barrett (Mrs. W. M.) Montgomery—noted author, educator, president of the Woman's American Baptist Foreign Mission Society, and first woman to preside over the Northern Baptist Convention (1921–22)—declared that "in the mind of the Founder of Christianity there is no area of religious privilege fenced off for the exclusive use of men." She went on to describe the unparalleled opportunities that existed in education, missionary societies organized by women, and service in the church.[28] At a well-attended women's session presided over by Woman's Missionary Union leader Minnie Kennedy (Mrs. W. B.) James of Baltimore, Maryland, various speakers extolled the efforts of women in witnessing and social action, and emphasized the important role they played in the Congress and the churches. Isabel James underscored that the British Baptist Women's League had created the Baptist Women's Training College in Hampstead, London, to prepare women for service as deaconesses (professional church workers), social workers, preachers, evangelists, Sunday School teachers, and foreign missionaries. Moreover, BU Secretary Shakespeare had implemented a policy that women should serve on every committee of any importance in the denomination.[29]

At the end of the session, it was announced that a Women's Committee meeting would take place on the last day of the Congress during which a plan by Lucy Peabody (who was not present) "for world-prayer and organization would be unfolded by Montgomery." No minutes were preserved of the event, but Mrs. F. C. Spurr, president of the Baptist Women's League in the United Kingdom, was elected chair and Montgomery was named general secretary. How the plan was presented or if it was ever implemented is not clear from the surviving records, but the committee itself continued in existence until the next Congress in 1928, when two women were given regular seats on the Executive and the separate body was disbanded.[30]

A significant initiative was the establishment of an organization that would coordinate Baptist youth ministries around the world. One could see how the war still shaped the delegates' thinking in the comments of Arthur Dakin of London: "We realize now as never before that nations are in the bundle of life together. Is there war, it is almost bound to be world-war. Is there peace, it must be achieved on the world scale." Therefore, what we need "is a religious consciousness independent of nationality, transcending nationality, as the Kingdom of God transcends all parochialism. We want a world-outlook corresponding with our world-gospel." He noted that since many of those present were "fast approaching the grandfather stage, they needed to plan for the future of the youth, for "[t]hey are the makers of tomorrow, and we, under God are the makers of them."[31]

James Asa White, general secretary of the Baptist Young People's Union of America, challenged his listeners to see the rising power and restlessness of young people around the world as an opportunity. He could see many things to take the thoughts of young people away from personal religion and church loyalty, but he believed firmly that the time would come "when the mighty hosts of young Baptists of the world will together make a tremendous impact upon the social, political, economic, and industrial problems of the world."[32] British Baptist Union Young People's Department Secretary E. E. Hayward reminded delegates that not only was the church created by people but, throughout history renewal movements were inspired by people under thirty. He called for the formation of groups for young men and women between the ages of sixteen and twenty-five, when they are most open to the challenge of the gospel. While willing to work with interdenominational groups, he believed our people should "band ourselves together as Young Baptists." He then moved the formation of the "World Baptist Young People's Union," whose aim would be to unite young Baptists in all countries. The World Baptist Young People's Committee would determine its structure.[33]

An evening session dedicated to Sunday Schools featured papers by the Southern Baptist Sunday School specialist Van Ness and British expert Carey Bonner of London. Van Ness argued that Sunday School was the chief means of growth for the Baptist churches in North America, with upwards of 80 percent of baptisms coming from the students. The movement was both future and people oriented, since the schools provided children with crucial education in religious themes and called for commitment to Jesus Christ. Bonner followed with an overview of the Sunday School movement among Baptists around the world.[34]

One day was dedicated to missions around the world and another to evangelism. The secretaries of the three largest boards delivered major addresses in the final missions session, while speakers from other societies and other parts of the world took part in the discussions during the day. Each of the keynote speakers argued that a new day in missions was coming when responsibility must be given to indigenous Christians rather than control coming from the old centers. They also acknowledged the increasing importance of nationalism.[35] In the afternoon session Asian voices were heard, with comments by J. W. Dall of Delhi, India; Yuguro Chiba of Tokyo, Japan; and C. S. Miao of Shanghai, China.[36]

A particularly memorable speech was given by C. H. Parrish of Louisville, Kentucky. Born into slavery, he had risen to be president of Simmons University, named for the founder of the National Baptist Convention. The title of his address was "Aspirations of Christian Africa." While speaking as an African-American, he was not hesitant to raise the issue of colonialism. He pointed out that in the United States the majority of blacks were Baptists, and the church was the center of their community. They had undertaken their own missionary endeavors but had difficulties with the colonial powers in securing permission to send their workers into parts of Africa. Parrish commended the European churches for bringing the gospel, hospitals, and schools to Africa, while urging them to see themselves in partnership with the Christians of Africa. He then frankly addressed the race issue in South Africa, criticizing the effort to make it a white society, and he prophesied trouble for the British because they ruled over forty million people in Africa. He closed by saying: "Let the United States and Great Britain apply the untarnished Gospel of Jesus Christ, and both will win out."[37]

Given the role of evangelism in Baptist life, it was appropriate that attention was focused on that topic. E. Arlington Wilson, National Baptist evangelist from Dallas, Texas, first paid tribute to E. C. Morris, one of the founders of the BWA, who had died in 1922 after having led the denomination for twenty-eight years. Then he pointed out that in "these critical days of doubt and skepticism" and "repudiation of the fundamentals of the evangelical faith," we can thank God that "Negro Baptists are free from the contagion of 'higher criticism.'" He explained the dynamic work of evangelism and church extension that his fellow Baptists were carrying out.[38] Following him were presentations by two outstanding evangelists of the day: Lee R. Scarborough, president of Southwestern Baptist Theological Seminary in Fort Worth, Texas, who talked about the training of evangelists; and A. Douglas Brown of London, who dealt with the spiritual forces in evangelism. Then the noted pastor-educator J. J. North from New Zealand; Northern Baptist pastor-journalist Curtis Lee Laws; and pastor J. E. Roberts of Manchester, England, addressed concrete problems of evangelization in the home base.

A subcommittee had been working for the past year on a statement to explain Baptist beliefs to the larger world. It was intended particularly to help the authorities see that Baptists are not "dangerous citizens." Mullins, the principal drafter of the document, read the text to the Congress, and it was adopted with only one dissenting vote, that of Dixon, who had wanted an even stronger statement.[39] Entitled *A Message of the Baptist World Alliance to the Baptist Brotherhood, to Other Christian Brethren, and to the World,* it spoke first of the Lordship of Jesus Christ and then of Baptist unity, based on the voluntary principle, Baptist willingness to work with others of like faith, their mission of proclaiming the gospel of Jesus Christ, and of the need for religious liberty in all nations. Other themes included were the integration of religion and ethics, the importance of family life, Christianity and social questions, stewardship, keeping the Sabbath, temperance, loyalty to the state, and the Baptists' role in international relations. With this comprehensive statement, Mullins hoped to create an environment where Baptists of diverse theological persuasions could work together in the cause of missions and evangelism.

The delegates also approved a resolution calling for total abstinence from alcoholic beverages, endorsing the idea of international peace, and condemning the Romanian government's restrictions on religious freedom. Historian Torbet points out that the "expressions of the Third Congress," as well as the resolutions adopted at the meetings of the Northern and Southern Baptists against "intemperance, Sabbath desecration, gambling, and indecency in the motion picture industry," revealed that Baptists continued to be within the Puritan tradition.[40]

Some minor modifications were made in the constitution. The office of Deputy President was eliminated, but Clifford, who would die four months later, was honored with the title of President Emeritus. Mullins was elected President, and Shakespeare continued as the Eastern Secretary. Northern Baptist Clifton Daggett Gray, president of Bates College in Lewiston, Maine,[41] replaced Pitt as the Western Secretary. Herbert Marnham of London continued as the European Treasurer, and Albert Matthews of Toronto, Canada, was named American Treasurer, replacing E. M. Sipprell, who died the previous year. The unwieldy list of vice presidents—one from each country—was replaced with "correspondents." Five new Vice Presidents and twenty-two Executive Committee members were chosen. The latter were named on the basis of a geographical quota, ensuring that both hemispheres and non-English-speaking bodies were fairly represented. The Executive Committee now functioned as the central administrative organ of the BWA. Rushbrooke's term as European Commissioner was extended. An invitation to hold the next Congress in Toronto was accepted.

The Next Five Years

Europe remained the chief focus for the BWA Executive, as various projects had to be supported and Baptist unions required encouragement. In the

Edgar Young Mullins

Edgar Young Mullins was already president of the Southern Baptist Convention (1920–24) and president of The Southern Baptist Theological Seminary (1899–1928) when the Baptist World Alliance elected him as President in 1923.

Born in Mississippi in 1860, reared in Texas and educated at that state's agricultural and mechanical college, by 1880, Mullins was working as a telegrapher and preparing to practice law. He had not yet been baptized.

Once he yielded his will to Christ, he experienced a call to preach. He studied at what was then the only Southern Baptist seminary and, before graduation, had begun to supply at what was to be his first pastorate in nearby Harrodsburg, Kentucky. He went to Lee Street in Baltimore, Maryland, where he wrote a weekly column in the Baltimore Baptist *and had his sermons published in the secular* Baltimore Sun. *Northern churches sought him, and in 1896 he went to Newton Centre, Massachusetts.*

But his seminary called: A president was needed who had not taken sides in the Whitsitt controversy. Mullins proved to be the healer and, in addition, improved the academic quality of the institution. His convention called when a consensus builder was needed, and his wise leadership helped keep the Southern Baptist Convention intact. When the Baptist World Alliance called, Mullins again answered yes. Unfortunately, he suffered a stroke shortly before the Congress of 1928. He died a few months later.

fall of 1923, Rushbrooke wrote a twenty-eight-page report on Russia that explained the situation there and the opportunities for ministry. It advocated starting preacher-training schools, supporting printing projects, providing hymnbooks, and choosing a single group through which to channel famine assistance to Russia. The All-Russian Union of Evangelical Christians then became the conduit for these funds.[42] By 1925, reports were circulating that there were over one million Baptists in Russia. Rushbrooke questioned the figure, but he did believe that it indicated "a spiritual awakening unique in our generation."[43] He visited the country some seven times in these years, but in 1928 the Soviet government denied him further admittance.

Some questions were raised about the role of the Commissioner, including the matter of accountability and his use of the BU headquarters in London. Rushbrooke replied that the BWA paid rent for the space in the Baptist Church House and that the participating mission boards funded the position, with separate accounts kept for each agency. He reported to the Continental Commission whose treasurer saw that the accounts were audited. His job description was: "To cooperate with the Boards in carrying into effect their programmes for missionary, education, and relief work in Europe, and in making such representations to governments as may be found necessary and desirable."[44]

Rushbrooke officially functioned as the director of European relief. He supervised local committees in the various countries, studied conditions so that he could make recommendations to the mission boards, handled the transfer of funds, and oversaw the expenditures and accounts kept by the national treasurers. He represented the world Baptist community to governments in questions of persecution and the legal status of Baptists. He acted for the British, Canadian, and Northern Baptists in general mission matters and for the Southern Baptist board whenever specially authorized to do so. His office served as a clearinghouse for remittances to Europe. Occasionally he undertook special tasks such as "a recent journey to Turkey and Greece to investigate the work of the Near East Relief so as to assist the American churches in determining their attitude towards that organization."[45] These activities gave him a high profile, and he was seen as "Mr. BWA" in much of Europe; and he was also a well-known figure in North America.

Between the Stockholm and Toronto Congresses the Executive met in Chicago, February 25–26, 1925; in Leeds, May 7, 1926; in London, September 8, and October 22, 1926; and in Toronto, May 11–12, 1927. At the Chicago meeting the Executive appointed Rushbrooke as Eastern

Secretary and combined the post with that of European Commissioner.[46] Shakespeare, whose health was rapidly deteriorating, had retired from both his BU and BWA jobs in 1924. (He died in 1928.) Since Rushbrooke continued to work out of the Baptist offices in London, it was the administrative and financial headquarters of the BWA. He was also directed to publish the *Baptist Directory* and the *Quarterly Bulletin* to provide news about the world's Baptists, but these initiatives did not get off the ground.

During 1925 and 1926 he endeavored to smooth out differences between Baptists in Britain and North America. Some Americans continued to be suspicious that the British were leaning to the left theologically and were too open to the ecumenical movement. Mutual discussions at regional conferences in Europe helped to foster understanding. E. C. Dargan, a former SBC president and then secretary of the Sunday School Board, even visited the BU's annual meeting in 1925 as a fraternal delegate and was invited to address the group. After sketching the history of the SBC and talking about its present problems and prospects, he affirmed a series of basic doctrinal tenets and stressed the importance of religious liberty. Acknowledging that these were the key doctrines to which the British Baptists also adhered, he assured them that the Southern Baptists stood with them in the defense of the faith.[47]

The ecumenical issue remained a sticking point. Baptists were invited to participate in the 1927 Lausanne Conference of the Faith and Order Group. Whitley responded with an article in the *Baptist Quarterly* comparing the Baptists' unity at Stockholm with the limitations of the ecumenical gathering. "Baptists made up their minds long ago, and have spoken clearly." Then he quoted from the 1923 Stockholm Statement drafted by Mullins. The Executive Committee itself ruled that representation at Lausanne would be a matter for the individual member bodies to decide.[48]

To stem the continuing undercurrent of confusion and uncertainly about the BWA, Mullins and Rushbrooke coauthored a statement defining the role of the organization. The widely distributed document clarified what had been said at Stockholm:

1. The Baptist World Alliance is a voluntary and fraternal organization for promoting fellowship and cooperation among Baptists.
2. It is not an administrative body, carrying on mission work or appointing missionaries.
3. It is not a legislative body, prescribing regulations binding on Baptists.
4. It is not a judicial body, handing down decisions governing other Baptist organizations.
5. It is not an authoritative body controlling churches or other organizations. Such authority as it possesses extends only to its own activities.

6. It is, in accordance with the principles of the Denomination, free, autonomous, and fraternal in all its relationships.
7. It is not responsible for financial obligations incurred by other Baptist bodies, or for controversies concerning matters of policy, doctrine and practice. It is prepared at any time to help by counsel or advice on matters properly pertaining to its aims and purposes; but always with careful regard to the rights of other Baptist Boards, Unions, and Conventions.
8. The aims of the Alliance are moral and spiritual. It seeks to express and promote unity and fellowship among the Baptists of the world; to secure and defend religious freedom; and to proclaim the great principle of our common faith.[49]

Two important innovations occurred in the mid-1920s—the introduction of the annual BWA Sunday and the holding of regional meetings. The *Baptist Times* announced "Baptist World Alliance Sunday, February 7, 1926: World-Wide Fellowship in Praise and Prayer."[50] Observing the first Sunday of February as a way of highlighting the ministry of BWA became an important tradition. It provided an opportunity for people around the world to join in prayer for the broader fellowship and especially for those Baptists who faced persecution.

Rushbrooke proposed the idea of regional meetings as a substitute for a European Congress like those before the war. Eight meetings lasting from two to four days took place between September 10 and October 21, 1926. President Mullins, Rushbrooke, various Executive Committee members, and representatives of the two American mission boards attended. They provided a BWA presence in a number of areas in Europe and demonstrated how the BWA reflected the international character of Baptists. Actually Mullins had intended to include these as part of a world tour, but health problems forced him to limit his travel to Europe. The series ended in London with a rally at Westminster Chapel, where Lloyd George, as one of the speakers, praised the Baptists for striving for religious liberty throughout Europe.[51] The fraternal visits were a significant aspect of BWA activity between the Congresses and gave public expression to the role Baptists were playing in the resurrection of Europe. Their value was revealed in the report of the Latvian delegate at the Toronto Congress, who expressed his deep gratitude that these leaders had come to his country.[52]

Fourth Baptist World Congress, Toronto 1928
Some 4,856 delegates from thirty-two countries and 2,174 visitors gathered at the Canadian National Exposition Grounds in Toronto for the Fourth Congress June 23–29, 1928. "Baptist Life in the World's Life," a phrase suggested by Mullins, was the theme, and the biblical text was "to sum up

all things in Christ." As the President's declining health precluded his attendance, Truett—pastor of the First Baptist Church of Dallas, Texas, and the current president of the Southern Baptist Convention—was the presiding officer. The delegates celebrated the accomplishments since the Stockholm Congress and made plans for the future.

Because the Congress was on their home turf, 893 Canadians registered as delegates and many more came as visitors. The Canadian Baptists had three regional conventions and a united Canadian Baptist Overseas Mission Board. One of those bodies, the Baptist Convention of Ontario and Quebec, had just experienced a division led by the cantankerous Toronto fundamentalist T. T. Shields, pastor of Jarvis Street Baptist Church, who charged that McMaster University (the Baptist school in nearby Hamilton) was teaching liberal theology. Whitley observed that Torontonians were surprised to learn that the one who was causing them so much grief actually "carried no weight in wider circles, and was unknown even by name to most."[53]

The keynote presentations were the opening sermon "The Universal Sovereignty of Jesus Christ" by Charles Brown of London; the address by Lacey Kirk Williams, president of the National Baptist Convention entitled "Some Contributions Negroes Have Made to the Progress of the World;" the opening message from President Mullins "Baptist Life in the World's Life," which was read to the audience; and Rushbrooke's "The Baptist World Alliance in Retrospect and Prospect." All used inspirational language and spoke optimistically of the Baptist future. They marvelled that a fraternal body without controls could exercise such an influence.

A noteworthy project was supporting the Romanian Baptists in their struggle for religious freedom. Rushbrooke felt the Alliance's actions were decisive in moving the government to relax its hard-line policy: "I ventured to tell one Minister of State that it was not a question of just a few thousand poor and isolated people in Romania: the treatment of these people had stirred the greatest Evangelical denomination on earth." He then pointed out that "Baptists have given . . . a President to the United States and a Prime Minister to Great Britain; in almost every land where we exist our people are found in the civil and the diplomatic service in higher or lower posts, and all men know that they are among the best citizens." But here in your country and here alone "we are scouted as anarchists and pariahs. The suffering may be confined to a few; the insult touches millions the world over, who will not rest until their brethren are free." In other words, our Alliance means "the message of Roger Williams uttered to the ends of the earth."[54] Those who had come to Toronto expected forceful rhetoric, accompanied by action.

Diversity was a prominent feature of the Congress, and placing sessions on China, Burma, and world evangelization right after the roll call of nations helped to set the tenor of the meeting. T. C. Bau, who presented the Chinese report, and Thra San Ba, speaking of his native Burma, were two of several people addressing the Congress who were not white males. A number of Asian Baptists spoke from their own perspective to the issues of evangelism, missions, nationalism, and racism. Women played an important part, with two speaking at plenary sessions and many others contributing short talks and participating in discussions. The Executive Committee had already decided in 1926 that women should be more directly involved in the overall work and that the Women's Committee would become organically connected to the BWA.[55] African-Americans again had a significant role, both as speakers and in their musical presentations. The variety of voices showed that the BWA was becoming a more international and inclusive movement. The stature of the younger national churches was enhanced by the roles their delegates played in the sessions and in the support they received from the Alliance.

The World Baptist Young People's Union, founded in Stockholm, held its own sectional meetings and decided to become more closely linked with the BWA. The youth would no longer have a separate organization but rather form "a Committee on Young People's Work, connected with the Baptist World Alliance." They expected to be involved in the choice of the committee and hoped to be represented on the BWA Executive.[56] They also proposed to organize a North American delegation that would travel at their own expense to Europe and meet with youth workers there.

The BWA had expanded its work to deal with needs resulting from World War I and in so doing discovered the rich possibilities for Baptists working together. To meet the next challenge—integrating into the global effort the young churches in those areas experiencing the stresses of newly gained political independence—it was felt that a full-time, salaried General Secretary would be necessary. Up to this point, all the BWA leadership positions were purely voluntary and people added BWA duties to already full schedules. Thus, to take the organization to a new and higher level, the Congress adopted a constitutional amendment to create the new position. Rushbrooke was named to the new post, while Gray continued as honorary (unsalaried) Associate Secretary with responsibility for North America. Elected as President was John MacNeill, pastor of Walmer Road Baptist Church in Toronto and soon to become principal of the McMaster University theological faculty. He had been involved in the BWA since its founding and was a speaker at the 1905 Congress. Since the first three

Presidents had come from England and the two American conventions, it was logical to choose a Canadian. These actions were confirmed at a grand finale, "Coronation Service," on the last night of the Congress.

Another constitutional change was enlarging the BWA Executive Committee. Added were two Vice Presidents (including the first non-western appointee, Joel W. Lall of India), all former Presidents, and four at-large members representing the women and young people.[57] More significantly, seven members of the Executive residing in Britain would now function as the Administrative Sub-Committee. It would exercise ad interim the functions of the Executive, i.e., conduct the day-to-day work of the BWA. Important actions would be referred to the main committee for approval at its regular session. The new body began meeting on September 12, 1928.[58]

Where Would the BWA Go from Here?

As those who had been there reflected, the Toronto Congress was a transitional stage in the BWA's development. For instance, Whitley was impressed with Truett's leadership as chair and Northern Baptist educator Clarence A. Barbour's guidance of the daily Executive meetings; he also recognized the importance of the Romanian problem and warned that the Russian Baptists had few resources and little real freedom to preach. He lamented that no blacks from Africa were present and hoped for a change by the next Congress.

The Congress was worthwhile if only to show thousands of white

John MacNeill

John MacNeill, the only Canadian to serve as President of the Baptist World Alliance in its first hundred years, was at the time of his election in 1928 pastor of Walmer Road Baptist Church in Toronto. He had come to that church in 1906, and under his leadership it had doubled its membership and increased its giving four-fold.

Walmer Road Baptist Church brought MacNeill home to his native province. He was born in 1874 of Scottish parents who had settled in Bruce County, which borders Lake Huron. He was educated at McMaster University in Hamilton, an institution to which he returned as president in 1930, serving until his death in 1937. His first pastorate, however, was in faraway Winnipeg, Manitoba, at the First Baptist Church.

MacNeill served with the armed forces during World War I. At the outbreak of war in 1914, he was on a visit to Great Britain. His sermon at the City Temple in London was so well received that it, together with other sermons on the war, was published in the book, **World Power—the Empire of Christ**, *a book that went through several printings in three countries. A later book,* **Many Mansions**, *was also popular.*

When elected as President of the Alliance, MacNeill challenged the Congress with a motto he said came from a missionary who had died in Africa: "Hats off to the past; coats off to the future."

> **Clifton Daggett Gray**
>
>
> *Clifton Daggett Gray served as a Baptist World Alliance Secretary for twenty-four years. Elected in 1923 as Western or American Secretary, a title that changed to Honorary Associate Secretary in 1928, he continued in office until the Copenhagen Congress in 1947.*
>
> *Gray was born in Somerville, Massachusetts, July 27, 1874, and in 1897 graduated magna cum laude from Harvard University. In the next two years he received both Masters and Bachelor of Divinity degrees from Newton Theological Seminary (now Andover Newton Theological School) and was ordained into the ministry. In 1900 he studied at the British Museum in London and at the University of Chicago, where he was awarded a Ph.D. in philosophy in 1901.*
>
> *Gray served as pastor of Free Baptist Church in Port Huron, Michigan, for four years; then returned to Massachusetts as pastor of Stoughton Street Baptist Church in Boston. In 1912 he began editing a Baptist newspaper* The Standard *and was soon president and treasurer of its Chicago-based publisher, Goodman & Dickinson Company. Bates College invited him to be its president in 1920.*
>
> *Gray was the third president of Bates, a college founded by Freewill Baptists and, after 1907, affiliated with the Northern Baptist Convention. Gray brought expansion in the 1920s, made certain the college survived the Great Depression, and renewed its growth as World War II began by arranging for Bates College to be a site for the U.S. Navy College Training Program. By 1944, when he retired, Gray could claim to have increased Bates' enrollment and doubled both the number of faculty and the size of the endowment. Gray died February 21, 1948.*

Baptists at first hand that there are now brown and yellow Baptists with a sense of responsibility and a power of enterprise. Some, who think in terms of missions, are dismayed to hear of Indian disaffection and Chinese civil war; they fear that the mission era in those lands is passing. The era may pass, Whitley believed, but Baptists may look with hope and confidence to young churches prepared to interpret Christ anew to their own races.[59]

Certainly the delegates had been exposed to ideas and persons who represented a wide range of perspectives. American Baptists of African descent played an especially positive role. Such speakers as Williams of Olivet Baptist Church in Chicago, then the largest Baptist church in the world, and President Parrish of Simmons University made a powerful impression. One African-American openly related the disabilities to which they were normally subject; spoke about the rising tide of indignation among the yellow, brown, black, and red races; and warned that white civilization was in danger of being swept away in a worldwide conflagration. "The grave pity was that he was treated like Ezekiel, applauded for his oratory, but not taken seriously." Whitley also expressed the wish that the Executive would free up more funds for regional conferences and visits by the President, especially to the Southern hemisphere, and praised the new

General Secretary. "The eight years since 1920 had convinced Baptists in all parts of the world that Rushbrooke was a man to whom they could safely entrust their affairs."[60]

President MacNeill began 1929 with greetings to the Baptists of the world, in which he declared: "Never was our witness as Baptists more needed than today. Never was our task more clearly defined." We are a New Testament people who assert Christ's claims in every relationship of men and nations.[61] At the time opportunity seemed to be everywhere but things were about to change.

For example, the Soviet Union had permitted worship and evangelization, Russians had come to Stockholm and Toronto, and a Baptist Preachers' School in Moscow was about to open. But as Stalin consolidated his power, the situation for Baptists, as well as for all Christians, became desperate. As the result of a new law adopted in 1929, places of worship were closed, children were denied the chance to receive religious education, the printing of Bibles was forbidden, the Baptist Preachers' School was shut down, and mass arrests of preachers took place. Since their numbers had grown so quickly and many of them were pacifists, the Soviet government saw Baptists as a threat and mercilessly moved against them. Religious liberty was even more endangered here than in Romania.

Meeting in Detroit on May 17, 1929, the Executive called on Baptists "of every race and tongue" to engage in "continuous and united prayer for their fellow-believers in Russia, and for all others who in that land in this twentieth century are denied religious liberty, and exposed to disabilities and persecution because of their loyalty to their conscience and their Lord."[62] In 1930, after returning from some regional conferences in Europe, MacNeill said: "We found a shadow of nameless terror hanging all along the Russian border . . . . The World Alliance would have fully justified its existence if only for the sense of brotherhood it has created and fostered among European Baptists."[63]

The BWA had come of age. The post-war uncertainties had been overcome, and Baptists were united to face communist tyranny in Russia and the economic catastrophe that was beginning to settle in over the world. The Alliance entered the decade of the 1920s in a very tentative situation but evolved into an integrated international movement with a purpose. It used the Baptist emphases on individual freedom and an active evangelism that included social concern, the training of leaders, and the sharing of the gospel to inspire people everywhere. By the Toronto Congress in 1928, the focus had begun to shift from North America and Europe to the whole world. For national Baptist leaders, the international organization provided status and a support structure that enabled them to speak more effectively to their own lands. Nationalism and racism were addressed as the organization sought to be both inclusive and nondirective in how local churches lived out the gospel. The issues of ecumenism and fundamentalism had not divided the body because most members were open to interaction with the wider church, while at the same time they upheld both the Baptist sense of uniqueness and the traditional understanding of the Christian message as found in the Bible and embodied in the risen and reigning Christ. Thanks to the people of vision who led the BWA, a strong structure had been raised on the foundation of love and acceptance laid in 1905 that enabled the organization to face the immense challenges that lay ahead.

---

1. Ernest A. Payne, *James Henry Rushbrooke, 1870–1947: A Baptist Greatheart* (London: Carey Kingsgate, 1954), p. 35; Payne, *The Baptist Union: A Short History* (London: Carey Kingsgate, 1959), p. 190.

2. Robert A. Torbet, *Venture of Faith: The Story of the American Baptist Foreign Mission Society and the Woman's American Baptist Foreign Mission Society, 1814–1954* (Philadelphia: Judson Press, 1955), p. 581; Payne, *Rushbrooke*, p. 35.

3. BWA IX. 1. 1. Minute Book; Charles A. Brooks and J. H. Rushbrooke, *Baptist Work in Europe: Report of the Commissioners of the Baptist World Alliance,* presented at the Conference in London July 19, 1920 (London: Baptist Union Publication Department, 1920), pp. 9–10. Copy in Angus Library, Regent's Park College, Oxford.

4. Brooks and Rushbrooke, *Baptist Work in Europe,* pp. 5–6; Bernard Green, *Tomorrow's Man: A Biography of James Henry Rushbrooke* (Didcot, U.K.: Baptist Historical Society, 1997), p. 73. I wish to express my appreciation to Bernard Green for the valuable insights on Rushbrooke and the broader Baptist community that he gave me in personal conversations in October 2002.

5. Green, *Tomorrow's Man,* pp. 73–78, provides details of the trip.

6. Ibid., p. 76; Payne, *Rushbrooke,* pp. 36–37.

7. Green, *Tomorrow's Man,* pp. 78–79, 150–153.

8. Charles W. Weber, *International Influences and Baptist Mission in West Cameroon: German-American Missionary Endeavor under International Mandate and British Colonialism* (Leiden: E. J. Brill, 1993), p.34.

9. Green, *Tomorrow's Man,* pp. 74–75; printed minutes in Minute Book, BWA IX. 1. 1.

10. F. Townley Lord, *Baptist World Fellowship: A Short History of the Baptist World Alliance* (London: Carey Kingsgate, 1955), p. 34.

11. Lord, *Baptist World Fellowship,* p. 38.

12. Brooks and Rushbrooke, *Baptist Work in Europe,* p. 28.

13. The proposals are detailed in Lord, *Baptist World Fellowship*, pp. 39–41, and Green, *Tomorrow's Man*, pp. 81–83.

14. Rushbrooke, *The Baptist Movement in the Continent of Europe* (London: Kingsgate Press, 1923), p. 202.

15. Lord, *Baptist World Fellowship*, p. 40.

16. Green, *Tomorrow's Man*, p. 82.

17. Ibid., p. 84.

18. Ibid., pp. 93–94.

19. J. H. Rushbrooke to J. H. Shakespeare, Knoxville, TN., November 3, 1922. Rushbrooke Correspondence, Angus Library, Regents Park College, Oxford. The Southern Baptists were so concerned about the issue that they discussed it at their 1922 convention and conveyed their disapproval to the BU. Carl W. Tiller, *The Twentieth Century Baptist: Chronicles of the Baptists in the First Seventy-five Years of the Baptist World Alliance* (Valley Forge: Judson Press, 1980), p. 4–6.

20. Peter Shepherd, *The Making of a Modern Denomination: John Howard Shakespeare and the English Baptists, 1898–1924* (Carlisle: Paternoster Press, 2001), p. 93.

21. C.E. Benander, "Baptists and the World's Crisis," *Baptist Quarterly* 1 (1922–3), pp. 193–195

22. Shepherd, *Making of a Modern Denomination*, pp. 154, 182.

23. Samuel S. Hill, Jr., and Robert G. Torbet, *Baptists North and South* (Valley Forge, PA: Judson Press, 1964), p. 64.

24. Lord, *Baptist World Fellowship*, p. 45.

25. *BWA Congress*, 1923, p. vii.

26. Torbet, *A History of the Baptists* (Valley Forge, PA: Judson Press, 1980), pp. 452–453.

27. *BWA Congress*, 1923, pp. 63–65.

28. Ibid., pp. 99–102.

29. Ibid., pp. 124–130.

30. Ibid., p. 130; Ferne Levy, *God's Command–Our Response: A History of the Women's Department of the Baptist World Alliance* (McLean, VA: BWA, [1985]), pp. 5–6.

31. *BWA Congress*, 1923, pp. 132–133.

32. Ibid., p. 134.

33. Ibid., pp. 136–137.

34. Ibid., pp. 140–152.

35. Ibid., 178–194.

36. Ibid., pp. 173–178.

37. Ibid., p. 173.

38. Ibid., pp. 200–201.

39. Ibid., p 194; BWA IX. 1. 2. Minute Book; Lord, *Baptist World Fellowship*, p. 50. Text in the *Baptist Times*, August 24, 1923.

40. Torbet, *History of the Baptists*, p. 452.

41. Biographical information about Gray is from The Edmund S. Muskie Archives and Special Collections Library at Bates College.

42. Report on Russia, November 6, 1923, Rushbrooke Papers, Angus Library.

43. Rushbrooke, "Near and Far," *Baptist Times*, November 26, 1925, p. 860.

44. Document 27, May 1924, Rushbrooke Papers, Angus Library.

45. Ibid.

46. He had also been offered the BU Secretary's position but felt he could not do both jobs and opted for the BWA one. Rushbrooke to Principal W. E. Blomfield at Rawdon, May 27, 1924. Rushbrooke Papers, Angus Library.

47. E. C. Dargan, "The Southern Baptist Convention. Address by Its Official Delegate, to the Baptist Union of Great Britain and Ireland, at the Annual Meetings, April 30, 1925," *Baptist Quarterly* 2 (1924–5), pp. 290–292.

48. W. T. Whitley, "Lausanne and Stockholm," *Baptist Quarterly* 3 (1926–7), p. 238; BWA IX. 1. 2. Minute Book.

49. Text in Lord, *Baptist World Fellowship*, pp. 57–58.

50. *Baptist Times*, January 7, 1926, p. 8.

51. Green, *Tomorrow's Man*, p. 108.

52. *BWA Congress*, 1928, p. 80.

53. Whitley, "The Toronto Congress," *Baptist Quarterly* 4 (1928–29), p. 150. I remember members of the Jarvis Street Church picketing the 1980 BWA meetings in Toronto because delegates had come from the recognized (registered) Baptist churches in the Soviet Union.

54. *BWA Congress*, 1928, pp. 66–67.

55. BWA IX. 1. 3. Minute Book.

56. *BWA Congress*, 1928, pp. 149–150.

57. BWA IX. 2. Constitution; Lord, *Baptist World Fellowship*, pp. 62–63.

58. BWA IX. 1. 3. Minute Book.

59. Whitley, "The Toronto Congress," p. 147.

60. Ibid., p. 152.

61. Lord, *Baptist World Fellowship*, p. 67
62. BWA IX. 1. 3. Minute Book
63. Lord, *Baptist World Fellowship*, p. 71.

4

THE YEARS OF ANXIETY AND WORLD WAR II
Erich Geldbach

The new decade opened with a flurry of activity. At the Toronto Congress the Baptist World Alliance (BWA) had agreed to hold the next Congress in Berlin in 1933, and the Executive Committee was busy with plans. General Secretary J. H. Rushbrooke, who had a deep concern for the worsening situation of the Baptists (and all Christians) in Russia, tried to persuade the Soviet authorities to relax restrictions, but his efforts went nowhere. He and President John MacNeill traveled extensively to strengthen BWA's international connections despite the deepening economic crisis that was affecting the organization's ability to function effectively.

Becoming a More Truly Global Organization
Brazilian Baptists organized the first "Latin American Baptist Convention," June 22–29, 1930, in Rio de Janeiro, Brazil, where some two thousand people gathered at the city's First Baptist Church to celebrate their achievements and to promote evangelism. Rushbrooke, Executive Committee member George W. Truett, and T. Bronson Ray of the Southern Baptist Convention Foreign Mission Board represented the BWA.[1] Rushbrooke and Truett then visited churches in Argentina and Uruguay. In August through November of that year, Rushbrooke with President MacNeill took part in regional conferences in several cities of Europe. They tried but failed to gain admittance to Soviet Russia.

The Committee on Young People's Work, formed in Toronto, sponsored the "first" Baptist International Youth Conference held in Prague, Czechoslovakia (now the Czech Republic), August 1–4, 1931. More than four hundred youth and their leaders from sixteen countries, mainly European, participated. The most memorable address was by the thirty-one-year-old German pastor and youth leader Herbert Gezork, who described his personal discovery of the oneness of people everywhere and appealed for a patriotism of service rather than privilege, of gifts rather than guns.[2] A prominent figure at the 1934 Congress, he emigrated in

1935 to the United States, where he became a professor of Christian ethics and eventually president of Andover Newton Theological School.

From September 1931 to February 1932, President MacNeill toured Baptist work in Asia, while earlier in 1931 Rushbrooke went to North America for the Executive Committee session and to speak at the annual meetings of both the Southern and Northern Baptist Conventions. In 1932 the General Secretary undertook a six-month around-the-world trip to South Africa, Australia, and New Zealand, speaking in congregations and large gatherings, meeting with public officials, and giving radio and newspaper interviews. Bernard Green pointed out that on the journey Rushbrooke played many roles: He was an inspiring preacher, an encourager, and one who publicly affirmed both the importance of Baptists in their own countries and the value of the Baptist World Alliance as a world confessional body. He used every opportunity to write, speak, and broadcast on matters of theological, moral, ecumenical, and social concern. Continuing on to the United States, he spoke in various cities and participated in the November Executive meeting in New York.[3]

Rushbrooke was a passionate advocate of peace, as he had been before the war, and the majority of the Executive Committee members shared his views. In 1931 the Executive called on the members of all BWA affiliates "to exercise their utmost influence . . . for the success of the approaching [World] Disarmament Conference." At its meeting in London on February 3, 1932, which happened to coincide with that conference, the Executive sent a cable to Geneva assuring conferees of united and eager support by Baptists in the effort to secure effective world-wide reductions of armaments."[4] Unfortunately, the conference broke up without any concrete achievements.

The Alliance's efforts on behalf of religious liberty also had little effect. The Romanian situation was an ongoing concern. In Russia the Soviets were unrelenting in their persecution of Baptists; so in 1933, when the United States gave diplomatic recognition to the Soviet Union, the BWA pressured that government to intervene. The Executive Committee addressed U.S. President Franklin D. Roosevelt directly on November 14 when Soviet foreign minister Maxim Litvinov was in Washington, D.C. It sent a telegram—signed by MacNeill, Rushbrooke, and Associate Secretary Clifton Daggett Gray—describing the nature of religious persecution in Russia and urging Roosevelt to use his influence to secure mitigation of the grave disabilities, suffering, and persecution, which believers in God were enduring under a policy whose ultimate purpose (frankly avowed by a large section of the supporters of the Soviet government) appeared to be the

> ## James Henry Rushbrooke
>
>
>
> James Henry Rushbrooke, better known to family and friends as Harry, was born into a working-class Anglican family in 1870. He moved to London at the age fifteen to work as a bookkeeper. An aunt took him to Westbourne Park Chapel, where he was soon involved in educational programs and attracted the notice of Pastor John Clifford. In 1887 he was baptized, and in 1894 he sought training in the ministry at Midland Baptist College in Nottingham. His abilities won him a scholarship to study in 1899–1901 at Halle and Berlin universities.
>
> His first pastorate was in Derby, but he was called to London's Archway Road in 1907 and to the newly organized Hampstead Garden Suburb Free Church (primarily Baptist and Congregational) in 1910. He soon had a leadership role in the Baptist Union and in its efforts to work with the Congregationalists on a national level.
>
> His participation in the Baptist World Alliance began in 1905, when he attended the first Congress. He was a featured speaker at each subsequent gathering. He first traveled for Baptist World Alliance in 1907. By 1920 the Baptist World Alliance saw Rushbrooke as the one person who had the experience and personal stature to be its Commissioner for Europe. Resigning his pastorate, he traveled in Europe and America, negotiated with governments and with and between fellow Baptists, appealed for funds and reconciliation. He gave the Baptist World Alliance credibility. In 1925 he became its Eastern or European Secretary and, in 1928, the Baptist World Alliance's first General Secretary.
>
> In Atlanta the Alliance elected him President. At sixty-nine he was considered too old to continue as General Secretary, but circumstances—World War II—kept him doing much of the same work. At war's end, he did not stop. He saw needs and opportunities that were even greater than those of 1920. Rushbrooke was planning the Congress in Copenhagen when he died in early 1947.

elimination of religion from the life of the Russian people.[5] There is no indication that Roosevelt paid any attention to this appeal, and certainly it had no impact whatsoever on Soviet antireligious policy.

The Deepening World Crisis

As the economic depression spread throughout the world, member unions found it difficult to meet their financial obligations to the BWA, a problem noted at the Executive Committee meeting in May 1931. In fact, throughout the early and mid-1930s, the London office carried on an extensive correspondence with various denominational leaders about their failure to send in their promised financial support. In June 1932 Rushbrooke warned the Administrative Committee that income had fallen short of budget.[6]

The deteriorating situation put the prospects of the Berlin Congress in grave doubt. The structure had already been worked out and the speakers identified. An innovation was the appointment of five commissions that would engage in inquiries before the meeting (by sending out questionnaires) and present reports on the topics of nationalism, racialism, family morality, temperance, and economics.⁷ The Administrative Committee noted on March 24, 1932, that the financial difficulties of the German Baptists were so great that they might not be able to carry out their obligations for hosting the meeting. Discussed at the meeting on June 20 was a letter from Associate Secretary Gray that suggested postponing the Congress. Unless conditions improved on his side of the Atlantic, there might be "a very small delegation from America." Rushbrooke reported that he had notified Friedrich Wilhelm Simoleit, director of the German Baptist Missionary Society and a denominational leader, that the BWA was monitoring matters about the convention and that the German committee should not enter into any contracts until the Executive met in the fall and made a final decision.⁸

When the full executive body assembled in New York on November 29, 1932, it took notice of the many letters from the United States, South America, Germany, and elsewhere in Europe calling for a delay. It then resolved the following:

> In view of the present economic situation and the serious burdens resting on the missionary enterprises of the denomination throughout the world, the Congress of Berlin be postponed until 1934. The Executive Committee hopes and believes that an improvement in world conditions will permit it then to take place without the disadvantages which would at present be difficult to avoid.

The resolution noted that a Congress in 1934 would fall in the centennial year of the birth of Charles H. Spurgeon and the beginnings of Baptist work in Germany. In addition, the Executive appointed a subcommittee to study the matter further and to determine at a May meeting in Washington, D.C. whether to recommend a further postponement.⁹

The rise to power of the National Socialist German Workers Party (commonly referred to by the acronym "Nazi") on January 30, 1933, added a new element of uncertainty. Now German Baptists grew fearful that if they tried to host the Congress, they would be accused of "internationalism hostile to the state." Since Adolf Hitler's regime responded to foreign criticism of its policies of anti-Semitism and terror by limiting all kinds of international activities, some Baptist Union (BU) leaders concluded that the Congress would have to take place elsewhere in Europe. They were reluctant to expose their movement to the charge of "internationalism" because they as well as the other free churches were fearful of forced unification into one national Protestant church (Reichskirche), which apparently would put them under the thumb of the pro-Nazi "German Christians."[10] Moreover, from the time Baptists had begun working in Germany, opponents charged them with being "international" rather than "national" in orientation. For decades, officials of the established church and the state had accused them of being a non-German, Anglo-American "sectarian" movement.[11]

Such cities as Copenhagen, Danzig, Rome, and Zurich now came under consideration. Rushbrooke rushed to Berlin and talked with Simoleit and other members of the German Congress committee. They were of the opinion that the situation made it difficult to continue preparations for a World Congress in Berlin. He then traveled to Kassel to meet with another top Baptist, Paul Schmidt, who was editor of the denominational paper *Der Wahrheitszeuge*. Schmidt strongly felt that Berlin should not be abandoned until they had had a formal discussion with the government and ascertained its attitude. To do otherwise would be to admit that a Baptist conference would conflict with the regime's desires, while relocating the meeting to a site near the German border would be seen as an attempt to escape its jurisdiction. Schmidt urged the brethren in Berlin to approach the government at once and to determine what its attitude would be about holding the Congress.[12]

On May 24 Associate Secretary Gray sent the report of the subcommittee meeting in Washington to the BWA office. That group insisted that the Congress should not be postponed beyond 1934. They were reluctant to abandon Berlin unless the German Baptists believed it was necessary, and in that event the Congress should be held in Zurich. The latest news from Germany seemed to indicate some moderation by Hitler, and the subcommittee felt that the present anti-Semitism and other aspects of German internal policy might change. Meanwhile, Rushbrooke had secured an agreement from the Swiss Baptists to host the Congress, but no action was to be taken until the November Executive meeting. Further complicating matters, the Baptist unions in Scotland and Australia asked the BWA to protest Hitler's anti-Jewish actions. The subcommittee cautioned the Executive against such an action. It argued that individual national unions were free to do as they wished, but a BWA resolution might "prejudice" any possible approach to the German government on behalf of the interests of the Baptists there.[13]

Meanwhile, unexpected movement came from official quarters. Hans Luther, the German ambassador in Washington, D.C., warned his Foreign Office on May 31, 1933, that canceling the Congress would be a "regrettable vote of mistrust" by the new regime. He had assured the BWA subcommittee that Berlin was the place to meet, and he even suggested that his government might give financial help to the German Baptists to stage the Congress. After consulting with the Protestant church's foreign affairs department, which did not offer any objections, on July 31 the Foreign Office notified the BU that the German government would welcome the Congress and if necessary, would assist "with word and deed."[14] The Nazi authorities obviously saw the Congress as being in their best interests, while the BWA and the German Baptists regarded this turn of events as a development in their favor. The BWA could hold its meeting in Berlin, while the denominational leaders saw this as an opportunity to avoid integration into the Reichskirche.

To ensure the Executive would favor Berlin, Simoleit traveled to New York for the November 14 meeting. Claiming to speak "on behalf of the Reich government," he urged the international Baptist community to hold its next Congress in Berlin. He maintained that his constituents strongly desired to welcome their brethren to Germany, that the government had looked over the program and was willing to allow the assembly in Berlin, and that the authorities were ready to grant full liberty of speech, since no resolutions attacking the Nazis or official policies were contemplated. Despite some anti-Semitic references and the glorification of the Führer (Hitler's title as Nazi party leader) in Simoleit's statement, the BWA Executive body accepted the invitation.[15]

Propaganda Minister Joseph Goebbels even sent a telegram to the Executive Committee supporting the action. He recognized the public relations possibilities of the Congress, as it could demonstrate to a large number of international guests, especially from the United States, that the new Germany was quite different from the "horror stories" about the Nazi regime that were appearing in the foreign media. The German Baptists, in their effort to achieve social respectability and to avoid being forced into a homogenized national church, failed to recognize that they were being used.

Preparations immediately went ahead, and the organizers bent over backwards not to offend the Nazi authorities. Thus, when Northern Baptist R. A. Ashworth of New York proposed that a leading Jewish rabbi be invited to bring greetings to the Congress, Rushbrooke rebuffed the request as "inexpedient." He said the Congress "will undoubtedly express itself on the racial question" and this action would do more harm than good. As conflicts between the Protestant church and Nazi state intensified during the spring and early summer of 1934 and critical reports filled the western press, the BWA leaders felt increasingly uneasy, but Simoleit assured them there was no cause for anxiety.[16]

Still, when the violent suppression of an alleged coup took place in Germany at the end of June, some Swedish Baptists, including their general secretary, decided to stay home.[17] Anxieties were further heightened when the two Russian unions, which up to then had been silenced by Stalinist oppression, in July sent a letter that called on the BWA to reject the invitation to the Congress. It labeled Germany as a country "that has amazed the civilized world by a repetition of mediaeval horrors," claimed that "under the present political regime no one can guarantee personal safety to delegated brothers," and pointed to "the injurious effect" upon the workings of the Congress that will occur in a country "where the fundamental Christian commandment of Peoples' Brotherhood is persistently violated."[18]

Fifth World Congress, Berlin 1934

The Berlin Congress, August 4–10, 1934, was the largest international gathering of Baptists yet held in the Eastern Hemisphere, and "it secured far wider public attention in all parts of the earth than was ever before accorded to a Baptist assembly," as General Secretary Rushbrooke noted in the official report.[19] Would the Baptists of the world be able to bear a meaningful witness in the capital city of the Third Reich? Colgate-Rochester church history professor Conrad Henry Moehlman raised doubts in a hard-hitting *Christian Century* article "The Baptists Are Going to Berlin."[20] Still, optimism reigned supreme at the Congress.

More than three thousand certified delegates, nearly thirteen hundred from outside Germany, and thousands of visitors met in the Kaiserdamm exhibition hall in Berlin-Charlottenburg. Behind the speaker's platform and tier of seats that could accommodate a large choir was a remarkable display: On the far left side hung a full-length Nazi (swastika) flag. In the center was a large painting of a cross, with a descending dove above it and beneath it the figures of Charles H. Spurgeon, William Carey, and Oncken. On the sides of the picture were the motto of the Congress: "One Lord, one faith, one baptism: One God and Father of all" (Eph. 4:5), the BWA logo, and the famous quotes of Oncken and Carey: "Every Baptist a Missionary" and "Expect great things from God: attempt great things for God." In front of the pulpit was a portrait of German President Paul von Hindenburg draped in black crepe. (He had died two days before the Congress opened, and the Nazi regime was making an enormous spectacle out of the state funeral that week.) It is interesting that no photo of the front of the hall appeared in the official BWA Congress volume.[21] Was the close association with the main symbol of the Nazi state too embarrassing?

There were more plenary addresses than at earlier Congresses, and they tended to be brief, except for the keynote address by Canadian J. B. McLaurin that was based on the Congress motto. Nine theological and devotional messages dealt with the person of Jesus Christ, implications of His lordship for the church, and His authority in the world. There were six missionary addresses and five speeches on present-day problems. British Baptist Ernest A. Payne, who would later be prominent in BWA life, made his debut with a well-received presentation on anti-God propaganda in Soviet Russia. The German-American educator Hermann von Berge delivered the Congress Sermon in German, a treatment of the "Thy will be done" petition in the Lord's Prayer. There were speeches on special topics, a colorful roll call, and words of greeting from various Baptist bodies around the world.

President MacNeill, who had remained home because of illness, sent a letter that was read from the podium. (Berlin was the third Congress in a row in which infirmity had kept the President away.) The Vice Presidents presided over the sessions. Special meetings for women, young people, and foreign missionaries and breakout sessions for the various language groups were scheduled. Groups from various countries and a united choir provided musical offerings. On Sunday visitors worshiped in various Berlin churches, with a youth service in the afternoon (noteworthy because the

George W. Truett

George Washington Truett, known as the Number One Baptist Preacher, was elected president of the Baptist World Alliance in 1934. He was born in the mountains of North Carolina in 1867. His first career was as a teacher of mountain children like himself. He began Hiwassee Academy, and his appeal to Georgia Baptists to fund that school assured its future.

Truett moved with his family to Texas, where his ability to speak movingly attracted attention. Texas Baptists asked him to raise money to pay Baylor University's debts, which he did by making appeals in nearly every church in the state. In 1893 he began his own studies at Baylor, graduating in 1897. Several churches sought him as pastor.

He went to First Baptist, Dallas, where he was to remain until his death in 1944. The Dallas church grew from a membership of five hundred to nearly eight thousand. Truett led it to begin missions in newer sections of Dallas and to initiate a citywide ministry to the deaf; he personally led annual camp meetings for cowboys in West Texas.

From 1910 Truett became increasingly active in the Baptist World Alliance, and his support, historian W. R. Estep believed, guaranteed its approval by Southern Baptists for many years. His greatest gift to the Alliance was perhaps his eloquent enunciation of the principles of religious liberty and the limitations of the state's jurisdiction in religious affairs. As he said in Atlanta, ". . . religion must be forever voluntary and uncoerced."

government had pressured the German Baptist youth organization to disband) and an "evangelistic meeting" in the evening.

The Congress chose Atlanta, Georgia, as the meeting site for 1939 and elected as President, Truett, pastor of the First Baptist Church of Dallas, Texas, and a prominent figure in the BWA. The Secretaries and Treasurers were reelected for the next five years, and some new people were named as Vice Presidents and members of the Executive Committee. The most significant constitutional change was the specification that the Executive must include at least five women. Past Presidents were also made regular officers.

The Political Context of the Congress

Two important aspects of the Congress require further discussion: First was the delicate political situation in which it was held and its impact on the German Baptists. Hitler had only been in office for eighteen months, and the Nazis were still consolidating power; but a brutal dictatorship had settled over the land. The press was muzzled, a ubiquitous secret police was watching the populace, many opponents had been thrown into concentration camps or forced to emigrate, the bloody purge a month before the Congress had eliminated potential rivals, and the death of President Hindenburg enabled the Führer to unite the powers of head of state with that of chancellor (head of government). The Nazis were systematically driving Jews out of public life and denying them basic civil liberties.

A bitter conflict, known to posterity as the Kirchenkampf (Church Struggle), was underway for control of the established Protestant church. The pro-Nazi "German Christians" were trying to seize control of the autonomous regional churches and unite them into one national Reichskirche with a Reichsbischof (Reich Bishop) Ludwig Müller ruling over it. They demanded the dismissal of all clergy of Jewish ancestry and the expunging of "Jewish influences" from Christianity. The "Confessing Church," whose leading figures included Martin Niemöller and Dietrich Bonhoeffer, mounted a fierce opposition to this nazification of the church. For the Baptists the Congress seemed to be a golden opportunity to get out from under official church pressures and to engage in evangelism unhindered. Hosting it in Berlin would testify to the Baptists' freedom and willingness to cooperate with the new order.

Public officials, including the mayor of Berlin and representatives of the established Protestant church, brought greetings at the opening session. The Congress adopted a formal resolution of sympathy about Hindenburg's death, and Hitler acknowledged it with a telegram of appreciation. BWA leaders were invited to a reception at the city hall. Rushbrooke and Gray were given tickets to the special session of the Reichstag (parliament) honoring President Hindenburg, and two representatives of the Congress were invited to the state funeral at Tannenberg. On August 8, Reich Bishop Müller invited a BWA delegation to his offices and assured them that his objective was to secure the preaching of the gospel and to reach the multitudes that have drifted away from the church. He explained that he was uniting only the established regional churches and that he desired friendly and brotherly relations with free churches, such as the Baptists. There was no intention of incorporating them into the Reich Church.[22] The Congress responded with a resolution of appreciation:

> We are gratified to learn of the solemn assurance of the Reichsbischof, made to a group of some twenty-five or so leaders whom he had invited to confer with him, that it is not the intention to bring about a union of the free churches with the Reichskirche or to exercise any compulsion upon them.[23]

In a resolution commemorating the German Baptist centenary, the Congress rejoiced "that the work of the Baptists enjoys today public recognition and honor." Since both the state and the established church had regarded them as a minor entity for the hundred years since Oncken and six others had been baptized near Hamburg, German Baptists felt that at last they had achieved social recognition. Five years later at Atlanta, Rushbrooke maintained that, despite the fact that "not all we said at the Congress was freely published," nevertheless "more appeared in the secular press in Germany [on the Baptist movement] in one month than had previously appeared in a whole century."[24]

Shortly after the Congress Carl August Flügge issued a compilation of positive statements in the German press about Baptists. One article marveled that delegates from sixty nations could sit peacefully side by side, "a Negro next to a Chinese, an Englishman next to an Argentine, a Swede next to a South African, a New Zealander next to a Laplander: A truly colorful mix of peoples, a picture which the German capital has never seen before. And all the thousands were one in the search for truth."[25] Several articles included references by leading Nazis that the party itself would not enforce any specific belief system but simply "positive Christianity," a vague concept contained in paragraph twenty-four of the party program adopted in 1920.

Within eighteen months all mention of the Congress had disappeared from the press. German Baptists soon learned that their newfound freedom was an illusion; they, like all other religious groups, would have to submit to the dictates of the Nazi state. They and the BWA had been victims of massive self-deception.

At this critical moment in their history, German Baptists rejoiced.

Never had a government seemed friendlier to them. By having the support of the international community, they retained their independence and were assured that they had "freedom" to worship and evangelize. The established church was struggling and divided, a situation some perceived as divine punishment for the mistreatment of Baptists in the past. When the Reich bishop promised not to force them into a unified Protestant church, they were convinced that separation of church and state was now operative. They failed to recognize that this "good" principle could be used by a totalitarian state to produce a withering away of the church, removing it as a rival to its own absolutist claims.

Like most of their fellow citizens, German Baptists believed the propaganda that the Nazis had saved the country from communism, had cracked down on indecent nightlife and the "culture of nakedness," and had done away with mass unemployment. They regarded the Nazi revolution as the rebirth of their nation and remained silent as the Holocaust unfolded and war began. What they failed to grasp was that submitting to the regime's every wish was the opposite of what the Christian witness demanded in dangerous and unpredictable circumstances. Rushbrooke, in his opening address at the Congress, spoke of a "higher loyalty" that transcended political, national, or economic programs and urged his hearers, "to resist any invasion of 'the Crown Rights of the Redeemer.' "[26] German Baptists missed that point completely; during this tragic time they obeyed rather than opposed the powers that be.

The Study Commissions
The second important aspect of the Congress was the introduction of study commissions. Three years earlier five topics were chosen and 155 members from forty-five countries were appointed.[27] Each commission had sent a questionnaire to BWA members around the world; its report, based on the data gathered, was presented at a plenary session. Given the tense political climate at the Congress, these reports were remarkably candid.

The strongly worded report of Commission One, "Nationalism," undoubtedly caused the Nazi authorities considerable discomfort. In fact, Schmidt had tried to soften it.[28] The report declared that nationalism constitutes one of the greatest obstacles to peace and understanding between nations. The Christian church, the one universal body of Christ, must not remain silent or indifferent. Jesus's teaching about the Kingdom of God is the criterion for determining what is legitimate patriotism, that which is compatible with loyalty to Christ, and illegitimate chauvinism. The latter was defined as a theory of the "absolute and unlimited sovereignty of the state" and the "application of this theory in national and international relations." Here, citizens must submit unconditionally to the authority of a state and lose their liberty. The results are separations, hatred, and enmity between nations. One people advances its own interests by using means that violate the rights of others.

In contrast to chauvinistic nationalism, the Christian is obliged to display universal love and sacrificial service to all fellowbeings and to promote the welfare of all, irrespective of race, nationality, religion, or social standing. The fundamental principle of moral action, both in private and public life, is the serving and sacrificing love that goes together with a new mind and a new relationship. If the state demands an action that would violate one's conscience, a Christian has no choice but to refuse: "Loyalty to Christ must be placed before every other loyalty." The report went on to say that nationalism is a menace to Christian missions and is most dangerous when in league with militarism. If these two forces "continue to exercise their destructive influence among the peoples, humanity will certainly face a very dark future."

National isolation must be overcome by international friendship and cooperation. Not only Baptists but all churches must "proclaim the incompatibility of selfish nationalism and warfare with the Christian spirit" and promote the principles of justice, peace, and reconciliation. This reconciliation can only be achieved if the church labors untiringly for an international standard of justice whereby disputes may be settled by an international court of arbitration. In this connection the report emphasized the work of the League of Nations and called on churches to provide the moral conditions for the League to attain success. One thing they could do is utilize their educational resources to teach the youth not "to look upon other nations as enemies to their own," but instead to create "a new mentality in youth in regard to international peace."

The report stressed that every great epoch in church history was connected with a new emphasis on some forgotten truth contained in the gospel. The time has come for the church to stress "human brotherhood and the obligations both for the individual and the nation which must follow the application of this truth." Through an uncompromising application of the gospel in all human relations, a fundamental change would result in the world. To achieve this change, however, the church must be ready to "travel the way of suffering, sacrifice, and self-denial." Such ideas clearly challenged the reigning political theory in Nazi Germany.

Equally as threatening to the Nazis was the report of Commission Two, "Racialism."[29] Although the issues of nationalism and racialism are often linked, the race question in itself is an urgent problem. Not only do people ask whether the world could survive another great war, but also "whether any civilization can live that tolerates the survival of cruelty and injustice of race toward race." To be sure, the biological fact of different races is divinely ordained and should be viewed positively. Racial antipathies, however, are an ethical matter and are based on fear arising from "pride, sordid greed, and economic rivalry." The antagonistic tendencies in the world—the mingling of races and the attempt to enforce absolute separation—should not preclude Baptists from declaring "constantly and without any uncertainty" in every land that "race differences are no justification or excuse for any exploitation or selfish racial domination." The Golden Rule of Christ is valid equally both for races and individuals.

The report then went on to apply these principles to specific situations:

1. A color or racial bar to worship and fellowship in the church "is a monstrous denial of the Lord—a violation of the very essence of His teaching."
2. The caste system in India is today "one of the most insidious of civilized sins."
3. The rivalry between Jews and Arabs in the British mandate of Palestine is not really racial, but economic and cultural. It can only be dealt with "under free and fair conditions of intercourse."
4. Anti-Semitism is neither racial nor religious in origin but a by-product of political and economic competition. If anti-Semitism were a question of religion, then Baptists as followers of Jesus Christ would need to declare that there is no other faith "for which we have more reverent honor" than that of the Jew. The report unequivocally deplored "the long record of ill-usage of Jews on part of professedly Christian nations" as a violation of the teaching and spirit of Christ and expressed "to the Jews by word and act the spirit of Jesus Christ our Lord, their Saviour and ours." Even though this statement did imply that the Gentile church had an obligation to evangelize Jews, its pro-Jewish sentiment was obvious and all the more remarkable, since the Nazis were systematically depriving Jewish citizens of their rights. Interestingly, the German delegates voted to approve the report.
5. The exploitation of "defenseless subject peoples of any race or colour" and the "appropriation of native lands" by powerful commercial interests to benefit a favored race are "shameless and contemptible greed" and forms of "robbery."

The reports of Commissions Three and Four, "Moral Standards, Especially in Connection with Marriage and the Family" and "Temperance," were predictable Baptist statements.[30] The one condemned gambling, called for more controls on the motion-picture industry, and affirmed the sacredness of love and marriage. The other expressed concern about the spreading use of intoxicating beverages and the need for controls on their production and sale.

The report of Commission Five, "Economics and the Mind of Christ,"[31] urged that democracy be extended "to industry and economic life" as an outgrowth of Jesus' social and ethical teachings. It affirmed that the philosophy of laissez-faire and uncontrolled competition not only was unethical and unscientific but also anti-Christian and called on Christians to assist in reconstructing the economic order. They should support a living wage, a planned economy to properly utilize capital and labor resources, and measures to combat unemployment. Churches should confront economic problems and engage in a new form of "social evangelism" that seeks "to convert the strong to the principles of Jesus." This social evangelism would "supplement the older individualistic evangelism" and make Christian capacity available for "economic reconstruction."

The reports and resolutions based upon them reflected the strong sense of idealism that pervaded the Congress. If only a worldwide program of evangelism and Christian education were carried out, Christ's rule would be accepted and all problems—war, race, divorce, gambling, drinking, or economic injustice—could be solved. Perhaps the solutions proposed diverged considerably from what the churches and Alliance could realistically accomplish, but, as Bristol Baptist College Principal Arthur Dakin pointed out, the reports were not a call to "Quietism." Baptists did not imagine that they had nothing to do with world conditions, politics, and economic arrangements: "We have heard the call in our time to vigorous social reforms and the application of our Faith to daily life."[32]

Especially important was the resolution against war and for peace. After identifying the problems besetting the world following "the last Great War," it urged governments to be ready to surrender whatever of their national sovereignty might be necessary to establish an international authority for the maintenance of world peace on the basis of equity and right. It also called upon all Christian men and women to constantly bear their personal testimony against the inhumanity and anti-Christian character of war, to earnestly promote the corporate and united action of the Christian Churches in the cause of peace, and to untiringly advocate and practice goodwill toward people of all nations. It ended by welcoming the calling of an international conference of the Christian church to avert war and to establish peace.[33]

Rushbrooke, who for three decades had striven to promote peace among nations, had made certain that the issue of peace and war would be on the Congress agenda.[34] President-elect Truett introduced this resolution and moved its passage. Rushbrooke and Gray successful beat back an attempt to water it down through a substitute resolution and other delaying tactics, and it eventually passed with only one negative vote.[35]

It is interesting to note that although the German government could not have been happy with the peace resolution or with those that deplored nationalism and oppression of Jews and other races, its secular press applauded the Congress and reported the sincerity of its discussions and the wide range of topics covered. The German Baptists' Oncken Verlag published the Congress proceedings with the full text of the reports and resolutions.[36]

From Berlin to Atlanta

The delegates left the hall with the choral strains of the *Hallelujah Chorus* ringing in their ears, a musical piece that soon would be banned in Germany because of its "Jewishness." Controversy continued about the meeting, and an editorial in the November 21, 1934, *Christian Century* criticized the Baptists in Germany for not standing by the principles they espoused the previous summer in their resolutions on race and church-state relations. The writer accused them of ignoring the persecution suffered by those Christians in the Protestant church who were defying Reich Bishop Müller's attempt to impose a Nazi dictatorship on the religious life of Germany.[37]

Rushbrooke affirmed the principles of the resolution on race in a speech to a conference of Jews and Christians in early 1935, when he expressed his "profound respect" for the Jewish race and the debt that Christianity owed to Jews. When in Berlin he condemned "the placing of a stamp of inferiority upon a whole race," it was not merely as a Baptist but in the name of all genuine and instructed Christianity that he spoke, and he strongly affirmed the pro-Jewish tenor of the resolution condemning all racial animosity.[38] General Secretary Rushbrooke clearly was not backpedaling on the commitment to racial justice made there, in spite of the regime's displeasure or the unwillingness of the German Baptists to risk official sanctions by pushing the issue. In fact, in Atlanta he claimed that the "Jews of America and Britain and other lands publicly thanked us" for the resolution on racial discrimination, and in Eastern Europe "they went further by thanking God in their synagogues for the witness Baptists had borne."[39]

In Berlin the sixty-four-year-old Rushbrooke had told the Executive Committee that he would serve only for another five years,[40] but he showed no signs of slowing down. After the Executive Committee meeting in May 1935 in Memphis, Tennessee, he went to Mexico to investigate the impact that stringent new religious laws there would have upon the Baptists. At the end of the year, he and President Truett went on a six-month world tour, visiting Baptists in Palestine, Burma, China, and India and taking part in a number of centennial celebrations. Before returning home, he delivered addresses at both the Northern and Southern Baptist conventions in the United States.

The two men made a good team: Rushbrooke was the forward-looking thinker, while Truett was more of a pastoral evangelist. Both admired each other's gifts and brought them to bear in their travels together or separately. In 1937 the two appeared at ten regional conferences at various cities in Europe, ending their journey at the Second Baptist Young People's World Conference in Zurich, August 8–13, where fifteen hundred youths from twenty-seven countries assembled, vastly exceeding the attendance in 1931. Truett made a tour of Western Canada in 1938. Other BWA dignitaries stepped in to represent the organization at ceremonial events, as the number was becoming too great for the General Secretary or President to be at all of them.

Religious liberty consumed a great deal of Rushbrooke's time. His attempts to secure any amelioration of the Russian Baptists' situation were fruitless, but he had somewhat more positive results with the Romanian regime. Rushbrooke went to Bucharest in 1935 to negotiate better conditions for Baptists, bombarded the Romanian government with letters and BWA resolutions calling for freedom of worship, and mobilized opinion in Britain and the ecumenical community against the official repression. The BWA files bulge with correspondence on the Romanian issue, which was discussed at every Executive meeting as well as at the Atlanta Congress.[41] Rushbrooke also directed considerable attention to Spain, where the bitter civil war followed by the victory of Francisco Franco threatened the modest freedom that Baptists and other Protestants had gained under the Spanish Republican regime. Townley Lord aptly summarized this aspect of BWA activity: "[W]herever Baptists were encountering tyranny the Alliance threw its whole weight into the defense and support of our people."[42]

The BWA acted on other international issues during these years, as the minutes of the Executive and Administrative committees reveal. Its support was critical for the resumption of the German Baptist mission in the section of Cameroon that the British controlled under a League of Nations mandate, and it channeled funds to help continue the work when the Nazi government blocked sending money to support foreign missions. In 1935, it appealed to the League of Nations to arbitrate the border dispute between Ethiopia and Italy and, once fighting broke out, urged negotiations. The BWA sent aid to hard-pressed Baptists in Czechoslovakia after the country was dismembered in 1938–39, provided assistance to Russian refugees in Manchuria and China, and expressed great concern about moves by the Japanese puppet regime in Manchuria to force Christian pupils in mission schools to participate in the ritual worship of the emperor.

Planning for the Atlanta Congress moved ahead rapidly. Concern was expressed about racial discrimination in that city, but President Truett assured his colleagues that any problems could be worked out.[43] The Executive decided that three commissions would be appointed to study: (1) what Baptists can do to avert war and promote peace; (2) the Baptist contribution to Christian unity; and (3) the report and findings of the Oxford [Life and Work] and Edinburgh [Faith and Order] ecumenical conferences of 1937. Named to chair the commissions were Swedish educator N. J. Nordstrom, Regent's Park College Principal Henry Wheeler Robinson, and Southern Baptist Seminary professor W. O. Carver. These chairpersons sent out questionnaires to Baptist leaders around the world for their opinions.

Sixth Baptist World Congress, Atlanta 1939

A record crowd turned out in Atlanta, Georgia, for the Sixth Baptist World Congress, July 22–28, 1939. The official registration was 12,445; tens of thousands more attended the large public gatherings that had to be moved from the air-conditioned city auditorium to Ponce de Leon Baseball Park to accommodate the crowds. At one event there, some sixty thousand people attended. The state's segregation laws had made the venue a controversial one. However, one-third of the local organizing committee was African-American, and the odious laws forbidding "mingling of the races" apparently were "suspended" during the time of the Congress. Several African-American pastors were on the program, more than at any previous Congress,[44] white Baptists from abroad were welcomed as guest preachers in black churches, and African-Americans were well-represented in the Congress audiences. Whether the seating was segregated cannot be determined from the Congress record, but Lacey Kirk Williams, president of the National Baptist Convention, did issue a statement that "while some few remote and more immediate, sincerely regrettable incidents have occurred," his denomination was grateful for the efforts of the "local entertainment committee" in making his people feel welcome.[45] J. Raymond Henderson of New Rochelle, New York, and Gordon B. Hancock of Richmond, Virginia, gave forceful speeches condemning racism and segregation.[46] Gray maintained that the Berlin Congress resolution on racial discrimination had now been implemented by deeds.[47] An unusual sense of racial cooperation prevailed throughout the Congress, and as Southern hospitality was displayed, people spoke of the "Atlanta Spirit."

President Truett[48] was the towering figure in a context where Baptists were essentially the majority religion. Working alongside him in the role of local arrangements chair was Atlanta pastor and Southern Baptist denominational leader Louie D. Newton. U.S. President Roosevelt sent a letter of greeting, while the Atlanta mayor, the state's governor, and a U.S. senator delivered words of welcome. An ecumenical spirit prevailed, as both the president of the Atlanta Christian Council and a local rabbi offered welcoming remarks. Presbyterian missions executive Robert E. Speer delivered a major speech. Just as remarkable was the national press and radio coverage that the Congress received.

Baptist leaders from many nations spoke on evangelism, missions, biblical authority, the doctrine of the New Testament Church, the ordinances (sacraments), and civil and religious liberty. Women and youth addressed plenary sessions as well as their own special meetings. Truett's presidential address entitled "The Message and Mission of Baptists in the World Today" and the concluding coronation address by C. (Charles) Oscar Johnson of St. Louis, Missouri, "The Uplifting Christ," were highlights, as was "Missionaries All," a pageant of Baptist history written by Payne of London. Featured performances by 750 local Baptists and a massed choir drew an overflow crowd to the ball park.

British BU Secretary M. E. Aubrey, U.S. professor William A. Mueller, and German Baptist leader Paul Schmidt had a sharp exchange over the political issues of totalitarianism, liberalism, and collectivism. The Germans had already complained to the BWA about strong criticism in the Baptist press in the west, and when platform speakers questioned their passiveness in the face of Nazi ideology,[49] Schmidt responded with a strong defense of the situation in Germany. Actually, he and colleagues Hans Luckey, a teacher at the Hamburg seminary, and Friedrich Rockschies, chair of the Union's council, were required to report in person to the German embassy in Washington, D.C., and to the authorities in Berlin about what they did in Atlanta to support the regime.

Schmidt later claimed he had secured the deletion of two sentences offensive to the German authorities from the text of Aubrey's hard-hitting speech printed in the Congress volume.[50] When he proclaimed in his own address—an advance copy of which he had provided to the Reich Church Ministry in Berlin—"We do not believe that Christian and Baptist ideals are necessarily identical with any political ideology," he essentially rejected the widespread criticism of the Nazi state in the west and justified the German Baptists' acceptance of the regime because it supposedly allowed them freedom to preach the gospel.⁵¹ The confrontation that had been avoided in Berlin occurred in Atlanta.

Each of the three commissions reported to the Congress. The report of the first commission, "What Baptists Can Do to Avert War and Promote Peace," set forth three Christian principles that were seen as applicable to international relations: (1) the imminent coming of the Kingdom of God; (2) the transcendent nature of this kingdom; (3) the inevitable tensions of the Christian life.⁵² It underscored the importance of an international judicial institution (such as the League of Nations or an International Court of Justice) to prevent anarchy and restrain transgressor nations, asserted the dual citizenship of Christians (both in the world and in the kingdom that is not of this world), stressed the need for them to exercise a transforming influence on societal life, and reaffirmed the Berlin pronouncement on nationalism that emphasized loyalty to God must stand above all other loyalties. Jesus's command to God and neighbor was unlimited in its scope.

The commission identified nationalism as a major cause of war, along with racial prejudice, war profiteering, and the selfish use of natural resources. The report viewed war in highly negative terms⁵³ and deemed it as "incompatible with the ideal of Jesus for human community-life" and as "something from which Christ wants to save us." It identified three approaches to war—pacifism, war as a necessary evil or last resort, and war justified for the purpose of maintaining law, order, and/or liberty—and reluctantly opted for this last approach. The report exhorted Baptists to function as peacemakers, reminding them that "none but changed people can change the world." Craig Sherouse, commenting on the report in his dissertation "The Social Teachings of the Baptist World Alliance, 1905–1960," noted that although the BWA throughout the 1930s consistently opposed nationalism and supported efforts for peace by such bodies as the League of Nations, it lacked any firm peacemaking program of its own. Religious liberty occupied a much higher level in its priorities for action.⁵⁴

The commission on Baptist contributions to Christian unity explored how Baptist distinctives could provide a basis on which to build unity. Baptists' essential beliefs are their emphases on liberty of conscience and biblical authority. Believers' baptism is a necessary outflow of both and derives from a high Christology; water baptism represents the gift of the Holy Spirit to personal faith and is a significant and enriching experience of grace. Baptists comprise the only church that can proclaim baptismal grace in its New Testament sense. As to whether the Lord's Supper is a sacrament, Baptists differ. Baptists prefer congregational government, which lies closest to their emphasis on individual faith; and although some may accept some modification in the direction of a presbytery, none see the "historic episcopate" as essential for Christian unity. There was no need for "organic" unity with other Christians—such unity would impair the truths for which Baptists stand—nor for a "federal" relationship to other denominations. Baptists should unite in the BWA and through that organization cooperate with other churches in Christian service.[55]

The third commission wrestled with issues of cooperation in light of recent events on the ecumenical scene. Its report urged those assembled to rethink their position on Baptist exclusiveness, an attitude that had resulted from their traumatic experience of persecution at the hands of other Christians, and to ask whether Baptists can retain their integrity if they refuse to fellowship with other Christians. The commission's answer was that "we will not choose separation, nor in our own spirit consent to be a sect in God's family." Its report concluded that Baptist ecumenism was best expressed at the International Missionary Council meeting in Tambaran (Madras, India) in 1938 with its emphasis on "Christian unity in the spirit." In the commission's opinion, the ecumenical conferences at Oxford and Edinburgh in 1937 focused too much on matters of church union and opted to create a World Council of Churches.

The commission could appreciate the services such a council could render but saw the danger that it might become an ecclesiastical union or an organization dominated by a central governing body that would supervise the belief and conduct of the free churches of Jesus Christ. In addition, some were reluctant to be associated with representatives of churches that were known to despise Baptist views or (like the Romanian Orthodox) were actively engaged in the persecution of Baptist communities. Most churches that would join the council would be "state churches" or would advocate hierarchy and sacramentalism, concepts inimical to Baptist principles. Still, there existed a "yearning for the ecumenical spirit on the part of Baptists" and a hope that unity could be cultivated on the basis of spiritual experience and practical participation in work in the world. Formal church union was out of the question, but still sectarianism and provincialism among Christ's followers was "deep disloyalty" to him.[56]

The Atlanta Congress adopted resolutions supporting religious liberty, expressing continuing concern about freedom in the Soviet Union and Romania, reaffirming the position on racialism taken in Berlin, and calling for ridding the world of intoxicating beverages. Retiring General Secretary Rushbrooke, was elected President. Walter O. Lewis, the longtime European staffperson of the American Baptist Foreign Mission Society, became

General Secretary. Gray stayed as Honorary Associate Secretary, and to ensure that the Southern as well as the Northern Baptists were represented, a constitutional amendment enabled Newton to be appointed a second Honorary Associate Secretary. Charles T. LeQuesne of London, a distinguished member of the legal profession, replaced deceased Herbert Marnham as Eastern Treasurer while Albert Matthews of Toronto continued as the Western Treasurer. A venue for the next Congress was not chosen because of the uncertain international situation, but Budapest and Rangoon were mentioned as possibilities.

This Congress reconstituted the Women's Committee, which had been discontinued after the appointment of women to the Executive Committee in 1928. Its membership consisted of the women on the Executive and an equal number that the women would co-opt, and it would report to the Executive. Eva (Mrs. Ernest) Brown of London was named chair.[57] An interesting innovation was the parallel conference on evangelism that took place during the Congress.

The Coming of World War II
Rushbrooke returned to London after the Congress and continued to

Walter O. Lewis

Walter Oliver Lewis, General Secretary of the Baptist World Alliance 1939–48, was a scholar and humanitarian. Born in Missouri in 1877, he had four earned degrees: an A.B. and M.A. from the Missouri Baptist college, William Jewell, a Th.D. from the Southern Baptist Theological Seminary, and a Ph.D. from the University of Erlangen in Germany.

His hobby was searching attics and archives in central Europe for handwritten and out-of-print writings of and about Balthasar Hubmaier and translating them into English. He was comfortable reading as well as conversing and preaching in several European languages.

From 1922 he served the American Baptist Foreign Mission Society as a representative in Europe. His job was to administer and deliver relief funds. His wife said that he invariably returned home with an empty suitcase and quite often without a coat. He gave his clothes to those in need.

Elected as General Secretary as World War II began, Lewis remained in the United States, which in time became home to the Baptist World Alliance office. He did visit European Baptists in 1941 and 1942, and at the end of the war he traveled to Germany to reestablish ties with the German Baptists and plan for reconstruction.

In 1948 Lewis resigned as General Secretary in order to direct the European relief operation. He was given the newly created position of Associate Secretary for Europe, based in London, where he could continue to do what he felt called to do. He resigned at the age of seventy-eight in 1955 and died in 1965.

oversee BWA affairs until the new General Secretary Lewis, arrived to take charge. As war seemed imminent, Rushbrooke took immediate actions to ensure BWA continuity. He arranged to have the minutes books placed in a secure, bombproof shelter at some distance from London, because duplicate records did not exist. He decided to have the Congress volume produced in the United States, as the largest market existed there and the possibility was real that wartime conditions might prevent its publication in Britain. He authorized Newton to take charge of the project, and the book was released within a short time.

On August 25 Rushbrooke sent out an appeal to all Baptists to pray for peace. Germany, however, unleashed World War II by invading Poland on September 1; two days later Britain and France responded by declaring war on Germany. On September 5 Rushbrooke issued a message defining the position of the British Baptists on the war and then began working on a statement in the name of the BWA that set forth "our Christian world outlook in war time." This statement called for the renunciation of hatred, bitterness, and falsehood; affirmed malice toward none; and stood for the rebuilding of broken fellowship as soon as possible. Fearing a plunge in the value of the British pound sterling and the Canadian dollar, Rushbrooke arranged for a special dollar account to be opened in the United States. A New York bank was selected, but it refused—because of a legal technicality—to accept an organizational account for the Alliance; the account was opened in the names of the three American-based Secretaries.[58]

The U.S. government, which had declared itself neutral in the war, prevented Lewis from relocating to England. He was ready to sail in October, but the State Department seized his passport, claiming that American passports were being stolen and used by spies. To get it back, he had to prove it was extremely urgent for him to travel; every attempt to secure permission in the next three months failed.[59] Meanwhile, since the Europeans were complaining that when they needed help the most the Alliance seemed to be inactive, Rushbrooke felt compelled to exercise his presidential role in a general secretarial manner. For example, he visited Romania in April 1940 and seemed to bring some alleviation of the ongoing religious freedom problem. Rushbrooke did all he could to "liaise with Lewis," but according to Rushbrooke's biographer, Lewis often acted without consulting him.[60]

The General Secretary represented the BWA in the United States, worked on religious liberty issues, and devoted considerable time to helping delegates to the Atlanta Congress from Eastern Europe who were unable to return home. His salary and travel expenses were paid through contributions from North American Baptist bodies that were deposited in the New York account.[61]

Because of the war, operating the London office was becoming increasingly difficult. Rushbrooke came to the United States in May–June 1940 to conduct BWA business and to take part in the annual Executive meeting. On May 21 the Executive decided to open a "temporary office" in Washington, D.C., and to function with a North American-based Administrative Committee that would supplement the London structure. Responsibility for the dollar account was then transferred from the Secretaries to the new committee.[62] To be sure, this resolved Lewis's shaky financial situation, but it meant control of the BWA had shifted from British to American hands. The move, however, did not strengthen the organization as neither the Administrative nor Executive committees met for nearly three years. Meanwhile, German bombs destroyed the Alliance office in London and Washington's "temporary" status quickly wore off, although it did not officially become the permanent headquarters until 1947.

In spring and early summer of 1941, Lewis traveled to Portugal, Spain, Vichy France (the area in the south under a puppet regime), and Switzerland to encourage the Baptist minorities there and to seek ways to get relief supplies from the United States to the European continent.[63] The BWA also endorsed former U.S. President Herbert Hoover's program for feeding starving populations in the areas overrun by Germany. Known as the National Committee on Food for the Small Democracies, it began in the fall of 1940 and functioned until early 1942. Its activities, however, were thwarted by the British government, which attempted to slap a total blockade on the European continent.[64] Finally, in May 1943, Rushbrooke was able to go to America for an Executive Committee meeting in Chicago. On May 27 the Executive launched a major relief effort, an action that breathed new life into the Alliance and put it once again on a firm footing.

---

1. F. Townley Lord, *Baptist World Fellowship* (London: Carey Kingsgate, 1955), p. 70.

2. Carl W. Tiller, *The Twentieth Century Baptist: Chronicles of the Baptists in the First Seventy-five Years of the Baptist World Alliance* (Valley Forge, PA: Judson Press, 1980), p. 7–5.

3. Bernard Green, *Tomorrow's Man: A Biography of James Henry Rushbrooke* (Didcot, U.K.: Baptist Historical Society, 1997), pp. 114–116.

4. BWA IX. 1. 3, Minute Book.

5. BWA IX. 1. 3, Executive Committee, November 14, 1933; text also in Lord, *Baptist World Fellowship*, p. 74.

6. BWA brochure, *Summary of Statistics 1930* (London: Offices of the Alliance, n.d.); BWA IX. 1. 3, Minute Book, Executive Committee, May 20–21, 1931; BWA I. 1. E, correspondence file.

7. BWA. *Fifth Baptist World Congress, Berlin, August 1933, Occasional Bulletin* No. 1 (March 1932), No. 2 (June 1932), copies in Southern Baptist Theological Seminary (SBTS) library.

8. BWA IX. 3, Minute Book.

9. Ibid.

10. Andrea Strübind, *Die unfreie Freikirche. Der Bund der Baptistengemeinden im Dritten Reich'* (2nd ed., Wuppertal: R. Brockhaus, 1995), p. 118.

11. Erich Geldbach, *Freikirchen–Erbe, Gestalt und Wirkung* (Göttingen: Vandenhoeck & Ruprecht, 1989), p. 130.

12. Administrative Subcommittee, April 27, 1933. BWA IX. 3, Minute Book.

13. BWA IX. 1. 3, Minute Book.

14. Strübind, *Unfreie Freikirche*, p. 119.

15. Ibid., pp. 120–121; BWA IX. 1 .3, Minute Book.

16. Administrative Subcommittee, April 30, June 19, July 16, 1934. BWA IX. 1. 3, Minute Book.

17. Green, *Tomorrow's Man*, p. 117. Green found out about this from a prominent Swedish Baptist.

18. BWA I. 1. 1. H. It was signed by I. I. Bondarenko for the Baptist Union and Y. I. Zhidkov for the Union of Evangelical Christians.

19. *BWA Congress*, 1934, p. v.

20. Conrad Henry Moehlman, "The Baptists Are Going to Berlin," *Christian Century* 51 (Feb. 7, 1934), pp. 183–185.

21. A picture of the front of the hall is contained in the report by William B. Lipphard entitled "The World Fellowship of Baptists," in the American Baptist Foreign Mission Society magazine *Missions* (vol. 25, October 1934, p. 460). A similar picture was not included in either the English or German edition of the 1934 Congress volume. Tiller, *Twentieth Century Baptist*, p. 7–5, has a smaller picture of the hall without the flag.

22. *BWA Congress*, 1934, pp. 228–229.

23. Ibid., p. 19

24. *BWA Congress*, 1939, p. 37.

25. C. A. Flügge, *Die Botschaft der Baptisten im Echo der Presse. Erklärungen führender Männer über religiöse Duldsamkeit im Neuen Deutschland* (Kassel: Oncken Verlag, 1934), pp. 38–39.

26. *BWA Congress*, 1934, p. 22.

27. Rushbrooke said this in his opening address. Ibid., p.26.

28. Ibid., pp. 30–38. Green points out that Schmidt asked Rushbrooke to send his suggested changes to the commission's chair, Principal N. J. Nordstrom of Bethel Baptist Seminary, Stockholm. Whether they were incorporated into the report is unknown. *Tomorrow's Man*, pp. 119–120.

29. *BWA Congress*, 1934, pp. 39–41.

30. Ibid., pp. 42–56.

31. Ibid., pp. 57–62.

32. Ibid., p. 118.

33. Ibid., p. 14.

34. Rushbrooke's lifelong involvement in the struggle for world peace is detailed in Paul R. Dekar, *For the Healing of the Nations: Baptist Peacemakers* (Macon, GA: Smyth & Helwys, 1993), pp. 76–85.

35. *BWA Congress*, 1934, pp.14–15.

36. Ibid., p. 17.

37. "Where Have the German Baptists Been?" *Christian Century* LI (Nov. 21, 1934), 1476.

38. BWA I. l. l. A. Rushbrooke addresses.

39. *BWA Congress*, 1939, p. 38.

40. BWA Executive Committee (EC), August. 6, 1934. Subsequent reference will be to the EC minutes housed in the Southern Baptist Theological Seminary library.

41. *BWA Congress*, 1939, pp. 14–15; Green, *Tomorrow's Man*, pp. 152–153

42. Green, *Tomorrow's Man*, pp. 158–161; Lord, *Baptist World Fellowship*, p. 93.

43. EC, June 29, 1937; May 11, 1938.

44. Lord, *Baptist World Fellowship*, p. 101.

45. *BWA Congress*, 1939, p. 17.

46. Ibid., pp. 266–272.

47. Ibid., p. 283.

48. For a brief biography see W. R. Estep, "George W. Truett, President of the Baptist World Alliance, 1934–1939," paper presented to the Baptist Heritage Study Commission, 1997. See also Quinn Pugh, "George W. Truett, Prophet of Freedom, Herald of Faith, 1867–1944," monologue presented to Baptist Heritage and Identity Study Commission, 2003. Text can be found on the commission's website.

49. *BWA Congress*, 1939, pp. 198–209; Tiller, *Twentieth Century Baptist*, p. 8–3.

50. The first: "Adolf Hitler said to Dr. [Hjalmar] Schacht, who in the previous spring together with others intervened for the release of [Martin] Niemoeller, 'It will either be Niemoeller or I.' It had to be Niemoeller." The other: "In that land the Bible may no longer be sold in bookstores and no efforts are being spared to prevent the publication of religious

tracts." Strübind, *Unfreie Freikirche,* p. 281. The citation is to the German translation of the oral text of Aubrey's speech contained in the Oncken Archive at Elstal, Germany.

51. Ibid., p. 282; *BWA Congress,* 1939, p. 203

52. *BWA Congress,* 1939, pp. 96–114.

53. War is "enforced enmity," "diabolic violation of human personality," "disregard of law and right," "systematic brutality," and "one of the most appalling expressions of human sin." Ibid., p. 101.

54. Craig A. Sherouse, "The Social Teachings of the Baptist World Alliance, 1905–1960," Ph.D. Dissertation, Southern Baptist Theological Seminary, 1982, p. 112.

55. *BWA Congress,* 1939, pp. 115–125.

56. Ibid., pp. 126–138.

57. BWA Women's Committee, "Jesus Shall Reign," pp. 8–9.

58. BWA I. 1. 1. F Undated (early fall 1939) memorandum by Rushbrooke; BWA IX. 1. 5. Report of General Secretary Lewis to the Executive Committee, May 21, 1940

59. BWA IX. 1. 5. Report to the Executive Committee, May 21, 1940.

60. Bernard Green makes this point. *Tomorrow's Man,* p. 129.

61. BWA IX. 1. 5. Report to the Executive Committee, May 21, 1940.

62. EC, May 21, 1940.

63. BWA IX. 1. 5. General Secretary's report of his trip to Europe.

64. Joan Beaumont, "Starving for Democracy: Britain's Blockade of and Relief for Occupied Europe, 1939–1945," *War and Society* 8 (October 1990), pp. 57–82.

5

RECOVERY FROM THE WAR AND THE ADVANCE TO MATURITY

W. Morgan Patterson and Richard V. Pierard

World War II brought to a standstill the Baptist World Alliance (BWA) efforts to unite Baptists. During the conflict, Baptist brothers faced each other on the fighting lines or as civilians loyally supporting their countries' war efforts. The German Baptists had compromised with Nazism, while those in Japan lost their independence and merged with other Christians into a united church that had to endorse the state ideology, including the deification of the emperor. Baptists in the areas under Axis (German, Japanese, and Italian) occupation suffered persecution and economic deprivation; many in Eastern Europe were taken to Germany as slave laborers. Relentless bombings had caused enormous harm to the churches themselves. In Britain, 660 Baptist chapels were damaged, with fifty completely destroyed. The Baptist Church House in London was gutted by an incendiary bomb. Both the German Baptist seminary in Hamburg and the publishing house in Kassel were heavily damaged, as were numerous chapels.[1] But as the war neared its close, the BWA sprang in action to aid the victims and through this initiative took on a whole new life.

Initiation of the Relief Effort

As mentioned in the previous chapter, in May 1940 the Executive Committee, the governing body of the Alliance, shifted the BWA office to the United States for the duration of the war and appointed an American Administrative Committee made up of of General Secretary Walter O. Lewis, the two Associate Secretaries (Clifton Gray and Louie Newton), and six other people. President J. H. Rushbrooke in London and General Secretary Lewis in Washington, D.C., essentially held the organization together through correspondence and Lewis's own travels, which included visits around the United States and Canada, journeys to southern Europe and Mexico City in 1941, and a risky Atlantic crossing to Britain to take part in the Baptist Missionary Society (BMS) sesquicentennial celebration in 1942.

At Rushbrooke's urging, when the Executive convened in Chicago on May 27, 1943, after a three-year hiatus, it adopted a resolution endorsing the creation of a BWA relief committee. It authorized the President to

> appoint a committee on World Emergency Relief to co-ordinate Baptist relief efforts in devastated countries, and to study and suggest to our constituent bodies methods and channels for relief work, both in general relief programs and in meeting the special needs of our Baptist brethren. And that this committee when appointed be authorized to act at its discretion in the disposition of such funds as may come to it.

Nine people, including the BWA President and General Secretary were named to the committee, but the specific charges were rather vague. It became Rushbrooke's task to define what the committee would actually do.[2]

In a seven-page memorandum dated October 12, Rushbrooke set forth his vision of what the program would entail. While expressing hope that the BWA could follow the same procedure as after World War I, he acknowledged that voluntary organizations would probably play a subordinate part in administering relief. The need was so massive that governments would have to take the leading role, and Baptists should encourage their young people to volunteer for service in that relief work. The Alliance was obligated to reestablish contact with its members to determine how they were faring and to offer assistance in developing pastoral leadership, producing religious literature, repairing and constructing church buildings, creating seminaries and other educational institutions, and establishing orphanages, hospitals, and homes for the elderly. The BWA focused on Europe because there it could deal with indigenous Baptist unions, not "foreign" fields where the local autonomous associations lacked the resources that the mission boards and the denominations behind them had. (Rushbrooke felt that the mission agencies were best suited to handle East Asian relief because they had the knowledge and resources.) The task of the BWA's Relief Committee was to gather and circulate information about needs in Europe, to help coordinate the work of various Baptist groups, and to actually distribute relief contributions that came from the member bodies.[3]

In September Dana M. Albaugh and George W. Sadler, chief executives of the Northern Baptist and Southern Baptist foreign mission agencies proposed that their boards assume the lead in planning for relief and suggested that a brief ad hoc meeting take place immediately following the New York gathering of the ecumenical Church Committee on Overseas Relief and Reconstruction (CCORR). (CCORR was the predecessor of

Church World Service, which came into being in 1946 and became the primary Protestant relief organization.) Nine Baptist leaders assembled, including General Secretary Lewis. The group was not thinking of replacing the BWA's World Emergency Relief Committee, although it had accomplished nothing concrete during the six months since its creation. After a discussion of what a relief effort would involve and whether there was a need for a distinctively Baptist program, the conferees agreed to invite the Northern, Southern, National, Canadian, and British Baptist mission boards and relief organizations to send representatives to a meeting that would further explore issues relating to world relief.[4]

Eight people, including the secretaries of the Canadian and British missionary societies, met at Eastern Baptist Theological Seminary in Philadelphia on January 19, 1944. The debate that ensued was vigorous. Earl F. Adams, a member of the Northern Baptist Convention's World Relief Committee, said his body did not directly administer relief funds and was working with CCORR. He did not see how the BWA committee on relief could function because it was impossible for it to meet. A telegram from Rushbrooke urged the group to initiate a single-coordinated Baptist effort, while Lewis argued that the United Nations Relief and Rehabilitation Administration (UNRRA), the international organization that had been chartered two months earlier to carry out reconstruction in liberated countries, might be a model for Baptists.[5] Noting that UNRRA had representatives from forty-four nations, he suggested that the BWA could set up an organization of its own that represented many Baptist bodies—large and small—one they would control and through which they could contribute. Others argued a united relief committee would duplicate denominational efforts already in existence; it would be sufficient just to have machinery in place to exchange information. Some questioned whether there would be any place at all for nongovernmental relief agencies. Clearly, the matter had not been resolved.[6]

The BWA did nothing until September 24, 1944, when the Administrative Committee authorized the General Secretary to co-opt an "American Baptist Relief Committee," made up of the U.S. members of the relief committee that Rushbrooke had appointed in May 1943, to carry out the spirit of the Chicago resolution. Leaders of the Northern and Southern Baptist mission boards held a joint consultation in New York City on October 2, 1944, and in Richmond on January 24, 1945, to discuss which actions to take. Lewis stated at the second meeting that the Administrative Committee had concluded that a broader world committee could not function at this time, because of transportation and communication difficulties, and that it decided to form a specifically American one. This "United States Relief Committee of the Baptist World Alliance" would be composed of three Southern and three Northern Baptists and one each from the National Baptist Convention, Baptist General Conference of America (the Swedish ethnic church), and the North American Baptist Conference (the German ethnic church). The committee's tasks were defined as coordinating relief activities of Baptists; sharing information as to plans and needs; stimulating relief giving from all Baptist bodies; receiving and channeling gifts from Baptist groups to areas of need where the donors had no administrative agencies but could assist through other Baptist groups; suggesting needs and ways of giving help in areas where there is no organized Baptist relief program; and bearing the message of the Alliance to our brethren in distressed areas who were cooperating with existing Baptist agencies.[7]

This arrangement meant the BWA World Emergency Relief Committee was divided into U.S. and European "sections," with the American one as the dominant group. Rushbrooke named the section members; he and Lewis belonged to both groups. At a meeting in Washington, D.C., on April 19, 1945, the U.S. section chose as its chair Theodore F. Adams, pastor of First Baptist Church in Richmond, Virginia. General Secretary Lewis functioned as treasurer. The committee formulated a plan for allocating funds that would come to the BWA through the constituent foreign mission boards.[8] The European section, made up of leaders in the British Baptist Union and the BMS, began working as well.[9]

At a meeting in London on February 13, 1946, the members of the two sections of the BWA World Emergency Relief Committee approved a structural modification to allocate undesignated funds that came to both the British and American offices. They authorized President Rushbrooke to appoint two "allotments subcommittees," one on each side of the Atlantic. Each of the bodies was composed of the President, General Secretary, and four members-at-large who were actively involved in relief activities. They consulted with the mission boards as they disbursed to the national unions the funds sent to the Washington, D.C., and London offices, thereby ensuring that the money would be wisely used.[10] The relief program accordingly began to take shape, but its more specific character was fleshed out over the next two years.

Meanwhile, in May 1945 General Secretary Lewis spent three weeks in San Francisco where the United Nations (U.N.) was being formed. He and Texan Joseph M. Dawson, the indefatigable advocate of religious liberty and founder of the Baptist Joint Committee on Public Affairs, lobbied for inclusion in the U.N. Charter a guarantee of full religious freedom for every human being and carried "a hundred thousand petitions from Baptists, North and South, white and Negro."[11] As a result of their efforts and cooperation with representatives from other churches, the idea of religious liberty was implied in the preamble to the U.N. charter and given full expression in 1948 in the U.N. Charter on Human Rights.

As soon as the European war ended, Rushbrooke went to the continent, visiting Denmark in July 1945 and northern Europe in November and December 1945, to restore contacts and to gain some idea of what the priorities for Alliance work should be. He was convinced that Baptists had to administer help to the people of Europe on a scale vastly larger than that following World War I and that they were not simply to depend on governmental and ecumenical bodies to do it. On May 29, 1946, he went to Washington, D.C., for the BWA Executive meeting—the first one to take place since 1943—and secured acceptance of the Danish Baptist Union's invitation to hold the next Congress in Copenhagen in the following year.

Lewis undertook a six-month trip to Europe in late 1945–early 1946, visiting nine countries and making it clear that his heart lay in the European relief effort. On February 11–12, 1946, he and Rushbrooke met with Theodore F. Adams, who was chair of the Southern Baptist Foreign Mission Board (FMB) committee for Europe, and Edwin A. Bell, the European representative of the American Baptist Foreign Mission Society (ABFMS), to discuss assistance to the Baptists in the Displaced Person (DP) camps in Germany as well as to the German Baptists themselves. This group of four recommended that the Alliance should be responsible for relief and reconstruction work in Germany and that Lewis would serve as the "Special Representative" for dealing with Baptists in that country. The Executive approved this action at its May 1946 meeting.[12]

The situation in Germany was dismal. Millions of people uprooted from their homes wandered around. The DPs, only a portion of whom had found shelter in camps, were mainly Eastern Europeans who had been brought to Germany as forced laborers or who had fled ahead of the advancing Soviet armies in 1944. Although the Soviet Union and countries under their control wanted them back, for many DPs repatriation would have meant certain death or incarceration. Other refugees were ethnic Germans (*Volksdeutsche*), persons who had been expelled at war's end from those Eastern European countries with newly drawn borders. They thronged into a country in ruins because of the Allied bombings, a country already overflowing with homeless people.[13]

Lewis, reelected General Secretary in 1947 in Copenhagen, continued to devote most of his time to relief matters. Working with him in Europe were two relief experts: Bell from the ABFMS office in Paris and Jesse D. Franks from the FMB office in Zurich. In early 1948 R. Paul Caudill, pastor of First Baptist Church in Memphis, Tennessee, replaced Lewis as the head of the BWA Relief Committee, which had become a united operation, thus freeing Lewis for his European endeavors. Shortly thereafter, he gave up his job as BWA General Secretary to assume a newly created position as Associate Secretary for Europe. In that position he was responsible for managing relief and the BWA's office in Baptist Church House, London. The Administrative Committee agreed that 75 percent of his salary would be covered by relief funds.[14] Replacing him as General Secretary, effective July 1, 1948, was Arnold T. Ohrn, former president of the Norwegian Baptist Theological Seminary in Oslo. Lewis remained at his new post until 1955, when he retired at age seventy-eight.[15]

The U.S. section, which renamed itself American Baptist Relief, took on some additional members and registered with the U.S. State Department's Advisory Committee on Voluntary Foreign Aid. In October 1946 it joined the American Council of Voluntary Agencies for Foreign Service,[16] which made it eligible to participate in the activities of the American Council of Relief Agencies Licensed for Operations in Germany (CRALOG); actual involvement began a year later.[17] American Baptist Relief also signed on with CARE (Cooperative for American Remittances to Europe), thus enabling it to direct thousands of packages to needy Baptists. The extraordinary efforts of CRALOG, CARE, the various Red Crosses, and Catholic, Protestant, and other private foreign voluntary relief agencies that engaged in the distribution of food and clothing to refugees and needy civilians saved untold lives in the first two years after the war's end.[18]

In August 1946 Rushbrooke made a three-week visit with BMS leader Harry L. Taylor to Germany where they held discussions with key military and church leaders, visited DP camps, and viewed the destruction of bombed cities, churches, and the Baptist seminary in Hamburg. They also conferred with the leaders of the German Baptist Union (due to wartime pressures now renamed the Union of Evangelical Free Churches). Rushbrooke's mastery of the German language and intimate knowledge of the continent and its problems helped him to assess the difficult situation and reestablish an amicable relationship with the brethren there. He was convinced that the Baptist World Congress in Copenhagen would mend broken relationships. The seventy-six-year-old BWA President plunged whole-heartedly into the preparations, but uncertainty clouded matters when he died from a stroke on February 1, 1947.[19]

Seventh Baptist World Congress, Copenhagen 1947

The Seventh World Congress, July 29–August 3, 1947, took place under the shadow of wartime destruction and growing East–West tensions. The prospect of a third world war loomed large on the horizon, and because of the awesome power of nuclear weapons it was certain to be even more devastating than the last one. Copenhagen had been selected as the venue because of its central location in Europe, and although Denmark had been under Nazi occupation, the city was largely intact. The small Danish Baptist community was prepared to welcome their colleagues from countries that had previously been enemies and to renew the old spirit of fellowship.

Travel was difficult, money exchange problems persisted, and several East European governments would not allow their delegates to come. Yet, more than five thousand people from fifty countries attended what some called the largest religious gathering hitherto held in Denmark. The theme was "Unity in Christ," and Rushbrooke had largely planned the program before he was stricken. Lewis at once stepped into the gap, completing the arrangements that made the Congress a success. In May the Executive Committee had named Vice Presidents Elmer A. Fridell of the United States and C. J. Tinsley of Australia as interim presidents until a new person could be elected. Tinsley presided over the Congress as his American colleague was unable to attend. The delegates keenly felt Rushbrooke's absence and lavished honor upon his memory.

The Danish prime minister, mayor of Copenhagen, and Lutheran bishop of Copenhagen all brought greetings. U.S. President Harry S. Truman, who was a Baptist, sent a message. Harold Cooke Phillips, pastor of the First Baptist Church of Cleveland, Ohio, delivered the stirring Congress Sermon on Christ as our one foundation. Speeches were given on a variety of topics, such as "The Challenge to World Evangelism" (Louie D. Newton, Southern Baptist Convention [SBC]); "The Limitations of Science" (E. C. Rust, U.K.); "Christianizing the Social Order" (Dores R. Sharpe, Northern Baptist Convention [NBC]); "The Colour Bar in Light of the New Testament" (J. Pius Barbour, National Baptist Convention); "Distinctive Notes in the Baptist World Mission" (Marion [Mrs. J. Edgar] Bates, Canada); "Christian Responsibility in Education" (Marjorie Reeves, U.K.); "Civic, National and International Responsibility of Christians" (Gunnar Westin, Sweden); "Baptists and World Tasks" (Brooks Hays, SBC); "The World Responsibility of English-speaking Baptists" (Edward H. Pruden, NBC); and "The Responsibilities of Baptist Laymen" (Eberhard Schröder, Germany). Informative reports on the relief program and conditions in Europe were presented. There were also the customary roll call of the nations; musical presentations; breakout sessions for various language groups; interest group meetings on Baptist history, church music, theological studies, Jewish evangelism, and foreign missions; three evangelistic services; a Sunday afternoon rally in a sport stadium that drew fifteen thousand people; and women's and youth meetings. Just before the end of the Congress, the members of the Relief Committee stood before a large table in the meeting hall and invited delegates to donate clothing and other articles from their luggage that would be distributed to needy pastors and laypeople in countries hit hard by the war.

Discussions of issues considered at Berlin and Atlanta continued here. The Executive Committee charged the Commission on Religious Freedom, chaired by Northern Baptist Stanley I. Stuber, with preparing a "Manifesto on Religious Freedom" and approved its wording in advance. The text stated that both civic and religious freedoms "are bound together," so that if "one is violated all are endangered." The "foundation of all freedoms" is the dignity of man created in the likeness of the eternal God." Our first duty is "to extend the rights of conscience to all people, irrespective of their race, colour, sex, or religion (or lack of religion)." The manifesto appealed to Baptists everywhere "to join hands, hearts, and minds with all others who are striving to make mankind free" and to support the U.N.'s efforts to win peace. It affirmed the Baptist concept of separation of church and state and criticized religious establishments: "No Church should be given special privileges by the State, nor should any Church seek such. There must be equality among Christian people." The freedom of conscience also applies within the church itself. "Let it never be said of Baptists that they are guilty of withholding from others what they desire for themselves, namely the right to follow the dictates of their own hearts."

The document concluded with a "Charter of Freedom," which had language identical to that used at the 1937 World Conference on the Church, Community, and State in Oxford It sought for all people, and particularly all minority groups, the following freedoms:

Freedom to determine their own faith and creed;

Freedom of public and private worship, preaching, and teaching;

Freedom from any opposition by the State to religious ceremonies and forms of worship;

Freedom to determine the nature of their own ecclesiastical government and the qualifications of their ministers and members, including the right of the individual to join the Church of his own choice, and the right to associate for corporate Christian action;

Freedom to control the education of their ministers, to give religious instruction to their youth, and to provide for the adequate development of their own religious life;

Freedom of Christian service, relief work, and missionary activity, both at home and abroad; and

Freedom to own and use such facilities and properties as will make possible the accomplishment of these ends.

The audience was then asked to stand and solemnly vow to help fulfill this manifesto.[20] The document is one of the most powerful statements on religious freedom every made, and its validity remains as firm as ever over the years since its drafting.

Another issue was ecumenism. British pastor Henry Cook, chair of the BWA Committee on Evangelism, addressed the question of the World Council of Churches (WCC), whose founding assembly was slated for 1948. He made a strong appeal for Baptists to participate in this ecumenical enterprise:

> If only all Christians in all denominations and in all lands would act together and put themselves at the disposal of the one Spirit, what tremendous things might we not see! And if we Baptist people, by joining this World Council of Churches, can stimulate it to evangelistic zeal, I say let us go forward to join it, believing that the hour demands our cooperation with all Christians, and resolved, as God will help us, to prove ourselves worthy of the challenge the world is presenting to us.[21]

Several Baptist bodies were open to involvement but strong opposition from Southern Baptists was voiced from the floor. However, the question essentially was moot because the WCC constitution excluded international bodies, such as the BWA, from membership. Still, the discussion moved away from the more ecumenical spirit that had prevailed in Atlanta. Since most unions and conventions making up the BWA did not join the WCC, they forfeited the opportunity that Cook had envisioned to bring Baptist distinctives to bear on the institutional expressions of the ecumenical movement.

Rushbrooke, who had a lifelong interest in peace, had introduced peace concerns into discussions in Berlin and Atlanta. He had the same intention at Copenhagen and had asked Dawson to speak on "The United Nations from a Christian Viewpoint." Dawson stressed that the U.N. sought no *Pax Romana* or Anglo-American or Soviet peace, "but the peace of a free, dynamical, creative society." Such a society would allow "the right of all to experiment and to seek by fair and tolerant methods to propagate their beliefs in the world." Dawson welcomed the International Bill of Rights and hailed the U.N. as an instrument, "the best yet devised," for ensuring "a good life for all peoples." The most objectionable feature of the United Nations was the veto power of the permanent members of the Security Council, and the churches had stoutly opposed granting that power.[22] In spite of its defects, the creation of the U.N. was for Dawson and the Baptist community gathered in Copenhagen a step in the right direction to ensure peace and human rights worldwide.

Strongly worded resolutions were adopted that (1) affirmed the idea that war is a crime against society and endorsed the U.N. as a means for achieving international peace; (2) urged Christians to confront the problems of race relations and condemned lynchings, race extermination, economic and racial discrimination, and denial of political rights; (3) denounced anti-Semitism, appealed to the nations to open their doors to Jewish refugees, and endorsed missionary work among Jews; and (4) called for the compassionate treatment of DPs and the relaxing immigration barriers to them. In an effort to avoid causing problems for Baptists in Soviet-controlled countries, no resolutions against communism were entertained.[23]

Evangelism was, as always, an important concern since Baptists believe that only people who have been changed by the power of God's gracious intervention can change the world. Thus, spreading religious liberty, maintaining peace, overcoming nationalism and racism, attaining high moral standards, and reconstructing the social order depend on evangelism and the mission of God's people. The report of the Committee on Evangelism noted that the war had produced no revival but instead created difficulties as so many millions were uprooted. People were careless about church when their lives were centered on the "bare necessities of existence." Still, the faithful had an opportunity "to witness more effectively than ever for Christ." The report recommended that the work of the committee be enlarged, that a five-year program of evangelism be launched, and that representatives of various nations should "go to other nations to carry an evangelistic message." This "cross-fertilization" would increase unity among Baptists.[24]

At the Executive Committee meeting, a number of constitutional revisions were approved and forwarded to the Congress for discussion. The most important was a seven-point statement on the nature and functions of the BWA, the requirement to live within an annual budget, the explicit creation of an Administrative Committee from within the Executive Committee to carry on the routine business of the Alliance (previously such business had been done informally), an increase in the number of Vice Presidents to seven, and the elimination of the unpaid Associate Secretaries.[25] The Congress also ratified the permanent relocation of the BWA headquarters to Washington, D.C. A London office was continued, with the British members of the Executive Committee as an advisory committee.[26] Elected as the new President was C. Oscar Johnson, the popular pastor of the Third Baptist Church of St. Louis, Missouri, who was active in both the Northern and Southern Baptist conventions. He made it clear that his intention was to serve only three years and that the next Congress would take place in 1950 so that the BWA could get back on a quinquennial schedule. Lewis agreed to a one-year term as General Secretary, and when he shifted to Europe in 1948, Ohrn succeeded him.

The BWA after Copenhagen

Now that the BWA was officially seated in the United States, it was legally incorporated, thus giving it the power to engage in commercial dealings without jeopardizing the personal finances of its officers and guaranteeing it tax-exempt status. The Alliance also purchased a building in conjunction with the District of Columbia Baptist Convention; each organization owned a half-interest in the structure and utilized it accordingly. The purchase required considerable fund-raising efforts, and President Johnson later acknowledged that he had personally borrowed the $27,500 down payment.[27] These actions, taken by the Administrative Committee, were ratified at the 1948 Executive Meeting.[28]

On August 13–14, 1948, the BWA organized a European Conference, the first such meeting since 1920. Present were twenty members of the Executive Committee, several people from the British Union's Continental Committee, thirty-two from the United States, three from Canada, and representatives from over a dozen Baptist unions in various countries. Committees were appointed to prepare reports on five matters: (1) Baptist cooperation in Europe, (2) theological education, (3) relief, (4) evangelism, and (5) religious liberty. The women present formed their own committee. The recommendations of these bodies were then discussed thoroughly.

The cooperation committee encouraged the European Baptists to plan a closer fellowship and suggested the creation of a European Baptist Committee on Cooperation. This committee's work resulted in the launching of the European Baptist Federation (EBF) in October 1950 in Paris. The EBF's constitution had been worked out the previous year at a meeting in Rüschlikon, Switzerland. The first European Baptist Congress took place in Copenhagen, July 29–August 3, 1952, with the theme "Baptists and the Evangelization of Europe."[29]

The theological committee expressed pleasure that the FMB was founding a seminary in Rüschlikon that would serve wider European—

> ### Charles Oscar Johnson
>
>
>
> Charles Oscar—better known as C. Oscar—Johnson, was President of the Baptist World Alliance for just three years. Elected at the first Congress after World War II (at Copenhagen in 1947), he presided at and served through the close of the 1950 Congress in Cleveland.
>
> While President, Johnson was also pastor of the Third Baptist Church in St. Louis, Missouri, a church that was aligned with and active in both the Southern and the Northern Baptist conventions. The Third Church, an inner city church near Washington University, was at that time the largest congregation in St. Louis. During Johnson's twenty-seven-year ministry, more than eleven thousand new members were added.
>
> Johnson was born in Tennessee in 1886. A graduate of a Tennessee Baptist College, Carson Newman, and the Southern Baptist Theological Seminary in Louisville, Kentucky, he pastored churches in the north, south, east, and west. Both the Southern and Northern conventions elected him as an officer. When he retired from Third Baptist in 1958, he went to Berkeley Baptist Divinity School in California as Distinguished Professor. He died in 1965.

rather than narrow national—interests. It also recommended giving assistance to existing seminaries in Poland and Germany and to new ones in other countries as well as increasing the number of exchanges of professors and students. The relief committee called attention to what was being done and urged cooperating groups to channel their relief through the Alliance. The evangelism group emphasized the importance of direct evangelism by every church member and discussed possible opportunities for outreach. The religious liberty committee expressed grave concerns over conditions in Spain, Italy, Romania, and various Soviet-controlled countries and called for a reaffirmation of the Copenhagen "Manifesto on Religious Freedom." The women's group recommended the formation of a European Baptist Women's Union to stimulate closer fellowship, greater cooperation, and deeper sympathy for and understanding of mutual problems; they roughed out its organizational structure on the spot. The reports were forwarded to the BWA's Executive, which met right after the conference.[30]

On August 3–9, 1949, the Third Baptist Youth World Conference took place in Stockholm, Sweden. In an impressive roll call, the delegates holding flags of their nations formed a circle to represent the world. A young man who stood at the side held a cross with which to set the world aglow. Copies of the four major addresses had been circulated in advance so that lively discussions could take place. According to the report given to the Executive, thirteen hundred delegates from thirty countries attended.[31]

The chief organizer of the conference was Joel Sorenson, executive secretary of the Swedish Baptist Young People's Union and a member of the

BWA Youth Committee. He had also served on the Stockholm city council before going to the United States for ministerial training. Since 1928 the Youth Committee (first called the Young People's Committee) had operated with a volunteer secretary, Frank H. Leavell, who was leader of the Southern Baptist Convention's Baptist Student Union. For years Leavell had agitated for a full-time youth secretary, and his committee had recommended such a position at its session in Copenhagen. The following year the Executive decided to authorize granting autonomy to the Youth Committee and the appointment of a full-time person.[32] The Administrative Committee carried out the mandate and announced it had selected Sorenson for the new position of Youth Secretary, to begin January 1, 1950. Leavell, who died in December 1949, saw his dream fulfilled.

In his new job Sorenson traveled extensively and transformed the Youth Committee's occasional bulletin into a regular *BWA Youth News*. He developed a constitution for the body that was approved at the 1950 Cleveland Congress.[33] Also elected then were new committee members, and the Southern Baptist Sunday School Board's youth secretary, Robert S. Denny, was named chair. In 1952 Sorenson convened the First International Baptist Student Conference at the Rüschlikon seminary, while 1,428 young people from thirty countries attended the Fourth Baptist World Youth Conference in Rio de Janeiro in July 15–22, 1953.[34] In thanking the BWA in 1950 for his appointment, Sorenson said he "did not feel his task was to sit at a desk and write letters, but to get out among the young people of the world."[35]

Relief activity continued to be a central BWA concern.[36] By 1947 relief funds were channeled to *Bruderhilfe* (Assistance to the Brethren), an organization founded by the ethnic German North American Baptist Conference that was working in Germany. To secure the permission of the U.S. military government in Germany for direct BWA involvement, the BWA affiliated with CRALOG.[37] At the beginning of 1948, former U.S. Army chaplain Otto Nallinger was sent to Germany as a CRALOG staff member. The BWA paid his salary, and his primary responsibility was overseeing the BWA relief effort. When Nallinger returned home in the summer of 1950, he was replaced by Kenneth Norquist, from the (Swedish–American) Baptist General Conference, who served until CRALOG was terminated in October 1951. The BWA also gave money to assist the German Baptists in reconstructing their seminary in Hamburg and publishing house in Kassel.

By this time the BWA's major focus had shifted to the DP program. In December 1947 the Relief Committee employed Adolf Klaupiks, a former Latvian DP who had come to America and become a Baptist pastor, to assist in resettlement efforts. In September 1948 it recommended setting up a structure under BWA auspices to assist in clearing DPs—especially those who were Baptists—for relocation in the United States, Canada, and elsewhere. Randolph A. Howard, who had just retired as a foreign secretary of the ABFMS, headed the operation in Washington, D.C., with Klaupiks assigned to handle correspondence and to secure sponsors for DPs. Fred C. Schatz, formerly assistant to the president of New Orleans Baptist Seminary, was in charge of the work in Germany. He opened an office in Munich under the supervision of Lewis, who was coordinating BWA relief in Europe. Two other men soon joined the staff to handle resettlement efforts.[38]

Over the next five years, the DP Committee labored diligently to bring Baptist refugees to the United States. The BWA first had to lobby the U.S. Congress to relax immigration quotas to allow DPs to come in, and even with legislative approval, the amount of paperwork and bureaucratic hassle was staggering. Anti-immigration forces put up every obstacle imaginable to hinder the influx of foreigners who might become a "public charge." Each refugee had to meet political and health requirements, as well as have a sponsor (a U.S. citizen) who would guarantee him or her a job and housing. In addition, the BWA was required to work with the WCC Ecumenical Refugee Division and Church World Service. From mid-1949 to the end of 1953, the BWA arranged for 5,710 persons to come to the United States, and working with churches of the North American Baptist Conference (NABC) in Canada, brought 1,700 ethnic German refugees into that country. In 1954 the BWA Relief Committee began working more closely with the WCC in refugee matters and, as other problems now attracted the committee's attention, it moved in new directions and eventually would evolve into the Division of Baptist World Aid.

Eighth Baptist World Congress, Cleveland 1950

After months of careful preparation, the Eighth Baptist World Congress opened in Cleveland, Ohio, on July 22 and ran through July 27, 1950. The approximately twenty thousand people from thirty-eight countries who registered for the Congress and filled to overflowing the city's Public Auditorium were treated to six days of addresses, sermons, devotionals, testimonies, short vignettes ("world glimpses"), reports from various interest groups and committees, and uplifting music. The presentations were stimulating, informative, and inspiring. One commentator described the occasion as a rare "speech-making jamboree."[39]

Presiding over the festivities was BWA President Johnson, who was described by observers as a "master of assemblies," "having a "radiant geniality," and contributing greatly to the "smooth running of the Congress." He was possessed of an "irrepressible humor," a "resonant voice," and "great stature."[40] U.S. President Truman had planned to make an appearance, but the war crisis in Korea forced him to stay in Washington, D.C. He sent a statement to be read that affirmed the importance of religion and called for "a rededication of this nation—individually and collectively—to the unchanging truths of the Christian religion."[41]

A banner over the platform displayed the Congress theme—"And the Light Shineth in the Darkness"—and drawing upon this scriptural reference, W. L. Jarvis of Australia entitled his keynote address "Christ, the Light of the World." Johnson's presidential sermon proclaimed "Our World Fellowship through the Light of the Gospel of Christ." Others who touched on facets of the theme were African-American educator Benjamin E. Mays, president of Morehouse College in Atlanta, who dealt with "Christian Light on Human Relationships," and Southern Baptist Theological Seminary President Ellis A. Fuller, whose paper focused on "Ye Are the Light of the World." There were more than twenty major speeches and addresses, including a sermon by the youthful black preacher, Gardner Taylor, pastor of Concord Baptist Church of Christ in Brooklyn, New York. The British Baptist Union's secretary, M. E. Aubrey, preached the Congress Sermon, "The Marks of the Church"; Theodore F. Adams spoke eloquently on "The Meaning of This Congress"; and F. (Fred) Townley Lord of London delivered the coronation address, "None Other Name." The list of presenters in the Congress volume is a veritable who's who of Baptist life at the time.

A highlight of the Congress was an opening-day parade from the auditorium to Cleveland Stadium, the city's baseball park. An estimated sixty thousand people lined the mile-long route to witness the spectacle: a motorcade of BWA and civic dignitaries, bands playing hymns and marches, thirteen hundred ministers and missionaries marching as a group carrying banners with Baptist slogans, people dressed in their national costumes holding their flags, and floats built by churches and Sunday Schools. In the stadium those not parading were waiting. The crowd swelled to an official thirty-two thousand. They were treated to an evening of song from a forty-two-hundred-voice choir and various soloists, a colorful roll call of nations, greetings from various dignitaries, and a moving address by Raleigh, North Carolina, pastor Edwin McNeill Poteat on religious liberty as "The Basic Freedom."

One noteworthy event was the dramatic presentation on the evening of

July 27, a pageant entitled "The Light of Religious Liberty," written by the local arrangements chair, Dores R. Sharpe. Some seven hundred Cleveland Baptists participated in the series of episodes that began with the life of Christ and was followed by scenes portraying the struggle for religious liberty through the centuries of church history. Another three hundred people made up the choir that sang hymns at appropriate moments.[42] A controversy over the pageant arose because of a criticism of the WCC, which was picked up by the press and declared as representing the view of the BWA. Since some BWA members had affiliated with the WCC, the Executive Committee was quite concerned. The Executive had not seen a copy of the script beforehand and clarified the situation with a resolution stating that "the Pageant does not represent the position of the Baptist World Alliance in these matters, and that the Alliance neither commends nor condemns any organized expression of the Ecumenical movement."[43]

The meeting in Cleveland was distinctive in a number of ways: For one thing, it was more international in scope and representation than the earlier Congresses. Also, it took place in a changing world. People in what had been colonies of western nations were demanding that their voices be heard, and many were calling for independence. By 1950 India, Pakistan,

Fred Townley Lord

Big and jovial, with a buoyant cheerfulness based on deep faith, Fred Townley Lord was the Baptist World Alliance's President 1950–1955. He was born in 1893 into the family of a Lancashire millworker, who was also a fervent Baptist. Lord won a scholarship to Manchester University and then went to study in London, where his doctoral dissertation examined the Christian conception of soul and body.

He pastored churches in Ipswich, West London, and Coventry before going to London's Bloomsbury Central Baptist Church in 1930. During World War I he volunteered to go to France as Staff Lecturer with the Army Service Schools. He thrived on presidencies, including the Baptist Union and the British Sunday School Union. He still found time to write. He edited the **Baptist Times** *from 1941 to 1956. He was on radio and later television; he even played the lead in a religious film,* **Generous Spirit.**

As Baptist World Alliance President, Lord traveled more miles than any previous holder of that office, and he spoke. The Georgia (U.S.) Baptist paper said, "He came into Atlanta on Saturday, having made 105 addresses in almost seventy days. He preached extemporaneously, rarely looking at notes, and he could be profound, challenging his hearers to give their minds and not just their wills to the service of Christ.

After retiring from Bloomsbury, Lord became Visiting Professor at Furman University, a Baptist college in South Carolina. There, in 1962, he suffered a fatal heart attack. At the memorial service his pastor described him as "a Christian, not daytime, not nighttime, but all time . . . . He was loyal to God and to God's church . . . . He took life tiptoe to the very end."

> ### Arnold T. Ohrn
>
>
>
> Arnold Theodore Ohrn served the Baptist World Alliance as General Secretary from 1948 to 1960. He was born in 1889 in the United States, in a Wisconsin parsonage. Ten years later his parents returned to Norway, the country of their birth, taking him with them. Ohrn remained in Norway until he accepted the Baptist World Alliance position.
>
> For thirty years he was associated with the Baptist Theological Seminary in Stabekk, Oslo, much of that time as a professor but also as its principal or president. During the five years of the Nazi occupation of Norway, he played an active role in the underground liberation movement, at great risk to himself and his family.
>
> Ohrn was active in the Baptist Union of Norway, holding offices related to its foreign mission as well as to its general work. Ecumenical in his outlook, he also served as president of the Free Church Council of Norway and as head of the Norwegian Sunday School Union. One of his books, **Gospel and the Sermon on the Mount** *(New York: Revell, 1948), was published in English.*
>
> *After Ohrn retired as General Secretary, he became lecturer on Baptist principles at both Baptist theological schools in California: Golden Gate and Berkeley. He died in 1963.*

and Indonesia had become independent nations. The so-called cold war was in full swing. The Soviets had installed "People's Democracies" in countries under their domination and tried to oust their wartime allies from West Berlin. Now Germany was divided into two countries, and the hostile regimes confronted each other along a five-hundred-mile border. The United States had begun rearming and had formed the North Atlantic Treaty Organization to counter Soviet moves in Europe. China had fallen under communist rule in 1949, and communist North Korea had invaded South Korea less than a month before the Congress opened. Finally, it was the first of these gatherings to have a "pre-Congress Conference." This innovation reflected General Secretary Ohrn's deep concern for the free discussion of theological and other issues. Some ninety-six theological and missionary leaders from nineteen countries gathered in Cleveland on July 17–21 and divided into seven groups or "commissions" that discussed "Religious Liberty," "Evangelism and Church's Life," "Social Justice," "Baptist World Missions," "Contemporary Religious Movements," "The Doctrine of the Church," and "The Doctrine of Baptism." There were also joint sessions during which, according to Ohrn's assessment, "a profitable cross-fertilization of Baptist thinking took place." The chairs of the commissions presented brief reports to the Congress and copies of the full reports were given to the Executive.[44]

The Congress featured the usual special conferences for women, youth, laymen, ministers, missionaries and mission boards, Baptist historians,

Sunday School workers, and those in urban ministry. It heard detailed reports from the Relief, Youth, and Women's committees. It approved a strongly worded manifesto, "Mid-Century Call to Religious Freedom," that spelled out dangers to liberty in communist and Roman Catholic countries and in those with Protestant establishments, reaffirmed the historic Baptist commitment to liberty, endorsed the U.N. Universal Declaration of Human Rights, and appealed for an end to religious persecution and discrimination.[45] It adopted several resolutions, including one calling for ratification of the U.N. Convention on Genocide. The resolution on race problems affirmed the actions of the last three Congresses that condemned racial discrimination and called on all Baptists to work for legislation to prevent the practice as well as to free themselves from racial and cultural prejudice.[46] The Congress accepted the British Baptists' invitation to hold the next Congress in London and elected Lord, pastor of Bloomsbury Central Baptist Church in London and a past president of the Baptist Union, as the new president.

A four-day post-Congress conference took place at Green Lake, Wisconsin, where several hundred delegates gathered to enjoy fellowship and the beauty of the Northern Baptist assembly grounds. General Secretary Ohrn paid tribute to both events as he wrote:

> The wonderful days at Green Lake served, one might say, as a quiet postlude in which the great organ voice of the Congress, where all the stops were pulled, softly "trembled away into silence" in the restful, Cathedral-like seclusion of the Wisconsin woods.[47]

Expansion of the BWA Women's Work

This period saw the maturing of the women's work of the Alliance. At the women's conference in Copenhagen, at which women who had been on opposing sides in the war forgave one another, it was clear that they wanted to increase their level of involvement. In August 1948, encouraged by the women members of the Executive, General Secretary Lewis invited representatives from women's organizations to the London conference, where they formed the European Baptist Women's Union.[48] The Executive agreed at their meeting in London that the BWA should form a Women's Committee, coordinate its work with the European body just created, seek to organize the Baptist women on each continent, and authorize the five women on the Executive to plan the program for the women's session at the 1950 Congress.[49] The women held two meetings at Cleveland. Addressing one of them was Nannie Helen Burroughs, president of the Women's Auxiliary of the National Baptist Convention, Inc., who had spoken at the

1905 Congress and at age seventy seemed as full of vitality as ever.

Delegates from every country where there was organized work among Baptist women met in Cleveland the week before the Congress to draft the organizational plan for the new Women's Committee of the Baptist World Alliance. The plan defined the committee's purposes: (1) to promote fellowship and understanding among Baptist women worldwide; (2) to encourage women to band together for Christian service; and (3) to exchange information concerning activities, ideas, and literature. Membership would include at least one person from each women's organization that was recognized by a constituent union, convention, or association of the BWA. The committee would choose its own officers, with one cochair from each continent, and would meet regularly before each Congress and at other times at the discretion of the officers. The chair would also sit on the BWA Executive.[50]

Elected as head of the new body was Southern Baptist Olive Brinson (Mrs. George R.) Martin. She had chaired the women's conference at Copenhagen, had been a member of the Executive since 1947, and deserves much of the credit for the achievements in women's work. In the next three years, regional women's unions were founded in North and South America. By 1958 all six continents had regional organizations. The committee also initiated the Baptist Women's Day of Prayer and a newsletter that since 1962 has been known as *Together* and organized women's conferences in various countries. At the 1955 London Congress the committee was elevated to the status of Women's Department of the BWA, with Martin continuing at the helm until her retirement in 1960. In her London Congress address, entitled "Baptist Women in the World Today," she sounded three notes: "joy for the privilege of service, thanksgiving for what has been accomplished, and courage for the future."[51]

Work of the BWA from 1950 to 1955

During the years between the Congresses in Cleveland and London, the work of the BWA continued and in fact expanded. President Lord[52] kept busy with speaking engagements and writing a history of the BWA. He traveled extensively, visiting Baptists in Europe, the United States, Canada, South America, and Australia. In 1954 the All-Union Council of Evangelical Christians–Baptists invited him to visit the Soviet Union. For the past twenty-five years, the only BWA connections with Baptists in Russia were the exchange of greetings. Accompanying the President on the two-week tour were Lewis and Executive member Ernest A. Payne (U.K.), and they were enthusiastically received. The event received considerable attention in the world press, and the visitors were gratified to renew contacts with the largest Baptist group in Europe.[53]

The work of the BWA Relief Committee led by R. Paul Caudill continued. Detailed reports given at the annual Executive meetings and at the Congress in London mentioned assistance rendered in Germany, Austria, Assam, and Korea. They also told of the ongoing work with refugees, which included opening a shelter in Munich for people ineligible for resettlement in the United States, distributing CARE food and clothing packages, and helping restore war-damaged church buildings. The impressive accomplishments of the Relief Committee reflected how meeting the physical needs of people had become a central element of the BWA's mission.

A major function of the BWA has been to keep Baptists around the world informed about fellow Baptists. To fulfill this purpose, General Secretary Ohrn launched *The Baptist World* in 1954. He and Marjorie Moore Armstrong of Missouri edited the publication that quickly became a vital organ for sharing news about the worldwide Baptist family.[54]

Ninth Baptist World Congress, London (Golden Jubilee Congress) 1955

On July 16–22, 1955, the BWA celebrated its fiftieth anniversary, and Baptists returned to the site of its founding in London. So many Baptists wanted to come to the eagerly anticipated Jubilee Congress that attendance had to be limited. The official delegate tally was 8,524 from sixty countries.[55] The Congress met in the spacious Royal Albert Hall with President Lord presiding.

Henry Cook, president of the Baptist Union (BU), and the Archbishop of Canterbury, who also was president of the British Council of Churches, brought words of welcome. The Congress sent greetings to the recently crowned Queen Elizabeth II and joined in prayer for the queen and her family. She responded with a personal note of appreciation.[56] A splendid and highly instructive 136-page booklet called the *Official Handbook* was made available to the delegates. The carefully prepared volume contained brief essays describing the history of the BWA, Baptists in Britain, the BU, and the BMS. It included many other features helpful to visitors to Britain, such as a map of central London, what to see in London, and places of special interest to Baptists. The handbook also included the Congress program, information about the Congress personalities, and hymns. No delegate could be without it.

The theme of the Congress was "Jesus Christ, the Same Yesterday, and Today, and Forever," and several speeches sought to illuminate some aspect of it. For example, the keynote address by Lawrence A. North, general secretary of the New Zealand Baptist Union, dealt with "The Changeless Christ," and the sermon of Josef Nordenhaug, president of the Rüschlikon seminary, focused on "The Fullness of Christ."

At the session of the Congress designated as the Jubilee Service, led by former BWA President Johnson, more than fifteen persons who had attended the Congress of 1905 were called to the platform and recognized. One of them—Gilbert Laws of Norwich, England—gave a brief and touching devotional address as he remembered the faces and personalities of those who had founded the BWA fifty years earlier. He declared: "My heart is strangely moved. Do not say they are dead and gone. They are not dead, and if they have gone, they have but gone before and call us from their heavenly seats to be faithful and carry on the work they began."[57] Lord delivered the Jubilee Address, which he entitled "The Baptist World Alliance in Retrospect and Prospect." In it he reviewed the events and the leaders of the Alliance over the preceding fifty years and then reminded his hearers of the challenges of the future.[58]

The BWA continued its unrelenting struggle on behalf of religious freedom. The Congress adopted a "Golden Jubilee Declaration on Religious Liberty." The five-point statement asserted: (1) the right to be free in religious matters is a gift from God; (2) one's right to choose or change his faith must be preserved; (3) mere toleration is not enough—we must be accepted as equals in Christ; (4) real liberty includes the right to teach, preach, publish, and advocate openly and without hindrance the gospel of Christ or other convictions; and (5) our churches, although willing to cooperate with the state, must be free from its interference. Baptists will not rest until such freedom is available to all throughout the world. This commitment is "an essential part of our contribution to the thought of the church, as well as to the establishment of Christ's reign in the earth."[59]

In addition, resolutions were approved on peace, race relations, Christian fellowship, evangelism, Bible study, and Sunday School work. The resolution on Christian fellowship was a carefully worded exhortation to join with non-Baptists "for the furtherance of the Gospel" and to demonstrate the unity of Christ's body. A "final Resolution" lamented the inability of Baptist brethren from China, Romania, Poland, Hungary, Czechoslovakia, and Bulgaria to attend the Jubilee Congress but rejoiced over the presence of a delegation of nine people from Russia.[60] Actually, the Russian Baptists were quite prominent in the London meeting. Claudia Tyrtova of Moscow gave her testimony as a Christian. Three others gave addresses and two offered prayers before the assembly. Yakov I. Zhidkov was elected a BWA Vice President.[61]

Increasing internationalism had become a basic objective of the BWA, as illustrated in the "Glimpses of Baptist Work" presented at the sessions; speakers from sixteen countries described the work and state of Baptists in their respective lands. A number of major speakers were from newer areas touched by the BWA. For example, João Soren, pastor of the First Baptist Church of Rio de Janeiro and president of the Brazilian Baptist Convention, delivered the Congress Sermon. Furthermore, constitutional changes approved in London required the "geographical distribution" of officers so that members of the Executive Committee should represent all six continents, and increased the number of Vice Presidents from seven to nine. These amendments assured worldwide representation in the activities and structure of the BWA.[62]

Another important action was changing the name of the "Youth Committee" to "Youth Department." Joel Sorensen resigned as Youth Secretary, saying he "felt a strong leading of the Lord to return to the pastorate," but he agreed to assume his former volunteer position as chair of the Youth Department. His successor, Denny, who had served as the committee's chair since 1950, assumed the title Associate Secretary for Youth. Unlike his predecessor, he relocated to Washington, D.C. Denny and Sorenson had worked together in organizing the 1953 youth conference, and together they planned the 1958 event in Toronto, the Fifth Baptist Youth World Conference, which drew 8,022 young people from sixty-seven countries.[63]

As a part of the overall activities of the London Congress, a variety of conferences brought together Baptists with special interests. Besides the women's and youth conferences, there were conferences of laypeople, ministers, theological teachers, missionaries, Baptist historians and librarians, Baptist deaconesses, and others. Their programs enabled participants to focus on their distinctive callings, to learn from each other, and to enjoy fellowship. They met in nearby Baptist churches and halls.[64]

In one session, C. E. Abraham, principal of Serampore College in India, spoke briefly about the work of the school founded by William Carey. At the end of Abraham's statement, Adams "proposed that the rule of no collections be broken and that an offering be made to help the needs outlined by the principal." The suggestion was warmly received, and an offering of four hundred and forty-six pounds was taken for the library of Serampore and the Carey Cemetery.[65]

As the next President of the BWA, Adams, who had been a member of the Executive since 1934, was the unanimous choice. Widely known and well informed, he had been pastor of the First Baptist Church of Richmond, Virginia, since 1936.[66] A minister with ties to both the Southern and Northern Baptist conventions with many distinguished achievements, he was an excellent choice to lead the BWA into the 1960s.

The closing rally of the Golden Jubilee Congress was held at the Arsenal Football Stadium, and about thirty thousand people attended. The weather was perfect, and the impressive congregational singing was accompanied by the massed bands of the Salvation Army. Retiring President Lord presented his successor, Adams, who spoke briefly. He reminded the crowd of four favorite words in the Baptist vocabulary: evangelism, fellowship, faith, and prayer. He urged his fellow Baptists to be committed to each and to be active in each. Billy Graham, the Baptist evangelist from North Carolina who was becoming known around the world, then brought the concluding sermon. His subject was "Crown Him Lord of All." It was relevant, practical, personal, challenging, and inspirational.[67]

Toward 1960

Following the successful and memorable Jubilee Congress, the work and activity of the BWA continued. At the close of the London Congress, Adams,

Theodore F. Adams

Theodore Floyd (Ted) Adams had a varied background. He was the son of a Baptist pastor considered fundamentalist and a graduate of Rochester Theological Seminary (now Colgate Rochester Crozer Divinity School) at a time it was known for its liberalism. Born in Palmyra, New York, in 1898, he lived with his family in Oregon and Indiana and visited Europe in 1910. Before entering Denison University, a Northern Baptist college in Ohio, he studied chiropractory in Chicago.

Adams's first two pastorates were in Ohio: first in Cleveland and then in Toledo. While in Cleveland, he was elected vice president of the national Baptist Young People's Union, an office that led to the Baptist World Alliance appointing him to the Youth Committee in 1928. He served as president of the Toledo Council of Churches and was elected to the Baptist World Alliance Executive in 1934.

The First Baptist Church of Richmond, Virginia, a Southern Baptist church with an impressive history of local and foreign ministry, invited Adams to be their pastor. The church had declining attendance and insurmountable debt. Adams said no, but God kept saying yes. In February 1936, Adams and his family arrived in Richmond, "feeling like strangers in a strange land."

Adams did not remain a stranger. The church recovered and thrived. Adams himself participated in numerous organizations, local and national. In Richmond he founded a hospital, a counseling service, and an interdenominational clergy association. He helped establish the national relief agency CARE. Virginia honored him. Time *magazine ran his portrait on the cover of its December 5, 1955, issue.*

Adams retired from the Richmond church in 1968 and embarked on a new career: teaching at Southeastern Baptist Seminary in North Carolina. He died in 1980.

Ohrn, Joseph H. Jackson (National Baptist Convention, Inc.), and V. Carney Hargroves (NBC) made a two-week tour of Baptist churches in Russia, traveling thirty-five hundred miles and preaching to more than fifteen thousand people. They were greeted everywhere by friendly and hospitable crowds. The next year five Russian Baptists spent a month in the United States. President and Mrs. Adams journeyed to the Caribbean, an area where no previous BWA President had gone, before joining Associate Secretary Denny in an extensive trip to southern Europe, the Middle East, and Asia. In Asia they spent six weeks visiting Baptists in ten countries. In 1959 Adams and Denny traveled to ten countries in the Middle East and Africa. These trips further reinforced the international character of the BWA.

Upon the retirement in 1955 of Lewis as Associate Secretary for Europe, Henry Cook, the retired general superintendent of Baptist work in London, filled the position on an interim basis. Finally, in 1958 Erik Rudén, former secretary of the Baptist Union of Sweden, was named associate secretary of the BWA with primary responsibilities in Europe; a year later, he moved to London to take charge of the office there. In 1957, Cyril E. Bryant (SBC) joined the BWA staff in Washington, D.C., as the first Director of Publications, serving as editor of an expanded *Baptist World* magazine and director of the newly established BWA News Service.

Ohrn and Adams revitalized the commissions by making them a feature of each meeting of the Executive. In 1957 they asked Baptists from around the world to gather in study groups to discuss evangelism, missions, religious liberty, and Bible study. In 1958, they added the subjects of doctrine, membership, training, and world peace.[68]

The period from 1945 to 1960 was an exciting and significant one for Baptists. As they continued to grow in unprecedented numbers and in new areas of the world, the BWA sought to encourage that expansion, the development of national leadership, and a feeling of fellowship and cooperation. Talented leaders offered support and inspiration through their travels to meet Baptists in dozens of countries. Relief efforts and programs enabled people in many lands to lead a better life and to have their faith and commitment deepened. Continental meetings, youth conferences, and the Congresses themselves provided opportunities for Baptists to get acquainted with one another, to become informed about fellow Baptists, to enjoy fellowship, and to engage in uplifting worship. In short the BWA played a crucial role in the maturation of the global Baptist community.

1. F. Townley Lord, *Baptist World Fellowship* (London: Carey Kingsgate, 1955), p. 113.

2. BWA Executive Committee (EC), May 27, 1943.

3. BWA X.1.1.B. Rushbrooke memorandum.

4. Ibid. Minutes, meeting of November 10, 1943.

5. George Woodbridge, ed., *UNRRA: The History of the United Nations Relief and Rehabilitation Administration* (3 vols., New York: Columbia University Press, 1950), is the official history of the body.

6. BWA X. 1. 1. B. Minutes, meeting of January 19, 1944.

7. Ibid., Minutes, meeting of January 24, 1945.

8. Ibid., Minutes, meeting of April 19, 1945.

9. Ibid., Minutes, meeting of March 27, 1945.

10. Ibid., Minutes, meeting of February 13, 1946.

11. Joseph M. Dawson, *A Thousand Months to Remember* (Waco: Baylor University Press, 1964), p. 161.

12. EC, May 29, 1946.

13. German Baptist layman Eberhard Schröeder gave a vivid account in his speech at Copenhagen of how miserable life was. *BWA Congress,* 1947, pp. 124–128.

14. BWA X. 3. 4. N.

15. An interesting sidelight is that Lewis considered retiring in 1949 and approached Ernest Payne, then a faculty member at Regent's Park College and later secretary of the British Baptist Union, about being his successor. Payne said he was not interested. He felt that he could not cope with the opposition of some member bodies "to wider ecumenical relations." He also demurred when Lewis suggested the job would put him on track for the general secretaryship. W. M. S. West, *To Be a Pilgrim: A Memoir of Ernest A. Payne* (Guildford: Lutterworth, 1983), pp. 69–72.

16. According to the official history, Elizabeth Clark Reiss, *The American Council of Voluntary Agencies for Foreign Service: Four Monographs* (New York: ACVAFS, 1985), after a year of periodic meetings that discussed common interests, representatives from ten American voluntary agencies concerned with planning relief and rehabilitation following World War II gathered on October 7, 1943, to ratify an agreement creating a council that could help such bodies to coordinate their activities. Within a year thirty-nine organizations, both secular and religious, had joined. The qualification for membership was that the agencies must be or expect to be "engaged in active work in foreign countries." (pp. 53–54). That three years passed before the Baptists joined reflected their hesitancy about ecumenical involvements.

17. BWA X. 1. 1. B. Minutes, meeting of September 16, 1946. In January 1946 a group of voluntary agencies created CRALOG. A similar body was formed for Japan–LARA, Licensed Agencies for Relief in Asia. Jørgen Lissner, *The Politics of Altruism: A Study of the Political Behaviour of Voluntary Development Agencies* (Geneva: Lutheran World Federation, Department of Studies, 1977), p. 63. The official history, Eileen Egan and Elizabeth Clark Reiss, *Transfigured Night: The CRALOG Experience* (Philadelphia: Livingston Publishing Co., 1964), describes its work but completely overlooks the Baptist involvement. It was created so that the American military authorities would not have to deal separately with the various

church and mission agencies sending aid to Germany. It enabled the military government to handle at one time, and often through one spokesperson, matters concerning assistance to the people of the devastated nation. pp. 63–64.

18. Malcolm J. Proudfoot, *European Refugees: A Study in Forced Population Movements* (London: Faber and Faber, 1957), p. 382.

19. Bernard Green, *Tomorrow's Man: A Biography of James Henry Rushbrooke* (Didcot, U.K.: Baptist Historical Society, 1997), pp. 132–133.

20. *BWA Congress*, 1947, pp. 118–120.

21. Ibid., pp. 56–59.

22. Ibid., pp. 67–74.

23. Ibid., pp. 98–100.

24. Ibid., pp. 26–32.

25. EC, July 29, 1947; *BWA Congress*, 1947, pp. 59, 114, 163–165.

26. EC, July 29, 1947.

27. EC, May 2, 1949.

28. EC, August 16, 1948.

29. Green, *Crossing the Boundaries: A History of the European Baptist Federation* (Didcot, U.K.: Baptist Historical Society, 1999), pp. 1–22.

30. *Minutes of European Conference called by the Baptist World Alliance, London, 13th–14th August 1948.* Printed copy in the Southern Baptist Theological Seminary Library.

31. EC, July 20, 1950.

32. *BWA Congress*, 1947, p. 24; EC, August 16, 1948.

33. Text in *BWA Congress*, 1950, pp. 357–358.

34. Lord, *Baptist World Fellowship*, p. 166.

35. J. D. Grey, "A Lengthened Shadow of Mighty Men," *Baptists of the World 1950–1970* (Fort Worth: Radio and Television Commission, 1970), p. 27.

36. Richard V. Pierard, "Baptist World Alliance Relief Efforts in Post-Second World-War Europe," *Baptist History and Heritage* 36 (Winter–Spring 2001), pp. 15–17.

37. BWA X .1. 1. C. Minutes of BWA Relief Committee, October 7, 1947.

38. For details of the DP program, see Pierard, "BWA Relief Efforts," pp. 18–23.

39. *BWA Congress*, 1950, p. 348.

40. Ibid., pp. 343–344.

41. Ibid., pp. 49–50. This message was one of U.S. President Truman's more forthright

affirmations of civil religion. On Truman and civil religion, see Robert D. Linder and Richard V. Pierard, *Twilight of the Saints: Biblical Christianity and Civil Religion in America* (Downers Grove, IL: InterVarsity Press, 1978), pp. 90–92.

42. Ibid., p. 158.

43. EC, July 26, 1950.

44. Lord, *Baptist World Fellowship*, p. 145. The list of commission members is in BWA Congress, 1950, p. 366.

45. *BWA Congress,* 1950, pp. 336–338.

46. Ibid., pp. 340–341.

47. Ibid., p. 348.

48. Yona Pusey, *European Baptist Women's Union: Our Story, 1948–1998* (Oakham, U.K.: European Baptist Women's Union, 1998), pp. 5–12.

49. EC, August 17, 1948.

50. EC, July 21, 1950; *BWA Congress,* 1950, pp. 280–282, 358–359.

51. *BWA Congress,* 1955, pp. 296–304.

52. For a biography focusing on Lord's BWA years, see Faith Bowers, "Fred Townley Lord, President of the Baptist World Alliance 1950–1955," paper presented to the Baptist Heritage Study Commission, 1997.

53. Lord, *Baptist World Fellowship*, pp. 159, 168.

54. Ibid., p.157.

55. Carl W. Tiller, *The Twentieth Century Baptist: Chronicles of the Baptists in the First Seventy-five Years of the Baptist World Alliance* (Valley Forge, PA: Judson Press, 1980), p. 10–1.

56. *BWA Congress,* 1955, pp. 18, 349, 353–356.

57. Ibid., p. 57.

58. Ibid., pp. 58–70.

59. Ibid., pp. 369–370.

60. Ibid., pp. 371–372.

61. Ibid., pp. 79, 260–262, 360–365.

62. Ibid., p. 356.

63. *BWA Congress,* 1955, pp. 357, 360; Paul Montacute, "Brief History of Youth World Conferences," paper presented to the Baptist Heritage Study Commission, 1994. See also *Christ for the World—Now! Official Report of the 5th Baptist Youth Conference Toronto, Ontario, Canada, July 27–July 2, 1958,* ed. Cyril E. Bryant (Washington, BWA, 1958).

64. Ibid., pp. 295–345.

65. Ibid., pp. 115–116, 355.

66. For a useful biography of him see Beth W. Harvey, "Theodore F. Adams: Baptist World Alliance President, 1955–1960," paper presented to the Baptist Heritage Study Commission, 1997.

67. *BWA Congress,* 1955, pp. 271–273, 277–282.

68. Cyril E. Bryant, "Baptist World Alliance," *Encyclopedia of Southern Baptists,* III, 1601.

6

THE INTERNATIONALIZATION OF THE ALLIANCE, 1960–70

James Leo Garrett, Jr.

The 1960s was an era of conflict and change: the ongoing cold war between the United States and the Soviet Union with its threat of a nuclear holocaust, the Vietnam War (1954–1975), and the Six-Day (1967) Israeli-Arab War; the Cultural Revolution (1966–1976) in Mao's China; and the achievement of national independence by numerous colonies, sometimes peacefully but often after considerable civil unrest. It was the epoch of growing ecumenism, the Second Vatican Council, the U.S. civil rights movement, the landing of a man on the moon, and the western cultural revolution with its sexual permissiveness, rock music, drugs, and youth rebellion. These happenings impacted the Baptist world as much as they did general society. As the winds of change blew through the Baptist World Alliance (BWA), it became more of an international organization than it had been in the past.

Tenth Baptist World Congress, Rio de Janeiro 1960
In 1956, the Executive Committee had accepted the invitation of the Brazilian Baptist Convention to hold the next Baptist World Congress in Rio de Janeiro. The dates chosen were June 26–July 3, 1960.[1] For the first time in its fifty-five-year history, a BWA Congress was to be held in a country outside Europe and North America. The theme chosen was "Jesus Is Lord," and elaborate plans were made for the eight-day event, a longer meeting than the previous ones had been.[2] Edgar F. Hallock, Jr., a Southern Baptist missionary in Brazil, chaired the local arrangements committee; William Jensen Reynolds of Nashville, Tennessee, was the music leader; and Theodore F. Adams presided. Brazilian Baptists provided the three thousand-voice Congress choir, a brass band, choral ensembles, and soloists. Sixty nations were represented on the program, and individuals from seventy countries carried their national flags in the roll call of nations. The number of registered delegates was 12,688, with 9,996 from Brazil,

1,986 from the United States, 186 from Argentina, and 173 from Canada.[3] The registration was the largest of any Congress held outside the United States prior to that time. That the Congress would be representing a great body of Baptists was seen in the latest membership figures of the constituent bodies that the BWA released. The report stated that as of December 1958 some twenty-two million people were members of Baptist churches, a growth of approximately three million since 1955.[4] The National Broadcasting Company (U.S.) sent a crew to film Congress events.[5] The Brazilian government also issued a special postage stamp to recognize the occasion.

In the presidential address, "Jesus Christ Is Lord," Adams first reviewed the travels he made during his five-year term at the helm of the BWA. He was indeed the first President to visit the continent of Africa. Then he summoned his fellow Baptists to evangelism and missions, Christian education, racial justice, the alleviation of poverty, and world peace; he also reaffirmed Baptist "convictions and principles." On the question of religious liberty he called for "freedom *for*," "freedom *from*," "freedom *through*," "freedom *in*," and "freedom *of*" religion. In the final session, Adams spoke again and reiterated the four themes that he had set forth when accepting the presidency in London in 1955: evangelism, fellowship, faith, and prayer.[6]

Arnold T. Ohrn, who had announced in 1959 that he would retire as General Secretary after the Congress, noted in his final report the growing contacts with the Russian and Romanian Baptists, warned of the violence against Christians in several newly independent nations, stated that eight more conventions or unions had become BWA member bodies since 1955, and pointed out that Europe was "the only continent where the various Baptist unions are associated in a continental federation." He rejoiced that Baptist women's unions had been "formed on every continent" and described how the Youth and Publications departments were advancing. He reported that changes were going to be made in the administration of the relief program and that a Men's Department was in the process of formation.[7] He also called attention to Operation Brother's Keeper, a work undertaken in 1958 by an interdenominational group of medical doctors. Under the leadership of American Baptist Robert Hingson, a professor at the Western Reserve University (Cleveland, Ohio) medical school, and, with financial support from the Tennessee-based Maxey Jarman Foundation, the team traveled forty-five thousand miles and visited twenty-seven nations in Asia and Africa, where they administered vaccinations, performed surgeries, delivered supplies, and gave medical instruction.⁸ Finally, Ohrn affirmed the lordship of Jesus Christ as the "basic principle" of Baptists and placed the very important Baptist emphasis on "the competency of the soul in religion" under Christ's supremacy.⁹

In their presentations at the Rio gathering, several speakers clearly articulated various aspects of Baptist beliefs and practice. In his keynote address, William Dodds Jackson, the London superintendent of the Baptist Union of Great Britain, urged Baptists to invite other churches to complete the Protestant Reformation. S. A. Lawoyin, president of the Nigerian Baptist Convention, warned delegates that Satan-employed racism continued to break the unity of Christians, while Willie Wickramasinghe, president of the Baptist Union of Ceylon (now Sri Lanka), celebrated the "expansion" and "universality" of the Baptist fellowship as a "foretaste" of the eschatological kingdom. For Alfonso Olmedo, an Argentine missionary-pastor, Baptist oneness was "not of authority but of [divine] paternity," "not of organization but of filiation [as sons of God]," "not of creeds but in deeds," and "not of succession but of subjection." Jitsuo Morikawa, director of evangelism for the American Baptist Convention (ABC, formerly the Northern Baptist Convention, now American Baptist Churches, USA), spelled out three issues for contemporary Baptist evangelism: (1) the lordship of Christ over the world as well as the church; (2) the missionary nature of the church; and (3) the ministry of the laity. Ernest A. Payne, general secretary of the Baptist Union of Great Britain, contended that the Baptist appeal to the Scriptures has a fivefold meaning: It is "to the writings gathered together by the early church and recognized as authoritative"; it is to both Testaments; it is "to the living word of God enshrined in, and conveyed by, the written word"; it is "to the living word of God . . . authenticated to us by the Holy Spirit at work within our own minds and hearts"; and it is "to the Lord Jesus Christ himself, made known to us by the Holy Spirit in and through the Scriptures."¹⁰

Baker James Cauthen, executive secretary of the Southern Baptist Foreign Mission Board, in the Congress Sermon argued that the distinctive Christian task of the twentieth century is worldwide evangelization. According to Louise Paw, associate secretary of the Burma Baptist Convention, Asian anticolonialism calls for greater unity on the part of the Christian churches; and George D. Kelsey, an American Baptist professor of ethics, maintained that Christ's lordship means obedient service, not cheap grace, and the redemption of body as well as soul. Longri Ao, an evangelist in Nagaland, India, informed his hearers: "Men who have been headhunters in all their past life have now become active soul-winners for Christ." Clarence Cranford, pastor of Calvary Church in Washington, D.C., reminded the audience that great Baptist thinkers had identified loyalty to the New Testament as the basic Baptist principle and added "to think only in terms of local congregations is to make meaningless the New Testament figure of the bride of Christ." Yakov I. Zhidkov, president of the All-Union Council of Evangelical Christians—Baptists (AUCECB) in the Soviet Union, cited the earlier BWA statements on world peace and the recent United Nations (U.N.) Declaration on Universal Disarmament as evidence of the growing desire for "the absence of any war" and urged Baptists to support moves for peace.[11]

Martin Luther King, Jr., whose reputation as a leader in the burgeoning civil rights movement in the United States was now well established, traveled with evangelist Billy Graham to the BWA gathering. King's father, Martin Luther King, Sr., a National Baptist, Inc., pastor in Atlanta, was honored at a dinner Graham hosted and also gave the closing prayer in the July 2 evening plenary session.[12]

In addition to sectional conferences for women, youth, men, theological teachers, and those involved in radio and television, three afternoon time slots were set aside for the five study commissions. Each was given an opportunity to report at a plenary session. Most of them had been meeting annually since 1957. The Commission on Evangelism called for the employment of an additional BWA staff member to facilitate the work of the several commissions and also to promote evangelism. It further recommended a worldwide evangelistic emphasis during 1964 and suggested that member bodies share data and materials on evangelism. The Commission on Bible Teaching and Membership Training identified eight principal areas of need in Baptist teaching and training, proposed that member bodies form committees to foster teaching and training. It also called for an international Bible study and membership training convention in 1965.

The Commission on World Missions gave a progress report on the directory and statistical survey of Baptist world missions (which it had undertaken in 1957), acknowledged that it would soon need updating, recommended the preparation of a world history of Baptist missions, and called for an observance of the bicentennial of William Carey's birth in August 1961. The Commission on Religious Liberty noted that the BWA had been "born in the midst of a battle for religious liberty" in the United Kingdom and encouraged "more biblical preaching and teaching on the reasons for our concern for religious liberty." The commissions on Doctrines of the Church and on Baptism made a joint report. It called attention to a statement from the Baptist Union of India in which the four ancient marks (one, holy, catholic, and apostolic) and two Reformation marks (the "Gospel is rightly preached" and the "Gospel ordinances rightly administered") of the true church were given a Baptist reinterpretation. It recommended a fivefold plan of action for the future of the commission so that Baptists could "come to take our rightful place within the *oikoumene*."[13]

The Congress approved two amendments to the BWA constitution that went into effect immediately: First, in Article IV the Executive Committee was empowered to choose the BWA secretaries. These appointments were limited to the quinquennium, with the possibility of reelection, and would be confirmed at the next regular Congress. The Alliance would continue to elect the president, vice presidents (set in 1955 at nine), and treasurers at the Congress; those chosen would take office at the conclusion of that meeting. Executive Committee members would also be elected or reelected at that time. Second, the section in Article V on Executive Committee membership was changed to allow any "duly established" department within the BWA to nominate two members to the governing body. Before, only the Women's and Youth departments had that right. Now, making up the Executive would be the current officers of the Alliance, the former presidents and general secretaries, the appointees of the departments, and thirty-nine members-at-large geographically apportioned and representing all six continents. The Executive Committee itself could co-opt up to nine additional members.[14]

Chosen to replace Ohrn as general secretary was Josef Nordenhaug, president of the Baptist Theological Seminary in Rüschlikon, Switzerland, and a native of Norway. Elected as president for the 1960–1965 quinquennium was João Soren, pastor of the First Baptist Church of Rio de Janeiro. Soren, a graduate of the Southern Baptist Theological Seminary, was the first president to come from outside Great Britain or North America. The appointments of the Associate Secretaries were renewed. Although Ohrn was leaving in September, Nordenhaug did not assume the post until November 1.[15]

Following the precedent of the previous Congresses, the delegates at Rio adopted a forceful manifesto on religious liberty. It affirmed three basic beliefs about religious liberty: "God created man in His own image and endowed him with freedom to respond to His redemptive love," "man is responsible to God for his religious belief and practice," and "religious faith and participation must be voluntary in order to be real." It then expressed three causes for rejoicing: "God gives grace to endure oppression and use freedom," "friends of religious liberty are found in all Christian communions," and "recent legislation in several countries is favorable to religious liberty." There were also three desires: a cessation of

> ## Josef Nordenhaug
>
>
>
> Josef Nordenhaug, General Secretary 1960–1969, was born in 1903 in Norway but spent much of his life outside of that country. He studied at the University of Oslo, earning M.S. degrees in chemistry, geophysics, and astronomy. While a student, he was active in many branches of church work, including being a part-time teacher at the Baptist Theological Seminary for four years. He also translated two popular spiritual classics from English into Norwegian.
> Feeling called to the ministry, he entered Southern Baptist Seminary in Louisville, Kentucky, where he earned Th.M. and Ph.D. degrees. After graduation he served as an assistant pastor in Norway and then as pastor for three churches in Kentucky and Virginia; he had been student pastor in two Kentucky churches while at Southern. For two years he edited the Southern Baptist Foreign Mission Board's monthly magazine, The Commission.
> In 1950, he became president of the International Baptist Theological Seminary, which had recently opened in Rüschlikon, Switzerland. His hard work in the next ten years—as well as his reputation as a scholar—was what established the seminary. There he again did some translating. His translation of Brothers in Christ: The History of the Oldest Anabaptist Congregation Zolliken near Zurich by Fritz Blanke was reprinted in 2003.
> He returned to the United States in 1960 to become General Secretary. He died unexpectedly in 1969, a year before his planned retirement.

"all forms of discrimination against religious minorities," "all religious bodies shall make an unequivocal commitment to full religious liberty for all people," and "all nations shall guarantee the right of all citizens to believe, to worship, to teach, to evangelize, to change their religious affiliation, and to serve their God as their consciences dictate." The manifesto concluded with a solemn three-point covenant: "to study and proclaim the freedom men have in Jesus Christ the Lord," "to show Christian understanding and love toward those whose beliefs and practices are different from our own," and "to pray and use our influence for the preservation and extension of religious liberty for all men."[16]

A pronouncement on world peace decried war in general and the horrors of nuclear war in particular; condemned the current arms race; acknowledged the weakness and sinfulness of the human race and our own need to seek reconciliation and peace with God and our fellows; supported the cause of international disarmament; emphasized the importance of the U.N. and other contacts among people; and called for peaceful solutions to the problems of racial injustice and world hunger. It concluded by affirming that "as fellow Christians and Baptists, we recognize that in prayer and in our worldwide fellowship, we have spiritual resources that transcend national boundaries and political differences and link us to the power and Spirit of Almighty God and of His Christ." Other resolutions urged an end

> ## João Filson Soren
>
>
>
> The first person to serve as President of the Baptist World Alliance who was neither British nor a North American was the Brazilian pastor and educator João Filson Soren. Pastor of the First Baptist Church of Rio de Janeiro since December 1934, he had led the executive committee of the Brazilian Baptist Convention since the committee was organized and had been president of the convention five times.
>
> Soren was born in Rio de Janeiro in 1908 and baptized by his father at age eight. Feeling called to minister among Brazil's indigenous people, he entered the Baptist Theological Seminary of Southern Brazil but after one year went to study in the United States. He earned an M.A in political science at a state university and Th.M. degree at the Southern Baptist Theological Seminary before returning to Brazil in 1933.
>
> Soon after he began teaching in the Baptist high school he had attended, his father died, leaving the First Baptist Church without a pastor. Members insisted that Soren be his father's successor. Although he longed to be a missionary, he accepted their invitation and remained pastor of that church for fifty years.
>
> Soren did not quit teaching. For four decades he taught theology courses at Rio's Baptist seminary; he was president of the seminary 1968–1971 and head of its theology department 1977–1980. He helped write two Brazilian Baptist confessions. He was a founder of the Brazilian Bible Society. His heart, however, was in the pastorate. He rarely missed a day in the office, and only twice did he fail to appear in the pulpit—once because of illness and the other when serving as a chaplain with Brazilian forces in Italy during World War II. He died in 2002.

to nuclear testing, commended measures that assisted underprivileged persons, and demanded the separation of church and state so that churches could freely teach and do charitable work.[17]

The final session of the Congress was a Sunday afternoon evangelistic rally in Maracana Stadium. Billy Graham preached on John 3:16 to an audience that numbered between one hundred and fifty thousand and two hundred thousand. President Adams triumphantly announced: "I am informed that this is the largest crowd ever to gather in this stadium for a religious meeting." It was subsequently called "the largest meeting ever held under Baptist sponsorship." There were a thousand ushers and ten thousand counselors. Approximately ten thousand persons responded to Graham's invitation by raising a handkerchief and by standing.[18]

The Rio de Janeiro Congress was not only the first to meet in the southern hemisphere but also the first in a predominantly Roman Catholic nation. The "breakthrough" of the BWA "into a genuine world organization," according to Duke K. McCall, president of the Southern Baptist Theological Seminary, "was the most obvious development" of this Congress. The BWA leadership was "beginning to make decisions in the light of a world Baptist strategy." It was "now becoming what its founders dreamed it might become."[19] The rapid growth among Brazilian Baptists subsequently attested to the impact of the Congress on the host nation.[20]

From 1960 to 1965

The level of activity in the BWA was increasing. Now that the Executive Committee numbered around seventy, its annual meetings became major events in themselves. The routine business was handled by the Administrative Committee, which according to Article VII of the constitution consisted of seven members (at least one had to be a woman) of the Executive who resided within "reasonable distance" of the headquarters city. The General Secretary and other officers were *ex-officio* members of this smaller committee.

The most pressing concern was that of relief. A committee, chaired by Memphis, Tennessee pastor R. Paul Caudill since its founding in 1947, oversaw the BWA's relief activities, but the program essentially functioned on its own. As Ohrn had mentioned in his Congress report, a restructuring was needed to bring it under the Executive Committee. The staff person who had actually run the program for the past decade was Adolf Klaupiks, a Baptist leader in Latvia in the 1930s who found his way to Germany toward the end of World War II and was classified as a displaced person (DP). As mentioned in an earlier chapter, the Relief Committee had employed him as a field coordinator for DPs in Europe. Then in 1949 he came to the BWA Washington, D.C., office to manage the European refugee settlement program. Then, he was reassigned to handling disaster aid contributions received by the BWA. In November 1960, as this situation was becoming increasingly anomalous, the Administrative Committee directed Nordenhaug to appoint a committee to study the relief program of the BWA. The seven-member group, made up of denominational and mission executives and chaired by R. Dean Goodwin, director of the ABC's division of communications, was first designated as the "relief subcommittee" but then became the new Relief Committee.

What necessitated a reorganization of the BWA's relief program was that more money was coming in and that new needs were emerging. Most notably, Angolans—many of them Baptists—were fleeing from the bitter fight for independence from Portugal, and Cubans were seeking refuge from the Castro government that officially declared itself communist in 1961. In fact, the BWA had settled nearly five hundred Cubans in the United States by August 1962. "World emergencies have become a permanent thing," Goodwin told the Executive Committee at its June 1961 meeting in Wake Forest, North Carolina, and the Alliance's relief work "is a channel and coordinating agency through which Baptists of all the world can join in meeting human need." The Executive decided then to officially appoint Klaupiks as Coordinator of Relief, a position he would hold until retirement in 1968, and to adopt a statement of policy for the Baptist World Alliance Relief Committee. The committee was to function as information center for all member bodies concerning relief needs; to develop programs to meet needs in those areas where Baptist bodies were active; to cooperate with existing Baptist bodies and mission boards that were sponsoring programs; to serve as a channel and coordinating agency through which Baptist bodies could join in meeting relief needs; and to respond to requests from Baptist bodies for help.[21]

Baptist physician Robert Hingson continued his work in non-western countries with BWA backing. He took a group of physicians to Liberia in 1962 for an extensive program of immunization, but a subsequent effort in 1964–65 to carry out a similar program in Nigeria came to naught because of press reports of racial conflict in the United States and an inaccurate evaluation by the World Health Organization of his previous venture in Liberia. Later, in 1966, his team worked with Nicaraguan Baptist pastor and physician Gustavo Parajon in a successful medical mission.[22]

Nordenhaug recommended continuing the practice of study commissions during the next quinquennium. Four were named together with their chairs: Religious Liberty and Human Rights, C. Emanuel Carlson (Baptist General Conference [BGC]); Baptist Doctrine, John E. Skoglund (ABC); Evangelism and Missions, Frank H. Woyke (North American Baptist Conference [NABC]); and Bible Study and Membership Training, Gaines S. Dobbins (Southern Baptist Convention [SBC]). Each had a central panel of seven members who would prepare the programs for commission meetings. These would be supplemented by about twenty regular members and assisted by area consultants chosen from leaders in the section of the world where the Executive Committee convened from year to year. The commission members would work through correspondence and face-to-face conferences to develop formal statements or papers that they would present to the Executive Committee for adoption as pronouncements of the Alliance or for circulation or publication as study papers. The study commissions met for the first time in August 1962 during the Executive Committee meeting at Stabekk, Norway.[23]

To hold the line on too rapid proliferation of agencies, the Administrative Committee declined the Rio Congress Radio and Television Conference's request for a representative on the Executive Committee and tabled for further study the proposal that a similar conference "be made a permanent feature of all future congresses."[24] On the other hand, Baptists were handed a publicity windfall when, on April 30, 1961, the U.S. National Broadcasting Company aired the special "Report from Moscow," a film about the Central Baptist Church in the Soviet capital.[25]

Thanks to high speed air travel, the General Secretary now traveled much more extensively than before, and Nordenhaug made a round-the-world trip in 1961, attending various functions and visiting Baptist bodies in Asia, the Middle East, and Europe.[26] In 1963 he visited Australia and New Zealand. In fact, such lengthy travels soon became commonplace and the General Secretary virtually lived out of a suitcase. An important stop on Nordenhaug's 1961 journey was the Third Assembly of the World Council of Churches in New Delhi, India, on November 19–December 5. In a public report giving his impressions of the assembly, he showed openness to ecumenical concerns. His interest was especially significant because eleven member bodies of the BWA had affiliated with the World Council of Churches (WCC), among them the ABC, the two National Baptist Conventions, the Baptist Union of Great Britain, and the Baptist Union of New Zealand.[27]

Another event with ecumenical implications was the Second Vatican Council, a landmark event at which the Roman Catholic Church recognized Protestants as fellow Christians. At the August 1962 Executive Committee meeting, a lengthy debate occurred in which no fewer than twenty-nine speakers took the floor. The issue was how the BWA should respond to the letter from Monsignor J. G. M. Willebrands of the Vatican Secretariat for Promoting Christian Unity. He had inquired as to the BWA's interest in sending an "observer" to the Council, slated to open in October. If the response should be positive, a formal invitation would follow. The accredited representative could attend the sessions but would not participate in the discussions. The Secretariat had extended the same offer to other world confessional bodies. Support for having a BWA observer came chiefly from the unions and conventions that belonged to the WCC, while representatives of U.S. groups who had no formal ecumenical links and of the predominantly Roman Catholic Latin American countries expressed opposition.

Ernest A. Payne of the British Union "argued eloquently" for having a Baptist presence at the Council, as did "several other outstanding leaders," and it was clear from the debate that sharp differences of opinions existed. Seeing that unanimity was nowhere near possible, Payne graciously backed away and moved that the Executive Committee reply courteously to Willebrands, stating that the BWA "could not agree on the desirability of encouraging an invitation to send an observer." But it hoped and prayed that the Council would "contribute to an increasing understanding of the will of God and the unity of his people."[28]

Reports of BWA activities, conferences and meetings around the world, and of the actions of Baptist denominations; statistics on Baptist membership, missionary work, and financial contributions; and accounts of Baptists suffering discrimination and persecution filled the pages of the *Baptist World*, whose circulation in 1962 had reached seven thousand copies with readers in ninety-one nations. Especially revealing of the BWA's concern for human needs were the accounts of various medical missions, refugee aid endeavors, and efforts to assist people experiencing hardship due to natural disasters, political conflicts, and war in such places as Nigeria and New Guinea. In April–May 1962 the Japan Baptist Convention, in cooperation with the SBC's Foreign Mission Board and the Baptist General Convention of Texas, conducted a "New Life" evangelistic campaign in Japan. This was a pioneering example of what soon would be known as partnership missions.[29]

In 1963, the *Baptist World* ran a series of essays in defense of religious freedom, giving special consideration to the deliberations of the Second Vatican Council. BWA leaders enthusiastically welcomed the council's readiness to consider the question of religious liberty; Nordenhaug even sent a letter to the Secretariat underscoring Baptists' interest in a possible document that would affirm freedom of conscience. Vatican II did eventually adopt a groundbreaking statement on religious liberty, but it fell short of what the BWA wanted, as several members of the Executive Committee mentioned at the 1963 meeting in Waco, Texas.[30]

In January 1963, after thirty-two "Evangelical Christians" from Chernogorsk, Siberia, appeared at the U.S. embassy in Moscow and voiced "their sense of religious persecution," Nordenhaug and Carlson, chair of the BWA Commission on Religious Liberty and Human Rights and director of the Baptist Joint Committee on Public Affairs, personally delivered a letter to the Soviet embassy in Washington. The letter asked the government of the Soviet Union to invite an impartial international committee to investigate charges of religious persecution and to provide a full report, "which can be shared with world Christendom and the governments of the U.N."[31]

Women's work had now become a major feature of BWA life. In addition to the leadership conferences the Women's Department sponsored in connection with every Congress, the regional unions sponsored meetings of their own. In November 1962 nearly one thousand North American Baptist Women gathered for their third "Continental Assembly" in St. Louis, Missouri. About seventy delegates from ten nations attended the third meeting of the African Baptist Women's Union in June 1962 in Kumasi, Ghana. The Asian and Latin American unions tried to reach larger numbers of their scattered constituency by having more localized meetings. In April 1963 women from twelve nations went to Iloilo City, Philippines, for the first meeting of the Southeast Asian Baptist Women's Union. Ten nations were represented at the November 1962 Congress for Southern Latin American women in Buenos Aires, Argentina, while a similar Congress for Northern Latin American women was held in Guadalajara, Mexico. The oldest body, the European Baptist Women's Union, held meetings in conjunction with the 1964 European Baptist Fellowship (EBF) conference, while the European Baptist Men had a separate conference in Switzerland in July 1963.[32] The Men's Department, created at the Congress in 1960, became active in efforts to organize men's work.

The major event of 1963 was the Sixth Baptist World Youth Conference in Beirut, Lebanon, July 15–21. The theme was "Jesus Christ in a Changing World." With 2,486 registered delegates from forty-eight countries, plus a few hundred visitors, the total attendance reached three thousand, somewhat short of the expected four thousand. Hosted by Lebanese Baptists, who actually only numbered four hundred, the delegates met in five different venues during the day for lectures, which were repeated. The evening sessions took place in a sports stadium. To accommodate local people who were invited to attend, the organizers even provided nine hundred earphones for Arabic translation of the speeches. They had planned to have Martin Luther King, Jr., as the main speaker, but he dropped out at the last minute. He felt that the civil rights movement in the United States was at such a critical stage that he needed to stay home and remain in the closest possible touch with the situation. Replacing King was William A. Lawson, a Progressive National Baptist pastor from Houston, Texas. Attendees said his closing address was one of the best at the conference. The best known of the ten speakers at the assembly was Lebanese Christian Charles Malik, a faculty member at the American University of Beirut and president of the U.N. General Assembly from 1946 to 1954. Local people commented that it was "the largest convention of any sort ever to meet in Lebanon."[33] Some two hundred and fifty delegates and observers from fifteen nations attended the second Asian Baptist Youth Conference in Tokyo, Japan, in July 1961.[34]

Seven North American Baptist bodies met together in Atlantic City, New Jersey, in May 1964, to commemorate one hundred and fifty years of organized denominational life. They had cooperated for six years in the Baptist Jubilee Advance, a united evangelistic witness that culminated in this celebration of the founding of the Triennial Convention. Soren presided and John G. Diefenbaker, former prime minister of Canada, delivered the keynote address. Other speakers included the noted American Baptist historian Kenneth Scott Latourette and Billy Graham.[35] Immediately following this event, both the American and Southern Baptist conventions held their annual meetings. BWA officials were hoping they would then vote to join the recently formed North American Baptist Fellowship, but the Southern Baptists opposed pursuing membership by a vote of 2,771 to 2,738. The SBC reversed this decision in 1965.[36]

In August 1964, the EBF held its fifth conference in Amsterdam, The Netherlands, attended by nearly five thousand people from twenty-two countries, including some Soviet bloc countries. Among the speakers was Martin Luther King, Jr. The BWA Executive Committee convened at the Baptist Theological Seminary in Hamburg, Germany, immediately afterwards. It chose C. Ronald Goulding, a suburban London pastor and former president of the EBF, as Associate Secretary for Europe to replace Erik Rudén, who was assuming the post of executive secretary of the Baptist Union of Sweden on July 1, 1965.

The Executive approved the recommendations of two committees appointed earlier in the year to suggest constitutional changes that would make the BWA more representative and to review membership standards with the idea in mind of attracting more new members. It forwarded to the 1965 Congress two constitutional amendments, one defining membership and the other expanding the Executive Committee. The first specified three requirements for the admission of a Baptist body to BWA membership: (1) it must have its own identity apart from any other convention or union; (2) it must contribute regularly to the BWA budget; and (3) it must have had a stable organization for at least three years. The other would guarantee that each member body would have representation on the Executive and that it would select its own delegate(s). As only thirty-one of the seventy-eight-member bodies were currently represented on the Executive, this action would double its size.[37] The Executive also refined the wording of the bylaws to bring them into harmony with the new membership provisions, prompting a query from the BGC leadership as to whether these changes would prevent a member body from belonging to the National Association of Evangelicals. Nordenhaug gave assurance that they would not.[38]

Preparations intensified for the next Congress in Miami Beach. In June 1963 a Florida steering committee had begun to work,[39] and efforts were made to enlist African-American and independent Florida Baptists in helping to host the Congress.[40] Early in 1964 four black Baptist churchmen in southern California—three of whom had been state convention presidents—along with a San Antonio, Texas, and a Pasadena, California, pastor wrote to the BWA Executive Committee requesting reconsideration of the venue for the 1965 gathering because of white resistance to civil rights demands, the prevalent segregation "in housing, schools, eating places and the churches" in Florida and other Southern states, and the existence of racial prejudice. Speaking for the local steering committee, chair Conrad R. Willard, pastor of Central Baptist Church in Miami, reassured those with misgivings that Miami Beach was relatively free from racial incidents and that all negotiations for accommodations were predicated on the assurance that the facilities would be racially integrated. Nordenhaug informed the Executive Committee of this correspondence.[41] The BWA also made a concerted effort to encourage the attendance of laypeople and students at the Congress.[42]

Eleventh Baptist World Congress, Miami Beach 1965

The attendance at the eleventh Congress, which met in Miami Beach, Florida, on June 25–30, 1965, was the largest to date. The overwhelming majority of the 19,598 registrants were from the United States (17,973), but substantial delegations came from Canada (410), Jamaica (158), and Brazil (138). Alan C. Prior of Australia exulted that it was "the most significant of all such gatherings in the history of the Alliance."[43] Numerous civic dignitaries and representatives of other denominational fellowships brought greetings; a Brazilian congressman who was also a Baptist pastor read a letter from the president of Brazil to the Congress; and Brooks Hays, former U.S. congressman from Arkansas (1943–59) and a past president of the SBC, read a message from U.S. President Lyndon B. Johnson in which Johnson paid homage to Baptist influences in his youth.[44]

On the opening day, a panel discussion of BWA leaders explained the nature and purpose of the BWA. General Secretary Nordenhaug followed with an address pointing out that fifty-five new nations had emerged during the past twenty-two years and emphasizing the important changes that were occurring in the world: instant communication; competition from atheistic communism and non-Christian religions; concern for Christian unity; and the impact of the Second Vatican Council. Herschel H. Hobbs, pastor of First Baptist Church in Oklahoma City, followed with the keynote address, an exposition of the Congress theme, "The Truth That Makes Men Free," from John 8:32. In his presidential address Soren dealt with four challenges to the truth and the light ("a divided world," "moral decadence," "waning freedoms," and "the quest for abiding realities"). On the following days Russell F. Aldwinckle, professor of theology at McMaster University in Canada, spoke on the nature and purpose of freedom; Billy Graham on the "new morality"; civil rights leader and Brooklyn pastor Gardner Taylor on freedom and responsibility; and Joseph H. Jackson, long-time president of the National Baptist Convention, Inc., on the relevance of Jesus and his message.

Martin Luther King, Jr., attended the Congress as a "delegate and a Baptist minister" but was not on the official program. As he arrived at the convention hall, a reporter asked him why he was not making a speech. King smiled and replied: "It isn't necessary for me to speak at every Baptist gathering."[45]

Two prominent attorneys addressed the Congress: Hays on the balancing of freedom and responsibility and Harold E. Stassen, a past president of the ABC (he also had been a drafter of the U.N. Charter in 1945 and a major contender for the U.S. presidency in the 1940s), on the possibility of implementing world peace characterized by freedom and justice. The Congress Sermon, entitled "Our God Is Marching On!" was preached by J. Ithel Jones, former president of the Baptist Union of Wales, while the coronation address by BWA stalwart C. Oscar Johnson was entitled "Our Unity in Christ." The acceptance speech of President-elect William R. Tolbert, Jr. focused on the theme of "Brethren, Let Us Love One Another.[46] Four different panel presentations with participants drawn widely from the BWA community focused on the central Baptist emphasis of "Witnessing to the Truth" in various situations and contexts: "in the Christian community," "where other Christian churches dominate," "in a secular society," and "amid other world religions."[47]

Glowing reports of Baptist work on the various continents reinforced the global nature of the movement. The plenary presentation of the Relief Committee addressed specific efforts among Angolan refugees in the Congo and assistance to poverty-stricken people in Haiti and announced that other programs were planned in Rwanda and Assam, India. The report of the Women's Department included a historical pageant on the Congress theme. A high point of the June 29 plenary was the presentation of the oratorio "What Is Man?" that Ron Nelson, director of the Division of Fine Arts at Brown University, had composed—with lyrics by Samuel H. Miller, an American Baptist minister and dean of Harvard Divinity School—for the 1964 sesquicentennial of the Baptist foreign missionary enterprise in the United States. The lavish production, however, was abruptly terminated during the second act because of a bomb scare that necessitated evacuation of the auditorium. Sectional meetings included

> # William R. Tolbert, Jr.
>
>
>
> The only African to serve as President of the Baptist World Alliance in its first hundred years was William R. Tolbert, Jr., of Liberia. A 1934 graduate of Liberia College (later a university), he was pastor of the Zion Praise Baptist Church in Bensonville and from 1958 president of the Liberian Baptist Convention of Missions and Education.
>
> Tolbert was Baptist World Alliance President 1965–1970. He had many opportunities to travel as at the same time he was vice president of Liberia. Whatever country he visited, he always said to his government hosts, "I would like to attend a Baptist service while I'm here."
>
> Tolbert gave his life to public service. He entered the Treasury Department in 1936, served eight years in the House of Representatives, and was elected vice president in 1951. In 1971, he became president of his country. He was shot to death on April 12, 1980, in a military coup that overthrew his government.
>
> While president of Liberia, he had been a guest of the National Press Club in the United States. He told his listeners there that churches have a role to play in making the world what it ought to be. He was quoted as saying, "Nothing can any longer deter (persons from seeking) to secure their God-given dignity and inherent rights. . . . Who are white people, or black people? I don't believe in color."

those of women, youth, men, pastors, theological teachers, and people involved in radio and television.[48]

Each of the four study commissions reported on its work to the Congress plenum and in their own separate sessions heard extended theological presentations: George R. Beasley-Murray (U.K.), "Baptists and the Baptism of Other Churches"; James Leo Garrett, Jr. (SBC), "The Biblical Basis of Religious Liberty"; Culbert G. Rutenber (ABC), "The Biblical Basis of Human Rights"; Albert McClellan (SBC), "The Biblical Basis of Evangelism"; and C. Penrose St. Amant (SBC), "The Teaching Church and Our Baptist Witness."[49]

The Congress accepted the Executive Committee recommendation to hold the 1970 Congress in Hong Kong (with Tokyo as an alternative); adopted a strongly worded manifesto on religious liberty and human rights; ratified the two constitutional amendments on membership in the BWA and the composition of the Executive; and approved resolutions on world peace, brotherhood and equality, and evangelism. A statistical report released later revealed that the total membership of the constituent bodies had risen to 27,127,983.[50]

Elected as the new BWA President was Tolbert, a Baptist pastor and vice president of Liberia since 1951. Wherever he traveled, which was often in the service of his government, he sought to meet Baptists and to participate in Baptist worship services. When Tolbert was introduced at the plenary session on the last day, Hobbs warmly embraced him in what the minutes described as "a mountain-peak experience" of the Congress. "The session made history . . . by electing an African as its president."[51] The General Secretary observed that the Congress demonstrated a greater awareness of the world situation and the recognition of honest differences among Baptists, but at the same time there was a "widening fellowship" with an increasing "absence of barriers of race and nationality."[52]

From 1966 to 1970

The emphasis on evangelism intensified in the period following the Congress. The Brazilian Baptists reported that a year-long (1965) national evangelistic crusade had resulted in one hundred thousand professions of faith, fifty thousand baptisms, and three hundred new churches, while in Ghana a February 1966 campaign in three metropolitan areas yielded 2,361 professions of faith and rededications.[53] Baptists were enthusiastic about Billy Graham's evangelistic crusades in the British Isles, Yugoslavia, and Japan, and thirty-one hundred decisions were reported from a preaching mission of thirty Southern Baptist pastors in South Africa.[54] At a meeting in Mexico City in December 1966, planning in earnest began for the projected three-year Crusade of the Americas, but its impact was lessened somewhat when the American Baptists decided not to participate.[55] In March 1967 a special conference on evangelism in Rüschlikon, Switzerland, attracted seventy Baptists from seventeen European nations, while in October 1968, four thousand people from thirteen North American Baptist conventions attended an evangelism congress in Washington, D. C., where they agreed that evangelism and social action "go hand in hand."

Efforts were also made at enhancing the evangelistic outreach to men. A Pan American Baptist Laymen's Conference met in Rio de Janeiro in July 1968 to focus on the Brazilian methods of evangelism that had proven to be so successful. Southern Baptist layman Owen Cooper of Yazoo City, Mississippi, was named president of the group, and periodic meetings were projected. Meanwhile, George W. Schroeder, executive secretary-treasurer of the SBC's Brotherhood Commission, was chosen to be chairman of the BWA Men's Department.[56]

Five of the Baptist women's regional fellowships held meetings in the period after the Congress. The European Baptist Women's Union convened in Worthing, Sussex, England, in midsummer 1967, and the North American Baptist Women's Union met in Washington, D.C., that October, with one thousand attendees from fourteen conventions. The

Baptist women of New Zealand and Australia gathered for the first time in March 1968 in Melbourne and adopted as their name the more inclusive title Baptist Women's Union of the Southwest Pacific. The next month 167 Asian women came to their conference in Hong Kong, and in June the Baptist Women's Union of Latin America met in Cali, Colombia.[57]

Baptist youth assembled at the Seventh Baptist World Youth Conference in Berne, Switzerland, on July 22–28, 1968, which had as its program theme "One World, One Lord, One Witness." The six thousand attendees from fifty-nine nations were challenged by such distinguished speakers as African-American pastor and educator Samuel D. Proctor; Swiss psychiatrist Paul Tournier who integrated psychology with Christianity; Gerhard Claas of West Germany; Goulding of England; BGC educator Carl H. Lundquist; Southern Baptist professor of evangelism Kenneth Chafin; Othelo D. de Leon of the Philippines, Solomon Gwei of Cameroon; Brazilian Baptist pastor Nilson do Amaral Fanini; and Billy Graham. Gunnar Hoglund (BGC), pastor and chair of the Youth Department, had primary responsibility for planning the event. The director of the Berne Tourist Bureau paid tribute to the Baptists when he said: "You have conquered the city . . . . You have conquered it with your behavior, and with your love, and with your happiness."[58]

Over one thousand young people from fourteen countries came to the first Latin American Baptist Youth Conference in Buenos Aires, Argentina, and more than two hundred and fifty young people from seventeen nations attended the Asian Baptist Youth Conference in Iloilo City, Philippines. Both of these events were held in 1966–67. In 1967, Asian leaders met in Hong Kong to discuss the organization of an Asian Baptist Fellowship. Australian Baptists were considering whether to join the Asian Baptist Fellowship or to seek to constitute a separate Southwest Pacific Fellowship as the women had done. The North American Baptist Fellowship (NABF) was finally launched by six participating conventions in March 1966. The Europeans met in Vienna, Austria, on August 6–10, 1969, and were pleased to welcome representatives from seven Soviet bloc nations: Czechoslovakia, East Germany, Hungary, Poland, Romania, Yugoslavia, and the Soviet Union.[59]

Regional meetings brought Baptists closer together, helping them to realize their unity. Extensive travels by President Tolbert and General Secretary Nordenhaug also promoted Baptist self-awareness. Tolbert made quite an impression on both Baptists and governments when he visited Eastern Europe in 1966. He traveled throughout the quinquennium, greeting Baptists in the name of the BWA in Western Europe, Asia, the Southwest Pacific, and throughout Africa. In the spring of 1967,

Nordenhaug—accompanied by Southern Baptist layman Floyd Harris of Annandale, Virginia—met with Baptists in nine South American nations. The preceding October he, Klaupiks, black Baptist pastor John W. Williams, and SBC president Wayne Dehoney were part of a seven-member Baptist–Mennonite delegation that visited Baptists and other evangelical Christians in the Soviet Union. The General Secretary used the trip not only to demonstrate the loving concern the worldwide Baptist community had for their brothers and sisters within the Soviet Union but also to instruct the constituency via the *Baptist World* about the history and current situation of Baptists inside that nation. A few weeks after the 1968 Soviet invasion of Czechoslovakia, Nordenhaug, Goulding, and Hamburg Seminary president Rudolf Thaut visited Baptists in that country to reassure them of BWA concern for their spiritual welfare.[60]

Assisting in the process of making Baptists aware of their worldwide family were the annual Executive Committee meetings. They convened in a different place each year—Britain (London) in 1966, North America (Nashville, Tennessee) in 1967, Africa (Monrovia, Liberia) in 1968, and Central Europe (Baden bei Wien, Austria) in 1969—and more people were attending. At these sessions, as was the custom, the Executive conducted the business of the BWA, heard reports, and passed resolutions. Among the last was a strong appeal to the Baptist churches of the world in behalf of world peace and racial justice, especially with regard to the Vietnam War and racial unrest in the United States in 1967. The 1968 resolutions concerned world peace, world relief, evangelism, and the violent death earlier that year of Martin Luther King, Jr.[61]

As the study commissions now met in conjunction with the Executive, the General Secretary appointed the leaders and central panel members prior to the 1966 session. Chairs for the quinquennium were: Baptist Doctrine, Jannes Reiling of The Netherlands; Religious Liberty and Human Rights, Southern Baptist missionary in Europe, John David Hughey; Evangelism and Missions, John W. Williams (National Baptist Convention of America); and Bible Study and Membership Training, Clifton J. Allen (SBC). In 1968, based on Nordenhaug's longtime dream of Baptist openness to cooperating with other Christians apart from any intention of union, the Administrative Committee created a fifth study commission—the Commission on Cooperative Christianity—and named Garrett as the chair.[62]

One indication of Nordenhaug's desire to keep the BWA in contact with the larger ecumenical world was his decision to attend the fourth assembly of the WCC in Uppsala, Sweden, July 4–20, 1968. He then reported on what transpired there to his Baptist constituency. His communication was

The Baptist Church House in London (sketch from 1905) served as headquarters for the Baptist World Alliance until World War II.

Nannie Helen Burroughs (National Baptist Convention) spoke to the crowds at Hyde Park while attending the 1905 congress in London.

Committee appointed at 1905 Congress to frame the constitution of the Baptist World Alliance: *(left to right, standing)* J. H. Farmer (Canada); J. S. Dickerson (Illinois Baptist General Association); A. T. Robertson (Southern Baptist Convention [SBC]); E. C. Morris (National Baptist Convention); Waldemar Uixkiull (Estonia); Timothy Richard (British missionary to China); H. F. Richardson (Australia); W. T. Whitley (United Kingdom [U.K.]); and Harold Knott (U.K.); *(left to right, seated)* S. B. Meeser (Michigan Baptist Convention); E. W. Stephens (SBC); H. L. Morehouse (American Baptist Home Mission Society); Lathan A. Crandall, chair (Minnesota State Convention); J. H. Shakespeare (U.K.); J. N. Prestridge (SBC); and W. C. Senior (Canada).

Baptist World Alliance

Russian delegates to the 1911 Congress in Philadelphia, Pennsylvania, U.S.A.

The World Baptist Young People's Union (forerunner of Youth Department) was organized at the 1923 Congress. The committee included: *(left to right, standing)*: M. D. Timoshenko (Russia); Frank H. Leavell (Southern Baptist Convention); P. Chiminelli (Italy); Arnold T. Ohrn (Norway); J. Lee Lewis (Burma); *(left to right, seated):* S. Saito (Japan); B. Fetzer (Germany); E. E. Hayward (United Kingdom); James Asa White (Baptist Young People's Union of America), Per Gunnar Westin (Sweden); and N. S. McKechnie (Canada).

British delegates to the 1923 Congress in Stockholm, Sweden, traveled by ship.

Some of the delegates and visitors to the 1928 Congress in Toronto, Canada, gathered in front of the Ontario Government Building, Canadian National Exhibition. (Panoramic Camera Co., Toronto)

A partial view of one of the sessions of the 1939 Congress in Atlanta, Georgia, U.S.A. Sessions were moved from the air-conditioned City Auditorium to the Ponce de Leon Baseball Park to accommodate the crowds. The largest attendance was nearly sixty thousand, with an estimated fifteen thousand turned away. (Reeves Studio, Atlanta, GA)

Memorial Service for J. H. Rushbrooke, the only person to serve as both General Secretary and President of the Baptist World Alliance, at the 1947 Congress in Copenhagen, Denmark. Rushbrooke had died earlier in the year. (Star Pressefoto, Copenhagen)

Estonia delegates wore their national dress at the 1947 Congress. (Star Pressefoto, Copenhagen)

Seated in the center of the front row at the 1948 European Conference in London were President C. Oscar Johnson, General Secretary Arnold T. Ohrn, and Associate Secretary for Europe Walter O. Lewis.

President F. Townley Lord *(third from left)* listened to greetings from Dr. Szorbo´, president of the Baptist Union of Hungary, on a 1954 visit to Eastern Europe. Those pictured are *(at table from left):* Ernest A. Payne (United Kingdom); Mrs. E. Hajos (interpreter); Lord; Hungarian pastor L. Haranti; and a representative of the Hungarian Reformed Church.

Baptist World Alliance Vice President Yakov I. Zhidkov *(pointing)* and Claudia Tyrtova, both of the Soviet Union, shared a bench with President Theodore F. Adams in this 1955 photo. Seated on the far right is V. Carney Hargroves (Northern Baptist Convention).

J. T. Ayorinde, a Vice President of the Baptist World Alliance, pastor of the First Baptist Church, Lagos, Nigeria, and president of the Nigerian Baptist Convention, was named the chairman of the Nigerian Broadcasting Corporation in 1957. His appointment was hailed as an indication that the new agency would encourage religious freedom. (Religious News Service)

Mobola (Mrs. J. T.) Ayorinde *(front row, center)* visited women's groups throughout Africa and in 1956, became the first chair of the Baptist Women's Union of Africa. This 1958 photo shows her with her own Nigerian Baptist Women.

Alan C. Prior *(left)* said farewell to fellow Australian Baptists as they boarded the ship to travel to the 1960 Congress at Rio de Janeiro, Brazil. Prior, who was editor of *The Australian Baptist* and chair of the Australian Committee for Baptist World Relief, flew to Rio later, where he was elected a Vice President.

Evangelist Billy Graham and incoming President João Filson Soren spoke at the final session of the 1960 Congress. The crowd at Maracana Stadium was estimated to be nearly two hundred thousand.

Pastors Abo and Keke baptized thirty-seven new converts at this 1959 service in the Sau Enga region of what is now Papua New Guinea. The Sau Engas had never heard the gospel message until it was brought by Australian Baptists ten years earlier.

In 1961, General Secretary Josef Nordenhaug *(second from right)* visited the U Naw Memorial Church, Rangoon (now Yangon), which was built on the site of the baptism of the first Burmese convert. Shown in the photo are *(left to right)*: Maung Maung Han (Burma [now Myanmar]); Harold C. Bonell (American Baptist Convention); Vice President Joseph H. Jackson and his wife (National Baptist Convention, Inc.); Nordenhaug; and Louise Paw (Burma [Myanmar]), who was also a Vice President of the Baptist World Alliance.

King Hussein of Jordan welcomed Associate Secretary for Youth Robert S. Denny to his palace in Amman. Denny was in the Middle East making preparations for the youth conference to be held in Lebanon. (1963)

In July 1963, more than three thousand Baptist youth from throughout the world attended the Sixth Baptist Youth World Conference held in Beirut, Lebanon.

Adolf Klaupiks, Baptist World Alliance Relief Coordinator, brought assistance to Angolan refugees in Congo in 1965.

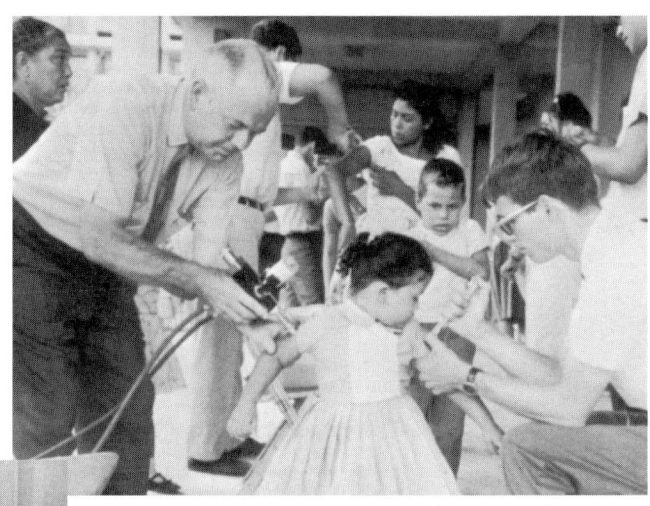

Former President Theodore F. Adams *(left in photo on left)*, examined a jet-spray gun, while Robert A. Hingson (American Baptist Convention) showed him a photo of the gun being used in a mass inoculation. In 1966, Harry C. Helm *(left, above)* and his son, Clay *(*Southern Baptist Convention), gave a young Nicaraguan protection against tuberculosis, leprosy, and smallpox. Hingson, a medical doctor, headed an organization that used volunteers to give inoculations throughout the world. (Carl Jones)

In 1966, visitors witnessed a baptism in the Moscow Central Baptist Church. Seated by the pulpit *(left to right)*: Harold E. Stassen, president of American Baptist Convention; Paul S. James, vice president of Southern Baptist Convention; and Alfonso Olmedo (Argentina), a former Vice President of the Baptist World Alliance. Standing to the left of the pulpit was Michael Zhidkov, who would be a Vice President 1970–75.

(Left) Yakov I. Zhidkov, long-time president of the All-Union Council of Evangelical Christians—Baptists in the Soviet Union and father of Michael *(above photo)*, was a Baptist World Alliance Vice President 1955-65.

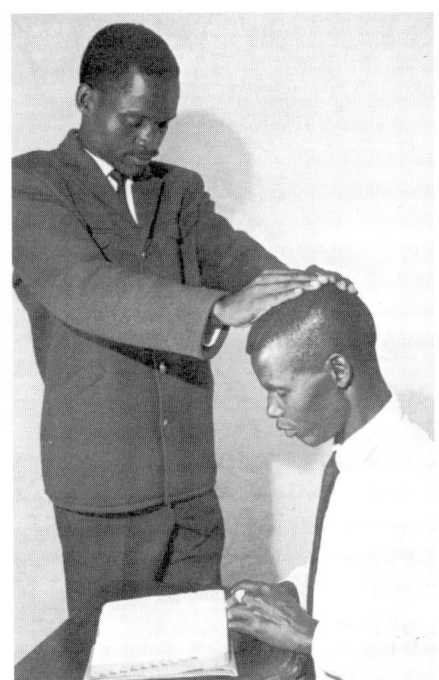

Pastor Edwin Mukumbo *(standing)* of Zambia led a prayer, setting Mwali *(kneeling)* apart for work as a lay preacher. In Zambia, as well as in many other countries, lay preachers fill a vital ministry in taking the gospel message to points beyond the reach of organized churches. (1966)

Baptist World Relief (now Baptist World Aid) provided help to refugees of the Nigerian-Biafran conflict in 1968. (Church World Service photo by Gerard Klijn)

especially important, since Payne, a current BWA Vice President, was elected one of the six presidents of the WCC at the assembly.[63]

Upon the retirement of Klaupiks in 1968, the Administrative Committee named as his successor Woyke, who had served for twenty-one years as executive secretary of the NABC. Born to Russian–German parents, he came to the United States as a boy, was reared as a German–American Baptist, was ordained in the NABC, and held a doctorate from Yale University. A veteran of BWA life, he had attended every Congress since 1934 and served on the Relief Committee since 1947 and on the Executive Committee since 1950. He was given the title of Associate Secretary and assigned responsibility for world relief, the study commissions, and the NABF. In 1970 American Baptist Chester J. Jump succeeded Goodwin as chair of the World Relief Committee.[64]

At the beginning of 1970, the constituent bodies reported a membership of 26,499,346, with the worldwide total of Baptists estimated at thirty-one million. In 1968 there were thirty-seven Baptist missionary-sending agencies, with 6,566 workers on 265 fields. In other words, the number of Baptists was growing, but BWA income was not keeping pace. The leadership sought additional funds to meet the shortfall in 1968, and the following year contributions from member bodies were even less. As it was, two-thirds of the funding came from the Southern Baptists. One economy measure taken was converting *Baptist World* from a monthly to a quarterly. On the other hand, contributions to Baptist World Relief increased steadily through the decade. The largest contributions in 1969 came from the German and Canadian Baptists.[65]

The Baptist world was stunned by the sudden death of Josef Nordenhaug on September 18, 1969 at age sixty-six. With his Scandinavian roots, North American education and pastoral experience, and continental European seminary presidency, Nordenhaug had brought a valuable mix of experience to the General Secretary's post. Actually, Nordenhaug had already announced that he would retire after the 1970 Congress, and only the month before his death, the Executive Committee had chosen Associate Secretary Robert S. Denny to be his successor. Denny assumed the job of acting General Secretary at once, and the responsibility for organizing the Tokyo World Congress fell on his shoulders. At its 1966 meeting the Executive Committee had selected Tokyo because Hong Kong could not guarantee its convention facilities would be completed by 1970. Denny and the BWA staff worked closely with Tokyo pastor and BWA Vice President Shuichi Matsamura (Japan Baptist Convention), the local arrangements chair, to make sure things went smoothly.[66]

During the decade of the sixties the BWA had become more international. Presidents and General Secretaries, often accompanied by other people active in the world organization, visited Baptists all over the world. The Alliance held its first Congress outside the Europe–North America axis, elected a Latin American and then an African as President, and expanded the Executive Committee to include delegates from each member body. The Executive also began meeting, at least occasionally, in places other than the United States and Great Britain, thereby giving better opportunity for delegates from other countries to attend. The BWA encouraged the existing regional fellowships and the formation of new ones and assisted with arranging the regular regional conferences as well as ones for such specific purposes as evangelism.

The Youth and Women's departments held their own regional and worldwide meetings, and the Youth Department's two world meetings were both in countries where Baptists did not ordinarily have a substantial witness. A newly formed Men's Department held two regional meetings and encouraged the involvement of laymen in the Alliance's global ministry. The BWA spoke and acted in behalf of religious liberty, world peace, racial justice, and meeting the physical needs of the people of the world. The organization took note of ecumenism and changes within the Roman Catholic Church, but it moved cautiously because of divergent views within its constituency.

---

1. BWA IV. 2. 6. H. Arnold T. Ohrn to João F. Soren, February 2, 1956; Frank K. Means to Arnold T. Ohrn, March 6, 1956; João F. Soren to Arnold T. Ohrn, April 16, 1956; Frank K. Means to Arnold T. Ohrn, May 14, 1956; *Baptist World,* June 1956, p. 1.

2. *BWA Congress,* 1960, p. 31.

3. Ibid., pp. 326, 17, 19, 219, 308. The total attendance was estimated at twenty-five thousand. *Baptist World,* September 1960, p. 3; BWA IV. 2. 5. H. "Registrations at Tenth Congress of the Baptist World Alliance."

4. *Baptist World,* May 1960, p. 9; *BWA Congress,* 1960, pp. 5, 22.

5. *BWA Congress,* 1960, p. 129. The telecast appeared in the United States on July 24. BWA IV. 2. 5. A. Telegram, Paul M. Stevens to Arnold T. Ohrn, July 21, 1960.

6. *BWA Congress,* 1960, pp. 21–30, 219–221. See also *Baptist World,* November 1960, pp. 3, 6.

7. *BWA Congress,* 1960, pp. 36–37, 40, 41–44. John A. Dawson of Chicago, an American Baptist layman, presented a proposed constitution to a laymen's conference on June 28 and was elected the first chairman of the Men's Department at a second meeting two days later. *Baptist World,* September 1960, p. 12.

8. *BWA Congress,* 1960, pp. 44–46; BWA I. 5. 6. B. Robert A. Hingson to C. E. Bryant,

January 13, 1961; Robert A. Hingson to Emmett Maum, January 25, 1961; *Crusader,* January 1959, p. 4.

9. *BWA Congress,* 1960, pp. 47–48. Ohrn had developed the case for the primacy of lordship more fully in "Christ Only Is King," his Holland Lectures at Southwestern Baptist Theological Seminary, Fort Worth, Texas, February 7–10, 1950 (four sound recordings, Roberts Library, SWBTS).

10. *BWA Congress,* 1960, pp. 63, 65–68, 70–71, 84–89, 111–115.

11. Ibid., pp. 132, 141–142, 145–147, 157, 192–194, 199–203.

12. Ibid., p. 294; Billy Graham, *Just As I Am: The Autobiography of Billy Graham* (San Francisco: HarperCollins, 1997), p. 360.

13. *BWA Congress,* 1960, pp. 75–76, 108–110, 138–139, 154–155, 168–172. Two specific proposals were the establishing of a special collection on Baptist ecclesiology at the American Baptist–Samuel Colgate Historical Library in Rochester, New York, and appointing a BWA "study director for a Baptist program of studies," p. 171.

14. Ibid., pp. 137, 290; *BWA Congress,* 1955, pp. 384–385; BWA IV. 2. 6. A, B. Arnold T. Ohrn to BWA Administrative Committee, May 9, 1960; V. Carney Hargroves to Arnold T. Ohrn, May 23, 1960; Arnold T. Ohrn to V. Carney Hargroves, May 24, 1960; Minutes of the Executive Committee, June 25 and July 2, 1960.

15. *BWA Congress,* 1960, pp. 172–174; *Baptist World,* September 1960, p. 2; October 1960, pp. 2, 7, 11. Nordenhaug's papers are held in the manuscript collection of the Samuel Colgate–American Baptist Historical Library, Rochester, NY. For biographical information on Soren see Israel Velode Azevedo, "João Filson Soren," paper presented to the Baptist Heritage Study Commission, 1997. This is drawn from his 1995 biography of Soren published in Portuguese.

16. *BWA Congress,* 1960, p. 296.

17. Ibid., pp. 300–303. Craig Alan Sherouse, "The Social Teachings of the Baptist World Alliance," 1905–1980, Ph. D. dissertation, Southern Baptist Theological Seminary, 1982, pp. 145, 168–170, reckoned the manifesto on religious liberty to be less Baptist and more ecumenical than previous Congress manifestos, noted that the resolution on nuclear testing was grounded in creation and referenced the Holy Spirit, and found the pronouncement on world peace to be "the broadest" of all Baptist World Alliance statements "in its understanding of the roots and horrors of war."

18. *BWA Congress,* 1960, pp. 219–231, 5; *Baptist World,* September 1960, p. 5.

19. *Baptist World,* October 1960, p. 5.

20. Ibid., May 1961, pp. 5–6.

21. Ibid., December 1960, p. 4; March 1961, p. 7; September 1961, pp. 5, 6; October 1962, p. 3; February 1963, p. 7; BWA I. 4. 6. J. Josef Nordenhaug to Baker James Cauthen, December 21, 1960; BWA, I. 4. 6. K. Administrative Committee Minutes, February 14, 1961, items 20–22.

22. BWA II. 1. 7. C. Administrative Committee Minutes, March 23, 1962, item 8; *Baptist World,* February 1962, p. 6; May 1962, p. 16. BWA I. 5. 6. C. Robert A. Hingson to Robert S. Denny, July 20, 1964; Robert A. Hingson to G. A. Ademola, August 7, 1964; Robert A. Hingson to Friends, September 11, 1964; Robert A. Hingson to Robert S. Denny, September 13, 1964; Robert A. Hingson to Vice President and Mrs. William R.

Tolbert, Jr., May 10, 1965; Robert A. Hingson to President William V. S. Tubman, May 10, 1965; Robert A. Hingson to Edward R. Briggs, November 4, 1965; *Baptist World,* October 1966, pp. 6–7.

23. BWA I. 4. 6. K. Administrative Committee Minutes, February 14, 1961, item 24. *Baptist World,* April 1961, p. 6; September 1961, p. 6; September 1962, p. 6; October 1962, pp. 1, 3–4.

24. BWA I. 4. 6. K. Administrative Committee Minutes, February 14, 1961, item 29.

25. BWA I. 4. 6. M. Paul M. Stevens to Arnold T. Ohrn, September 14, 1960; Theodore F. Adams to Josef Nordenhaug, March 8, 1961; Doris Ann to Josef Nordenhaug, May 9, 1961; clipping, Jack Gould, "TV: Baptists in Soviet Union," *New York Times,* May 1, 1961.

26. BWA II. 1. 7. C. "Itinerary for Dr. Josef Nordenhaug" (1961).

27. *Baptist World,* February 1962, pp. 4–5. Other Baptist World Alliance bodies that belonged to the World Council of Churches were the Baptist unions or conventions of Burma, Cameroon, Denmark, Hungary, and the Netherlands, and the Seventh Day Baptist General Conference in the United States. E. Roberts-Thomson (New Zealand) strongly advocated conciliar ecumenism in *With Hands Outstretched: Baptists and the Ecumenical Movement* (London: Marshall, Morgan, and Scott, 1962).

28. *Baptist World,* September, 1962, p. 6; October 1962, pp. 1–3; BWA. IV. 2. 9. A. Josef Nordenhaug, "Personal Notes on the Discussion in Oslo, August 22, 1962"; Nordenhaug to BWA Executive Committee, January 24, 1963.

29. BWA II. 1. 7. C. Administrative Committee Minutes, March 23, 1962, item 21; *Baptist World,* May 1962, p. 7; June 1962, pp. 6–7, 16; November 1962, pp. 5, 11; December 1962, pp. 7, 16; April 1963, pp. 4–5; May 1963, p. 5.

30. *Baptist World,* February 1963, pp. 3–4; March 1963, pp. 4–5; June 1963, p. 3; September 1963, p. 2; January 1964, pp. 5, 12; March 1964, p. 7; February 1966, p. 4; "Declaration on Religious Freedom" [December 7, 1965], in *The Documents of Vatican II,* ed. Walter M. Abbott, S.J. (New York: America Press, 1966), pp. 674–696.

31. *Baptist World,* February 1963, p. 5.

32. Ibid., October 1962, p. 15; December 1962, p. 15; January 1963, p. 15; February 1963, pp. 13–15; June 1963, p. 15; November 1963, pp. 13–15.

33. Ibid., May 1963, pp. 8–9; September 1963, pp. 4–5; C. E. Bryant, ed., *Jesus Christ in a Changing World: Official Report of the 6th Baptist Youth World Conference, Beirut, Lebanon, July 15–21, 1963* (Washington: BWA, 1963), pp. 10, 13.

34. *Baptist World,* September 1961, p. 7.

35. Ibid., November 1963, p. 6; February 1964, p. 12; April 1964, pp. 14–15. BWA I. 5. 11. K. "Background of the Baptist Jubilee Advance, 1959–1964;" *Baptist Advance: The Achievements of the Baptists of North America for a Century and a Half,* ed. Davis Collier Woolley, et al. (Nashville: Broadman Press, 1964). *Baptist Standard,* April 1, 1964, pp. 6–7, 9; April 15, 1964, pp. 6–7; April 22, 1964, pp. 6–7, 9–10; May 13, 1964, pp. 9–10.

36. *Baptist Standard,* May 27, 1964, pp. 6–7; June 10, 1964, pp. 4–5; *SBC Annual,* 1965, pp. 85, 280.

37. *Baptist World,* October 1964, p. 4.

38. BWA I. 4. 2. A. Lloyd W. Dahlquist to Josef Nordenhaug, November 17, 1964; Josef Nordenhaug to Lloyd W. Dahlquist, November 19, 1964.

39. BWA IV. 2. 9. C. Minutes of the Steering Committee, June 25, 1963; *Baptist World,* January 1964, p. 10.

40. BWA IV. 2 .8. C. Fred T. Laughon, Jr., to Josef Nordenhaug, February 26, 1963; J. Ray Dobbins to Josef Nordenhaug, April 1, 1963.

41. BWA IV. 2. 13. I. C. Albert Henson, C. H. Hampton, B. O. Byrd, and Fred D. Haynes to BWA Executive Committee, March 16, 1964; P. S. Wilkinson to Josef Nordenhaug, May 27, 1964; Conrad R. Willard to Brothers in Christ, June 2, 1964; Theodore F. Adams to Robert S. Denny, June 2, 1964; Josef Nordenhaug to BWA Executive Committee, June 19, 1964; Marvin T. Robinson to Josef Nordenhaug, July 3, 1964.

42. *Baptist World,* January 1965, p. 12; February 1965, p. 16.

43. *BWA Congress,* 1965, p. 538. Estimates of attendance at the four evening rallies in Miami's Orange Bowl stadium were 30,000, 45,000, 55,000 and 25,000. Ibid., p. 487. See also *Baptist World,* September 1965, p. 3.

44. *BWA Congress,* 1965, pp. 499–501.

45. *Miami News,* June 27, 1965, clipping in scrapbook of press reports on the Miami Beach Congress, BWA Office Library, Falls Church, VA

46. Ibid., pp. 3–100. Christian Witnesses against Communism, led by Presbyterian separatist Carl McIntire from Collingswood, NJ, together with four related organizations, expressed their opposition to the Congress by holding competing meetings and rallies. Marty Schram, "Rightists Rip Baptist Rally," *Miami News,* June 25, 1965, clipping in BWA IV .2. 13. A.

47. *BWA Congress,* 1965, pp. 113–149.

48. Ibid., pp. 150–175, 182–202, 490–491, 521–222, 360–463. The reports of the Youth and Men's departments to the plenary sessions consisted of testimonies, pp. 176–182, 202–207. See also *Baptist World,* November 1965, p. 6.

49. *BWA Congress,* 1965, pp. 208–255, 261–273, 280–287, 301–310, 321–325, 343–351.

50. Ibid., pp. 503–504, 510, 482, 512, 515–517. *Baptist World,* December 1965, p. 3.

51. *BWA Congress,* 1965, p. 526; *Baptist World,* September 1965, pp. 3, 6.

52. Ibid., October 1965, p. 4.

53. Ibid., March 1966, p. 10; April 1966, p. 7.

54. Ibid., September 1967, p. 4; December 1967, pp. 4, 7.

55. Ibid., February 1967, p. 2; May 1967, p. 6.

56. Ibid., May 1967, p. 7; December 1968, pp. 7, 8; December 1967, p. 13; May 1968, p.13; June 1968, p. 13; September 1968, pp. 9–10; October 1967, p. 13.

57. *Baptist World,* March 1967, p. 15; October 1967, p. 15; January 1968, pp. 14–15; December 1967, p. 14; June 1968, p. 14; February 1968, p. 15; April 1968, p. 14; June 1968, pp. 12, 15; November 1968, pp. 13–14.

58. Ibid., September 1968, p. 6. Cyril E. Bryant, ed., *One World, One Lord, One Witness: Official Report of the 7th Baptist Youth World Conference, Berne, Switzerland, July 22–28, 1968* (Waco: Word Books for the BWA, 1969) provides complete coverage.

59. *Baptist World,* October 1966, p. 16; December 1966, p. 8; March 1967, p. 4; June 1967, p. 14; April 1967, p. 3; November 1968, p. 9; October–December 1969, pp. 3, 7, 15; March 1966, p. 9; May 1966, p. 7.

60. Ibid., November 1966, p. 8; June 1966, pp. 4, 11; May 1969, p. 7; June 1969, pp. 6, 16; February 1967, pp. 4, 11; February 1969, pp. 4–5.

61. Ibid., October 1966, pp. 4–5; October 1967, pp. 4–5, 16; September 1968, pp. 3–4.

62. Ibid., May 1966, p. 6; November 1966, pp. 6–7; March 1968, p. 3; May 1968, p. 7; September 1968, pp. 3–4.

63. *Baptist World,* November 1968, pp. 6–8; Southwestern Baptist Seminary historian William R. Estep, Jr., authored a critical analysis of conciliar ecumenism: *Baptists and Christian Unity* (Nashville: Broadman Press, 1966).

64. Carl W. Tiller, *The Twentieth Century Baptist* (Valley Forge: Judson Press, 1980), p. 14–5, 6; *Baptist World,* January 1968, p. 8; February 1968, pp. 10–11; April–June 1970, p. 22.

65. Ibid., April–June, 1970, pp. 13–15; February 1968, p. 7; January 1969, pp. 8, 12; April 1969, p. 8.

66. Ibid., October–December 1969, pp. 4–6; June 1966, p. 16; September 1966, p. 2.

7

NEW STRUCTURES FOR A GROWING FAMILY: THE BAPTIST WORLD ALLIANCE IN THE 1970s
Faith Bowers

By 1970 the world Baptist family, now thirty-one million strong, was growing most rapidly in the non-western or developing parts of the world. Since in spite of the changes of the 1960s these areas were not adequately represented in the world organization, the Baptist World Alliance (BWA) needed to adapt more creatively to the new situation. In a period when international travel and communications were becoming easier, the BWA had to function with a more representative structure and to adopt a program that effectively enlisted worldwide participation.

Twelfth Baptist World Congress, Tokyo 1970

The first Congress to be held in Asia drew 8,556 Baptists from seventy-eight countries. They gathered in the spacious Budokan auditorium in the Japanese capital to celebrate their oneness as a community of believers. The theme of the meeting was "Reconciliation Through Christ," based on the biblical passage 2 Corinthians 5:18–20. An impressive feature was the presence of many "nonwhites" (in addition to the Japanese leaders) in prominent roles. Retiring BWA President William R. Tolbert, Jr., of Liberia eloquently challenged the delegates to go forth with cleansed hearts—having removed from the inner being all elements of hypocrisy, prejudice, racism, conceit, and many other vices—to carry the message of reconciliation to all people. Burmese Baptist U Kyaw Than, currently living in Bangkok, Thailand, where he served as general secretary of the East Asian Christian Conference, gave a moving address on Christ as our peace. Pastor Daniel Y. K. Cheung of Hong Kong spoke of Christ as the Savior whom all people need. John W. Williams, pastor of a large National Baptist church in Kansas City, Missouri, and a BWA Vice President, delivered the Congress Sermon, in which he expounded the importance of the whole gospel for the whole world.

Two former BWA Presidents delivered major addresses: Theodore F. Adams, the keynote speaker, gave an exposition of the Congress theme of reconciliation, and João Soren preached the coronation address entitled "The Song of the Morning Stars." He utilized the text Job 38:7 as the basis for his argument that there is great hope in God's world. In the concluding plenary, Billy Graham reminded the delegates of the youth revolution and emphasized that young people desperately needed the gospel. David S. (Syme) Russell, general secretary of the British Baptist Union, explained how the gospel was a force for reconciliation in a world of conflict, and Brazilian Nilson do Amaral Fanini, pastor of the Niteroi Baptist Church in Rio de Janeiro and a rising star in the BWA, proclaimed that reconciliation was the key to harmony and progress.[1]

Where previously Europe and North America had supplied most of the Congress hymns, the selections in the printed program book and the musical pieces performed at the sessions included works from Japan, China, Korea, Indonesia, Liberia, Angola, Colombia, Brazil, India, and Egypt. It was noted that during the previous five years the BWA had added ten new member bodies from Ethiopia, Israel, India, Nicaragua, Togo, Angola, Peru, East Pakistan (now Bangladesh), Burundi, and the United States. Two new regional associations received Executive Committee recognition: the Asian Baptist Fellowship (including the Southwest Pacific) and the Caribbean Baptist Fellowship. At the roll call, a representative from each continent noted the date when Baptist work began there and summarized the subsequent growth—or decline—that had occurred. Growth was most marked in the Caribbean and Central and Southern America.

There were other noteworthy firsts at the Congress, besides being the first one held in Asia, as Theodore F. Adams pointed out: It was the first to be presided over by a President and a Vice President from Africa and Asia. It was the first to have a woman as chair of the program committee and it was the first in which a black minister preached the Congress sermon. It was the first to have a portion of its proceedings broadcast across the Pacific by a satellite. And, as will be discussed later, it was the first to have a contested presidential election. Another significant first was the address by the current president of the United Nations (U.N.) Security Council, Angie Brooks-Randolph, a Liberian Baptist laywoman.[2]

Meeting at the time of the Congress, the Executive Committee approved the 1972 budget of $206,000, of which $171,000 was to come from member bodies and $2,500 from the new 500 Club initiated by Owen Cooper, the Southern Baptist layman from Mississippi who was a leader in the Men's Department. He was seeking five hundred donors who would contribute fifty dollars annually for five years to support the general fund. The remaining ten thousand dollars was to come from other sources, including the *Baptist World,* now changed to newsletter format. It was made clear that this publication was in no way connected with the new monthly of that name that the Landmark Baptists (not a BWA member body) in the United States were now publishing.[3]

The Relief Committee reported that over five hundred thousand dollars was distributed over the previous five years. Much of this money had gone to cyclone and flood relief in South India and to Nigeria to relieve widows, orphans, and other sufferers from thirty months of civil war. The Congress also celebrated the dedicated service of the recently retired Adolf Klaupiks, who as a BWA staff member had coordinated the relief work for two decades.[4]

The actions in the various regions dominated the reports of work among both men and women. The Baptist women had met at various places on all six continents during the previous five years. The men's organization was planning a progressive series of gatherings, beginning at the national level in 1971, then regional ones (including a meeting of the Pan American Union of Baptist Men in 1972, and a world conference in 1973). Hong Kong architect David Y. K. Wong, a person deeply committed to laymen's ministry, was elected chair of the Men's Department for the next quinquennium.[5]

News shared at this Congress included the ousting of foreign missionaries from Burma (now Myanmar) in 1966 and the release in Cuba of half the Baptists imprisoned in the past few years. Since the Second Vatican Council, Roman Catholic attitudes had noticeably relaxed; in Spain nonconformists now had access to public office and were allowed to build places of worship, to establish schools, and to print literature. Outside the BWA Congress hall, some Japanese youths distributed leaflets decrying U.S. participation in the war in Southeast Asia and the renewal of the U.S.–Japan security treaty.

The major initiative launched at the Tokyo Congress was the "World Mission of Reconciliation Through Jesus Christ."[6] The proposal came from the Commission on Evangelism and Missions, and this "program of evangelism and Christian ministry," embracing a wide range of gospel ministries, was the first such effort of the BWA to enlist worldwide participation.[7] Because the member bodies were asked to adopt a wide-ranging mission program, it moved the Alliance beyond fellowship activities. Each regional and national Baptist body was to determine the nature and expression of this mission within their own contexts. At the same time, a sense of mutual accountability existed since there would be annual progress reports. It was anticipated that the program would be underway by the beginning of 1973. The Southern Baptist Foreign Mission Board seconded Joseph B. Underwood to the BWA to direct the program.

The concept was carefully spelled out in the project statement:

> [R]ecognizing the extreme urgency for reconciliation of social, racial, economic and political structures, as well as of man with man, and believing that God calls us who have been reconciled to be instruments in His purpose to reconcile the world unto Himself and to create, out of the many diverse factions, one new humanity in Christ Jesus, we appeal to Baptists to join in the World Mission of Reconciliation through Jesus Christ, praying and working zealously for brotherhood and world peace.
>
> We believe the following ideas suggest practical, redemptive ministries of reconciliation and evangelistic endeavours that can help to achieve the ideals of this Mission: (1) spiritual renewal, (2) rediscovery and involvement of the laity, (3) co-operative and diversified evangelistic witnessing, and (4) positive expressions of the love of God through ministries of reconciliation.

Churches were called to engage in this program by
  I. Cooperative Evangelistic Endeavours
     A. Personal Witnessing
     B. Witnessing to and through small groups
     C. Witnessing through preaching
  II. Ministries of Reconciliation
     A. Social ministries that express the redemptive love of God in alleviating misery and in reconciling man with God and with one another.
     B. Fellowship meetings between those of various races and groups.
     C. Joint work or relief projects in which members of various churches of different races and groups work together to meet human needs—ministering to those of different races, languages, economic groups, etc.
     D. Counselling and assistance in Christian home building and spiritual education in the homes.
     E. A "Vision Walk-Through"—a South American pastor led his church to walk through its neighbourhood to become acquainted with the needs.
     F. Ministries to seamen, transients, migrants, people in the inner city, on holiday, and those too poor for holiday, etc.
     G. Person-to-person ministries and goodwill missions in active pursuit of better understanding between peoples of different countries, developing and strengthening bonds of friendship and goodwill.
     H. Ministries to those in hospitals, convalescent homes and other institutions
     I. Ministries in collaboration with other bodies, in harmony

with our basic principles, in active pursuit of world peace and social justice.
    J. Encourage Christian statesmen and businessmen to use their influence and relationships to promote Christian brotherhood, better international relationships, and improved mutual trust and understanding.
    K. Encourage youth and laymen to dedicate their life and abilities for a year, or more, to special Christian service in areas of special need and opportunity.
III. Special features, such as concerts, dramas, press receptions, special testimonies, etc.[8]

The program's structure reflected the BWA's growing consciousness of the need to stress Christian obligation toward social righteousness alongside the obligation to evangelism. American Baptist layperson Carl W. Tiller, Western Treasurer and later Associate Secretary of the BWA, included in his seventy-fifth anniversary commemorative volume, *The Twentieth Century Baptist*, along with the call for participation in the World Mission for Reconciliation, a quotation from the *New Zealand Baptist* that he approvingly highlights: "Christian responsibility is wider than evangelism. . . . Christians must have social and moral concerns and be prepared to translate these concerns into action."[9] This point was made repeatedly by other speakers at this and earlier Congresses.

In similar fashion a manifesto on the traditional Congress subject of religious liberty linked freedom with responsibility. Delegates pledged themselves to work for peace, religious liberty, civil rights, brotherhood, and the intimate relationship of personal faith with social responsibility.[10] The Congress resolutions repeated familiar themes. One called on world statesmen to intensify efforts for peaceful and just solutions of disputes, to support the U.N., and to suspend further deployment of nuclear weapons. Another expressed the BWA's willingness to work with other religious organizations toward world peace with justice and to overcome suffering and poverty. It instructed officers to report on progress at the next Congress. Opposition to racial discrimination, registered at every Congress since Berlin in 1934, was reiterated. Other resolutions addressed environmental concerns and economic justice: Wealthy nations were asked to devote at least one percent of their gross national product to aid developing countries.[11]

Apportioning vice presidencies among prospective nominees proved so difficult that a constitutional amendment was adopted to increase their number from nine to twelve.[12] The nominated Vice Presidents (a complete contingent of new people) and two Treasurers (Eastern and Western) were duly elected, but no changes in staff personnel occurred. Confirmed for a regular five-year term were Robert S. Denny, who had become General Secretary in 1969 after the death of Josef Nordenhaug; C. Ronald Goulding, who had been Associate Secretary for Europe since 1965; and Frank Woyke, the Associate Secretary for relief, the study commissions, and the North American Baptist Fellowship (NABF) since 1968. Cyril E. Bryant continued as Director of Publications, a position he had held since 1957. After the Congress the Executive Committee initiated a general review of the BWA's constitution, structures, and responsibilities of the General Secretary and Associate Secretaries.

For the first and only time in BWA history, the presidential election was contested between two Americans: Southern Baptist Herschel H. Hobbs of Oklahoma City and American Baptist (formerly named Northern Baptist) V. Carney Hargroves of Philadelphia. The latter was the choice of the fifty-one-member nominating committee, and his name was presented to the plenum in the July 16 morning business session. Normally, this was a routine action. However, Duke K. McCall, president of Southern Baptist Theological Seminary, stood up, referred to the provision in the constitution "Nominations from the floor of the General Meeting may also be in order," and nominated Hobbs.

The unexpected nomination threw the meeting into turmoil. Williams pleaded for unity and pointed out that many eyes were on the delegates in

Robert S. Denny

Robert Stanley Denny served on the staff of the Baptist World Alliance for twenty-four years. He was elected Associate Secretary for Youth in 1956, a position he ably filled until the death of Josef Nordenhaug in 1969, when Denny became General Secretary. He retired in 1980.

Denny was a layman who spent his life in Baptist youth work, a lawyer who never practiced law. Born in Kentucky in 1914, he earned degrees in both business and law at his state university. Upon graduation, he became director of Baptist student work at the First Baptist Church of Baton Rouge and at Louisiana State University, which is located in that city. He went next to Baylor University in Texas, where he was dean of religious activities. From 1945 to 1956 he was associate secretary for student work at the Southern Baptist Sunday School Board.

While employed by the Sunday School Board, he became an active participant in the Alliance. He served as chairman of the BWA Youth Committee for the quinquennium prior to his election as Associate Secretary.

After retirement, Denny continued to take part in the work of the Alliance and enjoyed greeting his many friends from around the world at the meetings of the General Council and Congresses. He died in 1996.

> ## V. Carney Hargroves
>
>
> Elected in Tokyo in 1970, Vernon Carney Hargroves served as Baptist World Alliance President into 1975. Born in 1900, he was a native of Virginia and was educated at Southern Seminary and Princeton University. While a student, he pastored the Princeton Baptist Church, going form there to the Weatherford Memorial Church in Richmond, Virginia. In 1932 he went to the Second Baptist Church of Germantown, Philadelphia, where he served as pastor until 1970.
> The American Baptist Convention elected Hargroves as its president in 1954, and from that year he became an active participant in the Baptist World Alliance. He took part in preaching and fellowship missions in the Soviet Union in 1955 and 1958, traveled for the Baptist World Alliance to other countries in Eastern Europe in 1964 and 1966. He was the first president of the North American Baptist Fellowship and served as a Baptist World Alliance Vice President from 1965 to 1970.
> Hargroves had a special concern for countries where Baptists were a minority. As President he tried to get permission to visit China and Cuba on behalf of the Baptist World Alliance. He believed that the Alliance could improve conditions for Baptists by providing Bibles and other materials, by granting funds for construction or rebuilding, and by interceding with governments.
> Hargroves's participation in the Baptist World Alliance did not cease when he was no longer President. He remained active in the organization into 1980. He died in 1986.

a country where Christians were a minority. Russell declared that the nominating committee was more representative than the geographical balance of the delegates themselves. Harold E. Stassen, who was upset by what he perceived to be a power play to deny the presidency to Hargroves (his own pastor), proposed that ballots be cast by delegates from each constituent union or convention weighted according to the size of the body. This way, groups who could not afford to send large delegations to the Congress would not be disadvantaged. Stassen's suggestion was reluctantly accepted and the balloting took place. That evening the tellers announced that Hargroves had been elected by a straight vote of 841 to 636. When the votes were tallied in accordance with the weighting formula, the results were the same.[13]

In his memoirs, McCall explained the mystery of this long-forgotten incident.[14] Hobbs had expected to be nominated in 1965, but he agreed to back off and leave the way clear for Tolbert of Liberia, with the understanding that his name would go forward in 1970. McCall, a member of the nominating committee, actually had wanted to nominate Leon (Lien-hwa) Chow of Taiwan "to break up the passing of the presidency back and forth between Europe and North America" but Chow, chaplain to the

Republic of China leader Chiang Kai-shek, was advised by his government not to stand.

Many Southern Baptists were unhappy with the nominating committee's choice of the American Baptist Hargroves, especially since the chair had unexpectedly rescheduled the meeting where the decision was to be made to a time when many of them could not be present. McCall himself was displeased with the chair's action, and when Hobbs asked McCall to nominate him from the floor, McCall agreed to do so, even though he expected Hargroves to win. Hobbs told McCall that it would be less embarrassing to return home to his church as a defeated candidate than to have been passed over altogether.

To ensure that such a debacle never happened again, the BWA quietly changed its nominating procedure. Included in the sweeping revision of the constitution approved at the 1975 Congress was a provision that the nominations would be made by the General Council (which would replace the Executive Committee) in the year preceding the Congress. Nominations from the floor could only be made in writing and no later than two days before the scheduled time for the election.[15]

The sixty-nine-year-old Hargroves[16] was quickly accepted as the new President. A native of Virginia, he had pastored in the North since the early 1930s and in 1954–1955 served as the president of the American Baptist Convention. He had long been involved in BWA life, having served on the Executive Committee, as a Vice President in 1960–1965, and as first president of the NABF.

The Study Commissions

By now the commissions had become a regular part of BWA life. Each of them had their own conferences, open to all who wished to attend, and made reports to the Congress on their work during the quinquennium. The Commission on Christian Teaching and Training had also arranged a pre-Congress meeting on "Christian Education for the Living Church," attended by eighty-five people from twenty-seven member bodies. The Commission on Evangelism and Missions heard reports on the Crusade of the Americas (a joint evangelistic effort of Baptists in the Western Hemisphere), hill-tribe evangelism in Northeast India, and evangelism in Europe. Baptist Doctrine focused on the Holy Spirit, "including but not limited to glossolalia." Religious Liberty and Human Rights looked at "goals and methods of social change," while the recently formed (1968) Commission on Cooperative Christianity considered New Testament teaching on the unity of the Church, Baptist involvements in interdenominational cooperation, and arguments for greater cooperation with other Christians.[17]

Commission membership now extended beyond the Executive Committee, although because of travel costs and other reasons some would correspond rather than attend meetings. Wider participation and growing diversity in topics discussed and ideas offered were desirable features, but the commissions lacked adequate structures to do as much as they would like, despite the changes that had been introduced in 1961. One positive development was that after the Tokyo Congress the commissions' new personnel were chosen in time for them to attend the Executive Committee meeting in Wolfville, Nova Scotia, in August 1971. At that meeting the structure and role of the commissions were more carefully defined:

1. A central panel of not more than twelve would prepare the program for meetings, conserve and circulate the results of study by the full commissions, and ensure continuity in their studies. This would include the chairman, co-chairman and secretary of the commission. They would normally serve until the next Congress.
2. The General Secretary would fill vacancies.
3. About thirty-five regular members would serve for the quinquennium.
4. All members of the Executive Committee would be assigned to a commission.
5. Area consultants might be invited to participate.

Commissions would meet at the Executive and report to it, but each central panel might arrange other meetings, full or regional. They were to "explore pertinent questions within their fields," and they might "present statements or papers to the Executive Committee for adoption as pronouncements of the BWA, or for circulation or publication as study papers." The Executive Committee also could assign specific tasks to the commissions.[18]

The BWA in the Early 1970s

On President Hargroves's initiative, six young people were invited to the Wolfville Executive meeting: "Recognizing the intelligence and the enthusiasm of many young people, we shall seek to bring them with their ideals, their hopes, their frustrations, their problems, into greater participation in the expanding work of the Alliance and in the work of its constituent bodies."[19] Four young men and two young women, all from North America, duly attended.

Several personnel changes occurred during this period: Bryant was elevated to Associate Secretary of Communications in 1971, with the same duties as he had had before. That same year Theo Patnaik, a native of India, filled the vacancy in the Youth Department left by Denny. In 1972, Tiller relinquished the (honorary) position as Western Treasurer that he had held since 1956 and succeeded the retiring Woyke as Associate Secretary. In his purview were relief and development, the study commissions, and the NABF. Added to these in the next few years were responsibility for statistics, the U.N. liaison, staffing, and the International Mission Secretaries Conference (IMSC). Formed in 1974, within a year this conference had come to involve thirty-one national bodies and was informally linked with the BWA, which provided a clearinghouse for personnel placements.[20]

Hargroves delighted in the unity-in-variety of the Alliance:

> When I sit in the president's chair at each annual Executive Committee meeting I marvel at what it is that holds such a mixed group together. The variety in the Baptist World Alliance can be seen in the diversity of the people who took part in one worship service. A Nigerian read the Scripture in a language spoken by one in twenty of all people who live in Africa; a Hungarian prayed; a Swiss announced "Old Hundred" as the hymn and suggested that the congregation sing in English, French or German. An Australian preached the sermon. A trio of men from Moscow, Soviet Union, sang; a black man from America sang a spiritual; and the pianist was a New Testament scholar from England.[21]

The Executive meetings clearly were changing in character. More interested people had been invited to attend and special tours were organized, making Executives more like a mini-congress, "though with a strong American predominance."[22] Regional conferences also were becoming a regular feature of BWA life. European Baptists in Zurich in 1973 had considered "The Church of the Future and the Future of the Church." NABF held a two-day course on management in January 1975 in Toronto. The Caribbean Fellowship arranged various conferences and also a consultation on theological education and publishing.

The departments as well were active. The First World Conference of Baptist Men took place in Hong Kong in November 1974, while the Women's Department sponsored meetings for Europe at Rüschlikon, Switzerland; for Africa in Blantyre, Malawi; for North America in Toronto; for Asia in Singapore; for Latin America in Mexico City; and for the Southwest Pacific in New Zealand. Four thousand attended the women's meetings that preceded the Congress in Stockholm. In 1974, the Eighth Baptist Youth World Conference in Portland, Oregon, drew six thousand from fifty-four countries.

In December 1974 General Secretary Denny, accompanied by several European Baptist leaders who were in Moscow for the European Baptist Fellowship (EBF) executive meeting, spent two hours "pleading for our people" with Victor Titov, the deputy chairman of the Council for Religious Affairs in the Soviet Union. Knud Wümpelmann, who was present, said later that this meeting was "unforgettable."[23] A similar thing happened in Kiev. The BWA was granted consultative status (nongovernmental organization or NGO) at the U.N., "which has been important in our common struggle for religious freedom and other human rights." [24]

Commission papers from the period indicate the extraordinary range of issues that interested Baptist scholars.[25] In 1971 the Doctrine Commission was chiefly concerned with religious authority, thus Norman H. Maring's paper considered a timely topic in his denomination: "Fundamentalism and American Baptists: an attempt to deal with the problem of biblical authority."[26] Following the path of the discussions that began at the Tokyo Congress, the theme of "Reconciliation in Christ" dominated the deliberations of Evangelism and Mission,[27] appeared in Christian Teaching and Training,[28] and was foundational to the work of Cooperative Christianity.[29] Religious Liberty and Human Rights focused on the use of power.[30] In 1974 Doctrine was concerned both with authority and with charismatic issues.[31] In a particularly interesting paper, Southern Baptist W. Morgan Patterson considered "The History of Baptists and Human Rights."

The Commission on Cooperative Christianity produced a significant book, *Baptist Relations with Other Christians,* edited by James Leo Garrett, Jr. (1974). There were sections on Europe; the Americas, including all the major Baptist bodies in the United States; Asia; Australasia; and Africa. "Most surprising," judged Wümpelmann, "was the paper on the Southern Baptist Convention (SBC), written by a Roman Catholic lay theologian and giving a very interesting historical reason for the attitude of the SBC towards the present day ecumenical movement."[32]

Denton Lotz's 1973 paper, "Baptist Attitudes Toward Relations with Other Christians in Eastern Europe," makes interesting reading thirty years later. It underscores the reality that a changed political situation does not always mean improved ecumenical relations. Before World War II, Baptists had suffered psychological and sometimes physical persecution as "sectarians" at the hands of governments strongly influenced by Orthodox or Roman Catholic churches. Many Baptists actually found the communist regimes in some ways liberating, since former state churches lost their privileged positions, and smaller church groups were treated equally before the law. Working under the same restrictions drew Protestant groups together and eased relations with Catholics and Orthodox. In Poland and Yugoslavia Lotz found positive contacts between Baptists and Catholics. He observed that ecumenism, like evangelism, took place at the person to person level.

Other Christian international movements were touching Baptist life. The International Congress on World Evangelization convened in Lausanne, Switzerland, at the invitation of the Billy Graham Evangelistic Association in 1974, launched a fresh movement among evangelicals that encouraged holistic approaches to mission—tying evangelism and social concerns firmly together as gospel imperatives. As mentioned in previous chapters, some Baptist unions and conventions were members of the World Council of Churches (WCC), but others were suspicious of this body's social and political activity. Many Baptists welcomed the mission emphasis contained in the WCC's 1975 Nairobi Assembly report, "Confessing Christ Today," and in "Mission and Evangelism: An Ecumenical Affirmation," a paper that the WCC Commission on World Mission and Evangelism issued. Also encouraging was general secretary Philip Potter's declaration that "Evangelization is the test of the ecumenical vocation." Raymund Fung, a Baptist from Hong Kong, was the WCC staff member most closely involved in the preparation of the Mission and Evangelism document. The Faith and Order Commission's discussion of baptism attracted some Baptist attention, and that commission even held a consultation with Baptists in Louisville, Kentucky, in 1979.

Thirteenth Baptist World Congress, Stockholm 1975

Some 9,612 people from eighty-four nations, representing one hundred and six conventions and unions, gathered in Stockholm, Sweden, July 8–13, 1975, for the Thirteenth Baptist World Congress. The theme "New People for a New World—Through Christ" effectively continued the idea of the Mission of Reconciliation for another five years. Greetings were brought from ecclesiastical and state dignitaries, including Prime Minister Olof Palme (who would be tragically assassinated a decade later). Alma Hunt, the recently retired Southern Baptist Woman's Missionary Union executive secretary and a BWA Vice President, presided over some of the sessions.

Among the main speakers were Rüschlikon seminary's current president C. Penrose St. Amant, who talked about how Christians were really new people; prominent Los Angeles African-American pastor Edward V. Hill, who spoke of the joy of working for reconciliation; Japanese educator and Women's Department secretary Ayako Hino, who explained that the primary task of education is to integrate a person's character into that which Jesus Christ exemplified; Nlandu Mpanzu of Zaire (Congo), who explained the responsibilities of Christians from the west in missions to the Third World; Thomas Kilgore, Jr., of Los Angeles' Second Baptist Church, who addressed the matter of fellowship beyond the frontiers of race; and BWA Associate Secretary Goulding, who looked toward the new world promised by Christ. After four of the plenary addresses, panel discussions interacted with the speakers. Erling Oddestad, the president of the Baptist Union of Sweden, delivered the Congress Sermon on how Christ provides new power. Retiring BWA President Hargroves gave the keynote address on the conference theme, and the incoming President Wong laid out a series of seven priorities for the organization. The Congress concluded with an open air rally at Stockholm's Skansen Park, where Billy Graham preached to a crowd of thirty thousand.[33]

Since 1970, the number of member bodies had risen from eighty-nine to one hundred and six, possibly the largest five-year increase in the BWA's history. They included bodies from Kenya, Tanzania, Mozambique, Bolivia, Guyana, Rhodesia (now Zimbabwe), Central Africa, Bangladesh, Indonesia, the Bahamas, Singapore, the English-speaking European Baptist Convention, and two each from Malawi and Zaire. According to General Secretary Denny, the Baptist family had grown from six million in 1905 to thirty-four million located in 141 countries.[34]

While English remained the primary language at BWA meetings, in Stockholm simultaneous translation was provided in Swedish, German, Spanish, French, and Serbo–Croatian. English, German, and Swedish hymns were sung. Bible studies took place in seven languages in twenty-two small groups, with leaders from twenty nations. More than one hundred eighty people from fifty nations exercised some kind of leading role in this Congress.

At the time, the BWA, with a staff of five men and nine women, carried on a worldwide program with a budget of two hundred forty thousand dollars. Of this amount, 84 percent was given by member bodies, some of whom were very poor; individual supporters contributed 13 percent, and the remaining 3 percent came from other sources. The work of the 500 Club was continued and extended by the new "Friends of the Alliance." The BWA was financially solvent only "because we determined to hold to that pattern, even though many needed services have been deferred."[35] There were no funds, for example, to help Vice Presidents travel in order to keep in contact with Baptists within the regions they represented.

The appointment of two new Associate Secretaries was announced:

> # David Y. K. Wong
>
>
>
> The first layman and the first Asian to serve as President of the Baptist World Alliance was David Yue Kwong Wong. Wong was born in Wuzhou (Wuchow) in 1910 and lived in Guangshou (Canton) on the mainland of China until 1949, when he went to Hong Kong. He was an architectural engineer, semi-retired during the years of his presidency.
>
> Shortly after his election in 1975, Wong received permission to visit China for three weeks. He was the first Baptist official allowed in that country since the 1940s. For him it was a wonderful experience to return to those places he had once known so well. He visited schools, former church buildings, and in Guangshou the Christian cemetery. He was disappointed to fail in contacting former pastors and church leaders, but he did meet Christians. He noted, "People could tell I was an overseas Chinese back for a visit. I was received warmly."
>
> A warm and enthusiastic person himself, Wong delighted in visiting Baptists in various parts of the world. Prior to becoming President, Wong had served as chair of the Baptist World Alliance Men's Department and as president of the Asian Baptist Fellowship. The year after his visit to China, he went to the Soviet Union. He urged Baptists to work for peace.

Gerhard Claas of West Germany, who would replace Goulding as Secretary for Europe in September 1976, and Alan C. Prior of Australia, who offered to work without pay in a continuing effort to develop a spirit of fellowship within the Asian Baptist Federation (new name of Asian Baptist Fellowship). Patnaik resigned as Youth Secretary. The newly-elected President Wong of Hong Kong,[36] was an "optimist of shining faith," who had presided over the BWA Men's Department and the Asian Baptist Fellowship. The sixty-five-year-old architect was the Alliance's first Asian and first lay president. He retired from his job and spent most of his time in the BWA's service. During his term in office he visited over seventy countries.

Underwood of the Southern Baptist Foreign Mission Board, who, as mentioned earlier, directed the Mission of Reconciliation program initiated in Tokyo, summarized its achievements:

1. *A deepened commitment to evangelism in its total significance,* with forty-five countries giving special emphasis to training both lay and ordained for personal evangelism. There was a huge response, which was especially striking in Nigeria and Telugu, India.
2. *A great variety of ministries to serve people* with diverse and particular needs. The emphasis was on reconciling man with God and man with man. This effort generated a new sense of harmony between New Testament evangelism and loving service.
3. *A new and increased spirit of oneness in Christ.* The call to co-operative witness had revived interest in the BWA, giving a sense of family unity and greater sense of common purpose and direction.

4. *A greater recognition of Christian responsibility to personal involvement* in this continuing mission, which increased the service given.[37]

The eyewitness accounts of the needs faced in trying to provide relief and development were at times depressing, but the relief program achieved some success. Efforts included famine assistance in Nicaragua and the Sahel, and emergency aid in Honduras following a devastating hurricane. Other projects included irrigation and farming aid in Haiti, digging wells in India, and school construction in Liberia. Money for assisting pastors and providing medicines was earmarked for Eastern Europe. The main refugee needs were in Rwanda because of the renewed fighting between Tutsis and Hutus in neighboring Burundi.[38]

BWA officials had directed appeals to the governments in various countries where religious freedom was threatened, including the Soviet Union, Romania, Hungary, and Spain. Denny's stance was: "We plead for the freedom of our people; and we respectfully say that we think your laws are too strict regarding the exercise of religious rights."

> Perhaps the most important function of the BWA is its strong voice for religious liberty, freedom and dignity for all men. We Baptists, along with other believers, espouse the freedom of all people to propagate our faith....
>
> The laws of nations vary regarding the degree of freedom and the method of expressing religious convictions. Perhaps the most delicate operations conducted by your BWA staff are those of assessing these laws for the most effective way of negotiating and interceding for Christians under restrictive governments. Many times the obvious course may not be the best course. For example, a widely publicized resolution condemning certain governments may do more harm than good to the very people it was meant to help. When to proclaim or demonstrate and when to negotiate quietly is a sensitive judgement.[39]

A single Stockholm resolution covered many social concerns. The Alliance once again defined religious liberty, affirmed the U.N.'s Universal Declaration of Human Rights, and in those years of the cold war encouraged arms limitation, control of nuclear weapons, arbitration efforts, and the current détente (easing of tensions between the communist and noncommunist nations). The international body called on Baptists to launch a thrust for public morality; to work to eliminate arbitrary treatment on the basis of race, nationality, sex, or creed; and to work for improvements in information and entertainment from the mass media.[40]

Before the Congress, youth leaders met at Sjovik, Sweden, and developed a new constitution for the Youth Department. Karl Heinz Walter of Germany, who served as president of the department in 1970–75, gave direction in this effort. The most significant business of the Stockholm Congress, however, was a comprehensive renewal of the organizational structure that had functioned for seventy years of Alliance life.

Restructuring

The expanding Alliance was outgrowing its structure. The constitution claimed that "the BWA should have a global function," but for this globalization to happen the structure needed serious revamping. Running the BWA between the Congresses was the Executive Committee that met annually with an Administrative Committee whose members were chosen because of their easy access to Washington, D.C. Russell recalled the situation then:

> I had the impression that the BWA was largely run by an executive of very worthy Baptist leaders, mostly American, who enjoyed and encouraged the worldwide fellowship of Baptists which such gatherings provided, but [it] was quite inadequate if it were to function as an orderly and progressive body representing a worldwide force of Baptist witness, albeit diverse in its expression. The tendency had been to "run" the Alliance as we did our own Unions and Conventions "back home." A wider vision was needed and with it a greater sense of accountability and a more adequate structure to enable it to carry out clearly defined aims.[41]

Recognizing that this situation could not continue indefinitely if the Alliance were to grow and maintain an effective witness, a Committee on Structural Changes and Constitutional Revision was appointed at the 1970 Congress. It members were: Russell as chair, J. T. Ayorinde (Nigeria), F. J. Church (Australia), Warren R. Magnuson (Baptist General Conference, U.S.), T. B. McDormand (Canada), Azariah McKenzie (Jamaica), Jose das Reis Pereira (Brazil), Erik Rudén (Sweden), James L. Sullivan (SBC, U.S.), M. L. Wilson (Lott Carey Baptist Foreign Mission Convention, U.S.), and Wong. Russell commented on the difficulty of chairing such a scattered group:

> A small representative group was appointed to draw up a Constitution and I found myself appointed chairman and convenor! It was a thankless task, as such a group could not be called together very readily by reason of distance and expense. The outcome was that I was largely left on my own to put forward suggestions and carry on discussion by letter. In this I was greatly helped by a skilled lawyer, Mr. Fred Church of Sydney, Australia, with whom I shared draft after draft![42]

The process may have been cumbersome and quite troubling to a Baptist chairman who did not want to impose his thinking on the committee, but it ultimately resulted in:

> the creation of the General Council and the setting up of the four Divisions through which the Alliance was able, I believe, more effectively to carry out its defined tasks. . . . The General Council assumed greater responsibility and was able more effectively to do work which had hitherto been done by the Assembly which met only at lengthy intervals and the Executive which was necessarily limited in its powers. These developments went hand in hand with developments at the regional and international levels with the result that the work of the Alliance assumed greater cohesiveness, more clearly defined objectives and more adequate expression. The regions, I believe, had as a result a greater sense of belonging and assumed greater responsibility in the ordering of Alliance affairs. The changes came about at the right time and prepared the way for changes in the Christian world at large and within our own worldwide Baptist family.

> Several important areas were identified at the outset:

> 1. The creation or recognition of regional groups. The Alliance needed a strong regional structure and good liaison with the center. There were related questions about the Men's, Women's and Youth Departments.
> 2. The constitution needed clarification. The Administrative Committee should be more representative. Voting procedure and power at Congresses needed clear definition, "in such a way that no single Convention can control the machinery of the Congress." It was necessary to distinguish which of those present had the right to vote.
> 3. The Nominating Committee should be more representative and the process should begin earlier. The voting system should be fairer.[43]

Over the next years the committee reported annually to the Executive regarding progress made. The revisers finally met on July 7–8, 1975, gave formal notice on July 9 that constitutional amendments were going to be presented, and brought their recommendations to the Congress on July 10. These recommendations consisted of fourteen amendments, detailed in a booklet, to be taken seriatim but moved as one "since they hang together." Russell, "the architect of the new BWA constitution and bylaws," presented them at Stockholm "with much elegance and clearness," explaining their nature and purpose.[44] Although there were "alterations in expression and terminology" and the objectives were set out differently, the proposal remained true to the original spirit and intention of the constitution. The most important changes were that the Executive Committee would become the General Council and that the

Administrative Committee would be renamed the Executive Committee.

> More important is the proposed recognition of regional fellowships or federations (four of which exist already) "through which the Alliance shall operate" and whose "constitution and organizational status" shall have been approved by the General Council. It is proposed that the Alliance shall provide service to these regional fellowships through Area Secretaries. . . . Recognition of additional regional fellowships is possible and is authorized. It is confidently hoped that such regional fellowships will serve as channels for Alliance operations in a number of ways and not least in matters relating to Relief and Development and to Research and Studies (with particular reference to the Study Commissions which, it is hoped, will be organized on a regional basis and be integrated with the Alliance Commissions).[45]

The BWA would give recognition to the regional bodies (they would cover Europe, Africa, the Middle East, Asia and Oceania, the Americas, and the Caribbean), approve their constitutions and structures, and provide service through the secretariat.

> Alterations are recommended, too, in representation on certain committees and in the process of nomination and election of officers. For example, membership of the Administrative Committee is no longer limited to people living within easy reach of Washington as hitherto. Where the election of officers is concerned, it is proposed that the new General Council shall serve as a Nominating Committee in this connection, nominations being announced preferably in the year preceding the congress. Provision is made for other nominations to be received from messengers or delegates.[46]

To the existing divisions of Relief and Development, Study and Research, and Communications was added a fourth: Evangelism and Education. "The need for such a division became evident as a result of the success of the World Mission of Reconciliation through Jesus Christ." the program required "a worldwide committee" and implied "that Secretariat time will be apportioned to provide continuing attention to the subject." Another new committee would coordinate Study and Research, relating to the study commissions but also guiding staff studies. The Revision Committee also sought, through detailed bylaws, to bring the departments into closer relationship with the Alliance. There were financial implications involved in all of these changes—staffing the new division; supporting the enlarged Executive Committee; and providing for regional staff, committees, and commissions. Carefully husbanding limited resources, the Executive Committee at Louisville in 1974, approving the proposed changes, had added "as necessary funds available."

The seven objectives defined in the 1947 revision of the constitution as

"Nature and Functions" were revised to become nine "Objectives":

> Serving as the nerve center and corporate will of Baptists throughout the world, the Alliance shall:
>
> 1. Promote Christian fellowship among Baptists throughout the world.
> 2. Promote understanding and unity among Baptists and with fellow Christians.
> 3. Assist member bodies in making known the Christian Gospel according to the Scriptures and seeking the evangelization of all peoples.
> 4. Act as an agency for the expression of distinctive Baptist principles and practices.
> 5. Act as an agency of reconciliation with a view to the establishment of peace among all men.
> 6. Act to further uphold for all people the claims of fundamental human rights and to further and maintain full religious liberty everywhere, both for our constituent churches and all other religious faiths.
> 7. Cooperate with Baptists and others in expressing social concern and in alleviating human need.
> 8. Act as an agency for cooperation in mission: (a) by informing its member bodies concerning new forms and spheres of work and witness, and (b) by the use of Baptist World publications and other forms of communication.
> 9. Serve as an agency through which member bodies may voluntarily cooperate in matters of common concern.[47]

The amendments passed easily, and the President, General Secretary, and General Council were authorized to implement the restructuring as funds permitted. The new General Council was constituted on July 12, 1975.

BWA Activity, 1975–80

Russell, who had devoted so much effort to restructuring the BWA, was a champion of human rights. He pursued the same concerns about persecution and torture through BWA and EBF channels and through the British and World Councils of Churches. The BWA, EBF, and the Soviet Union's All-Union Council of Evangelical Christians–Baptists (AUCECB) repeatedly interceded for Georgi P. Vins and others who refused to register their churches with authorities of the Soviet Union, a demand to which the AUCECB itself had submitted. Vins, a leader of the separate Baptist "Initiative Group" was eventually released from prison and internal exile in April 1979 and sent to the United States in exchange for captured Soviet spies.

There were some hopeful signs from Eastern Europe. Billy Graham was well received in Hungary and Poland. To commemorate the four hundredth anniversary of the appearance of the Kralice Bible, the Czechoslovakian authorities granted permission to print one hundred and twenty thousand Bibles if Christians could obtain paper from external sources. In Russia circulation of *Bratski Vestnik,* an eighty-page Baptist periodical, rose steeply. The fifteen hundred delegates to the 1979 EBF Congress in Brighton, England, included groups from Romania and Poland. Every European country was represented except closed Albania and Bulgaria, whose delegates were refused permission to travel.

That same year churches reopened in Shanghai, Beijing, and Amoy, China. In 1978, however, Israel passed an Anti-Missionary Law, making it a criminal offense to encourage a change of religion, punishable by fines or imprisonment. The BWA observed soberly that "even a simple act of kindness may be construed as a benefit." Argentina's military government decreed that all religions except Roman Catholicism must register or be banned. And in Nicaragua civil war brought severe economic dislocation, resulting in calls upon Alliance relief. The Relief and Development Division also took part in the immunization campaign to mark the U.N.'s Year of the Child, 1979.

The Study and Research Division ran four study commissions in the 1975–80 period: Church Life; Christian Ethics; Freedom, Justice, and Peace; and Doctrine and Interchurch Cooperation. Noting an increased willingness to discuss issues, the division claimed to deal "at the world level, with the command 'Always be prepared to make a defense to anyone who calls you to account for the hope that is in you.' " In 1978, the commissions on Doctrine and Inter-Church Cooperation and on Freedom, Justice, and Peace jointly issued a cautionary "Summary Statement and Guidelines on the Charismatic Movement." Under the leadership of Doctrine and Interchurch Cooperation, the BWA conducted a four-year program of conversations with the World Alliance of Reformed Churches (1973–77). In 1975, the BWA began corresponding with the Lutheran World Federation about a possible dialogue, but the actual conversations did not take place until the next decade. Each commission sponsored two open sessions at the Congress in Toronto; attendance was reported to be "phenomenal."[48]

Both the 1977 and 1979 General Council meetings focused attention on younger churches, with open sessions arranged by Study and Research assisted by the IMSC. The Council sought ways for older and younger churches to work together, "rising above cultural limitations and the tendency toward a paternal relationship."[49] Delegates reaffirmed the principle of equality of standing among all member bodies and asked the BWA officers to implement suggestions to improve the responsible participation of the younger churches, including consideration of financial aid.

The first Asian Baptist Federation congress took place in 1979. An estimated sixty-five thousand Baptists in Burma (now Myanmar) met for the four-day Kachin Centenary, culminating in a baptismal service in which one hundred pastors baptized 6,215 believers in the Irrawaddy River. In 1978 the Men's Department held its Second World Conference in Indianapolis, Indiana, while the women had conferences in every region. The European Baptist Women's Union now embraced the Middle East and North Africa. Both the Women's and Men's departments sponsored their own sessions immediately before the Toronto Congress. The Youth Department, whose president from 1975–80 was Daltro Keidann of Brazil, held its Ninth Baptist World Youth Conference in Manila in July 1978, where fifteen hundred delegates from thirty-four nations celebrated "Jesus Christ—the One Light for All People."

There were further changes in personnel: Betty Lee Smith of Virginia, who had been a clerical staff person in the office for ten years, was in 1976 appointed as an Assistant Secretary with responsibility for youth and conferences. Goulding, who transferred to the Washington, D.C. office in 1976 after relinquishing his post as Associate Secretary for Europe, was responsible as Associate Secretary for the two divisions of Evangelism and Education and of Relief and Development. He retired in 1980. Claas, general secretary of the Baptist Union of West Germany, had assumed the position of Associate Secretary for Europe and moved the European office to Hamburg. When Tiller retired in 1978, Charles F. Wills of the American Baptist staff was named Associate Secretary for Study and Research and the NABF. He served two years.

In Brighton, England in 1979, following the report of a Long-Range Planning Committee, the General Council approved forty goals, with both five-year and twenty-year strategies for attaining them. Specific propositions included a millennium emphasis, centenary celebrations in 2005, doubling endowments by 1990, maintaining the headquarters in or near Washington, D.C., holding regular conferences at five-year intervals, increasing study and cooperation with other Christian bodies, and accelerating communications.[50]

Further Structural Revision

At the Diamond Jubilee Congress in Toronto in 1980, there was further adjustment to the constitution and structures. The election of the General Secretary was moved from the Congress to the General Council, and Associate Secretaries would no longer hold General Council membership. Gender-neutral language was coming in. For example, "brotherhood" was changed to "fellowship" in the preamble to the constitution. The 1975 bylaws were expanded, spelling out the duties of the President, Vice Presidents, and the divisions.

The revision committee, chaired by Duke K. McCall, consolidated the nine objectives in the constitution to eight and reworded them to some extent. The opening clause became "Under the guidance of the Holy Spirit, the objectives of the Baptist World Alliance are . . . ." The second and third clauses were inverted, the second now reading "Bear witness to the gospel of Jesus Christ and assist unions and conventions in their divine task of bringing all people to God through Jesus Christ as Savior and Lord." The fourth was expanded to ". . . expression of biblical faith and historically distinctive Baptist principles and practices." The old fifth and sixth were amalgamated to read "act as an agency of reconciliation seeking peace for all persons, and uphold the claims of fundamental human rights, including full religious liberty." The eighth and ninth were combined as number seven: "Serve in cooperation with member bodies as a resource for the development of plans for evangelism, education, church growth, and other forms of mission." The new eighth dealt with communication "through all possible media."[51]

The Alliance in membership and structure had substantially become a global body. Although North America still dominated because of the large numbers of Baptists there and their greater wealth and ability to travel to meetings, the new structures encouraged wider participation, especially through the regional fellowships.

---

1. *BWA Congress,* 1970, pp. 15–77.

2. Ibid., pp. 127–130, 395–396.

3. Ibid., p. 267; Carl W. Tiller, *The Twentieth Century Baptist* (Valley Forge: Judson Press, 1980), pp. 14–3, 4.

4. *BWA Congress,* 1970, pp. 187–192.

5. Ibid., p. 268.

6. Ibid., p. 418.

7. Tiller, *Twentieth Century Baptist,* p. 15–1.

8. BWA Executive Committee (EC), August 2–6, 1971, pp. 24-25. Minutes in Archives 2d3, Angus Library, Regent's Park College.

9. Tiller, *Twentieth Century Baptist,* p. 14–2, 3.

10. *BWA Congress,* 1970, pp. 248–250.

11. Ibid., pp. 251–254.

12. Ibid., pp. 411, 415.

13. Ibid., pp. 411–515.

14. Duke McCall, *An Oral History* (Nashville: Baptist History and Heritage Society, 2001), pp. 354–357.

15. Article X. Officers. *BWA Congress,* 1975, p. 295.

16. Hargroves's Baptist World Alliance correspondence 1956–80 is in the American Baptist Historical Society Manuscript Collection at the American Baptist–Samuel Colgate Historical Library in Rochester, New York.

17. *BWA Congress,* 1970, pp. 206–237.

18. EC, August 2–6, 1971. Minutes in Archive 2d3, Angus Library, Regent's Park College, Oxford.

19. V. Carney Hargroves, quoted in ibid.

20. Knud Wümpelmann suggested this initiative at the 1973 Executive meeting in Einsiedeln, Switzerland. As chair of the Danish Baptist Foreign Mission Committee he had seen the value of "an ecumenical Scandinavian Congo Committee where secretaries from the various mission societies and committees could exchange experiences and challenges. During the Executive Committee meeting, I felt that it might be helpful if under the umbrella of the Baptist World Alliance, we could have a similar set-up, so I shared this idea with the General Secretary, Bob Denny, in a handwritten note, and the following year the IMSC was established, which among its activities got a Missionary Personnel Exchange Program." Letter to Faith Bowers, June 28, 2000. See also Tiller, *Twentieth Century Baptist,* p. 15–3.

21. Hargroves, 'The Phenomenon of the Baptist World Alliance,' *Foundations* 17(January–March 1974), p.4.

22. Tiller, *Twentieth Century Baptist,* p. 15–4.

23. Knud Wümpelmann to Faith Bowers, June 28, 2000.

24. Robert S. Denny, "Report of the General Secretary," *BWA Congress,* 1975, pp. 115–118. Denny was accompanied by David S. Russell (U.K.), Gerhard Claas (West Germany), Andrew MacRae (Scotland), Knud Wümpelmann (Denmark), and Jose Goncalves (Portugal).

25. A box of Baptist World Alliance materials in the Angus Library, Oxford, contains many commission papers, mainly from the early 1970s and not all clearly named or dated. A more complete collection is in the Baptist World Alliance archives at the American Baptist Archive Center in Valley Forge. Several of the commission papers were eventually published in a variety of places or incorporated into larger works, but this treasure trove of Baptist scholarship remains largely unexplored and underutilized.

26. Other Doctrine papers that year were: John P. Newport, "Biblical Language and Religious Authority"; Elmer Leslie Gray, "Sources of Revelation"; Millard J. Erickson, "Scepticism, Subjectivism, Nihilism, and the Crisis of Religious Authority"; and R. F. Aldwinckle, "Does It Matter What a Man Believes?" (His answer was "Yes.")

27. A. S. Clement, "The Church's Mission and Message in Reconciliation through Christ:

Some Problems of Unreconciled Relations"; David Gomes, "Global Preparation for Global Reconciliation in Christ"; Chester J. Jump, Jr., "Priorities for the Seventies"; John W. Wims, "Missions and Evangelism"; and Francis M. DuBose, "Evangelization and Reconciliation: The Mission of the Church."

28. Papers by two Australians: G. Noel Vose, "Teaching and Training for Reconciliation", and John H. Knights, "Claiming the Future through Teaching and Training", and "Education and the Church's Reconciling Mission."

29. Jarold K. Zeman, "Baptists in Canada and Cooperative Christianity" in 1971. Later papers deal with "Baptist Attitudes Toward and Relating with Other Christians: Negro Conventions U.S.A."; "Ecclesiology and Ecumenicity in Israel"; "The American Baptist Convention's Attitudes Toward and Relations with Other Christians"; and "Liturgical Issues in Anglican-United Church Discussions."

30. Thomas B. McDormand, "An Historical Survey of the Baptist Use of Power (Including the Magistracy)"; E. A. Payne, "British Baptists, Participation in Politics, and the Use of Power"; and James E. Wood, Jr., "A Theology of Power."

31. Dale Moody, "Authority and the Holy Spirit"; Nils J. Engelsen, "Spiritual Gifts with Special Reference to Tongues"; John H. Boyle, "The Authority of Christian Experience within the Christian Community"; G. R. Beasley-Murray, "The Authority of Scripture"; and G. Noel Vose, "Authority and the Church."

32. Wümpelmann to Bowers, June 28, 2000. The Catholic theologian was Raymond O. Ryland.

33. The texts of the sermons are in *BWA Congress,* 1975, pp. 43–112.

34. Ibid., p. 115.

35. Ibid., pp. 118–119.

36. Wong's Baptist World Alliance correspondence and related items are in the American Baptist Historical Society Manuscript Collection.

37. *BWA Congress,* 1975, p. 127.

38. Ibid., pp. 140–152.

39. Ibid., pp. 115

40. Ibid., pp. 255–259.

41. Letter from David S. Russell to Faith Bowers, June 14, 2000.

42. Ibid.

43. Ibid.

44. Wümpelmann to Bowers, June 28, 2000.

45. Russell, "Revision of the Constitution," *BWA Congress,* 1975, pp. 263–264.

46. Ibid.

47. "The Constitution of the Baptist World Alliance," *BWA Congress,* 1975, p. 292.

48. *BWA Congress,* 1980, p. 135.
49. Tiller, *Twentieth Century Baptist,* p. 16–2.
50. *BWA Congress,* 1980, pp. 148–153.
51. Ibid., pp. 238–239; 283–284.

8

PRO-EXISTENCE NOT CO-EXISTENCE: THE BAPTIST WORLD ALLIANCE IN THE 1980s
Ian M. Randall

The 1980s began well for the Baptist World Alliance (BWA). The organizational restructuring during the previous decade had placed it on a firmer footing. In spite of the significant numerical dominance of British and North American Baptists, the BWA had become a truly international body. Continental European and non-western Baptists now occupied places of leadership, and two Congresses had taken place in countries outside of the BWA's European–North American axis. More and more unions and conventions in Africa, Asia, and Latin America were being received into membership. An excellent corps of leaders enabled the BWA to exercise effective stewardship of its limited financial resources.

Fourteenth Baptist World Congress, Toronto 1980
A total of 20,275 people from ninety-three countries registered for the Fourteenth Baptist World Congress in Toronto, Canada, July 8–13, 1980. The attendance at this assembly marking the seventy-fifth anniversary of the founding of the BWA surpassed previous records. Actually, only twelve thousand had been expected. The plenary sessions were held in Maple Leaf Gardens, a large sports arena. Nearly every hotel in Toronto was utilized, and many participants stayed in the homes of Canadian Baptists. The theme of the Congress was "Celebrating Christ's Presence through the Spirit," and there was a strong sense of the BWA's achievements throughout the world. As had been the case at every Congress since 1955, Billy Graham was the closing speaker.

Duke K. McCall was elected the new president. A member of the BWA General Council (formerly the Executive Committee) since 1947, he decided to retire at the beginning of 1982 from his position as president of the Southern Baptist Theological Seminary in Louisville, Kentucky, so that he could devote full time to the work of the Alliance. He also had served a term as the Southern Baptist Convention (SBC) president. McCall recalled

Acting General Secretary Robert S. Denny *(left)* conferred with Shuichi Matsamura, a Vice President of the Baptist World Alliance and pastor of Tokiwadai Baptist Church in Tokyo, and his wife about the upcoming 1970 Congress to be held in Tokyo. (1969)

Baptists from seventy-eight countries met in the Budokan auditorium in Tokyo for their first World Congress in Asia. (1970)

Gifts from Baptists around the world through Baptist World Relief (now Baptist World Aid) provided stone homes to flood-wrecked communities in India. (1971)

Two wells developed by the Samavesam of the Telugu Baptist Churches were dedicated by the governor of Andhra Pradesh, India, April 9, 1972. The well above was named for Associate Secretary for Relief Frank H. Woyke; the other was named for Joseph I. Chapman, executive minister of the Ohio Baptist Convention (U.S.). Funds for the pumpsets and overhead reservoirs came from Baptist World Relief and the Ohio Baptist Convention.

David Y. K. Wong presided at the First World Conference for Baptist Men in Hong Kong in 1974. Wong, then President of the Baptist World Alliance Men's Department, would be elected Baptist World Alliance President at the 1975 Congress.

Leaders of the International Mission Secretaries Conference (now International Mission Secretaries, an organization formed in 1974 and affiliated with the Baptist World Alliance) met with Associate Secretary Carl W. Tiller in 1975. In the photo are (left to right): J. D. Williams (Australia); A. S. Clement (United Kingdom); Tiller; Sven Ohm (Sweden); and Winston Crawley (Southern Baptist Convention).

Some 9,612 people from eighty-four nations enjoyed the northern sunshine in outdoor sessions during the 1975 Congress in Stockholm, Sweden.

Baptist World Alliance 199

Spontaneous gatherings, such as this at the 1975 Congress, bring Baptists together. People living on opposite sides of the world discover they share a common commitment to Jesus Christ.

General Secretary Robert S. Denny and his wife and outgoing President V. Carney Hargroves and his wife sat in the audience for at least one session of the 1975 Congress.

(Left to right) Baptist World Alliance Vice President Advertus A. Hoff of Liberia spoke with his fellow Vice President, Arthur Kinyanjui of Kenya, and Associate Secretary C. Ronald Goulding. (1978)

U.S. President Jimmy Carter, a Baptist, addressed the 1980 Congress in Toronto, Canada. He would also address the 1985 Congress, and in 1995 he was the first recipient of the Baptist World Alliance Human Rights Award.

Latin American women were among the non-English-speaking delegates who listened to speakers at the 1980 Congress in Toronto through earphones that provided simultaneous translation.

More than twenty thousand people from ninety-three countries gathered in Toronto for the 1980 Congress. Most of them seem to have been at the World Fellowship Celebration at the exhibition center on the shore of Lake Ontario.

Edwin I. Lopez of the Philippines *(right)*, Baptist World Alliance Regional Secretary for Asia, and fellow countryman Johnnie de la Fuente at the 1981 General Council meeting in Puerto Rico.

Baptist World Alliance President Duke K. McCall *(center)*, and former General Secretary Robert S. Denny *(right)* talked with Michael Zhidkov of the Soviet Union at the 1981 General Council meeting. Zhidkov was a Vice President.

These were five of the sixteen students at the Buckow seminary in 1981—all of whom combine theological studies with volunteer labor to renovate the facilities. Buckow seminary was established by the East German Baptists, and since German reunification, it has become part of the new German Baptist seminary in Elstal.

Regional Secretary for Europe Knud Wümpelmann *(left)* and General Secretary Gerhard Claas enjoyed a presentation at the 1982 Soviet-sponsored conference of people of faith for the protection of life from nuclear catastrophe. Billy Graham was a featured speaker.

Singers entertained delegates and guests at the 1982 General Council meeting in Nairobi, Kenya.

Heads bowed in prayer at a rally during the council meeting in Nairobi. (1982)

Samuel Libert *(left)* of Argentina accepted congratulations from Bob Taylor (Southern Baptist Convention), president of the Youth Department, and Bernard Green *(right)*, general secretary of the British Baptist Union, after the Council, at its 1982 meeting, refused to move—without further study—the proposed Baptist World Youth Conference from Argentina to the United States. The youth event took place in Buenos Aires in 1984.

The Third World Conference of Baptist Men took place in Nairobi, Kenya, in July 1982.

Latin American theological educators gathered in Buenos Aires, Argentina, in June 1983. Regional conferences, such as this one sponsored by Baptist World Alliance, enabled educators to relate theology to their own context.

(Left to right) Tomas Mackey of Argentina, Associate Secretary for Youth Denton Lotz, Beverly Sutton of the Southern Baptist Convention, Raoul Scialabba of Argentina, and Associate Youth Director Samson S. K. Mathangani of Kenya made plans for the 1984 Baptist Youth World Conference in Buenos Aires.

Regional Secretaries met together at the Executive Committee meeting in March 1987 *(left to right)*: Azariah McKenzie of Jamaica (Caribbean); Knud Wümpelmann of Denmark (Europe); Samuel T. Ola. Akande of Nigeria (Africa); Edwin I. Lopez of the Philippines (Asia); Archibald R. Goldie of Canada (North America); and José Missena of Paraguay (Latin America). Goldie served as Regional Secretary as part of his duties as a Baptist World Alliance Associate Secretary.

Effective 1980s Baptist World Alliance leaders were Floyd Harris (Southern Baptist Convention), president of the Men's Department, and Edna Lee de Gutiérrez (Mexico), president of the Women's Department. (1987)

Singapore hosted the Asian Youth Leadership Conference of the Baptist World Alliance in June 1986.

Asbjorn Bakkevoll of Norway *(third from left)*, chair of the program committee, met in Glasgow, Scotland, with *(left to right)* British Baptist Union Youth leader Paul Montacute, Douglas Inglis of Scotland, and General Secretary Gerhard Claas to make plans for the 1988 Baptist Youth World Conference.

More than seven thousand young people from eighty-four countries gathered in Glasgow, Scotland, in the summer of 1988 for the Eleventh Baptist Youth World Conference.

> ## Duke Kimbrough McCall
>
>
> Duke Kimbrough McCall, Baptist World Alliance President from 1980 to 1985, first experienced the fellowship offered through the Baptist World Alliance at the Youth Conference in Prague in 1931 when he was sixteen. Born in Mississippi in 1914, he grew up in Memphis, Tennessee, where his father was a lawyer. His mother wanted him to be a preacher, but he felt no call until a fellow student at Southern Seminary gave him the opportunity to preach at the Sunday night service in a small rural church.
> While working on his doctoral dissertation at Southern, McCall pastored one of Kentucky's most prestigious churches, Broadway in Louisville—one faced with many challenges. In 1940, he accepted the presidency of the Baptist Bible Institute and led in its transformation to New Orleans Theological Seminary. From 1946 until 1951 McCall served as executive secretary of the Southern Baptist Executive Committee.
> That position entitled him to be one of the Southern Baptist Convention's delegates to the Baptist World Alliance, and at the 1947 Congress he was elected to the Baptist World Alliance's Executive Committee. He admired Baptist World Alliance President C. Oscar Johnson, helped him raise funds for the Baptist World Alliance's first office in Washington, D.C., and traveled with him overseas. McCall chaired the program committee that planned the London Congress in 1955.
> By 1955 he was president of Southern Seminary, and he remained there until he retired in 1982. He also remained active in the Alliance, but his nomination as President surprised him. As President his goals included new offices, a larger staff, better funding, and broader participation in decision-making. He wanted third-world voices to be heard.
> In December 2004 McCall called a meeting of Southern Baptists who declared, " We serve the Baptist World Alliance . . . because it has inspired and instructed world Baptists in their intention to be Biblical Christian witnesses to our Saviour Jesus Christ."

that his first contact with the BWA was in 1931 when as a sixteen-year-old he traveled to the first Baptist Youth World Conference in Prague, Czechoslovakia (Czech Republic). Commenting on the many different nationalities present there, McCall said: "For the first time, this provincial southern boy saw the love of Christ at work in a way he'd never seen before." Since then, inspired by the example of J. H. Rushbrooke, he seized every opportunity during his life to serve the Baptist world.[1]

The dominating feature of the new decade was the increasing opportunities for witness and service, and significant new developments reflected the BWA's maturing. These included: the continuing internationalization of the BWA; a stress on the strategic roles of the Alliance staff and of the divisions; and fresh initiatives in the areas of evangelism and education, human rights, conversations with other churches, and relief and development. The worldwide Baptist family generated, nurtured, and carried through work in all of these areas.

At the same time, leadership by the Alliance staff was vital. The key person here was Gerhard Claas, who became General Secretary in 1980 upon the retirement of Robert S. Denny. He served until his tragic death eight years later. Claas's wide experience included service as an Associate Secretary of the Alliance, secretary-treasurer of the European Baptist Federation, and pastoral and administrative posts in the West German Baptist Union. At the Toronto Congress, Claas appealed for Baptists to move beyond "peaceful co-existence," a common phrase at the time in international relations, to "pro-existence"—a "real relationship of serving each other."[2] This call was the vision that would give direction to the Alliance's ministry during the decade.

The Process of Internationalization

For mutual service to take place, the Alliance had to continue the process of internationalization. The Toronto Congress had a roll call of nations, with a parade of flags, and speakers at plenary sessions who came from Africa, Asia, Europe, North America, South America, and the South Pacific region. The Kentucky Baptist newspaper noted that there was disagreement as well as agreement in the meetings but "not one indication that one suspected another of heresy or that one wanted to impose his position on another."[3]

Although the story of the BWA in the 1980s was not as straightforward as that, the evidence was that Baptists could work together. In the new BWA secretariat—now made up of eight people—the General Council wanted a "multi-cultural, multi-lingual staff if at all possible." The Personnel Committee believed this diversity had been achieved.[4] Claas took up his position as General Secretary and moved from Germany to Washington, D. C., in September 1980. He was known as an evangelist, a campaigner for human rights, a skilled negotiator with governments, and someone who could associate with church leaders of many traditions.

Others in the team were to play important roles. Although Associate Secretary Charles F. Wills retired at the end of the year, Ruby J. Burke (since 1978 an aide to two of the directors) and Betty Lee Smith (Assistant Secretary for Conferences) continued in place. Cyril E. Bryant relinquished his post as Director of Communications but stayed on as an administrative assistant to the general secretary until his 1982 retirement. The two most significant new appointments were those of Denton Lotz and Reinhold J. Kerstan. The youthful Lotz was named Associate Secretary, with responsibilities for the divisions of Evangelism and Education and of Relief and Development, and one of his first actions was to rename the relief program as Baptist World Aid, often shortened to BWAid. A graduate of the University of North Carolina, Harvard Divinity School, and Hamburg University (where he studied missions and ecumenics), Lotz had spent the previous fifteen years in Europe, much of the time as an American Baptist missionary and fraternal worker. He also taught at the Baptist Theological Seminary, Rüschlikon, Switzerland. The German-born Kerstan, a trained historian, had been director of communications for the North American Baptist Conference, and his BWA position was Associate Secretary for Communications and Study and Research. Erna Redlich, a Canadian already employed by the BWA, was named as Assistant Secretary in Relief and Development. Two Regional Secretaries were chosen: Edwin I. Lopez, general secretary of the Convention of Philippine Baptist Churches, became Secretary for Asia; and Knud Wümpelmann, general secretary of the Baptist Union of Denmark, became secretary for Europe along with serving as general secretary of the European Baptist Federation (EBF).

For those from different regions of the world to play a full part in BWA deliberations, consideration had to be given to travel assistance. The twelve Vice Presidents, named to work alongside McCall, came from ten countries, including Brazil, Burma (Myanmar), India, Mexico, South Africa, and Zaire (Congo). In his report to the General Council meeting at San Juan, Puerto Rico, in 1981, the President said that he wanted "to provide appropriate travel funds to facilitate the widest possible representation on committees and commissions." He claimed that the development of the regional offices represented "the most important new development in BWA life for the last half-century." He believed that Baptists had "yet to explore fully the concept of the church as the body of Christ encompassing the world." More global participation was needed. There was, he suggested, "a certain provincialism not only in our loyalties but also in our knowledge." McCall was not pointing the finger at others. Speaking very personally, he said: "I call upon my fellow members of the General Council to help me and come grow with me to be, in fact, a Baptist ambassador for Christ in the whole world."[5]

McCall took up his own challenge. He launched out to visit Baptists in Romania and the Soviet Union. He also acted as a Baptist representative in wider conferences, including a three-day peace conference in Moscow in May 1982. There the five hundred and fifty participants considered the subject "Religious Workers for Saving the Sacred Gift of Life from Nuclear Catastrophe."

At the 1983 General Council meeting in Buenos Aires, McCall reflected on the fellowship of the BWA. He did so in the light of the death of his wife on Easter Sunday 1983, and he described the BWA as "a fellowship which binds the strength of some to the needs of others." Again he stressed internationalism. By this time the Caribbean Baptist Fellowship had a full-time Secretary, Azariah McKenzie of Jamaica. The All Africa Baptist

Fellowship had formed in 1982 with Samuel T. Ola Akande as its Secretary, and the Union of Baptists in Latin America (originally founded in 1983 as the Baptist Union of South America) decided to become a regional body of the BWA. McCall argued that the regional leadership was radically altering the ethos and style of the BWA and that by its very nature the BWA could not be paternalistic. For him this internationalization meant everyone was working together. His hope was that BWA programs of action, as well as fellowship, would continue.[6]

Action was evident. The first assembly of the All Africa Baptist Fellowship convened in Harare, Zimbabwe, January 17–22, 1984. There were 136 registered delegates and observers from nine African countries, and among the items discussed was the urgent need for food in Ethiopia. The July 1984 BWA General Council session in West Berlin attracted more than four hundred and fifty people from nearly eighty countries, a record attendance. Main meetings were held in the ultramodern International Center, which the Berlin authorities provided free of charge. Worship took place in Baptist churches in both East and West Berlin.[7] There McCall reported on a visit he had made to Asia, where he found that sharing in leadership was a key element for the growing Baptist movements in the region.[8] New Baptist voices were definitely being heard. In fact, José Missena, Secretary for the Union of Baptists in Latin America, said that he hoped the next leader of the Alliance would come from the Third World. He then proposed the name of Nilson do Amaral Fanini of Brazil, since there had not been a president from Latin America since 1960.[9] His wish would be fulfilled a decade later.

At the 1985 General Council, which took place at the time of the World Congress in Los Angeles, the issue of wider representation came up again. The main concern was how to bring about greater international representation at Council meetings. It was agreed that the Executive Committee (formerly Administrative Committee)—a body that, in terms of attendance, was weighted towards North Americans—would consider the matter more closely at its meeting the following March. President McCall reiterated the argument he had put forward in 1981, that the only way to achieve this diversity would be through funding travel scholarships. The Executive voted to use 1 percent of BWAid money for this purpose.[10]

But internationalization was still problematic. During the 1986 Council in Singapore, at which about three hundred attended, unhappiness was voiced about holding meetings in expensive hotels. Although in 1984 the Council had agreed to choose venues that would accommodate everyone, it was noted that those from the west, particularly from the United States, were accustomed to and could afford first-class hotel accommodations. Those from elsewhere could not. The result was that the 1987 Council meeting took place in Jordan, at Amman's modern Royal Cultural Center; 1988 in Nassau, Bahamas; and 1989 in Zagreb, Yugoslavia. These cities and the hotels chosen had more moderate prices.

Secretariat and Commissions

Without the dedicated work of the BWA's secretariat, the more public international endeavors of the Alliance in the 1980s would not have been possible. Claas was central to what took place in this period. He gave evangelism a high profile. Wherever in the world he preached, people welcomed his clear evangelistic message. He was also keenly aware of the needs in the poorer parts of the world, and his reports to the BWA staff after returning from overseas visits were always marked by the desire to accomplish more for needy people. He was a gifted communicator in a variety of settings, speaking effectively to small and large groups alike. Recognizing the importance of this aspect of the ministry, he elevated the communication operation to BWA division status in 1985, with John Wilkes as Director.

The contribution of Claas, with his ability to cross over cultural boundaries, was widely recognized as crucial to international BWA communications. He was greatly valued, too, on account of his character. His death on March 21, 1988, from injuries sustained in an automobile accident near Lodi, California, was a severe loss to the Alliance. As G. Noel Vose (the 1985–90 President) pointed out, Claas was a shepherd, a preacher who communicated to people of all cultures, an evangelist, and a statesman.[11]

Yet the work of the secretariat did not focus on one person. Teamwork was the key to the wide-ranging activity of the divisions and departments, which sponsored many conferences during the decade in various parts of the world. As will be discussed later, the BWA's Relief and Development work was growing fast. Lotz relinquished responsibility for this aspect of the BWA ministry and concentrated on supervising the Evangelism and Education Division and the Youth Department. Replacing him was Archibald (Archie) R. Goldie, secretary of the North American Baptist Fellowship and chair of the Relief and Development committee, who was named Associate Secretary for Relief and Development. Redlich remained Assistant Secretary. In order to strengthen the Youth Department, Samson S. K. Mathangani of Kenya was appointed its Associate Director. He was involved in youth leadership training and helped organize the Tenth Baptist Youth World Conference, held in Argentina in 1984. In the

Alliance's Women's Department, Kerstin (Mrs. Erik) Rudén from Sweden served as president; in 1982 June Totten, an ordained American Baptist minister, was employed as its first full-time executive secretary (later renamed executive director). The 1984 General Council meeting underscored the crucial place of women in the Baptist family: "While we acknowledge that there are strong cultural and theological differences about the role of women in the church, we wish to affirm the teaching of Galatians 3:28 that in Christ, male and female are equal."[12]

The Alliance's commissions, subsumed under the Division of Study and Research, were also active and influential. The four commissions of the previous quinquennium were converted into five. Church Life was divided into two: Ministry of the Laity and Pastoral Leadership, and Freedom, Justice, and Peace was renamed Human Rights. For the period 1981–85 the chairs were: Christian Ethics, James M. Dunn (SBC); Doctrine and Interchurch Cooperation, Vose (Australia); Human Rights, Pearl L. McNeil (American Baptist Churches [ABC]); Ministry of the Laity, George W. Peck (ABC); and Pastoral Leadership, William E. Hull (SBC). At the 1985 Baptist World Congress in Los Angeles, commission reports were submitted under the heading "Baptist Identity in Global Perspective." Although the leadership of the commissions was almost entirely American, membership was broad.[13]

In the 1986–1990 quinquennium, the leaders of these five commissions were: Cora Sparrowk (ABC), Russell Dilday (SBC), Thorwald Lorenzen

Gerhard Claas

Gerhard Claas, General Secretary of the Baptist World Alliance from 1980 to 1988, was born in 1928 in a unique place in Germany. His native community of Volmarstein in the Ruhr valley had neither a Lutheran nor a Catholic church, but it did have a Baptist church.

Claas was converted and baptized in 1942 and in 1945, heard a call to the ministry. Educated at both the Baptist Theological Seminary in Hamburg and the International Seminary in Rüschlikon, Switzerland, his first pastorate was at the First Baptist Church in Düsseldorf. He also taught religion in the state gymnasium (high school) at Düsseldorf.

Noticing how well he related to young people, the Baptist Union of West Germany asked Claas to be its youth secretary in 1958. Six years later he answered the call to pastor Oncken Baptist Church in Hamburg. In May 1967 the Baptist Union chose him as its general secretary.

When the BWA turned to Claas in 1976, prevailing upon him to be Associate Secretary for Europe, he insisted in moving the office, which had always been in London, to his home city of Hamburg. His impressive service in that job, plus his commanding personality, made him the natural choice to succeed Denny as General Secretary in 1980.

He was killed in a traffic accident in 1988, a tragedy felt by Baptists around the world.

(Germany), Birgit Karlsson (Sweden), and Welton Gaddy (SBC). A new and sixth commission, Baptist Heritage, was created, chaired by American Baptist historian William H. Brackney. An important action was the publication of a BWA study book at the end of the quinquennium. Entitled *Faith, Life, and Witness* and edited by Brackney and Burke, it contained forty-five of the papers presented at the annual sessions of the six commissions.[14] Since in the past the study papers were circulated among the commissions in mimeographed form and were not systematically preserved, this innovation made the work of these Baptist scholars available to a wider audience.

Fifteenth Baptist World Congress, Los Angeles 1985
The Fifteenth World Congress, July 2–7, 1985, did not attract many more than nine thousand people. The organizers had hoped that up to thirty thousand might attend, but a great many Southern Baptists had already gone to their own convention the previous month and did not have the time or financial resources to attend another large meeting so soon.[15] It was still a step forward in serious engagement with world issues. People from ninety-three countries came, with the largest delegations outside of North America being those of Australia and the Philippines.

The Congress theme was "Out of Darkness into the Light of Christ," and the presentations by President McCall and Evangelist Billy Graham, for example, stressed the need to walk in the light. Former U.S. President Jimmy Carter addressed the Congress on the issues of human oppression and suffering. Southwestern Baptist Theological Seminary President Russell Dilday spoke about "To Set at Liberty" on July 4th, U.S. Independence Day. Other international plenary speakers were Billy Jang Hwan Kim of Korea, Alexei Bichkov of the Soviet Union, and Douglas Waruta of Tanzania. Some twenty choirs from various parts of the world performed, as well as soloists from eight countries.

Strong resolutions were adopted endorsing the United Nations (U.N.); condemning racism in general and apartheid in particular, criticizing the conflict in Nicaragua (and by implication U.S. policy there); affirming the need for religious liberty; condemning terrorism; urging a more simple life so more could be shared with the needy; and calling for an end to the arms race. Elected as President was Vose, principal of the Baptist Theological College of Western Australia since its founding in 1963.[16]

Departments
Women continued to be prominent in the BWA leadership. Two had served

as Vice Presidents in the 1980 quinquennium, and the number increased to three in 1985: Christine Gregory of Danville, Virginia, former president of the SBC's Woman's Missionary Union; Atinuke Bamijoko, a Nigerian who had presided over the Baptist Women's Union of Africa; and Karlsson, general secretary of the Baptist Union of Sweden. Serving as president of the Women's Department were Rudén of Sweden, 1980–85, and Edna Lee de Gutiérrez of Mexico, 1985–90.

President Vose was committed to raising the profile of the Women's Department in the BWA. He was convinced that Baptists needed to give more attention to and learn lessons from women's work. In his report to the 1988 General Council, Vose spoke about the ministry of the "silent majority," the women in Baptist churches: "There was a time when, through lack of educational opportunities and organizational experience, women had very little place in the decision making aspects of church life. In the last quarter of a century, the position has changed radically. Highly gifted women are beginning to make an impact in every area of life, including the church. In the BWA the women's work has a strength and dynamic from which we could all learn . . . . I commend this whole question to the careful, and biblical, attention of the Alliance."[17]

Whereas the attendance at regional women's conferences meant that in any one year around four thousand women from about ninety countries

G. Noel Vose

The only person from the Southwest Pacific elected president of the Baptist World Alliance in its first century was G. Noel Vose, whose home is in the far west corner of Australia. He did not immediately prepare for the ministry but, after service in the Royal Australian Air Force in World War II, went back to school. As a student, he served churches in Sydney. He is the first Baptist pastor Ken Manley knew. Back in Perth his fellow pastors recognized his gifts and sent him to the United States for further education so that he could start a theological college in their part of Australia

Returning to Perth, Vose made the Baptist Theological College of Western Australia a center of pastoral and academic excellence. His own loves are the Anabaptists (before it was fashionable); theology, which he taught; and expository preaching. In a setting often critical of scholarship and ecumenical involvement, he worked hard to advance these causes. But his most outstanding quality is his keen pastoral compassion for others, which shines through his very being. To meet Noel Vose is to know you have a friend—more than a friend, someone who truly cares about you.

Vose retired in 1991. His beloved wife, Heather, had died unexpectedly during the Baptist World Alliance-sponsored Baptist Mennonite Conversations in 1990. He now lives in the hills outside of Perth, enjoying time to read and garden but continuing to preach and teach occasionally, as well as keeping in touch with his many friends around the world.

came together in different parts of the world, the BWA Men's Department operated on a smaller scale. In 1987, for example, the World Conference of Baptist Men attracted approximately seven hundred men from thirty-six countries. The Men's Department, however, was working to set up regional organizations and to develop lay activities.

The Youth Department drew large numbers for its conferences. At Buenos Aires in 1984, four thousand delegates from sixty-eight nations gathered to celebrate "Jesus Christ, the Truth, Our Faith, Our Commitment, Our Peace." The 1988 Eleventh Baptist Youth World Conference in Glasgow, Scotland, was an even greater success in numerical terms. More than seven thousand young people from eighty-four countries came to hear inspiring speakers. A highlight of the gathering was the varieties of worship experiences that took place. The youths returned to their home countries with fresh dedication to evangelism. Leading this conference was a British Baptist youth official, Paul Montacute. In 1985, Vose had expressed his desire for greater involvement of young people in the BWA, and the Executive Committee noted in 1989 that scholarships amounting to $180,000 had enabled youth from around the world to attend.[18]

In 1985 the BWA relocated its office. The Washington, D.C., building that it shared with the D. C. Convention was no longer adequate for the growing organization's needs, and the General Council approved the purchase of a building in the suburbs at 6733 Curran Street, McLean, Virginia. The move was costly. Although the Alliance generally avoided deficits, its financial position was not strong, and in 1988 it launched a campaign to raise two million dollars.

Early in that year, Claas highlighted the need to rethink the structure of the Alliance. He asked radical questions: Should there be departments based on gender and age? How could the BWA be financed? Should the many different (and expensive) conferences continue? Andrew D. MacRae of Canada (formerly general secretary of the Baptist Union of Scotland) chaired a Structure Committee working on these fundamental questions, but its proposals for change were shelved with the unexpected death of Claas. The acting, and soon-to-be-elected General Secretary Lotz underlined and affirmed the concern that Claas had always shown for world evangelization and justice.[19] These matters, rather than structural change, clearly had priority in BWA thinking.

Evangelism and Education
In his strong emphasis on the importance of evangelism and education, Claas was in tune with the BWA as a whole. His report to the General

Council in 1981 mentioned a visit he had made to Eastern Europe, during which he baptized seventeen new believers at one church.[20] In 1982 the Books and Translation Committee of the EBF, which David S. Russell (general secretary of the Baptist Union of Great Britain) chaired, endeavored to support Baptist witness in that area by securing a license to send books.[21] The Evangelism and Education Division also initiated a program to provide mini-libraries for lay ministers whose resources were limited. At the 1983 Council, Grady Cothen (SBC), chair of the division, praised the work of the recently formed World Evangelization Strategy Work Group.[22] A resolution adopted that year called upon Baptist bodies around the world to renew their efforts and to accept the challenge of world evangelization. The hope was expressed that a draft strategy for an evangelization program would be ready for the 1984 Council meeting.[23]

At the Berlin General Council, the International Mission Secretaries (IMS, previously known as the International Mission Secretaries Conference) held two joint sessions with the World Evangelization Strategy Work Group. The emphasis that emerged was to train national leaders for evangelism. Claas also referred within his report on lay development to a new Southern Baptist initiative, "Bold Mission Thrust," which he saw as "one of the finest and most effective mission programs Baptists have ever had." But he emphasized that Baptists were aware that they could win the world for Christ only when *every* Baptist was a missionary.[24] In this statement Claas echoed the vision of his German spiritual forebear Johann Gerhard Oncken.

An ongoing concern was the need for religious literature in the Soviet Union, where the demand greatly exceeded the supply. In 1984 it was reported that the Russian Baptists had finally received permission to print or import fifteen thousand New Testaments plus thousands of hymnbooks and concordances. The *Baptist World* reported in 1985 that the Soviet government had granted a permit to import one thousand copies each of a Russian translation of the first five volumes of William Barclay's *New Testament Commentaries*. The BWA continued working behind the scenes, and eventually another hundred thousand Bibles were shipped to the Soviet Union.[25]

The aforementioned *Baptist World* news item in 1985 also stated that the Baptists had received permission to begin looking for a suitable site in Moscow to establish a seminary and that Baptists in Poland and Hungary had been authorized to proceed with construction of seminary facilities. The communist world was a prominent topic in BWA discussions, both because of the ongoing cold war and also because of the strong influence of the EBF.

Communism was, however, only one global issue. A major challenge was Islam. In their 1985 report the IMS mentioned the rise of the Islamic movement and its implication for missions. Dennis Dilip Datta from the Bangladesh Baptist Fellowship commented that this raising of the issue of Islam was the first time he had seen any reference to a matter that was critical for missions in the southern hemisphere. He asked whether or not the IMS had planned further exploration of this subject. IMS secretary Sven Ohm (Sweden) said that one of the next two conferences would deal with the Islamic question.[26] A significant action of the 1986 Council was the approval of a "Baptist Fund for World Evangelization and Discipleship," proposed by the Division of Evangelism and Education, to support national workers.[27]

For the BWA education was closely linked to evangelism, and this included theological training as well as the provision of literature. In 1983, President McCall encouraged theological reflection among Baptists in the light of their differences in history, culture, economic, and sociopolitical experiences.[28] One result was the formation of regional theological education committees. Another was the convening of the first Baptist International Conference on Theological Education (BICTE) at Ridgecrest in North Carolina in 1982. Thereafter, BICTE became a regular BWA event with two further conferences in the decade: one in Los Angeles (1985) and the other in Zagreb (1989). J. Ralph McIntyre—a Texas-born pastor, evangelist, and educator who had just retired from his position with the Southern Baptist Sunday School Board—became the temporary Director of Evangelism and Education and of Study and Research after Lotz moved to the General Secretary's post. He reported at the 1989 General Council meeting that the third BICTE meeting had attracted 131 educators from thirty-seven countries.

There was progress in providing the above-mentioned mini-libraries. Some 6,370 of these packages, making up a total of 66,612 books, were sent to pastors and students in seventy-three countries at a cost of $500,000.[29] The Alliance also worked closely with the United Bible Societies to help publish a new Moldovan edition of the Bible, as well as to assist in sending Armenian, Estonian, Latvian, and Ukrainian language Bibles to these Soviet republics.[30]

Claas highlighted the remarkable worldwide growth of Baptists at the March 1987 Executive Committee. He reported the ongoing revival in Korea, where the number of Baptists had reached five hundred thousand, and pointed out that in Burma they were now the strongest Christian denomination.[31] The following year, Claas welcomed the chairman of the Council for Religious Affairs in the Soviet Union to the Executive meeting at the new BWA office in McLean, Virginia, and spoke of his own experiences in that country.[32]

The General Council often convened in places where its presence might reinforce Baptist witness, hence gatherings were held in Singapore (1986), Amman, Jordan (1987), and Zagreb, Croatia, in what was then Yugoslavia (1989). At the meeting in the primarily Islamic country of Jordan, an unforgettable "Sunrise Worship Service" took place on Mount Nebo—where all the participants gazed as Moses had into what for him was the Promised Land.[33]

In 1989, Daniel E. Weiss (ABC), the Evangelism and Education Division chair, asked L. A. (Tony) Cupit of Australia (soon to become Director of the division) to present to the General Council its "Vision 2000" recommendation for accelerated world evangelization. The Council promptly endorsed the document. Lotz, as the new BWA General Secretary, appealed for commitment to evangelism and social justice. His words echoed the missionary call of the early twentieth-century Student Volunteer Movement "to work for the evangelization of the world in this generation," and he proposed that 1990–2000 be declared a "Decade of Evangelism" for Baptists.[34] He intended to maintain the evangelistic direction Claas had set out.

Human Rights, Religious Liberty, and Peace

In his commitment to human rights, Claas continued the emphasis of his predecessors. At the 1980 Congress, Denny said Baptists had discovered that "the voice of thirty-three million Baptists can make an impact in speaking for human rights. We are part of an organization which insists on the dignity of all peoples and on protecting the rights of all to have the freedom of worship, especially those in the restricted areas in the world."[35] At Toronto resolutions were approved on evangelism, religious freedom and human rights, family life, world peace and disarmament, world hunger, refugees, and ecology. A resolution on disarmament called on the world's governments to stop the production of and trading in the weapons of war—conventional and nuclear.[36] The 1980 Congress also adopted a separate declaration on human rights. The statement affirmed that "concern for human rights is at the heart of the Christian faith," and Baptists acknowledged their responsibility to "strive to promote and defend human rights within churches and society at large."[37]

Resolutions at the General Council in 1981 included one supporting the U.N. "Declaration on the Elimination of all Forms of Intolerance and Discrimination based on Religious Belief" as being consistent with both the Baptist heritage and contemporary commitments. That Council also condemned the folly of relying on nuclear weapons, describing them "as abhorrent as bacteriological or chemical warfare."[38] In 1983 the Council made an even stronger statement: "The presence of nuclear weapons is a direct affront to our Christian beliefs and commitment."[39] Carl W. Tiller, who was serving as the BWA representative at the United Nations (the U.N. recognizes the BWA as a nongovernmental organization or NGO), worked to make Baptist influence more effective on the international scene.

Heather Vose, an academic historian in Australia and wife of Noel Vose, argued in an article published in 1990 that by the time of the Congress in Toronto the BWA clearly stood for "peace and reconciliation among all nations." She noted that resolutions with this theme were becoming part of national Baptist conventions, regional assemblies, and local meetings, reflecting changes taking place in Baptist thinking worldwide. The Vietnam War had brought into focus the question of the morality of war. Heather Vose maintained that Baptists, who had often been better at fighting than making peace, now had a greater concern for peacemaking and peacekeeping.[40]

As noted above, former U.S. President Carter received a resounding ovation at the 1985 World Congress when he urged Baptists and other Christians to meet human need and fight oppression. He asked those present to follow Christ's example in exhibiting the qualities of "peace, humility, concern for others, forgiveness, mercy, generosity, [and] a willingness even to be persecuted in God's name."[41] Human rights themes also pervaded the resolutions passed by the Congress.

Yet, it seemed that little was being achieved. So the General Council in 1986 once again condemned racism, terrorism, and apartheid in South Africa and called on nations to stop the arms race. A new topic was Afghanistan: A resolution expressed concern for the three million refugees and urged international agreements for restoring peace and the withdrawal of all foreign forces from the country. Tiller updated the Council on matters at the U.N. He reported that there was no progress on arms limitation and that the United States had blocked the holding of a peace conference that might address the continuing problems of the Middle East. The most positive development was that human-rights issues were receiving more international attention.[42]

The role of women in church life was a matter on which Baptists were divided. Shirley Bentall, president of the Canadian Baptist Federation, in a paper given to the Commission on Human Rights (1988), pointed out that in 1984 the SBC had adopted a resolution excluding women from pastoral functions or leadership roles that entailed ordination. Bentall saw "masculine determination to stifle or subordinate their womanhood, even when it is wrapped in scriptural references" as something "more like a manifestation of fallen human nature or fallen human relationships than redemption and the fellowship of the redeemed in Jesus Christ."[43] On the other hand, a 1988 General Council resolution commended "progress toward the increasing contribution women make to church life through leadership in local churches and regional, national and international bodies" and encouraged Baptists to give "biblical and careful attention" to the matter of "the enabling of women and their gifts."[44]

Lorenzen, professor of systematic theology at the Rüschlikon Seminary and 1985–90 chair of the Commission on Human Rights, praised the substantial papers presented to his body and published in *Faith, Life, and Witness*. Along with the Bentall paper cited above were substantive discussions on such themes as: a biblical perspective on human rights (Athol Gill, Baptist Seminary, Melbourne, Australia); a biblical basis for concern about refugees (Wolfgang Lorenz, West Berlin); evangelism and human rights (Saverio Guarna, Italian Baptist Union); human rights in relation to Baptist thinking (James E. Wood, Jr., Baylor University, Texas); and the gap between BWA pronouncements on human rights and what was actually achieved (Per Midteide, Norwegian Baptist Seminary). Tiller suggested ways that Baptist influence could become more effective at the U.N.[45]

In 1988, Tiller reported to the General Council that the U.N. had honored the BWA as a "peace messenger" and presented a certificate to the BWA to that effect.[46] In 1987 and 1988, the Council also adopted resolutions containing a peace emphasis. One commended the Baptist Peace Fellowship of North America for advocating that the year 2000 be recognized as a Year of Peace, while the other applauded a U.S.–Soviet agreement that eliminated intermediate-range nuclear missiles.

Political Tensions and Internal Relationships

Although the BWA encouraged world peace, it was not always able to ensure peace within Baptist ranks. Strains emerged in 1980 when Bichkov addressed the General Council meeting in Toronto. Speaking on behalf of the All-Union Council of Evangelical Christians—Baptists (AUCECB) in the Soviet Union, he expressed deep regret that Georgi P. Vins, the exiled leader of the "unregistered Baptists" in the country (a group not holding membership of the BWA), was accorded delegate status at the Baptist World Congress and given press accreditation. Bichkov angrily said that this action was "a violation of the Baptist World Alliance constitution" and spoke of "the irresponsible action of certain groups both before and during the Congress." Russell, who knew the Russian scene well, assured Bichkov that Vins had no right to register as an official delegate and that the registration must have been an oversight or mistake. The Council received his statement with applause. Some wanted to cancel Vins's registration, but McCall said that would be contrary to the nature of Baptists. In his speech to the Congress, McCall expressed his regrets for any embarrassment that the Soviet delegates may have suffered.[47]

At the 1982 General Council meeting, Claas recommended moving the 1983 Council from Buenos Aires to Fort Worth, Texas, because of the conflict between Argentina and the United Kingdom over the Falklands Islands/Malvinas. Some on the Council favored the idea. Others insisted that the BWA should support Latin American Baptists and seek to "demonstrate our unity in Christ and the reconciling power of the gospel." Following the General Council sessions, Claas went to Buenos Aires to view the situation firsthand. He reported to the Executive Committee in November that he learned the Baptists of Argentina would be very disappointed if the Council was not held there. He then recommended that the Council should follow its original meeting plan and the Executive agreed.[48]

The Tenth Baptist World Youth Conference, scheduled for Buenos Aires in 1983, however, was postponed until 1984. Most of the four thousand young people who attended were Latin Americans. Lotz noted that for the first time a World Youth Conference was not dominated by Europeans or North Americans and that "the Gospel's evangelistic and social dimensions were held together in a wholistic and Biblical way."[49]

In Eastern Europe it was evident that internal Baptist tensions were lessening, but some difficulties remained. At an Executive Committee meeting in November 1984, McCall reported that during a recent visit to the Soviet Union he had felt a "new sense of relationship" between those in the AUCECB and pastors of the independent (unregistered) churches. He had met with both. He was also impressed by the distinct ethnic identity of different parts of the Soviet Union, from Latvia in the north to Ukraine in the south.[50]

But in 1985 a dispute arose when the Council sought a nominee for BWA Vice President who would represent Eastern Europe. The name of Josip Horak of Yugoslavia was brought forward, but AUCECB leader Bichkov stated his opposition, saying that this country could not represent Eastern Europe. The real issue was that Yugoslavia did not belong to the Warsaw Pact (the Soviet-controlled military alliance). Bernard Green, who in 1982 had succeeded Russell as general secretary of the Baptist Union of Great Britain, said it would be very unfortunate if the BWA made decisions on political grounds. In a secret ballot Horak was elected, but to assuage the Russian concerns Adam Piasecki of Poland was also given vice-presidential rights and privileges but not the title itself.[51]

Tensions were also likely when new groups sought to join the BWA. For example in March 1985, Bichkov objected when Claas mentioned that a second Baptist Union was being organized in West Germany. The reason for his unhappiness was that it would include people of German ethnicity who had emigrated from the Soviet Union and still spoke Russian.[52] Although not stated openly, it was known that some of these Baptists had links with unregistered churches in the Soviet Union As it turned out, the group did not seek membership in the BWA.

Two guests from the People's Republic of China were present at the Los Angeles Congress. This was reckoned to be the first time that delegates from Communist China had attended a denominational conference elsewhere in the world. Han Wen Zhao, the associate general secretary of the China Christian Council, gave a description of the "Three Self Movement" (self-government, self-support, and self-propagation) in the church in China and spoke of three million Chinese brothers and sisters.[53] He did not mention Christians in churches outside the "Three-Self" official group.

Cold war tensions were reflected in two incidents at the Los Angeles Congress. During the parade of flags, the pastor of an independent fundamentalist Baptist church in the city jumped on the stage and attempted to rip the Soviet flag off its pole. The Chinese visitors, however, were insulated from such pressures as they viewed the Congress proceedings from a glass-enclosed booth.[54] During his address U.S. President Carter read—no doubt without consulting the Soviet Baptist leaders—a letter he received a few weeks earlier from Vins, whom he had assisted in leaving the Soviet Union. In this letter Vins spoke of two hundred Baptists in prison camps and appealed to the former president: "My dear brother, please say something on behalf of the persecuted church. No one else will speak out for the prisoners—only you." Carter insisted that it was not his purpose to "berate the Soviets, many of whom share our basic desires for peace, understanding, and the alleviation of human suffering," but he wished to encourage those crossing political boundaries in the name of Christ.[55] Considering the problems in 1985, the General Council decided to dispense with the parade of national flags at the 1990 Congress,[56] but by then the political landscape had become very different.

Conversations with Other Churches

A further area of possible tension was Baptist conversations with other churches. Earlier, in 1973–77, the BWA had engaged in fruitful talks with the World Alliance of Reformed Churches. This process continued in the 1980s. First, the BWA conducted discussions with the Lutheran World Federation, and four sessions took place in 1986–89 without any noticeable problems occurring. Similarly, in 1989–92, four meetings took place between representatives of the BWA and the Mennonite World Conference that examined questions of authority, the church, and mission.[57]

Arranging conversations with Roman Catholics, however, proved to be more difficult. In 1980 the retiring chair of the Commission on Doctrine and Interchurch Cooperation, R. J. Thompson of New Zealand, recommended that efforts should be made to open a theological dialogue with the Roman Catholic Church.[58] The BWA office received a positive reaction from the Roman Catholic Secretariat for Promoting Christian Unity, so the Executive Committee voted in November 1980 that "three or four Baptist scholars should be nominated to represent the Baptist World Alliance in such bilateral talks with the Roman Catholic Church . . . and it should be guaranteed that the voice of Baptist minorities in so-called Catholic countries is heard." The Executive also proposed forming a preparatory committee to work out the procedures for such dialogues. At the 1981 General Council some expressed concern about the process, as it might assume that participants were coequal and such equality was not acceptable to them. When the Council could not agree on a course of action, it referred the matter back to the Executive to clarify the purpose of the talks.[59]

Since no progress had occurred on the Roman Catholic conversations, a planned visit to the Vatican in December 1981 was cancelled. The matter was referred to the Commission on Doctrine and Interchurch Cooperation, which was sensitive to the problems. The commission then created from its membership a four-person committee—Glenn Igleheart (SBC); Kerstan from the BWA staff; Manfred Grellert (Brazil); and Günter Wagner from the Rüschlikon seminary—to explore the conditions for any meetings.[60] Objections continued to be raised, especially by Latin Americans, but the majority favored conversations. Tiller, for example, said that the BWA would be paralyzed if it accepted the view of the minority of Baptists opposed to such dialogue.[61] This more open approach was what prevailed.

Igleheart and Kerstan met in Frankfurt, Germany, with Roman Catholic representatives. The talks were productive, and commission chair Vose proposed to the 1983 General Council the initiation of conversations "in order to come to a mutual understanding of convergences and divergences [in the] ecclesial, pastoral, and mission concerns between the Baptist and Roman Catholic world confessional bodies." The plan was to have five meetings over five years with a small group of Baptist participants. Vose explained that these conversations would allow raising questions about the denial of Baptist human rights in Catholic dominated areas, while by entering into talks Catholics would acknowledge Baptists as a world confessional body. Baptists could point out the emphasis in the statements of Vatican II on liberty of conscience and the primacy of Scripture, and Catholics could discover the centrality of the doctrine of the church for Baptists and how they understood that doctrine. After a lengthy discussion, where some members expressed concern that such talks could be misinterpreted or misused and others argued they could help ease Catholic-Baptist relationships, a motion to oppose dialogue was defeated.[62]

Sponsored by the BWA Commission on Baptist Doctrine and Interchurch Cooperation and the Vatican Secretariat for Promoting Christian Unity, five sessions took place between 1984 and 1988. Besides the BWA conversations with the Catholics, Lutherans, and Mennonites, the BWA General Secretary regularly took part in the low-profile meetings of the Christian World Communions (CWC). One result of this interchurch activity was that representatives of the various CWCs met at the Prayer for Peace at Assisi, Italy, in 1986. Pope John Paul II had suggested that they be invited, and this occurred after the various churches, including the Baptists, had been contacted.[63] Vose, who participated in the Baptist–Roman Catholic conversations, reflected that "there were notes of positive appreciation on both sides, without any attempt to conceal the doctrines that divide our world communions."[64]

The commission presented its report of the conversations, "Christian Witness in Today's World," at the 1989 General Council. It stated that those involved "discovered a remarkable amount of consensus." American Baptist Sparrowk moved acceptance of the report, while Brazilian Irland Pereira de Azevedo spoke in opposition heatedly and at great length. After much discussion the Council voted to receive both the report and Azevedo's response.[65] Very different attitudes remained, but the conversations were of great significance.

Baptist World Aid
Baptists were united in their desire to provide relief and development. Claas, in his inaugural address to the 1980 Congress, stressed that "Christian pro-existence manifests itself in financial support and aid." To be sure, the BWA had worked in this area for a long time, but Claas issued an even stronger challenge. As a member of the organization "Bread for the World" that worked for systemic global change, he had come to believe that often Christians offered only "crumbs for the world." He suggested that Baptists

give greater attention to environmental concerns and make an "alternative life-style" a characteristic of Baptist discipleship. "We are called," he declared, "to set signs in our personal life-style—by renunciation of consumption, by working for peace and social justice, by struggling against exploitation of resources and pollution, by supporting the underprivileged and minority groups, and most of all by serving the poorest and lowest brothers of Jesus."[66]

In 1983 both McCall and Claas highlighted the importance of aid. McCall said that some people had expressed the view that the BWA should exist for fellowship only and not have programs of action. He pointed out that there had been a program of world relief since the close of World War I.[67] Claas illustrated what the BWA was doing by referring to the effectiveness of the distribution of food, clothing, and medicine in Poland. Along with permission to give aid had come the permission to print one hundred thousand Bibles and build new Baptist churches.[68]

Many of the most pressing needs, however, were outside Europe. Here again, McCall and Claas were bringing the same message. At the Executive Committee in March 1984, McCall reported on his visit to Asia. He had been to Japan, Korea, Hong Kong, the Republic of China (Taiwan), Sri Lanka, and Thailand.[69] While noting a special emphasis that year on evangelism—together with lay development, education, peacemaking efforts, conferences, and fund-raising—he and Claas both highlighted BWAid, with its involvement in well-drilling, community health projects, housing, and skills training.[70] Later in the summer the General Council authorized a special "Africa Response Appeal" for famine relief in Africa. In that year Baptists gave more than twenty-one million dollars for relief and development. This amount was a composite figure, representing work done by BWAid, Baptist unions, conventions, and mission agencies. A large portion of this money went to world hunger and disaster relief.

At the 1985 Congress, Waruta, principal of the Theological Seminary of East Africa, delivered a powerful address in which he asked what Baptists would do about the pressing misery of the world. Berhanu Habte, a medical doctor from Ethiopia, told of the plight of his people and spoke with appreciation about BWAid. He gave additional personal testimony to God's help. On his way to the Congress, he had been a passenger on a flight hijacked by terrorists after taking off from Beirut, Lebanon, and was a hostage for thirty-three hours.[71]

Goldie, director of the Division of BWAid and of the Men's Department, described in 1986 how BWAid had responded to the disaster of a volcano and avalanche in Colombia and had channeled aid through the country's Baptist convention. Help was sent to Karen and Lahu Baptists in Thailand who had suffered crop failures as well as resettlement problems. In the later 1980s BWAid was helping Eastern Europe, Bangladesh, Burma (Myanmar), Colombia, Costa Rica, India, Jamaica, Mexico, Nepal, Nicaragua, the Philippines, Rwanda, and Sudan. Money was coming in at a greater rate than ever. In 1987, as the receipts were approaching two million dollars, the chair of the Division of Baptist World Aid, Carolyn Weatherford (SBC, later Carolyn W. Crumpler), summed up the range of work being done. BWAid was seeking to assist the victims of floods, disease, earthquakes, violence, hurricanes, and volcanoes. In addition to this disaster relief, there were extensive development programs in agriculture and medicine.[72]

Vose summed it up with his characteristic precision: "The Baptists of the world, with their deep spiritual resources and their expertise and financial resources, have a unique opportunity to present the claims of Christ in a holistic fashion through programs of assistance and development."[73]

A Decade of Achievement

There was a sense of confidence within the BWA in the 1980s. The number of Baptists affiliated with the Alliance continued to grow—from just under thirty-one million at the beginning of the decade to over thirty-five million at the end. It was reckoned that membership of BWA's affiliated bodies represented 87 percent of the total number of Baptists in the world. Each year more unions and conventions joined the Alliance.

Internationalization was a marked feature. Claas, McCall, and Vose all encouraged this process. In 1988, Vose welcomed the growth of regional fellowships, although he pointed out that the regions could "lose their sense of global relationships and responsibilities." For him the European Baptists provided a model: "strong, multifaceted and efficient, but always sensitive to and supportive of its parent body."[74] Perhaps the idea of "fellowship" was more appropriate than parenting. It was this fellowship that the secretariat, departments, divisions, and commissions sought to foster.

Reflecting the Alliance's increase in size and variety of endeavors was the logo approved by the General Council in 1986. The previous November the Executive Committee had authorized a worldwide competition for an entirely new BWA logo to replace the one with the clasped hands that it had used since 1905 (it had been somewhat modified in 1976), and some sixty-eight entries were received. The winning design, by Michael J. Buckingham, a freelance graphic artist from Kentucky, with its symbolic representation of the three key elements of the BWA's ministry—the world, the open Bible, and the cross—and the scriptural passage—One Lord, One Faith, One Baptism—has continued since then to serve as the organization's symbol.[75]

Yet, the BWA was not simply a fellowship to enjoy. It was highly active in the fields of evangelism and education and, increasingly, in the area of human rights. The work of the Alliance was not achieved without difficulty. Tensions were evident over geopolitical, ecclesiastical, and ecumenical issues. Those involved in the commissions did an admirable job in directing the attention of Baptists to important issues of belief and practice. It is arguable that in the 1980s a healthier balance was achieved between study and active ministry. BWAid was a potent expression of holistic mission, deriving from a fuller view of the mission of God in the world. Claas, the central BWA figure of the 1980s, had called for Baptist "pro-existence"—a "real relationship of serving each other." Many responded to this call.

1. *Baptist World,* July–August 1980, p. 5. For the life of Duke Kimbrough McCall, see his memoir, *Duke McCall: An Oral History* (Nashville: Baptist History and Heritage Society, 2001).

2. *Baptist World,* October–December 1980, p. 1.

3. *BWA Congress,* 1980, p. 15.

4. *Baptist World,* July–August 1980, p. 1.

5. General Council, 1981, President's Report, item 9.

6. General Council, 1983, President's Report, item 8.

7. *Baptist World,* October–December 1984, pp. 1–2.

8. General Council, 1984, President's Report, item 8; Minutes, p. 19.

9. General Council, 1984, Minutes, p. 19.

10. Executive Committee, Minutes, March 10–11, 1986.

11. *Baptist World,* January–March 1988, pp. 2–3.

12. Ibid., October–December 1984, p. 7.

13. *BWA Congress,* 1985, pp. 112–123; *Baptist World,* October–December 1985, p. 11.

14. William H. Brackney and Ruby J. Burke, eds., *Faith, Life, and Witness: The Papers of the Study and Research Division of the Baptist World Alliance, 1986–1990* (Birmingham, AL: Samford University Press, 1990).

15. *The American Baptist,* October 1985, p. 6.

16. *BWA Congress,* 1985, pp. 215-222.

17. *General Council,* 1988, President's Report, item 9.

18. *Baptist World,* October–December 1985, p. 9; Executive Committee, Minutes, March 7–9, 1989.

19. General Council, 1988, General Secretary's Report, items 10, 10a.

20. General Council, 1981, General Secretary's Report, item 10.

21. General Council, 1982, Report on Europe, item 17c.

22. General Council, 1983, Minutes, p. 14.

23. Ibid., Appendix V.

24. General Council, 1984, General Secretary's Report, item 9.

25. Ibid., item 9, addendum; *Baptist World,* October–December 1985, p. 12; General Council, 1988, Minutes, p. 13.

26. General Council, 1985, Minutes, p. 12.

27. Ibid., 1986, Minutes, p. 17; *Baptist World,* July–September 1986, p. 1.

28. General Council, 1983, Minutes, p. 4.

29. *BWA Congress,* 1990, p. 113.

30. General Council, 1988, Minutes, p. 28; 1989, Minutes, p. 13.

31. Executive Committee, Minutes, March 4–5, 1987.

32. Ibid., Minutes, March 9–10, 1988.

33. General Council, 1988, General Secretary's Report, item 10.

34. General Council, 1989, Minutes; General Secretary's Report, item 8.

35. *BWA Congress,* 1980, Report of the General Secretary, p. 109.

36. Ibid., pp. 241–245.

37. Ibid, pp. 246–250; James E Wood, Jr., "Toward a Theology of Human Rights: A Baptist Perspective," *American Baptist Quarterly* 9 (December 1990), pp. 216–217. This issue was devoted to human rights.

38. General Council, 1981, Minutes, Appendix III, pp. 40–41.

39. Ibid., 1983, Minutes, Appendix V, pp. 61–63.

40. Heather M. Vose, "Attitudes Toward War and Peace Reflected by Some Puritan-Separatist Spiritual Descendants—the Baptists," *Mennonite Quarterly Review* 64 (October 1990), pp. 382–383.

41. *BWA Congress,* 1985, p. 40.

42. General Council, 1986, Minutes, pp. 18–19; Appendix V.

43. Shirley F. Bentall, "Baptists and 'Freedom of Expression Without Distinction as to . . . Sex,'" *Faith, Life, and Witness,* p. 283.

44. General Council, 1988, Minutes, Appendix VIII, p. 73.

45. *Faith, Life, and Witness,* pp. 241–313.

46. General Council, 1988, Minutes, p. 20.

47. General Council, 1980, Minutes, p. 25; *BWA Congress,* 1980, p. 92.

48. General Council, 1982, Minutes, pp. 21–22; Executive Committee, Minutes, November 23, 1982.

49. *Baptist World,* October–December 1984, p. 5.

50. Executive Committee, Minutes, November 19, 1984.

51. General Council, 1985, Minutes, pp. 17–19.

52. General Council, 1985, Minutes, pp. 17–19.

53. General Council, 1985, Minutes, pp. 17–19.

54. *The American Baptist,* October 8, 1985, p. 6.

55. *BWA Congress,* 1985. p. 39.

56. General Council, 1987, Minutes, p. 17.

57. The BWA Division of Study and Research published the reports of these theological conversations as a booklet in the mid-1990s.

58. General Council, 1980, Minutes, p. 27

59. Ibid., 1981, Minutes, pp. 7–8.

60. Ibid., 1982, Minutes, p. 17.

61. BWA VI. 2. 15. Carl Tiller, "Personal Response," July 14, 1982.

62. General Council, 1983, Minutes, p. 15.

63. Ibid., 1986, Minutes, p. 6.

64. Ibid., 1989, President's Report, item 7.

65. Ibid., 1989, Minutes, p. 13.

66. *BWA Congress,* 1980, pp. 99–100.

67. General Council, 1983, President's Report, item 8.

68. Ibid., 1983, General Secretary's Report, item 9.

69. General Council, 1984, President's Report, item 8.

70. Executive Committee, Minutes, March 11, 1984.

71. *BWA Congress,* 1985, p. 77; *Baptist World,* October–December 1985, pp. 3, 12.

72. *Baptist World,* January–March 1987, p. 5.
73. General Council, 1986, BWAid Report, item 35a.
74. Ibid., 1988, President's Report, item 9.
75. *Baptist World,* July–September 1986, p. 3.

9

THE NEW WORLD, 1988–95
Albert W. Wardin, Jr., and Richard V. Pierard

As the decade of the 1980s neared its end, the Baptist World Alliance (BWA) had to deal with two unexpected challenges—the death of General Secretary Gerhard Claas in March 1988 and the dramatic fall of communism in Eastern Europe in 1989. The BWA was suddenly left leaderless. The reshuffle of officials that followed made it possible for the organization to continue on an even keel. Accompanying the change was a partial restructuring of the BWA, one that did not go as far as the Structure Committee had wanted.

Meanwhile, Baptists continued to grow in non-Western regions—Africa, Asia, and Latin America—and new BWA President Knud Wümpelmann, acknowledged this reality when he wrote in the *Baptist World:* "The older part needs the inspiration and challenge from the often fast growing younger part, 'the two-thirds world.' It is my intention during my period as president to try to strengthen the ties between the two."[1] With this expansion the BWA faced increased responsibilities in developing relationships, extending its evangelistic outreach, meeting calls for social and humanitarian aid, solving problems in church-state relations, and conducting dialogue with other religious communions.

The Demise of Communism
The cold war was not really a central concern of the Alliance, although during the years the organization resolutely faced the issues that war created. The BWA reached out to Baptists in the Soviet Union and Eastern Europe and endeavored to make them an integrated part of the group. From 1955 forward a leader from one of the churches in a communist-ruled country alternately served as a Vice President of the Alliance: Yakov Zhidkov (Soviet Union) 1955–70; Janos Laczkovski (Hungary) 1970–75; Michael Zhidkov (Soviet Union) 1975–80; Rolf Dammann (East Germany) 1980–85; and Josip Horak (Yugoslavia) 1985–90. At least one East European member sat on the Executive

Committee as well, and their numbers had increased to ten by the 1970–75 term. With the formation of the General Council in 1975, each of the six East European unions had at least one member, and the All-Union Council of Evangelical Christians–Baptists (AUCECB) in the Soviet Union had three members. Only officially atheistic Albania lacked a Baptist body. As a result, the BWA did not concern itself as much with international politics. Instead it focused on evangelism and community building.

As mentioned in previous chapters, human rights were a BWA concern. "Human Rights" had been added to the purview of the BWA's Commission on Religious Liberty by 1965, and over the next years broader issues of human freedom received regular attention in its papers. The Helsinki Accords, adopted at the end of the first Conference on Security and Cooperation in 1975 and signed by the Soviet Union as well as every country in Europe except Albania, recognized as permanent the national borders drawn up at the end of World War II. More importantly the signatories (including the heads of the communist states) agreed to respect human rights. The agreement appeared to give some teeth to the United Nation's 1948 Universal Declaration of Human Rights and was a stimulus to the growing human rights movement in Europe. The BWA welcomed this development in a resolution at Stockholm.[2]

Even as the cold war heated up again with the Soviet invasion of Afghanistan in 1979 and the United Sates refusal to participate in the 1980 Olympic Games in Moscow, the BWA focused as strongly as ever on the need for securing human rights and world peace. While U.S. President Ronald Reagan promoted his Strategic Defense Initiative antimissile program and in 1983 labeled the Soviet Union an "evil empire" before a cheering crowd of evangelicals, the BWA continued to advocate peace and nuclear-arms limitation, concerns that strongly animated its international membership. Former U.S. President Jimmy Carter also highlighted the need for the expansion of human rights at the Los Angeles Congress.

In 1979, The European Baptist Federation (EBF) welcomed the SALT 2 arms-limitation agreement that the leaders of the United States and Soviet Union had signed. People from the East and West regularly took part in EBF meetings; several easterners held leadership posts; and money was channeled to Baptist projects in the East. In an especially poignant act of reconciliation, at the EBF congress in Hamburg in 1984 the West German Baptists (Bund Evangelisch-Freikirchlicher Gemeinden, as they had been known since World War II) made a public confession of guilt for having remained silent during the Nazi regime, and the others warmly responded with words of thanks and forgiveness. The ever-increasing communication between European Baptists and their working as partners in the federation helped lay the groundwork for the dramatic events at the end of the 1980s.[3]

The new era opened in 1985 with the appointment of Mikhail Gorbachev as general secretary of the Communist Party of the Soviet Union He ushered in a new spirit of glasnost (or openness) and reform at home, and recognizing that the Soviet economy was on the verge of collapse, engaged in arms-limitations negotiations with the United States and withdrew troops from Afghanistan. As more and more reform-minded government officials in Poland and Hungary urged economic and political liberalization, the Soviet bloc began to come unglued.

In 1988, the millennium of the coming of Christianity to Russia, Gorbachev acknowledged the important role that Christians had played in the society. Soviet officials responded favorably to the BWA offer to give one hundred thousand Bibles to their country as a contribution to the millennium celebration. The ensuing changes in the Soviet government's treatment of religious bodies marked a real breakthrough in relationships between the Baptists and the state. As Bernard Green wrote:

> Baptists eagerly shared in the events, using them as the opportunity to start public evangelism, distribution of religious papers and magazines, Sunday Schools and youth work, and, perhaps one of the most surprising outcomes, to accept the invitation to visit prisons and provide volunteers for pastoral care in hospitals.[4]

They now were able to conduct public meetings as well as begin giving theological education and hold a "congress" where they would draft a new constitution. At that convention, the retiring general secretary of AUCECB, Alexei Bichkov, publicly called on the government to immediately adopt a law, granting freedom of conscience for the people and full freedom for religious associations.[5]

Gorbachev's reform measures in the Soviet Union set off a chain reaction in other communist countries. Public pressure forced the government in Poland to negotiate with the Solidarity labor movement of Lech Walesa and to allow free elections to take place in 1989; the voters turned out the old government. One of the first acts of the new one was to pass a law granting religious freedom. The Polish Baptists immediately began an aggressive program of evangelizing, training leaders, and establishing new churches,

In Hungary political negotiations brought an end to the communist regime and resulted in the formation of a multiparty state. Seeing the changes that were occurring, the EBF decided to hold its Eighth Congress in Budapest in July 1989—the first such meeting ever to be held in Eastern Europe—and people from the East and West poured into the city. It was the largest crowd of Baptists ever to gather in continental Europe. The president of the Hungarian Parliament gave an official welcome and told the delegates that the Baptist emphases on individual faith and the responsibility of every church member to share in the government would be a key factor in the building of a new Europe. Speeches and discussions took place on such issues as human rights, torture, the death penalty, and the suppression of the democracy movement in China the month before. Billy Graham spoke to ninety thousand people at an ecumenical rally in the country's largest stadium. As Green assessed it: "The most exciting testimony to the power of God to cross the boundaries which communism had erected" was the response of seventeen thousand people to Graham's evangelistic appeal.[6]

In Czechoslovakia in November 1989, students peacefully marched day after day calling for changes. On November 17 armed-police units forcefully suppressed their demonstration; several young people were injured, and one person was killed. On the following Sunday the congregation at the Fourth Baptist Church in Prague issued a public declaration to all Baptists in the world, pleading for them to intervene however they could and to pray for the protestors, the perpetrators of violence, and the innocent victims. Three days later the leaders of the Baptist Union of Czechoslovakia sent a protest letter to the country's prime minister and president calling for the democratization of society and responsible dialogue with those of different convictions. "We are convinced that this harsh use of force against peaceful citizens, perhaps other opinions, is an abuse of human dignity and an attack on the freedom of speech." They grounded their protest in the gospel of Jesus Christ, who was the bearer of new life and peace.[7] Within a short time the communist government had fallen, and democratic elections in the new year brought full freedom to the land. The "Velvet Revolution" in Czechoslovakia had succeeded.

The most dramatic events of the upheavals of 1989 were played out in East Germany and Romania. The story in the former country is detailed by East German evangelist Jörg Swoboda in his inspiring 1990 book *Die Revolution der Kerzen,* made available to Western readers in an English translation in 1996.[8] The peace initiatives of East German Protestants in the early 1980s helped undermine the communist state's claim to a monopoly over peacemaking; the Baptists, though small in number, played an active part in these endeavors. These included the "peace decade," a ten-day program each November of prayer, religious services, and peace workshops; the "Swords to Plowshares" youth movement that publicly demonstrated for peace; the Monday evening prayers for peace that began in Leipzig and soon were replicated in churches around the country; and the nonviolent marches that followed the prayer meetings, often with people carrying lighted candles. Baptist congregations suffered like other churches from the loss of members who emigrated to the West, but members who remained struggled valiantly to maintain a gospel witness in the troubled country. Swoboda tells of several courageous acts of resistance by East German Baptists. Thus they rejoiced, as did people across their country and the whole world as well, when on November 9, 1989, the East German borders (including the odious Berlin Wall) were opened to free passage and families and congregations could be reunited. Baptists actively participated in the free elections held in March 1990, served in the new parliament, and welcomed the reunification with West Germany that came later in that year. Even the two Baptist unions, divided since 1964, were rejoined into one body.

In Romania, run by the Stalinist President Nicolae Ceausescu, large crowds in the city of Timisoara protested communist repression, and Baptists were among the demonstrators who were attacked by armed forces. Over a thousand people were killed in this and other such protests. In those tense days Baptist and other Christian leaders expressed solidarity with the people in their demands for freedom and justice. On December 22, 1989, even as the hated security police were brutally attacking dissenters, Peter Dugulescu, pastor of Timisoara's First Baptist Church, courageously addressed a crowd of thousands in the city square. He proclaimed that in spite of what the communists had said "God exists," and he urged those assembled to pray. The crowd spontaneously repeated after the pastor the words of the Lord's Prayer.[9]

As word of the violence reached the outside world, BWA General Secretary Denton Lotz immediately released a statement deploring the use of force against innocent people and calling on the state president and his government to recognize the "new reality" of a Europe where freedom of religion and conscience could be enjoyed by all. The EBF immediately seconded Lotz's challenge, as did several ecumenical bodies in Europe. The climax of the Romanian revolution came on December 25 when Ceausescu's own forces turned against him and summarily executed him. Freedom gradually returned to the land, and within eighteen months the Baptists held their first freely convened assembly in over half a century. They now could practice their faith openly.[10]

Communist rule also fell in Bulgaria and Yugoslavia, thus freeing the Baptists to evangelize openly, although the rapid breakup of the latter state led to a host of new problems. Even the atheistic regime in Albania fell, and Baptists were able to begin work there in 1992. The Soviet Union, which already had begun to come apart with the secession of the Baltic States, finally disintegrated in 1991. At this point separate Baptist unions were formed in the former republics that were now independent states. The EBF reached out to embrace Baptists in these countries just as it had in 1986 when it welcomed the small Baptist bodies in the Middle East into the organization.

The EBF also faced the daunting challenge of providing physical assistance to the impoverished brethren in the East. In cooperation with Baptist World Aid (BWAid) and the Southern Baptist Foreign Mission Board (FMB), the EBF formed the Baptist Response–Europe (BR–E) aid program in 1990. It provided books, money for buildings, and humanitarian aid for Eastern Europe. The *BWA News* reported that in 1992 alone BR-E contributed almost two million dollars to Eastern Europe by sending Bibles, food, medicines, wheat and corn seeds, and clothing, while also giving assistance to some indigenous evangelists and missionaries.[11] In fact that year 80 percent of BWAid contributions, including gifts-in-kind, went to projects in that area. As Paul Montacute said later, the massive effort in coordinating responses to the challenges in Eastern Europe following the end of communism was comparable to the work that the BWA had done after World Wars I and II.[12]

General Secretary Lotz exulted about the new opportunities for Baptists and all Christians to evangelize but warned of the pitfalls that lay ahead: difficulties in maintaining unity, excessive nationalism, secularism, proliferation of irresponsible parachurch movements, loss of Baptist identity, and materialism. Referring to the planning for the BR–E, he stressed how the BWA is again prepared to serve as a catalyst for aiding our churches in their new mission: "We want to seize the moment and see the new thing God is doing."[13]

Leadership and Organizational Changes

The unexpected collapse of communism came just as the BWA had undergone a major change in leadership. The accidental death of the fifty-nine-year-old General Secretary Claas in March 1988 was an enormous blow to the Alliance, and the Executive Committee quickly named Lotz, the Director of Evangelism and Education and of the Youth Department, as the acting General Secretary. He was elected to the permanent position at the General Council meeting in the Bahamas that summer. Lotz, who had been on staff since 1980, brought years of experience to the job. His energy, administrative skills, broad educational background, knowledge of a second language (German), and vision uniquely equipped him for the world post. Reinhold J. Kerstan, Director of Promotion and Development and of Study and Research, left in the summer to take a teaching position at McMaster University. Also, John Wilkes, the Director of Communications, retired. Five out of the six directorates were vacant at the same time.

Lotz moved quickly to appoint capable new staff members. In October 1988 Wendy Ryan was named Director of Communications. She had been involved in radio and television work in her native Trinidad and Tobago; after coming to the United States for studies at Eastern College in suburban Philadelphia, she joined the staff of the American Baptist Board of International Ministries as a writer and producer of videos. As mentioned in the previous chapter, J. Ralph McIntyre came out of retirement as an interim replacement for Lotz in the Evangelism and Education and the Study and Research divisions, and General Secretary Lotz reached out to Australia to recruit L. A. (Tony) Cupit, the general superintendent of the Baptist Union of Victoria, for the two positions. Cupit (who came on board in October 1990) was well qualified, since he had served as a missionary under the Australian Baptist Missionary Society in Papua New Guinea from 1965 to 1971, then as a pastor and from 1978, as a denominational administrator. He was also an author, conference speaker, and visiting lecturer at various theological colleges.

The post of Director of Promotion and Development, which had only been created in 1987, remained unfilled, and the duties were subsumed under the General Secretary. Soon it became necessary to appoint two special assistants to work in Promotion and Development; finally in 1995, Douglas Inglis of Scotland was appointed Director for this branch of the BWA endeavor.

In 1990 Paul Montacute of Berkhamsted, England, was chosen to succeed the retiring Archibald (Archie) Goldie as Director of BWAid. Montacute, who had begun his career as an employee in the British tax office in the 1960s, attended his first Baptist Youth World Congress in 1963. He then studied for the ministry but remained active in BWA youth work. He had served as the national youth officer for the Baptist Union of Great Britain since 1982 and from 1985 to 1988, was president of the BWA Youth Department. Because of this background, he was assigned the additional duty of directing the BWA Youth Department, with the bulk of the work to be carried out by Associate Director Regina Claas of Germany, daughter of the former General Secretary and a rising star in Baptist circles. (In 2003 she would become the general secretary of the German Baptist Union.) In 1994 Emmett F. Dunn of Liberia was appointed Director of the Youth

Department, thus enabling Montacute to devote full attention to the expanding work of BWAid.

At first, Montacute was to be in charge of BWA finances. However, in 1990 a constitutional change brought back the position of Treasurer, and John R. Jones, Jr., a Southern Baptist layperson, was elected for the 1990–95 term. Ruby J. Burke, who had left in 1987 after nine years on the BWA staff in order to complete a degree at Eastern Baptist Seminary, returned in 1990 to serve in the new position of Assistant to the General Secretary. W. J. (Doc) Isbell, Jr., who had been involved in men's work in the SBC for over three decades, had become director of the Men's Department in 1988; in 1987 Elizabeth (Beth) Hayworth MacClaren, also a Southern Baptist, had been named director of the Women's Department. Both individuals were reelected in 1990. Isbell retired in 1994 and was replaced by Doyle Pennington of Atlanta. In 1990 Catherine Bryant Allen (a former staff member of Woman's Missionary Union [SBC]) was elected president of the Women's Department and Walter Cade (National Baptist Convention, U.S.A., Inc.) president of the Men's Department.

On the staff but not at the headquarters were the six Regional Secretaries, of whom the newest were Karl Heinz Walter of Germany, who had replaced Knud Wümpelmann of Denmark as general secretary of the EBF, and Carolyn Weatherford Crumpler of the North American Baptist Fellowship. Continuing as Regional Secretaries were Samuel T. Ola Akande (Nigeria), All-Africa Baptist Fellowship, who would be succeeded in 1992 by Eleazar Ziherambere (Rwanda); Edwin I. Lopez (Philippines), Asian Baptist Federation; Azariah McKenzie (Jamaica), Caribbean Baptist Fellowship; and José Missena (Paraguay), Union of Baptists in Latin America. When illness prevented Carl W. Tiller from serving as the BWA representative at the U.N., Southern Baptist Glenn Igleheart filled in until George Younger, a retired American Baptist denominational executive and historian, took on the task on a regular basis. In addition, many persons throughout the world served as officers and members of the various committees, departments, divisions, workgroups, and commissions of the Alliance.

Although not part of the executive staff, the President of the BWA was more than just a presiding officer at annual meetings. Elected to serve in 1990–95 was Knud Wümpelmann. His years as a pastor, general secretary of the Danish Baptist Union, and general secretary of the EBF brought a much-needed European dimension to the BWA. His quiet demeanor complemented the more robust personality of Lotz, and the two worked together. Wümpelmann was noted for his graciousness and kindly disposition, as well as an encourager and patient counselor. His ecumenical relationships and

Parade of banners at the Sixteenth Baptist World Congress in Seoul, Korea, 1990.

Ten thousand new converts were baptized in the Olympic Rowing Area off the River Han during the congress in Seoul, Korea, 1990.

The Girls Brigade of Baiyer River, Papua New Guinea, welcomed General Secretary Denton Lotz in February 1992.

Jamaicans and 1992 General Council delegates worshiped at a street rally in Montego Bay.

A choir of young Karen women in Yangon, Myanmar.

Choir in Baptist church in Moldova.

Mizo Baptists and visitors filled the hillsides to celebrate the Mizoram (state in northeast India) Gospel Centenary. The British Baptist Missionary Society sent the first missionaries in 1894. Today, most Mizos are Christian.

Baptist World Alliance 247

A parade of flags held at the celebration of the Mizoram Gospel Centenary. The Baptist World Alliance sent representatives, as did the Baptist Missionary Society and Baptist groups in the neighboring states. (1994)

Mizo children enjoyed the Mizoram Centenary, 1994.

Delegates crowded the auditorium for plenary sessions of the 1995 Congress in Buenos Aires, Argentina.

Emile D. E. Sam-Peel *(center)*, general secretary of the Liberian Baptist Convention, at an elementary school, "displaced" by civil war. S. Augustine Yeahgar, director of evangelism for the convention is to the right. (1995)

General Secretary Denton Lotz visiting Liberia in 1995 spent time with the children.

Bonny Resu of India spoke to the General Council at its 1996 meeting in Hong Kong. In 1997 Resu became Regional Secretary for Asia.

Associate Secretary L. A. (Tony) Cupit talked with lepers living out in the open during a visit to Andhra Pradesh (state in southeast India) in 1997.

Baptist World Alliance 251

Cuban Baptists have the joy of the Lord as they meet to worship. (1997)

Cubans knelt in prayer during a training session led by a team of theological educators sent by the Baptist World Alliance in April 1997.

Participants in the Baptist World Alliance-sponsored International Summit Against Racism and Ethnic Conflict in Atlanta, Georgia, U.S.A., January 1999.

Coretta Scott King, an honorary chair of the 1999 Summit, greeted Daniel Carro *(center)*, Regional Secretary for Latin America. Behind Carro was Samson S. K. Mathangani of Kenya. General Secretary Denton Lotz preceded them.

Baptist World Alliance 253

German Baptists and the government of Saxony (state of Germany) welcomed delegates to the 1999 General Council at a reception in a government building on the Elbe in Dresden.

Baptists from around the world greeted the new millennium at the 2000 Congress in Melbourne, Australia. One special event was a cultural celebration on the banks of the Yarra River.

(Left to right) Harry Monro, president of the Asian Baptist Federation; Ken Stanley, treasurer of the Baptist Union of Australia; and Baptist World Alliance Vice President Emmett Johnson of the American Baptist Churches met in Melbourne, Australia, to make plans for the 2000 Congress.

(Left to right) Past Presidents, Noel Vose and Knud Wümpelmann, and current President Nilson do Amaral Fanini prayed for the newly elected Billy Jang Hwan Kim at the Congress. Kim would become President in the summer of 2000.

(Left to right) General Secretary Denton Lotz, outgoing Baptist World Alliance President Nilson do Amaral Fanini, and incoming President Billy Jang Hwan Kim met with Cuban President Fidel Castro when in Havana, Cuba, for the 2000 General Council meeting.

The Baptist World Alliance's 21st Century Committee met in Berlin (2000): *(first row, left to right)* General Secretary Denton Lotz and David Emmanuel Goatley (Lott Carey); *(second row, left to right)* Associate Secretary L. A. (Tony) Cupit; Louise Kretzschmar (South Africa); Bathsheba Stewart (Bahamas); Associate Secretary Wendy Ryan; John Simpson (Australia); Young Shim Chang (Korea); *(third row, left to right)* Emile D. E. Sam-Peel (Liberia); Rodney Beaumont (United Kingdom); Lutz Reichert (Germany); Michael Okwakol (Uganda); George Bullard (Southern Baptist Convention).

Wati Aier of Nagaland (state in northeast India) led reflective/meditative worship in the prayer tower of the Hyderabad (city in south-central India) Baptist Church at the Baptists in Worship Conference (2000).

Rosalio Ramirez Rivas of Guatemala, president of the Union of Baptists in Latin America (UBLA), addressed participants at a UBLA gathering. (2000)

Leena Lavanya *(right, holding sign)* pictured at a Baptist rally. Lavanya leads a number of ministries, most of them to benefit women and children, in her native Andhra Pradesh (state in southeast India).

A worship service in Myanmar. (2000)

Moscow Seminary President Alexander Kozynko *(left)* with Ian M. Chapman of the American Baptist Churches, General Secretary Denton Lotz, and George Boltniev of the Russian-Ukranian Baptists in the United States at the dedication of the seminary's new home. (2002)

Five young Nepali students at the Baptist Bible Institute in Kathmandu.

earlier outreach to East European Baptists from his neutral Scandinavian base provided him with invaluable experience for the presidential role.¹⁴

During his first year as General Secretary, Lotz spent much of his time on the internal organization of the BWA. In 1989, he reported at the General Council meeting that with the assistance of outside professional analysis and the help of an executive staff retreat, changes were made to define clear lines of responsibility and to place each staff member under a supervisor. Retiring President G. Noel Vose agreed with the new direction, stating in his report at the same General Council: "new staff members, new approaches to old duties, new demands and responsibilities all call for new vision and commitment."¹⁵

The General Council had decided in 1986 to appoint a Structure Committee to do a thorough review of the BWA's constitution and bylaws and to recommend revisions that would improve the functioning of the Alliance.¹⁶ Chaired by Andrew D. MacRae, principal of the Acadia University Divinity School in Canada, the committee worked diligently and presented a detailed report to the 1988 General Council.¹⁷ The seven-page document clarified the relationship between the BWA and the regional fellowships, called for a General Council that would mirror more adequately the age and gender makeup of the constituency to be the legislative body of the Alliance, and recommended a reconfiguration of

Knud Wümpelmann

Knud Wümpelmann, President of the Baptist World Alliance 1990–1995, was born in 1922 in Odense, Denmark, the birthplace of Hans Christian Anderson. Reared in a Christian home, Wümpelmann accepted Christ and was baptized on Easter 1936. During World War II, at a time when Denmark was occupied by Nazi Germany, he trained for the postal and telegraph service. But feeling God's call, he prepared for a different career at the Baptist Theological Seminary in Tollose. In 1947 he graduated, married Karen, and first met the worldwide Baptist family at the Copenhagen Congress.

He served as assistant pastor in two churches and then traveled to Central Baptist Seminary in Kansas City, Kansas, for two years further study before returning to be senior pastor of Köbner Memorial Church in Copenhagen 1955–1964. He was general secretary of the Danish Union in 1964–1980 and served the European Baptist Federation as president in 1977–1979 and as general secretary in 1980–1989.

Wümpelmann is an encourager and reconciler. Throughout his life he has worked for harmony among and between Baptists, other Christians, and people of other faiths. In his native Denmark he has had long experience in working with Lutherans (established church of Denmark) and gained acceptance from them for Baptists as full members in that country's ecumenical groups. He enthusiastically supports holistic ministry—evangelism with full attention to the needs of the dispossessed of the world, including that for peace with justice. His last message as Baptist World Alliance President was, "Love one another, because love won another."

> **Denton Lotz**
>
>
>
> Denton Lotz, General Secretary of the Baptist World Alliance since 1988, finds his greatest joy is telling the good news of Jesus. He learned that joy as a child. His father, an electrical engineer and bi-vocational pastor of American Baptist churches in and around New York City, was a street evangelist and personal soulwinner. His mother, a dental hygienist, always provided Sunday dinner for twenty or more people.
>
> Denton was the youngest of four brothers, all of whom have had successful careers. He and wife Janice, a Southern Baptist from Mississippi, have three children—all born in Europe, two of the three currently living in Europe. Denton's parents were the children of European immigrants. Denton loves his family, dislikes being away from them, and treasures the times they can get together.
>
> Denton always wanted to be in politics and was involved in student government. As president of the student body of Harvard Divinity School, he presided over discussions, including some with Paul Tillich, and led a student demonstration around the federal building in Boston.
>
> Body bags provided his defining moment: Denton was a U.S. Marine on Okinawa. Seeing body bags coming back from Vietnam made him realize that he wanted to be an ambassador for Christ and not for any government.
>
> He earned a doctorate at the University of Hamburg, studying with Stephen Neil, and then, served as American Baptist fraternal representative in Eastern Europe. Denton came to love these Christian saints. He believes his experiences there—negotiating over issues of religious freedom and the need for seminaries and buildings—prepared him for his present ministry.
>
> Denton loves books, history, and languages. He and Janice both enjoy the Washington Symphony and when in Germany, go to hear the great cathedral organs play Bach.

the BWA's support, ministry, and faith and life services. The most controversial proposals were to reduce the term of the President to two years so that a wider range of people could serve and to run the Congresses in a four-year instead of a five-year cycle.

The Council discussed the report and decided to submit it to all the member bodies to consider and propose changes. The Structure Committee would then review the suggestions, work with the Executive Committee to refine the proposals, and bring a final report to the 1989 General Council.[18] When MacRae moved the revised report at Zagreb, the abbreviated Congress term was no longer on the table, and the Council voted down the committee's new proposal to limit the presidential term to two and a half years. The amendments that were accepted set forth the legislative authority of the General Council, affirmed the role of the General Secretary as the Chief Executive Officer, and separated the function of Treasurer from the General Secretary, thereby repealing an amendment passed at the 1985 World Congress.

Moreover, the officers of the Alliance were to be nominated by the General Council and elected at the Congress. No last-minute nominations could be made from the floor. The General Council would establish all committees and the President would make appointments to them. Auxiliaries of the Alliance (Women's, Men's, and Youth departments) would be self-governing, but their bylaws were to be approved by the General Council; they were to generate their own funding and to appoint their own staff. Only the General Council could amend the BWA Constitution and Bylaws, and a one-year's notice was needed for adopting a proposed amendment. The existing provision whereby one hundred delegates to the Congress could propose an amendment was repealed. Also specified was that the number of delegates a convention or union would have on the General Council was proportional to the number of church members within that body; larger delegations were required to have a numerical balance of clergy, laypeople, women, and young persons. Explicitly stated was that regional fellowships were not intermediaries between the conventions/unions and the BWA.[19] The constitution and bylaw changes were ratified at the World Congress in Seoul in 1990.[20]

The General Council approved further amendments in 1995, and they were voted on in 1996. The most important were that a member body "assumes responsibility for assisting in the support and furtherance of the purposes and work of the Alliance"; the Executive Committee was to consist of ten members (including two women) chosen from the General Council's membership, the officers of the BWA, the elected presiding officers of the regional fellowships, and the chairs of the departments and program divisions; and the number of Vice Presidents was no longer specified (it had been twelve; in 2000 it was increased to sixteen).[21]

Sixteenth Baptist World Congress, Seoul 1990
In August 1990 the Sixteenth Baptist World Congress met in Seoul, Korea.[22] Because of communication and logistical problems, the BWA almost changed the site of this meeting, but in the end the Seoul Congress proved to be one of the most successful in the Alliance's history. A total of 10,649 registered delegates from eighty-six countries gathered to celebrate the new freedom for Eastern Europe; to enjoy music from places as diverse as Nagaland, Brazil, Korea, and the Soviet Union; and to hear great preachers from more than half a dozen different traditions. Especially noteworthy was the presence of 199 delegates from the former Soviet countries, including 171 from the Soviet Union itself. Previously the largest Baptist delegation that had been allowed to leave that country was six people.

Featured speakers came from all six continents: Kwan Suk Oh (Korea); Mercy Jeyaraja Rao (India); Sergei Nikolaev (Soviet Union); G. Noel Vose (Australia); Atinuke Bamijoko (Nigeria); Pablo Deiros (Argentina);

Burchell Taylor (Jamaica); Joel Gregory (U.S.); and Roy D. Bell (Canada). But no one made a greater impact than Charles G. Adams from Detroit, Michigan, the first vice president of the Progressive National Baptist Convention, Inc. Waves of spontaneous applause broke out as Adams, using both the Congress theme "Together in Christ" and the text 1 John 4:16b, expounded on the supreme significance of love. His final cadence—Go back home and demonstrate love, explicate love, accentuate love, perpetuate love. God is love! Together in Christ—we love—left no one unmoved.[23]

This was a Congress of prayer. Korean Baptists, by far the majority in attendance, did not pray silently even during a service; every person prayed aloud, not in unison but in what General Secretary Lotz described as "Old Testament-like ecstatic utterances." They arose each day to gather for prayer at 4:30 a.m. On the Friday of the Congress they held an all-night prayer meeting, at which, according to Lotz, you could "hear thousands groaning in sweet anticipation of the Spirit."[24] For many from abroad participating in such prayer-filled gatherings was truly a life-changing experience.

The Congress closed with the Lord's Supper, conducted by outgoing President Vose, assisted by the twelve Vice Presidents. While the elements were served, all in attendance read together the words of the Seoul Covenant, dedicating themselves "anew to the task of world evangelism with the aim that by AD 2000 every person will have the opportunity to respond to the message of God's love in Jesus Christ in an authentic and meaningful way." The BWA designated 1990–2000 as a "Decade of Evangelism." Cupit, who in his first assignment as the new Director of the Division of Evangelism and Education had drafted the covenant, led the reading. Australian Baptists later prepared a set of Bible studies based on the covenant that they published under the aegis of the BWA.[25]

Korea was a most fitting venue for such an evangelistic initiative. It was one of the most successful Baptist mission fields in the world, one in which the new Christians immediately became missionaries themselves. Korean Baptists were committed to witnessing and they now numbered almost three hundred twenty-five thousand. They showed their great strength on the eve of the Congress with a welcoming rally, where over fifty thousand persons filled the Olympic Stadium. In addition, in two large baptismal services held at the Olympic Rowing Arena beside the Han River, they baptized a total of ten thousand new converts.

An editorial in the *Baptist World* summed up the significance of the Seoul Congress. The BWA had met its goals here: We were united; we contributed to the identity of the Korean Baptists; we learned much from the Koreans; we emphasized evangelism; and above all Jesus Christ was exalted.[26]

BWA Programs

Although the BWA engaged in relief programs after the two World Wars and endeavored to support religious liberty wherever it was infringed, most Baptists in earlier years thought of it as an organization for fellowship. In later decades it became increasingly program oriented and served as an agency for evangelism, education, social service, and human rights.

Cupit was deeply committed to evangelism. His Division of Evangelism and Education sought to actualize the principles of the Seoul Covenant by convening conferences on evangelism. Some focused on establishing new congregations ("church planting"), especially the "first" Baptist International Conference on Establishing Churches in Swanwick, Derbyshire, England, in March 1992, where the two hundred and fifty delegates from forty-five countries endorsed a document known as the Derbyshire Declaration. This ten-point call reaffirmed the task of world evangelization and invited "every Baptist congregation in the world to establish, or to explore the possibility of joining with other churches in establishing, at least one new congregation by AD 2000 "[27] As a result of the Swanwick conference, a European Conference for Church Growth hosted by the German Baptist Union was held in Berlin in 1993. Regional meetings on church planting also took place in Moscow, Russia (1993); Bratislava, Slovakia (1993); Calcutta, India (1993); Pokhara, Nepal (1994); and Toulouse, France (1995).

Other meetings, called "Conferences on Unevangelized People," focused on training Baptists to witness to people who knew very little about Christianity. A meeting in Larnaca, Cyprus, in January 1994 produced the Cyprus Guidelines for reaching those who had not heard the gospel.[28] They were reformulated at a second conference in Madras, India, a year later. Entitled "Hope for a Needy World: Reaching Out to Unevangelized Peoples," these guidelines for action urged Baptist mission agencies to redistribute their personnel and resources in order to give priority to evangelization of the unreached. The statement also stressed gathering and sharing research data on these peoples; developing effective strategies to reach them; raising human rights issues where religious freedom is restricted; developing holistic responses to their socioeconomic needs; providing them with the Scriptures; mobilizing Baptist women to reach the unevangelized women in these cultures; and learning from and respecting peoples of other religions while remaining totally committed to the uniqueness of Jesus Christ as the only way to find salvation and peace with God.[29]

The Madras meeting was followed by regional gatherings later in 1995 in Tura (Northeast India) and North Thailand. Earlier, in 1989, the BWA and the Asian Baptist Federation had cosponsored an education and evangelism conference in Singapore. Evangelistic preaching ministries took place in Cuba (1991 and 1992), Ukraine (1992), and Poland (1994).

Education was an ongoing concern. As a missionary in Europe, Lotz had been deeply interested in educational matters and, in 1978, had founded the Summer Institute of Theological Education at the Baptist seminary in Rüschlikon. Thus in November 1989, the BWA under Lotz's leadership sponsored an International Christian Writers' Conference at the seminary. Then in October 1990, in Moscow at a BWA-sponsored meeting of theological educators from the West, Lotz announced the appointment of a Theological Assistance Group (TAG) to further the development of theological education in Eastern Europe. Its purpose was to function in a consultancy role and to provide guidance to Baptist unions in establishing seminaries, planning buildings, setting up libraries, developing courses, and selecting teachers. There were to be two sections—one for Europe and the other for North America—but coordination of the two proved difficult, and the EBF executive decided that the TAG–Europe would follow its own agenda.[30]

In 1993, after many years of work, the BWA and the Mennonite Central Committee completed their joint project of translating a Bible commentary into Russian. Director of Communications Ryan led or organized a number of training workshops. A notable one was the Christian Writers' and Communicators' Conference in Papua New Guinea in 1992. A well-attended Baptist International Conference on Theological Education (BICTE) was held in 1989 in Zagreb, Yugoslavia, and another in 1993 in Johannesburg, South Africa. At the latter, conferees asked the BWA to facilitate the process of theological dialogue and to implement "a more contextual, effective, and relevant theological education in South Africa." They also urged that the work of the BWA's TAG be extended into other areas besides Eastern Europe.[31]

Unfortunately, a serious crisis erupted in Europe that foreshadowed the later rift between the SBC and BWA. The FMB was indigenizing the Baptist Theological Seminary in Rüschlikon by gradually turning control over to the EBF, and by 1989 the process was essentially completed. The FMB had agreed to continue providing a subsidy for some years while the seminary worked to get on a sounder financial footing, but the EBF rejected the FMB's request that a modest doctrinal affirmation be included in the seminary's new charter. In 1991 an American seminary professor, whom some regarded as a liberal, was invited to lecture at the school, and the FMB responded by completely defunding the institution as of January 1, 1992. In spite of protests from the Europeans, the mission board stood by its decision. The Hamburg Agreement of September 1992 mended relations between the FMB and EBF to a certain extent, but the EBF leaders saw no other alternative than to sell the Swiss property and relocate the school in a less expensive and more centrally located part of Europe. With financial help and volunteer workers from various Baptists in the United States, the EBF purchased and rehabilitated a new campus in Prague, Czech Republic, and the International Baptist Theological Seminary moved there in 1995.[32]

As mentioned earlier, human rights were an ongoing BWA concern. Tiller and his wife, Olive, who were among the most forthright exponents of human rights, had decided to donate $10,000 to fund a Baptist World Alliance Human Rights Award. The General Council, at its meeting in Montreal on July 10, 1991, voted to accept it just two days after Tiller passed away after a long struggle with cancer. The first recipient was former U.S. President Jimmy Carter. The award was presented to him at the Carter Center in Atlanta in a ceremony that was videotaped and shown at the Buenos Aires Congress.[33] When this dedicated layman was awarded the Nobel Peace Prize in 2002, the BWA publicly congratulated him.

To express its concern about human rights, racism, peace, and religious liberty, the BWA used resolutions, personal contact through visits and correspondence, and dialogue; at the same time it informed the Baptist constituency about these issues. Wümpelmann and Cupit led a BWA delegation to El Salvador in January 1992 to investigate reported violations of human rights. In June 1994 Lotz and Cupit visited Myanmar, a country with many Baptist constituents who felt disenfranchised by the hard-line regime there. The BWA had repeatedly expressed its disapproval of apartheid in South Africa, and Wümpelmann and Regina Claas represented the BWA as observers at the country's first fully democratic elections in 1994.

Because of its nongovernmental organization (NGO) consultative status at the U.N., the BWA was able to participate in the U.N. World Conference on Human Rights in Vienna in June 1993. This convocation was the first time that NGO representatives were allowed to meet with official conferees and to participate in the discussions. President Wümpelmann and Vice President Eudora Mary Kalil (El Salvador) led the BWA delegation; he wrote in his *Baptist World* column that those present seemed to agree on the need for a "holistic approach" to human rights. Those from the northern hemisphere usually spoke of individual rights, whereas those from the south emphasized freedom from poverty and freedom to develop as the most urgent rights. The result was that the final conference document stated: "All human rights are universal, indivisible and interdependent, and inter-related." The President emphasized that freedom of conscience and freedom from poverty must go hand in hand, and that the international community, of which the BWA is a part, "must treat human rights globally in a fair and equal manner, on the same footing, and with the same emphasis." Kalil talked to a thirteen-year-old girl from El Salvador whose father had been tortured and killed and learned that Kalil had known the father through their common fight for justice and against violence.[34]

Deeply concerned about the riots that had swept southern California over the beating of an African-American man by a white policeman, in May 1992 the BWA formed a Special Commission of Baptists Against Racism. It was charged with investigating the causes of racism; examining the biblical and theological issues raised by racism; and finding ways in which Baptists could help to overcome its evils and to challenge racist attitudes and actions that prevent people from living in harmony with each other. The honorary chair of the commission was former U.S. President Jimmy Carter, and the chair was Progressive National Baptist pastor John O. Peterson. The thirty-five-member interracial and international body presented a report with several thoughtful papers and a series of hard-hitting resolutions for the General Council to consider at its meeting in Harare, Zimbabwe, in August 1993.[35]

The commission also formulated the Harare Declaration, which the General Council adopted and used as a liturgy for worship at its meeting. It is a ten-point document that acknowledges God's work in redemption; affirms that the BWA will—through evangelism, worship, education, fellowship, and prophetic action—expose and challenge the sin of racism and engage in a ministry of reconciliation; and commits members of the BWA to recognize and accept all humankind as God's creation and to affirm with joy the unity and diversity of their membership in the community of faith.[36] After the Harare General Council, the body was renamed the Special Commission of Baptists Against Racism and Ethnic Conflict.

BWAid engaged in a dizzying array of projects. Its report to the General Council in 1991 declared that it was engaged "in a holistic response to the whole gospel." The three sections of work—disaster relief, development, and fellowship assistance—covered a wide range of activities. BWAid concentrated heavily on Eastern Europe after the fall of communism, channeling nearly $9 million in assistance, including very large gifts-in-kind to the area in 1992, and it donated $178,000 to help launch the Moscow Theological Seminary in 1993. Wümpelmann declared 1993 "the year of Africa," describing it as "a most needy and forgotten continent." BWAid responded with relief in areas of civil conflict—Somalia, Angola, Liberia, Burundi, and Rwanda—and provided assistance to refugees in neighboring countries. It sent significant amounts of food and medical supplies to Rwanda, where in 1994 at least a half million were massacred and two million fled the country, including Ziherambere, the BWA Regional Secretary for Africa.

In Asia BWAid helped people affected by cyclones, floods, and an earthquake, as well as providing assistance to refugees and people with AIDS. It supplied aid to victims of an earthquake and a volcanic eruption in Central America and to persons impacted by a major hurricane in the Bahamas and southeastern United States and an earthquake in California. It also provided pastors in Cuba with bicycles and travel assistance for people in poor nations to attend BWA meetings. In its report to the 1995 General Council, the division listed cash income, including funds from the EBF, of over two million dollars and gifts-in-kind of seven and a half million dollars. In a review of its work between 1990 and 1995, BWAid noted an increase in the number of projects, as well as in cash contributions and gifts-in-kind. Electronic communications enabled it to respond to needs more quickly; because of improved monitoring procedures, it had gained increased trust from Baptist bodies and other agencies. Also, an important shift had occurred. In the past BWAid funneled funds and supplies through missionaries, but increasingly it empowered, enabled, and entrusted indigenous Baptists to meet the needs in their own communities.[37]

The Departments, Regional Fellowships, and Other Activities
The Women's, Men's, and Youth departments were valuable auxiliaries. The Women's Department was particularly well organized with its own meetings prior to the World Congresses, special consultations on the evangelization of women, a newsletter called *Together*, and links to six continental women's unions and numerous national women's groups. Its budget income grew from a little over one hundred and sixty thousand dollars in 1987-88 to almost three hundred and fifty thousand dollars in 1994. It was very successful in raising funds through its annual Day of Prayer offering, half of which was retained by the continental unions. In August 1993 it provided leadership training for women from Russia, Moldova, Estonia, and Romania; in October on the scene in Moscow, it trained Russian women who were starting their own mission organization. It also helped women in Eastern Europe acquire literature not readily available from local sources and enabled networking between women's groups in Eastern Europe and those in the West.

On the other hand, the Men's Department was much less active. It did hold its Fifth World Conference at the same time as the Baptist Congress in

Seoul in 1990 and an enthusiastic Sixth World Conference at a prominent black church in Nashville in 1993.

The Youth Department sponsored an International Youth Leadership Training Conference prior to the Seoul Congress and a youth rally during the conclave. In 1993 the Twelfth Baptist Youth World Conference in Harare, Zimbabwe, with a registration of three thousand, was a great success. In 1994—the year that Dunn of Liberia became the department's full-time director—the Youth Executive Committee gave its blessings to "True Love Waits," a program initiated by Southern Baptists that encouraged unmarried young people not to engage in sexual intercourse.

The six regional fellowships, each with their own officers, budget, and congresses or conferences, extended the work of the BWA. The presiding officers of the fellowships were members of the Executive Committee of the BWA, and their regional secretaries were also Regional Secretaries of the Alliance. In 1989, the Structure Committee was fearful that the regions might become competitive with the Alliance and drain resources from it. In 1993, a consultation between the executive staff of the BWA and the Regional Secretaries was held in Tollose, Denmark, to clarify roles and relationships of the regions. A second consultation followed in 1994 in Buenos Aires.

In Europe the major effort was the full integration of the Eastern European unions into the EBF and helping them to find their way in the post-communist era. In Africa it was dealing with civil strife, refugee problems, the intensifying AIDS epidemic; overcoming barriers to communication; and dismantling apartheid in South Africa. In Asia were four major events: the celebration of the two-hundredth anniversary of William Carey's arrival in India; a Relief and Development and a Communications Seminar; a Nagaland tour; and the Indian Evangelism Conference. In the Americas the Caribbean Baptist Fellowship and Union of Baptists in Latin America functioned well, but the North American Baptist Fellowship had difficulty in finding its way. Although Baptist denominations in that continent were strong, the regional organization was the weakest of all the fellowships. Few representatives of the member bodies attended meetings and, except for the period 1990 to 1992 when Crumpler served as Regional Secretary, the BWA office assumed the work of the fellowship.

The BWA did not neglect lands still under communist rule, such as Cuba and China. Lotz visited Cuba in March 1989, and this successful experience was followed by a visit by twenty-three Baptist leaders representing ten countries. They called on government officials and gave out Bibles. In the early 1990s evangelistic tours in Cuba began occurring regularly. Similar efforts were made to develop relationships with the official Christian leadership in China. In 1986 the BWA conducted a Friendship Tour of China, and in November 1991 Lotz and several others visited Nanjing Seminary and the head of the Amity Foundation, which published Bibles and hymnals for the Christian community in China. In April 1994 Lotz and a thirty-four-person group that included President Wümpelmann traveled in China as guests of the China Christian Council and took part in a conference at Nanjing Seminary.[38]

Problems

The BWA leaders had a number of concerns. For example, who should be accepted as members? Lotz had told the General Council in 1990 that the BWA was not a "doctrinal" body and was open to Baptist diversity worldwide. In 1994, nevertheless, he acknowledged in a report to the Executive Committee that some guidelines for membership were needed. One guideline had to be an emphasis on believers' baptism. Another concern was insufficient internationalization. Although the officers and professional staff had become much more diverse, the leadership of committees, workgroups, and commissions remained heavily weighted in favor of males from the western world. Wümpelmann desired greater participation from the Two-thirds World, but he recognized at the General Council meeting in Buenos Aires in 1995 that 63 percent of the member conventions/unions had fewer than twenty-five thousand church members and consequently, did not have the financial resources for full participation.[39]

Language was another problem. English is essentially the official language of the BWA, but at Congresses some accommodation was made—for example, providing through headphones translations into one or two other languages. At Seoul, Korean was the primary language at the welcoming rally, and the Congress book was in both Korean and English. The workshops at the Congress in Buenos Aires were conducted in both English and Spanish, and the daily bulletins were bilingual. Used in congregational singing at Buenos Aires was *World Praise*, a new hymnal produced through the efforts of the Worship Commission that incorporated numerous hymns from outside the western world. A Spanish edition of the *Baptist World* was published in May 1995, followed by a second one just prior to the opening of the Congress. The possibility was raised that in future issues some pages might be printed in Spanish.[40] At other meetings, both regional and local, the BWA secured translators but did comparatively little to provide adequate conference materials for those who did not know English.

Membership was continuing to grow, with the greatest gains occurring in Africa, Asia, and Latin America. The number of bodies increased from 140 to 187 but much of this growth was due to the breakup of the Soviet Union, Yugoslavia, and Czechoslovakia, as well as the dissolution of the Council of North East India. Eight new countries or territories, all in the Two-thirds World, had also been added. With adjustment for inflated and duplicated figures, the membership of the BWA grew from slightly over thirty-one million in 1990 to almost thirty-four million in 1995, a gain of almost three million. Three-quarters of this growth was in Two-thirds World churches.[41]

But income did not keep pace with the expansion in numbers of members, and the Alliance was constantly faced with deficits. At the General Council in Harare in 1993, Lotz lamented that the operating budget of the BWA was "a pathetic and paltry sum" and pointed out that numerous churches in North America had budgets four times greater than the Alliance. The year 1993 proved particularly devastating with a net revenue loss of $136,000. Lotz reported to the General Council in Buenos Aires that deficits in 1993 and 1994 brought reserves "dangerously low," reducing them from almost four hundred thousand to around two-hundred and ninety thousand dollars.[42]

For one thing, the annual contributions of member bodies had remained relatively static. Many of them gave nothing, not even token amounts. A number of these were small and poor or were located in countries with currency restrictions. It was reported at the 1994 General Council that in 1975 84 percent of the BWA's revenue had come from member bodies, but in 1993 less than 50 percent did. An increasing number of churches and individuals were giving, but the donor base was "astoundingly low for a world organization." The General Council approved requesting an offering from the churches in 1995 to be followed by subsequent offerings in the year of each Congress.[43] Fortunately, the BWA did gain some new income. The Combined Federal Campaign enabled U.S. government employees to designate gifts that would be matched by equal gifts to the BWA. In 1994, Charlotte Hoover (U.S.) gave $200,000 to establish the Charlotte and Lawrence Hoover BWA Conference Fund to assist Baptists from the Two-thirds World to participate in conferences and training. In 1990, the BWA inaugurated an endowment, the 21st Century Fund and sought pledges of $2,000 for the year 2000. The BWA also received income from its investments.

Lotz was not hesitant to note that that many Baptists gave money to parachurch groups while neglecting their own Baptist world body. In an editorial in the *Baptist World,* he insisted that the BWA was not simply another parachurch organization but that it had an "ecclesial function" that demanded Baptist support.[44]

He was also concerned that the extensive activities of parachurch groups in Eastern Europe were assisting the Orthodox churches in regaining the established position they had before the advent of communism. The Orthodox used the western-based parachurch movements to cast doubt on all non-Orthodox groups, including Baptists, even though the governments had officially recognized their unions. In each Eastern European country, the Orthodox Church urged its government to limit religious freedom, and as in previous years the BWA protested and sought to represent Baptist interests.[45] The BWA also decided to initiate conversations with the Orthodox churches, which will be discussed in the next chapter.

Seventeenth Baptist World Congress, Buenos Aires 1995

Over six thousand delegates from 136 member bodies gathered in Buenos Aires, the beautiful capital city of Argentina, for the Seventeenth World Congress, August 1–6, 1995. Each day began with Bible studies, which met in different places around the city. In the afternoon there were elective workshops, featuring subjects as diverse as "Using Music in Worship" to "Rights of Women and Children" plus a new initiative called "Love in Action." Participants could witness on the street, distributing tracts and copies of the Gospel of John; visit hospitals and homes for children or the elderly; or build wooden tables and benches for use in feeding centers for children. The Congress Hall housed the auditorium for the evening plenary sessions as well as the exhibition center that was open daily and became a crossroads, featuring a bookstore and displays presented by each BWA entity as well as other Baptist agencies. Adjacent was a small café where strong, sweet Argentine-style coffee was available and where Baptists from various countries met and exchanged ideas.

The plenary sessions opened with music in which Spanish and Portuguese singers exuberantly expressed their praises to God. There were reports and short messages by such noted people as Bernice King, daughter of Martin Luther King, Jr., who used John 4:1–29 as her text to exhort Baptists to oppose racism. The president of Argentina, accompanied by a large official contingent, spoke at length of his own Christian faith. The plenary speakers represented every regional fellowship except the Caribbean. Two were from North America: a Southern Baptist man and an African-American woman. They had each been assigned one facet of the theme, "Celebrate Christ: The Hope of the World," and the impact of all the messages was to challenge listeners to bring Christ to a world that needs him.

The entire Congress focused on evangelism, as was appropriate in this "Decade of Evangelism." In addition to the plenary sessions, the several workshops on evangelism, and "Love in Action" activities, there were outdoor rallies: one at the famous Plaza de Mayo and two at the Obelisk on the city's widest boulevard, one of which was led by the Women's Department and the other by the Youth Department. The youth also presented a musical drama at various locations around the city. The Men's Department sponsored street evangelism.

Elected as President for the next quinquennium was South America's outstanding evangelist, Nilson do Amaral Fanini of Brazil. Fanini, who had preached the gospel in eighty-seven nations, challenged each person at the Congress to return home to lead evangelistic campaigns: "Let us use all possible resources: radio, television, newspapers, the printed word, as well as the spoken word to proclaim with one voice,

Jesus Cristo é o Senhor
Jesus Christ is Lord
Jesu cristo és el Señor."[46]

---

1. *Baptist World*, October–December 1990, p. 2.

2. *BWA Congress*, 1975, pp. 256-257.

3. This process is discussed at length in Bernard Green, *Crossing the Boundaries: A History of the European Baptist Federation* (Didcot, U.K.: Baptist Historical Society, 1999).

4. Ibid., p. 114.

5. *Baptist World*, April–June 1990, p. 11.

6. Green, *Crossing the Boundaries*, p. 118.

7. Text of the letter is in a release of the European Baptist Press Service, November 24, 1989, quoted in Green, *Crossing the Boundaries*, p. 115.

8. *Die Revolution der Kerzen* (Wuppertal: Oncken Verlag, 1990); translated by Edwin P. Arnold and edited by Richard V. Pierard as the *Revolution of the Candles: Christians in the Revolution of the German Democratic Republic* (Macon, GA: Mercer University Press, 1996).

9. Bud Bultman, *Revolution by Candlelight* (Portland, OR: Multnomah Press, 1991), p. 240.

10. Green, *Crossing the Boundaries*, pp. 119–120.

11. *BWA News*, September 1993, p. 1.

12. *Baptist World*, July–September 1945, p. 16.

13. Ibid., January–March 1990, pp. 5–7.

14. For biographical information, see Bent Hylleberg, "Knud Wümpelmann," paper presented to the Baptist Heritage Study Commission, 1999.

15. General Council, 1989, p. 30.

16. *BWA Yearbook*, 1986, p. 13.

17. BWA Structure Committee Report, July 1988. Copy in the BWA Office Library, Falls Church, VA.

18. *BWA Yearbook*, 1988, p. 14. Responses to Structure Committee Report," March 1989, photocopy in BWA Office Library, Falls Church, VA

19. *BWA Yearbook*, 1989, pp. 5, 7, 17–22.

20. *BWA Congress*, 1990, p. 156.

21. *BWA Yearbook*, 1995, pp. 101–106.

22. See the report in *Baptist World*, October–December 1900, pp. 4–5.

23. *BWA Congress*, 1990, p. 55.

24. Ibid., p. 7.

25. Ibid., p. 257, has the text of the Seoul Covenant. It is also found in Tony Cupit, ed., *Baptist World Alliance Covenants and Declarations* (McLean, VA: BWA, 1999). The study book is Harry Monro, ed., *Seven Study Guides on Local and World Evangelism Based on the Seoul Covenant of the Baptist World Alliance* (Melbourne: Baptist Union of Australia, 1992).

26. *Baptist World*, October–December 1990, p. 6.

27. Ibid., July–September 1992, pp. 3–4; Cupit, *BWA Covenants and Declarations*, pp. 7–9.

28. BWA Division of Evangelism and Education, *Seoul Covenant, Derbyshire Declaration, Cyprus Guidelines* (McLean, VA: BWA), 1940, pp. 8–11.

29. Cupit, *BWA Covenants and Declarations*, pp. 14–18.

30. Green, *Crossing the Boundaries*, pp. 166–167.

31. *Baptist World*, October–December 1992, p. 8.

32. Green provides a nuanced account of this painful situation in *Crossing the Boundaries*, pp. 185–196.

33. *BWA Congress*, 1995, pp. 97, 100–102.

34. *Baptist World*, October–December 1993, p. 2, 11.

35. Ibid., July–September 1993, pp. 5–8. *Baptists Against Racism: Report of Special Committee Baptists Against Racism, Harare, Zimbabwe*, August 1993 (McLean, VA: BWA, 1993).

36. Text in ibid., pp. 46–47, and Cupit, *BWA Covenants and Declarations*, pp. 10–12.

37. General Council, 1995, pp. 99, 105.

38. For BWA relations with China, see *Baptist World,* January–March 1992, p. 7.

39. General Council, 1995, p. 54.

40. For a few years in the 1970s the Baptist Spanish Publishing House in El Paso, Texas, had printed a Spanish edition.

41. Membership statistics are a matter of contention. The people in the BWA office who compile the figures are obligated to utilize the figures furnished by the conventions and unions. It is no secret that some have churches that are aligned with other bodies, and their members may be double-counted. Moreover, there are churches that baptize children as young as four or five years old and count them as members.

42. General Council, 1995, p. 61.

43. *BWA Yearbook,* 1992, p. 111.

44. *Baptist World,* January–March 1993, p. 2. At a church growth conference in Berlin in March 1993, Lotz sounded a warning about parachurch groups, especially "lone-ranger" individual evangelists and sectarian, heretical types, and he offered some guidelines for cooperation with parachurch organizations. Ibid., July–September, p. 12.

45. For an account by Denton Lotz of the threats to religious freedom in Eastern Europe, see General Council, 1994, pp. 87–88.

46. *BWA Congress,* 1995, p. 95.

10

FORWARD INTO THE NEW CENTURY, 1995–2005
Ken R. Manley

As the delegates left Buenos Aires in July 1995 with the theme of the Seventeenth World Congress, "Celebrate Christ: The Hope of the World," echoing in their hearts, few realized how desperately hope would be needed during the ensuing decade. A new world was emerging, and vivid images dominated public awareness. Some radiated hope, such as the celebrations to mark the new millennium as the year 2000 dawned around the world. But there were sadder and depressing images. Fearsome fighting continued in the Balkans, with equally disturbing eruptions of ethnic conflict that brought bloodshed and heartache to Africa and Asia. The dramatic scenes of September 11, 2001, when hijacked planes destroyed the twin towers of the World Trade Center in New York and killed almost three thousand people, dominated the memory of billions. Never before had the much-vaunted "global village" shared so intimately in a disaster as television replayed the horrific scenes. Other images of terrorism, seemingly endless fighting between Israelis and Palestinians, masses of refugees seeking security and a better life, appalling levels of hunger, the ravages of HIV/AIDS, tensions within the United Nations (U.N.), and the controversial war in Iraq all confirmed this as a decade of despair. Nothing could conceal the suffering of millions.

The Global Baptist Community
In a highly influential book, Samuel P. Huntington popularized the term *clash of civilizations*, and it underscores how much resurgent religion is at the heart of the global shifts and world conflict. Fundamentalist movements in the major religions are "committed to the militant purification of religious doctrines and institutions," as well as "the reshaping of personal, social, and public behavior in accordance with religious tenets."[1] In such an era Baptists need the Baptist World Alliance (BWA) as never before. Christ as the hope of the world remains their motivation and message, but how to live and serve in such a tumultuous time is a searching challenge.

The increasing internationalization that has marked the life of the world body of Baptists was symbolized by the two BWA Presidents in this decade: Nilson do Amaral Fanini, a leading pastor-evangelist from Brazil, 1995–2000, and Billy Jang Hwan Kim, an equally distinguished Korean pastor-evangelist, 2000–2005. The era of the domination of the BWA by European and North American Baptists was clearly at an end. The growth of Baptists in Latin America, Asia, and Africa brought new leaders to the forefront. Baptists from around the world were chosen to serve as Vice Presidents and on the various divisions and committees. David Coffey of the United Kingdom was nominated in 2004 to be the new President of the BWA for 2005–10.

Impressive personalities continued to provide strong leadership in the BWA regional bodies, even as changes occurred among the full-time Regional Secretaries. In the All Africa Baptist Fellowship (AABF) Eleazar Ziherambere of Rwanda was replaced by Frank Adams of Ghana in 1997. Edwin I. Lopez of the Philippines concluded a remarkable term of service (1980–97) with the Asian Baptist Federation (ABF), to be succeeded by Bonny Resu of India. In the Caribbean Baptist Fellowship Peter Pinder of the Bahamas commenced service in 1995. In the Union of Baptists in Latin America (UBLA), Daniel Carro of Argentina began serving in 1995 and was followed by Alberto Prokopchuk of Argentina in 2001. In the European Baptist Federation (EBF) Karl Heinz Walter of Germany retired in 1998

Nilson do Amaral Fanini

When Nilson do Amaral Fanini was elected at the Buenos Aires Congress in 1995, no one was surprised when he announced that his main focus as President of the Baptist World Alliance would be evangelism. Fanini is a world-renowned evangelist.

But he has never overlooked the physical needs of people. Reencontro, the humanitarian organization he founded, works throughout Brazil to feed the hungry, clothe the naked, give medical attention to the sick, and provide vocational education for the unemployed. His church, First Baptist of Niteroi, Brazil, has adopted thousands of slum babies. And the adoption program is only one of the church's many ministries in a vast urban area.

Fanini has a doctorate in law from the Fluminensi Law School of the University of Rio de Janeiro and a masters in theology from Southwestern Baptist Theological Seminary in Fort Worth, Texas. He is also a graduate of the highest level of the Brazilian war college, a privilege reserved for the nations's outstanding leaders. His government has recognized him for his work on behalf of the poor.

As President in the 1995–2000 quinquennium, he appealed to governments on behalf of those whose human rights were violated. He traveled throughout the world, greeting Baptists and bringing the good news of Christ to those who had not heard it. Although no longer in office, he continues to be a spokesperson for Baptists and for the Christ he serves.

and was replaced by Theo Angelov of Bulgaria. By the time Tony Peck of the United Kingdom succeeded Angelov in 2004, the EBF office was centrally located in Prague, Czech Republic, illustrating how active Eastern Europeans were becoming in the BWA.

At each annual General Council there was a strong focus on the local region where it was meeting. In Hong Kong (1996) support was given to Christians preparing for the reversion of the colony to China in 1997. (Since the 1980s the BWA has maintained meaningful contact with the China Christian Council and Alliance leaders have made numerous visits to the churches of China.) The Vancouver gathering (1997) provided the opportunity for various Canadian groups to act together. The Council meeting in Durban, South Africa (1998), focused on reconciliation. Distinguished guest Archbishop Desmond Tutu spoke powerfully about the work of the South African government's Peace and Reconciliation Commission in bringing the country together after the end of apartheid, and Baptist leaders reported significant steps towards reconciliation among their conventions. In 1999, the Baptists met in Dresden, Germany, and in this city—largely destroyed by bombs during World War II and a center in the struggle that brought down the communist regime in East Germany—the theme of new hope was again powerfully embraced.

Baptists in Havana, Cuba, were thrilled to welcome the General Council in July 2000. To those who had endured years of persecution and restrictions, it was like a dream come true. A huge banner hung outside the massive State Capitol Building with the slogan *¡Cuba para Cristo!* (Cuba for Christ!) and affirmed the 2000 Congress theme *¡Jesu Cristo para Siempre, Si!* (Jesus Christ, Forever. Yes!). A vigorous evangelism program accompanied the meetings, and BWA leaders stressed the importance of the Baptist teaching about separation of church and state in a lengthy meeting with Cuban President Fidel Castro.

Picturesque Charlottetown in Prince Edward Island, Canada, was the site for the 2001 meeting where racism was highlighted. In 2002, more than five hundred and fifty people from sixty-five countries gathered in Seville, Spain, and encouraged the local Baptists who live in a largely Catholic country. Rio de Janeiro, Brazil, hosted the Council in 2003, and the 2004 meeting was in Seoul, Korea, where President Billy Jang Hwan Kim extended a warm welcome to the delegates. The Council had wanted to meet in Beirut, Lebanon, during this decade but decided against this venue because of political unrest in the region. Nonetheless, the EBF did meet there in 2004.

In January 1998, the BWA staff outlined what they thought "BWA does best."[2] The impressive list (slightly adapted here) summarized the

Billy Jang Hwan Kim

Billy Jang Hwan Kim is President of the Baptist World Alliance for its centenary celebration at Birmingham, England, July 27–31, 2005. He was elected during the Melbourne Congress in the first month of the second millennium after the birth of Jesus Christ.

Kim also serves as director of the Far East Broadcasting Company, Christian Services, Inc., Youth for Christ in Korea, and as area director for Youth for Christ in East Asia. Until December 19, 2004, he was senior pastor of Central Baptist Church in Suwon, a suburb of Seoul, Korea. Central is today a church of some fifteen thousand members. When Kim arrived there on January 1, 1960, the membership was ten people.

Kim graduated from Shinpoong Primary School in Suwon and earned a Bachelor of Arts and Master in Theology degrees from Bob Jones University in Greenville, South Carolina. In 1973, he had the opportunity to interpret for Billy Graham in Graham's 1973 Korea Crusade, where more than one million people attended a single service, an experience that Kim has never forgotten. Kim became a noted evangelist, invited by people throughout the world who want and need this loving man with a fiery message.

As President, Kim led Baptists to come together for evangelism, church planting, and to fight racial and ethnic conflict. Inspired by Christ's prayer in John 17, his theme is unity.

emphases and concerns of the decade:

1. Be an advocate for religious freedom and human rights, giving extra effort to combat racism.
2. Act as a catalyst for mission and evangelism through conferences and training opportunities.
3. Entrust, empower, encourage, and enable local churches, pastors, and people in their mission. Baptist World Aid (BWAid) has deliberately adopted this strategy in helping Baptists offer compassion and service to a needy world.
4. Afford opportunity for Baptists to demonstrate unity in Christ while facing the challenge of working for reconciliation among Baptist groups.
5. Help establish a clear understanding of Baptist identity. Identity awareness is sharpened in constructive conversations with other church traditions.
6. Provide a worldwide forum where crucial issues are discussed and differing views expressed. To develop an authentic global Baptist view on key topics is helpful, not in any sense as being prescriptive for member bodies but to affirm the rationale of being Baptist, and to articulate guidelines on pressing social and religious concerns. Belonging to the BWA, with a community of at least a hundred million, gives credibility and status to Baptist groups when dealing with governments. BWA gives a global focus to Baptist cooperation and life.
7. Provide structures to facilitate fellowship and networking. The increased importance of the annual General Council meetings supplements the larger Congress gatherings and the regional assemblies.

Religious Freedom and Human Rights

The BWA promoted racial reconciliation and ethnic harmony as well as actively defending religious freedom and human rights in general. Problems of racism are everywhere, but the BWA—choosing to address it in the country where Baptists are strongest—sponsored a Baptist Leaders U.S.A. Summit Against Racism in December 1995. This gathering paved the way for the significant International Summit of Baptists Against Racism and Ethnic Conflict, which convened in the historic Ebenezer Baptist Church in Atlanta, Georgia, January 8–11, 1999, with Billy Graham and Coretta Scott King as honorary chairs.[3] BWA General Secretary Denton Lotz spelled out the impact of the meeting:

> We heard the cry of aboriginals from Australia, of the tragedy of ethnic conflict amongst the Tutsis and Hutus of Rwanda, of the destruction and loss of life in the conflict between Kukis and Nagas in North East India. British participants and Americans of African descent shared the pain of continued prejudice in their own countries. The sad story of ethnic cleansing in the Balkans, even today, was cause for prayer and repentance.[4]

This summit produced the Atlanta Covenant and challenged Baptists around the world to observe a decade (2000–10) to promote racial justice by "efforts to eradicate racism wherever it emerges and engaging in the struggle against ethnic conflict."[5] Another timely conference, Baptist Identity and National Culture, held in Berlin May 26–29, 2001, declared that nationalism or adherence to a national ideology which exalts one nation over others, or is used to exclude others is a form of idolatry and not compatible with our Christian beliefs.[6]

After the fall of communism, the BWA promoted religious freedom in the former Soviet republics, many of which were dominated by authoritarian religious establishments. Lotz played a key role in these endeavors and even served a term as president of the International Religious Liberty Association, an agency that worked with governments everywhere to advance religious freedom. Only a few of the instances of Baptists experiencing persecution can be noted here, but the cumulative effect reveals the importance of this aspect of BWA ministry. In 1995 public attention was drawn to the situations of Baptists in Armenia, Bulgaria, Mexico, and Nigeria. In April 1996 Lotz and Angelov met with the president of Bulgaria to press for freedom for Baptists in that country. Protestant churches in Surabaya in Indonesia were attacked by mobs that same year. During 1997 the BWA protested against the police persecution that Baptists in Tashkent, Uzbekistan, were experiencing and pressed the authorities in Macedonia to allow Baptists the right to exist legally. In Turkmenistan a Baptist pastor was imprisoned, and in Azerbaijan consistent harassment took place. At various time, concerns were expressed with regard to incidents in Lebanon, Belgium, Romania, Russia, Estonia, Sri Lanka, and Pakistan.

The problems ranged from a resurgent Orthodox Church claiming sole religious authority to dominant non-Christian religious groups opposing Christians. Savage attacks on Christians by militant Hindu zealots in India reached a tragic climax in the deaths of Australian Baptist missionary Graham Staines and his two young sons on January 23, 1999, in Orissa. Lotz claimed that "the Baptist idea of religious freedom, now embedded in the United Nations Declaration of Human Rights, is under threat as never before." In November 2002, Belarus introduced a new law about religion thought to be the most repressive in Europe. New laws have created problems in Moldova and Russia. Even in the secular west, French Baptists protested against a new antisect law, "Human Rights and Public Liberties," which the BWA feared represented a renewed attempt in various Western European countries to place religious groups under state control.

The BWA's ongoing representation as an officially recognized nongovernment organization (NGO) at the U.N. in New York, Geneva, and Vienna is an important factor in influencing governments. When the BWA obtained "consultative status" in 1973, that designation gave it a higher level of access to all parts of the U.N. and the privilege of circulating its views to the General Assembly and the various commissions.[7] Eleanor Schnur, followed by Carl W. Tiller and George Younger, did yeoman service for the Alliance as its NGO spokesperson. Ruth Watson succeeded Younger in New York after his death in November 2001. Representing the BWA at U.N. agencies in Europe are Lauren Bethell in Vienna and Walter in Geneva.

Baptists have continued to advocate human rights for all people. The second Sunday in December is designated "Human Rights Day," while at each General Council meeting human-rights issues have been considered and resolutions addressing these concerns were regularly adopted. At Hong Kong (1996) resolutions deplored the persecution of Christians and the incidents of church burnings in the U.S. The fiftieth anniversary of the U.N.'s "Universal Declaration of Human Rights" prompted the Vancouver Council (1997) to record gratitude for the declaration's "great moral influence in the cause of justice, peace and religious tolerance." The prospect of peace in the Middle East and the horror of landmines were also featured in resolutions at Vancouver. In Durban (1998) resolutions dealt with peace among the Nagas in India; reconciliation in South Africa, Burundi, and Rwanda; nuclear proliferation; and the Jubilee 2000 campaign encouraging the forgiveness of debts by banks and government agencies. At Dresden (1999) the leaders of the "G 8" nations, the world's wealthiest, were congratulated for approving a hundred billion dollar debt forgiveness package for some of the poor nations.

At the 2000 Congress in Melbourne, Australia, resolutions reaffirmed the conviction that "human rights are God-given and that violations of human rights are violations of the laws of God." The BWA urged governments and citizens to seek peace with justice and "to strive to eradicate social injustice and eliminate human rights violations wherever these deplorable and intolerable conditions exist." Immediately prior to the Congress, 141 persons, mostly from the Two-thirds World, participated in a special conference, "Hearing the Cry, Acting in Hope." The Havana General Council (July 2000) endorsed resolutions deploring the sexual exploitation of children and protesting economic sanctions, specifically those that prevented food and medicine from reaching the people of Cuba. At Seville (2002) attention was given to problems in the Middle East and to terrorism, denouncing "the use of violence in the name of God and the service of religion." The BWA affirmed its willingness "to engage in debate and conversation with other religions and ideologies to resolve areas of tension." Concern for religious liberty and peace in the Middle East were recorded at Rio de Janeiro (2003). Issues raised at Seoul (2004) included the division of families and communities in the two halves of the Korean peninsula and the dispute over the inspection of nuclear-power facilities in North Korea. Resolutions by church bodies, such as the BWA, may not have a dramatic effect on world governments, but they undoubtedly serve as a stimulus to their own members to consider these issues.

In 1996 General Secretary Lotz, ABF Secretary Lopez, Study and Research director L. A. (Tony)Cupit, and Human Rights Commission Chair Thorwald Lorenzen surveyed the dismal situation that the twenty-five thousand Karen Baptist refugees from Myanmar faced in Thailand. Although regularly attacked by troops infiltrating from Myanmar, the refugees had established homes, schools, churches, and a Bible college on the Thai-Myanmar border. In 2000 the BWA Human Rights award went to the man known simply as Rev. Simon, a former teacher in a theological school in the Myanmar capital, who joined his fellow Karens at the Maele refugee camp and established the Kawtholei Baptist Bible School. Since Simon was unable to travel to receive his award, it was delivered to him at the camp on March 19, 2000. Other human rights visits were made to support the Baptists of Chiapas, Mexico, as well as to Myanmar, Indonesia, Azerbaijan, and Manipur in India.

The BWA's Human Rights Commission issued a series of booklets on Baptists and Human Rights: James E. Wood, Jr., *Baptists and Human Rights*

(1997); Lorenzen, *The Rights of the Child* (1996); Lorenzen, *Freedom of Religion as a Human Right* (1998); Cupit, *Peace I Leave with You* (2001).

Mission and Evangelism

Mission and evangelism have always been primary concerns of the BWA. The 1990 Seoul Covenant had called upon Baptists to give every person the opportunity to respond to the message of God's love in Jesus Christ in an authentic and meaningful way by the year 2000.[8] In 1995, President Fanini issued the challenge to double the number of Baptists and churches by the year 2000. While these goals were not reached, Baptists have grown dramatically. Some conventions/unions even exceeded Fanini's goal: For example, the number of churches in the Ukraine had increased from one thousand to two thousand by 1999.

This decade has evidenced significant changes in missions. Lotz repeatedly spoke of the "paradigm shift" in missions.

> The great new fact of our era is the new and bold missionary thrust from the Two-thirds World! Missionaries from Brazil go to Angola, from Japan to Thailand, from Korea to Bangladesh, from Nigeria to Ghana, from Hungary to Sierra Leone, from Nagaland to Nepal, from Mizoram to Bhutan. . . . More than twenty thousand missionaries from the Two-thirds World are now involved in cross-cultural mission.[9]

Though not a missionary agency, BWA has assumed the responsibility to assist Baptists in mission. A Baptist Fund for World Evangelization and Discipleship offers assistance to smaller groups. The International Mission Secretaries meet regularly under BWA auspices. A good example of BWA's influence was a conference held in Madras, India, in January 1995, with the theme of "Hope for a Needy World." The special focus on evangelizing previously unreached peoples led to a call for all Baptists to "develop holistic responses to human need" and to learn from and respect other religions while remaining totally committed to Jesus Christ as the "unique and only way to find salvation and peace with God."[10] Later that year similar regional conferences were held in Thailand and Tura, India. President Fanini conducted effective evangelistic meetings in association with these gatherings, and thousands indicated their desire to be committed to Christ. Indeed, both Presidents in this decade regularly conducted missions around the world and constantly urged their fellow Baptists to be faithful in their witness.

Lotz convened a "Summit on Baptist Mission in the 21st Century" at Swanwick, England, May 5–9, 2003. Some one hundred and fifty prominent Baptist missiologists and missionaries from sixty-five countries gathered to respond to the new directions and needs of mission. The vital question they faced was how could the wealthier western churches partner with the new missionary movements from the dynamic Two-thirds World? In other words, how could the west be "reevangelized"? The summit formulated a new vision for the task of evangelism and fostered significant networks of Baptists committed to world mission. Also proposed was an international Baptist mission agency. It would not be organized by the BWA per se, but its resources would serve as a catalyst. The conferees challenged the existing Baptist mission agencies to explore ways to support the economically poor missionaries from Africa, Asia, and Latin America.[11]

Aware that many Baptists can never travel to the larger BWA meetings, Evangelism and Education Division Director Tony Cupit made strenuous efforts to take BWA resources to more isolated regions. Accompanying the various conferences on evangelism have been separate meetings focusing on church leadership, church planting, Christian writing, and discipleship. At times local circumstances forced changes: In April 1996, a major conference in Liberia had to be canceled because of civil war, and alternative meetings were held in the Ivory Coast and Ghana. In October 1996, Cupit visited Cambodia, Vietnam, and Myanmar to encourage churches there and to take part in significant gatherings. The following December, Lotz, Cupit, Kim, and Regional Secretary Resu visited Diphu, India, to encourage the Northeast Indian Baptists. Despite intense opposition from Hindus, large numbers indicated a desire to become Christians.

A large group shared in a conference on evangelism for Nordic and Baltic countries in Sweden in August 1997. In November of that year, Cupit led a BWA team to Andhra Pradesh, India, for conferences and evangelistic meetings among the Telugu people. Immediately afterward was a seminar in Nagaland held at the celebrations marking the 125th anniversary of the coming of Christianity to that part of India. During the UBLA Congress meetings at Guatemala City in March 1998, seminars were held both on evangelism and Christian writing. In April 1998, Communications Director Wendy Ryan and Youth Director Emmett F. Dunn traveled with Cupit to lead an evangelism and leadership conference in war-ravaged Monrovia, Liberia. The next month Ryan and Cupit made a historic visit to the large Baptist community in the remote Baleim Valley in Irian Jaya, Indonesia; they also conducted meetings in Jakarta and Jayapura. Subsequent visits and conferences included Venezuela and Colombia (December 1998); Nepal, Myanmar, Uganda, Sri Lanka, Finland, Ukraine, and Lebanon (1999); Philippines, Cuba, and Nigeria (2000); Myanmar, Russia, Bolivia, South Africa, Cameroon, and Togo (2001); India and Jordan (2002); Peru and India (2003); and Malawi, Mozambique, Tanzania, Zambia, Zimbabwe, and South Africa (2004). Simply to list places and dates cannot capture the evangelistic vitality of Baptists. But this outline of activities does illustrate the unique role of the BWA in fostering Baptist mission and evangelism on a truly global scale.

A major new initiative was announced at Seoul in 2004. Following the receipt of a significant gift, the General Council appointed Cupit to coordinate the "Christ the Living Water" evangelistic strategy "to enlist and equip Baptists for evangelism and leadership" for the period 2005–10. This plan involves evangelistic conferences around the world and is a fresh example of the BWA's deep encouragement to evangelism by all Baptists.

Baptist World Aid

Named Director of BWAid in 1990, Paul Montacute popularized the term *glocalization*—"Think globally, act locally." His approach has been to entrust, empower, and enable local leadership and foster partner organizations. Education has also been a priority. For example, a disaster preparedness seminar was held at Cochabamba, Bolivia, in April 2001. Audiovisual tools are also used to introduce the work of BWAid to churches and unions.

To review the work of this division is to recall a never-ending story of natural disasters, wars and conflicts, and impoverished peoples struggling with hunger, disease, and oppression. But the challenges are opportunities, and figures on paper can never adequately reflect the sacrificial giving and energetic service of numerous Baptists throughout the world. An annual "Project Book" or "Project Catalog" lists numerous possibilities for prayer and support. Included are disaster relief, sustainable development projects, and fellowship assistance (scholarships, building projects, literature supplies, etc.), each with an estimated cost to cover these projects. Local churches or unions can adopt any one or more of them. In 1996–97 aid went for refugees from Rwanda, refugees and medical supplies in Angola and in the former Yugoslavia, flood relief in China, and provision of food in Mozambique. Africa—where famine, the HIV/AIDS crisis, and the devastating effects of war have created desperate needs—continues to be a major focus of assistance. In November 2002, Montacute chaired a meeting in southern Africa to consider the crisis caused by drought. Heartbreaking stories and statistics were shared, and it was shown that an estimated fourteen and a half million people in the six affected countries would need food aid. The BWA was asked to intercede with governments and to request that politics not interfere with the distribution of food.

Faced with such overwhelming need, Baptists have responded. On average, they have given annually one million dollars through BWAid and another six million through their unions. Each year there are new projects, such as a caring for street children in Brazil and providing medicines and powdered milk to Baptists in Cuba. In a striking initiative, Hungarian Baptists enabled sending over seven hundred thousand dollars worth of food, seeds, and medicine to North Korea in 1998. Hungarian Baptist Aid, with its specialized teams, led the BWAid effort in Iran after the disastrous earthquake in December 2003 and again in Southeast Asia after the earthquake and tsunami a year later. BWAid has funded HIV/AIDS projects in Uganda, Rwanda, and Bangladesh. In 2003–04, special appeals were made to assist Iraqis in their war-torn land. Relief for those suffering hurricane losses in the Caribbean was made available in 2004. BWAid also launched an appeal to assist families devastated by the terrorist attack in Beslan, Russia, when hundreds of children were massacred. Among the victims were six children of Baptists, including four children of the local pastor and his wife. Such sad needs unfold daily.

In July 2004, at Seoul the General Council commended the Micah Challenge (based on Micah 6:8) to all its constituent bodies. The Council authorized BWAid to cooperate with 270 evangelical Christian organizations to provide relief, development, and social-justice ministries throughout the world. It also encouraged Baptists to take seriously the Millennium Development Goals of the U.N. in an effort to halve the current level of world poverty by 2015.[12]

Is there hope for the future in such a needy world? Only in Christ can Baptists find the inspiration, motivation, and example to engage in this aspect of authentic witness. Once again BWA, through its multifaceted aid program, has offered a truly global perspective to Baptists.

Unity

The extraordinary diversity among Baptists is not only of culture but also of theology and practice. The Alliance encourages greater unity among all Baptists and provides a place for those who wish to identify with the larger fellowship in Christ. New bodies admitted during the decade were located in the following countries: Slovenia and Nepal (1996); El Salvador, Benin, and Burkina Faso (1997); Democratic Republic of Congo (1998); India, Democratic Republic of Congo, and Cambodia (1999); Gambia, Madagascar, South Africa, India, and Sudan (2001); South Africa, India, Canada, and Myanmar (2002); Central African Republic, Bosnia and Herzegovina, Democratic Republic of Congo, Cuba, and the United States

(2003); and India (2004). The BWA grew from 186 bodies (154,116 churches and 40,983,465 members) in 1995 to 206 bodies (181,747 churches and 46,879,650 members) in 2003. Some 211 Baptist bodies were BWA members in 2004. Unity, however, is not always easy to achieve. Baptists do differ and, despite the efforts of the Alliance, are not always willing to work together. For example, the request for membership in 2001 by a new body of Baptists in the United States—the Cooperative Baptist Fellowship (CBF)—led to a major crisis outlined later in this chapter.

The story of unresolved tensions in North America is especially sad in light of the achievements made in reconciliation during this decade. BWA teams have sought to reconcile Baptist groups in Cuba, India, Indonesia, South Africa, and Zambia, as well as in the United States. In Chiang Mai, Thailand, in November 1996, a special conference on conflict resolution was held with the ABF, which resulted in the formation of a task force to work for peace and reconciliation in the region, where there have been significant issues of long-standing tension. One complex division was in Manipur, India between the Nagas and the Kukis, which was marked by fierce fighting in spite of various mediation attempts. A BWA team visited the region in 1995 and again in 1996, but the Kuki leaders still refused to join the Nagas in the 1997 centennial celebration of the Manipur Baptists. Fortunately, relationships have gradually improved, and in 2002, a significant decision to relocate the Manipur Theological College to Kangpopki Mission was greeted favorably. A long dispute over property and other concerns within the Samavesam of Telugu Baptist churches—the largest body in India with over five hundred thousand members—was partly ended in 1996, and a further positive move occurred in late 2003. The two Bengal Baptist Unions resolved a long and bitter dispute at the Bengal Baptist Peace and Unification Celebration in Calcutta in November 1997.

Africa has also been the focus of concern for unity. Reconciliation between the Baptist Convention of Zambia and the Baptist Mission of Zambia was achieved in 1997, and similar tensions over ownership and possession of church property in Zimbabwe were addressed with BWA assistance in 1997. Rwanda was an area of profound tragedy, with the ethnic conflict between the Hutus and the Tutsis leading to the massacre of thousands of people. BWAid has worked closely with the leadership of both the Baptist Union and the Baptist Association in trying to help returning refugees and to act as an agent for peace and reconciliation.

In the midst of so much heartache, there was great joy over developments in South Africa. The BWA had begun negotiations in 1993, and in November 1995, provided a delegation, which met with leaders of the Baptist Union (composed mostly of white South Africans) and the Baptist Convention (formed in 1987 with mostly black South Africans). Issues involved theological education, property, and movement of churches from one group to another, but underlying all was the painful legacy of the apartheid era. Divisions were deep, but a remarkable breakthrough came after a prayer retreat at Kempton Park in November 1996. A spirit of openness, affirmation, repentance, and forgiveness led to a renewed commitment to seek unity. Desmond Hoffmeister of the Convention and Terry Rae of the Union proved to be strong leaders in the process; at the General Council meeting in Durban July 1998, they reported genuine progress. Subsequently, other groups—the Afrikaans Baptists, the Baptist Association, and the Baptist Mission—joined in the movement to form the South African Baptist Alliance in August 2001.

Another encouraging move toward unity occurred during a BWA-sponsored worship conference in Niteroi, Brazil, in March 2000. The two Brazilian Baptist groups, divided for thirty-five years, came together in a public reconciliation. The call of Christ for unity is still being sounded by the BWA. The continuing challenge of division in North America makes President Kim's plea for Baptists to pray and work for "unity in Christ" powerfully relevant.

Baptist Identity

One "ecclesial function" of the BWA is helping Baptists discover their international identity. Lotz said that the 2000 Congress demonstrated powerfully that Baptists from Asia, Africa, and Latin America are "proud and committed to their Baptist identity." On the other hand "many of our older member bodies have lost a certain sense of pride in their Baptist heritage."[13] Why denominationalism continues in the twenty-first century is an open question.

Discussion of Baptist identity has become a growth industry among Baptist scholars. Of course, Baptists share a common body of beliefs and practices, even though most reject the need for a specific creedal statement of these. The BWA study commission dealing with Baptist heritage has been expanded to deal with Baptist identity. In North America the question has been vigorously discussed and the various bodies have produced statements. Faced with a variety of understandings of what it meant to be a Baptist in the new Europe, the EBF produced a statement on Baptist identity in 1995. Then, as already noted, the BWA and EBF joined with the German Baptists to sponsor a conference on "Baptist Identity and National Culture" in Berlin.

In order to help Baptists understand their beliefs and explain them to others, in 1999 the Study and Research Division published a small book, *We Baptists,* edited by James Leo Garrett, Jr.[14] The six chapters were prepared by the study commissions and introduce Baptist history, beliefs, ethics, worship, church life and leadership, and human rights. This work has proved invaluable in many regions and has been translated into several languages.

Another way in which Baptists have come to understand their identity better is through interchurch conversations. As discussed in earlier chapters, the BWA engaged in talks with the Reformed Churches, Roman Catholics, Lutherans, and Mennonites.[15] Conversations with the Vatican and the Mennonites have continued. In November 1996 Fanini and Lotz met with the Secretariat (now Pontifical Council) for the Promotion of Christian Unity in Rome. In December 2000, a delegation of twelve Baptists met in Rome with leaders of the Pontifical Council and expressed opposition to the controversial Vatican document "Dominus Jesus." They agreed to meet again the following year in Buenos Aires, where a positive discussion took place. A Baptist-Mennonite conference on "Evangelism and the Peace Witness of the Church" took place at Eastern University in Philadelphia, January 10–12, 2002.[16]

Through his involvement in the annual conferences of the secretaries of the Christian World Communions, Lotz has widened Baptist contacts with other churches. He also has been able to carry out further talks with Anglicans and the Eastern Orthodox Churches. The conversations between BWA and the Anglican Consultative Council (ACC) introduced a novel process. A core committee of three people from each denomination plus a representative from the BWA office and the ACC was formed. Chair of the Baptist committee was Paul Fiddes of Regent's Park College, Oxford, England. The two core committees met in various parts of the world, and individuals from the region in which they were meeting were invited to join the talks. There were six meetings: the European phase in Norwich Cathedral, England (September 2000); the Asian phase in Yangon, Myanmar (January 2001); the African phase in Nairobi, Kenya (January 2002); the Latin American phase in Santiago, Chile (January 2003); the Caribbean phase in the Bahamas (January 2003); and the North American phase in Wolfville, Nova Scotia (September 2003). A preliminary report was presented to the General Council in 2004, with a final report submitted to the Executive Committee in March 2005.[17]

Because tensions between the various Orthodox churches and Baptists at times resulted in discrimination and persecution, the BWA welcomed the possibility of conversations. Preliminary meetings were held in 1994, followed by a major dialogue in Istanbul in May 1996. It was apparent that the two churches had deep-rooted differences, especially about the place of mission in the life of the church. The BWA hoped that these conversations—or more accurately preconversations—with the Ecumenical Patriarchate would lead eventually to full conversations between the BWA and representatives from the fifteen autocephalous and autonomous Orthodox churches. The last preconversation took place at Oxford in May 1997. Since then, relations between Baptists and Orthodox in a number of European countries have become quite difficult, with Baptists characteristically accused of being a "foreign sect."

Hope remains that conversations might resume. As the General Secretary declared to the 1996 Council

> our understanding of evangelism and proselytism may differ, as well as our understanding of church and state, and authority. Nevertheless, we rejoice at the Orthodox defence throughout history of the trinity, the divinity of Christ, the cross and resurrection, and the triumph of Christ and His kingdom. We pray that conversations will take place for the edification of both communions.[18]

The 2001 General Council endorsed continuing the interchurch dialogues, noting the purposes of the conversations:

1. enhance the understanding by other Christian communions of Baptist distinctives, such as the believers' church, believers' baptism, religious liberty, mission and evangelism;
2. support Baptists who find themselves oppressed by a dominant Christian communion;
3. strengthen the ministry of participating communions by discovering areas of cooperative Christian work;
4. search for an expression of the apostolic faith which adequately represents the understandings of participating communions; and
5. seek to fulfill the plea for spiritual unity in Christ's prayer "that all may be one . . . that the world may believe" (John 17:21).[19]

Forum

The BWA provides Baptists with a forum for sharing needs and concerns. News is disseminated through publications—most notably the quarterly magazine the *Baptist World* and the monthly news sheet *BWA News*, both edited by Communications Director Ryan—and through its Web site www.bwanet.org. A variety of views are expressed in the workgroups, study commissions, and special conferences. The workgroups of the Evangelism and Education Division and commissions of the Study and Research Division have become increasingly important to the world family of Baptist scholars, pastors, and leaders. More than five hundred people are appointed to these bodies for five-year terms; and although many of them are unable to attend the meetings regularly, they can share as corresponding members. No similar forum exists where Baptists can address urgent and topical questions in an atmosphere of free inquiry and concern.

Workgroups exist for academic and theological education, Christian education and literature, church renewal, and mission and evangelism. The study commissions are Baptist Doctrine and Interchurch Cooperation, Christian Ethics, Baptist Heritage (expanded in 2000 to include Baptist Identity), Church Leadership, Human Rights (renamed Freedom and Justice in 2000), and Baptist Worship (Spirituality was added in 2000). Representative papers from the commissions during the period 1995–2000 were published,[20] and the appearance of a similar volume for the next quinquennium is anticipated.

Aware of tensions among many Baptists over approaches to worship, Cupit arranged a series of conferences to explore this central issue. The first meeting in Berlin in October 1998 attracted six hundred delegates from fifty-eight countries. The conference featured worship songs and music from every continent, modeled five different styles of worship, and provided a variety of elective sessions on every aspect of worship.[21] The success of the Berlin meeting inspired others to sponsor conferences. Swedish Baptists organized one of their own, while the BWA assisted regional leaders in arranging a conference in Rio de Janeiro in March 2000 for which more than two thousand people registered. During the years 2000–03 other worship conferences took place in Hyderabad, India; Denia, Spain; Managua, Nicaragua; and Kiev, Ukraine. They were successful because they were all clearly related to the contexts of the regions in which they took place, and they illustrate how the BWA is uniquely placed to lead Baptists in consideration of issues central to the life of the churches.

Theological education is another BWA concern. Hundreds of Baptist educators, teaching in isolated colleges with few resources, struggle to prepare those called by God for effective ministry. Other teachers have many resources but lack the insights they might gain from interaction with their brothers and sisters around the world. The BWA encourages the sharing of resources and insights through scholarships, travel grants, and the provision of books and visiting teachers. The Division of Evangelism and Education has helped by sponsoring Baptist International Conference of Theological Educators (BICTE) and assisting those from disadvantaged regions to attend. During this decade two successful BICTE conferences took place. BICTE—which met in Vancouver, Canada, in July 1997, with the theme "Educating Leaders for the 21st Century Church"—attracted eighty educators. BICTE VI in Seville, Spain, July 2003, focused on the theme "Nurturing Spiritual Leaders for the Service of the Church." The significant presence of theologians from Africa and Latin America added to the value of the discussions at these conferences.

The BWA has also given attention to theological education in the various regions, where local teachers share in the planning of and discussions at strategic conferences. The meeting in Buenos Aires in August 1995 gave special attention to listening to theologians from the South, as opposed to the more traditional centers in the North.[22] In April 1997 Cupit organized a team of English- and Spanish-speaking theological educators from North and Latin Americas to teach in Cuba, where revival was adding so many to the churches that the need for trained pastors was urgent. The visiting teachers worked in Havana and Santiago de Cuba, thereby providing valuable learning experiences for the students and teachers at the seminaries in these cities.

Theological education in Eastern Europe has been a concern of BWA almost from its very beginning. Soon after the EBF gained full control of the International Baptist Theological Seminary (IBTS), the regional body moved the school from Rüschlikon, Switzerland, to Prague, Czech Republic. When the new facilities were dedicated in April 1997, EBF Secretary Walter declared it would be the "bridge both of east-west and north-south."[23] As local seminaries sprang up throughout Europe, the IBTS focused more on graduate education and short-term courses and programs.

International Baptists had a special interest in the needs of the former Soviet Union As mentioned earlier, the BWA had long been interested in establishing a seminary in Moscow, but Stalinist oppression had destroyed any hope of doing so. With the end of communism, a new seminary was launched in Odessa, Ukraine, and the founding of a seminary in the Russian capital itself became possible. The Moscow Theological Seminary opened in 1993, utilizing facilities provided by the Russian Baptist Union in its building. Finally, in 2002, thanks to generous gifts from the Lindner family foundation (U.S.), other British and North American Baptists, and the BWA, it secured a home of its own: a refurbished factory daycare center that had accommodations for about sixty students. Seminary President Alexander Kozynko hailed the development as a great miracle and the answer to a century of prayers by faithful people. President Ian M. Chapman of Northern Baptist Theological Seminary played an important part in channeling assistance—both through his own school and the BWA—and helping secure volunteer teachers from the west. Another key figure in this effort was George Boltniev, president of the Russian-Ukrainian Evangelical Baptist Union, U.S.A.

The BWA offers other forms of training. Ryan of the Communications Division organized seminars for Baptist groups in all the regions. For example, she introduced various Asian groups to new media technologies at a seminar in Seoul in November 1996. At another conference in Bamenda, Cameroon, in August 2002, she focused on how to use media to help educate people about HIV/AIDS.

Similarly, the BWA dedicated itself to developing leadership among Baptist youth. Youth Department Director Dunn worked energetically to arrange conferences for young people in each of the regions. For example, youth leaders from across southern Africa came together in an important meeting in November 1995 to discuss the social and economic problems that threatened the very survival of youth. The ABF held its youth congress in 2000 (in association with the BWA Congress in Melbourne, Australia), and a large number of young people experienced a sense of belonging to the global Baptist family.

The main focus for the development of Baptist young people has been the world conferences. The Thirteenth World Conference at Houston, Texas, in July 1998 brought together more than eight thousand young people from eighty-seven countries. Inspiring speakers, challenging Bible studies, and exciting music drew a huge response and numerous lives were changed. The Fourteenth World Conference was postponed by a year because of the SARS epidemic in East Asia, but in August 2004 some four thousand young people from seventy countries joined in a joyful celebration in Hong Kong under the theme "Jesus Christ is the Life . . . . Live!" For five days they shared inspiration and music from their various cultures—an experience that will undoubtedly have an impact on future worship in every region.

In these conferences many Baptists made commitments to the Christian ministry. A striking example is the story of Leena Lavanya, a young Indian woman who went to the Baptist World Youth Conference at Harare, Zimbabwe, in 1993. There, she was challenged to commit her life to the service of those in need. Soon after, while witnessing to a prostitute, Leena realized that something practical needed to be done for the woman and her children. This first encounter led Lavanya to develop an amazing variety of ministries: ministering among lepers and prisoners, a sewing and computer ministry to give women skills, and a school for destitute children. Attending a world youth conference awakened this amazing Christian woman, who has touched so many lives, to her life's potential.[24]

Lavanya also illustrates the strategic place women have in Baptist life.

Many women serve on commissions, workgroups, and committees; and five hold vice-presidential positions in the 2000–05 quinquennium. Even more important is the BWA Women's Department, which maintains international networks and offers encouragement to Baptist women. An annual Day of Prayer unites Baptist women around the world, and the offering taken supports women's work in each region, as well as internationally. Willene Pierce (U.S.) succeeded Elizabeth (Beth) Hayworth MacClaren as director in 1995, followed by Patsy Davis, a former Southern Baptist missionary in Venezuela, in 1998. The president of the Women's Department traveled regularly to support the staff director and to bring a global understanding to the many regional women's conferences and ministries. A social dimension has also been present at these gatherings. For example, following a conference of Asian women in Chiang Mai, Thailand, in October 2000, a group of participants took two hundred hygiene kits and two hundred Bibles in the Karen language to refugees in the Maela refugee camp. Mercy Jeyaraja Rao of India (president, 1995–2000) and Audrey Morikawa of Canada (president, 2000–05) were greatly loved and respected leaders. The Women's Department also sponsors a "leadership conference" before each Baptist World Congress. The 1995 conference ended with an evangelistic meeting on a major thoroughfare in Buenos Aires. Over three hundred and fifty women came to the 2000 conference in Melbourne, with the theme "On to Greater Heights."

In recent years the BWA Men's Department has not been as successful in organizing laymen, but a number of men did meet for a rally during the 2000 World Congress. Under the new president, Samson Olaniyan (Nigeria), planning has begun for world conferences similar to those that had occurred in the heyday of the Men's Department, when Owen Cooper and Floyd Harris provided such dynamic leadership. Doyle Pennington, a Southern Baptist from Georgia, was appointed director in 2003.

Structures

To provide leadership for the BWA in its multitude of tasks has been a challenge. General Secretary Lotz has enjoyed the strong support of each of the BWA presidents, and his executive staff has been an effective team. Division directors Cupit, Montacute, and Ryan with Youth Director Dunn have served the entire decade. Douglas Inglis (Scotland) retired as Promotion and Development Director in 2000, and his successors have been Alan Stanford (U.S.) in 2001 and Ian M. Chapman (U.S.) in 2004. Ellen Sims Teague (U.S.), who began working at the BWA office in 1991 and has been responsible for financial matters since 1994, became the head of the new Finance and Administration Division in 2001. Lotz maintains a prophetic edge that complements his administrative skills and constantly seeks to identify what he refers to as "paradigm shifts" in denominationalism, missions, and church life generally. To assist him in envisaging the needs of Baptists in the next generation, he established a think tank, known as the 21st Century Committee, to consider changes in BWA life.[25]

By 1999, BWA officials had become aware that the headquarters building in McLean, Virginia, was inadequate to meet the needs of the steadily expanding organization. Then a suitable building in nearby Falls Church, Virginia, became available. It was a huge challenge to raise the more than two million dollars needed, but individuals and conventions gave generously and the goal was reached. On September 22, 2001, President Kim opened the new "home for the BWA family," and it has provided a much more suitable base for administrative work and conferences.

Lotz has often referred to the change in denominational giving in the west. In 2002, he noted that for the first time in North American history more than 50 percent of local church funds designated to causes beyond the congregation went not to the denominational headquarters but to parachurch organizations. Baptist conventions and unions that once contributed liberally to the BWA were no longer able to do so. In 2002, less than 40 percent of the Alliance budget came from the member bodies. That fact, plus instability in the international monetary market, has made the financial situation of the BWA increasingly problematic.

Accordingly, the General Council authorized a Baptist World Offering to be collected once every five years. It also inaugurated a Centennial Fund, with a target of ten million dollars, to aid theological education and the regional fellowships, and to fund travel and study scholarships. Baptists around the world continue to celebrate Baptist World Alliance Day on the first Sunday in February and to contribute to a BWA Day Communion offering.

An extremely important action taken was to open membership in the world organization to others beside national bodies. The General Council proposed a constitutional amendment in 2003 (approved after the second reading in 2004) that would allow individuals, local churches, and Baptist organizations to join as personal or associate members.[26] The BWA then invited each local congregation to become a "Global Impact Church" by contributing a certain amount of money annually. The expanded membership was designed not only to extend the financial support of the BWA but also to provide additional networks for mutual ministry and prayer.

Withdrawal of the Southern Baptist Convention

On the eve of the centenary, a question of membership produced a major rift within the BWA. The story is too long to recount in detail, but a brief outline is necessary. The CBF was formed in 1991 in reaction to conservative changes within the Southern Baptist Convention (SBC), and there was considerable tension between the groups. The CBF applied to join the BWA, and at the 2001 General Council the Membership Committee reported that it could not recommend approval because the CBF had not clarified its separate existence from the SBC. The difficulties between the two groups remained unresolved. The 2002 Council, despite SBC opposition, accepted the Membership Committee's special report on the matter. The report spelled out what the CBF needed to do to establish a separate identity as a Baptist denomination and indicated that in 2003 the committee might then recommend its acceptance.

The SBC Executive Committee responded two months later by appointing a "study committee" to consider the question of BWA membership. In February 2003 the SBC reduced their annual support for the BWA (previously $425,000) by $125,000 and spoke of relating to "other like-minded Christian bodies worldwide." At the 2003 Council Ian Hawley (Australia), chair of the Membership Committee, who was handling the difficult task of trying to bring this complex issue to completion with grace and patience, recommended the admission of the CBF. Thereupon, the SBC's Executive Committee decided to recommend withdrawal from the BWA. President Kim and Baptist leaders from around the world, deeply appreciative of the significant role that the SBC had played within the BWA since its inception, pleaded with its leadership to reconsider. Although much prayer for unity within the Baptist family was being offered, the messengers (delegates) at the annual convention in Indianapolis in June 2004 nevertheless voted without discussion to sever the SBC's ninety-nine-year connection with the BWA. The largest convention (over sixteen million members of the BWA's total of almost forty-seven million) and most significant financial supporter had decided to go its separate way.

Immediately, an outcry arose from Baptist bodies around the world. The BWA and its leadership received overwhelming support, and pleas went out to the SBC to reconsider its action. In justifying their withdrawal, SBC leaders made serious allegations that Lotz and others insisted slandered the BWA and indeed Baptists everywhere. In a forthright statement released on February 23, 2004, Lotz categorically rejected the contention that the BWA was "anti-American" and a theologically "liberal" organization.[27] He also refuted the charge that he and the BWA promoted women as pastors by pointing out that a variety of positions are found among member bodies and by emphasizing that the Alliance does not have an official policy on this issue and other controversial questions. Baptists worldwide were especially incensed when one prominent SBC figure charged the BWA with supporting homosexuality as an acceptable lifestyle for Christians. These accusations and counteraccusations were widely publicized in both the religious and secular press. Fortunately, not only the CBF but various Southern Baptist state conventions, churches, and individuals have assured the world organization of continuing support.

The General Council that met in Seoul the month after the SBC departure welcomed representatives from the Woman's Missionary Union, an auxiliary of the SBC that had resolved to continue active support for the BWA, as well as a significant number of individual Southern Baptists who were there. It adopted a resolution about the controversy that acknowledged with gratitude "the enormous contribution made by the Southern Baptist Convention in the formation of the Baptist World Alliance a hundred years ago and in the continued development and effectiveness of the Baptist World Alliance since its inception." The Council regretted the SBC decision "resulting in loss of unity and a compromise of the worldwide testimony of all Baptists." It rejected the charges made against the BWA and expressed support for the officers and staff who were responding to the charges. The Council also recorded its hope "for a future reconciliation and renewal of SBC membership" and assured a warm welcome to all from the SBC who "wish to participate in the life of the BWA."[28] The whole saga was a sad development in the last year of the BWA's first century of life and witness, but notes of hope and renewal were sounded as the BWA prepared for the great Centenary Congress in 2005.

Eighteenth Baptist World Congress, Melbourne 2000

In the middle of the decade, a jubilant Baptist World Congress was held in Melbourne, Australia, January 5–9, 2000. This departure from the traditional midyear timing enabled global Baptists to greet together the new millennium (in the southern summer's warmth)—right at the start of what came to be thought of as a new era in world history—and to meet in one of the younger western nations within the larger BWA region of Asia. The chosen theme "Jesus Christ Forever. Yes!" provided a positive note for the new millennium. General Secretary Lotz eloquently declared:

> Baptists of the world entered the twenty-first century with an affirmative and resounding YES! Whereas many prophets of doom predicted computer failure, widespread disorder, riots, and general upheaval, all

under the name Y2K, more than ten thousand Baptists from one hundred countries gathered confidently under another name, Jesus Christ! The Congress . . . entered the twenty-first century with hope and with the simple and age-old Biblical affirmation that in Jesus Christ God has definitively acted, spoken and given to all humanity hope, courage and a future.[29]

Australian Baptists lived up to their promise of a friendly, hospitable, and relatively informal Congress and delegates enjoyed the unique Australian flavor of the meetings. Held in the Melbourne Exhibition Center on the banks of the River Yarra in the heart of the bustling metropolis, the Congress was a glorious celebration of Jesus Christ through music, art, drama, preaching, and rich exchanges of fellowship. A striking feature was the large number of delegates from Asia and the South Pacific: 452 from India, 62 from Indonesia, 375 from Korea, 133 from the Philippines, and a colorful group of 95 from Papua New Guinea mixed with the 32 from New Zealand and 2,336 from Australia. The opening ceremony not only featured the traditional roll call of Baptists by a parade of national flags but also a special performance by Baptist Aboriginal singers and dancers from the Warlpiri people who live in the desert heart of the continent. An international festival held on the riverbank provided a bold and entertaining witness to the gospel.

Other features included a pastors' stream with over a thousand participating, a children's program that attracted some seventy children, and fellowship breakfasts that gave further opportunities to hear speakers from around the world. Mission in Action groups provided opportunities for witness and social action in the city. There were the traditional morning Bible Studies in eighteen groups and also thirteen Focus Groups, in which some four thousand delegates tackled a wide range of themes. The highlights, however, were the large evening celebrations with H. Beecher Hicks, Jr. (U.S.), Bruce Milne (Canada), Fanini (Brazil), Tim Costello (Australia), and Anne Graham Lotz (U.S.) as preachers. Outstanding music, singing, and dramatic presentations added to the inspiration of the services.

Kim, enthusiastically hailed as the new President, called on Baptists to strive for unity, renewal, and revival. He invited the delegates to prepare for the Centenary Congress at Birmingham, England in 2005, and he underscored that its theme, "Jesus Christ Living Water," promised refreshment and hope for a needy world.

A Concluding Challenge

On the eve of the new millennium, Lotz challenged his fellow Baptists to look to the future with optimism and to be prepared to deal with changes that were certain to come.

> Our faith in Christ does not change. Christ is the center to whom we belong and to whom we move. Is the Baptist ecclesiology, or denomination, sufficient for the twenty-first century? All of our denominations need a re-examination. When Pope John XXIII called for "opening windows," he shook the foundations of Catholic ecclesiology . . . . In the same way we need a Baptist opening of the windows, not only to let the old and worn air out, but to allow a fresh blowing of the Holy Spirit in our midst. If we do that, then indeed the Baptists as a denomination will continue not only to exist but to flourish in the new century! May that be our prayer and may we so act and work for those changes! To God be the glory![30]

---

1. Samuel P. Huntington, *The Clash of Civilizations and the Remaking of the World Order* (London: Touchstone Books, 1998), p. 96. See also Philip Jenkins, *The Next Christendom: the Coming of Global Christianity* (New York: Oxford University Press, 2002).

2. General Council, 1998, pp. 97–100.

3. The addresses and papers are contained in Denton Lotz, ed., *Baptists Against Racism* (McLean, VA: BWA, 1999).

4. Ibid., p. 7.

5. Tony Cupit, ed., *Baptist World Alliance Covenants and Declarations 1990–2000* (McLean: BWA, 1999), pp. 23–35.

6. *Baptist World,* April–June 1999, p. 3.

7. *Baptist World,* July–September 2001, p. 31.

8. Cupit, *BWA Covenants and Declarations,* pp. 5–6.

9. *Baptist World,* July–September 1989, p. 11.

10. Cupit, *BWA Covenants and Declarations,* pp. 14–18.

11. Lotz, ed., *Proceedings of the Summit on Baptist Mission in the 21st Century* (Falls Church, VA: BWA, 2004).

12. *BWA Yearbook,* 2004, pp. 86–87.

13. General Council, 2000, p. 89.

14. Franklin, TN: Providence House, 1999.

15. See Ken R. Manley, *The Baptist World Alliance and Inter-Church Relationships* (Falls Church, VA: BWA, 2003). An earlier version of this, "A Survey of Baptist World Alliance Conversations with other Churches and some implications for Baptist Identity," was

presented to a joint meeting of the Baptist Heritage and Identity Commission and the Doctrine and Interchurch Cooperation Commission in Seville, July 2002.

16. Cupit, ed., *Evangelism and the Peace Witness of the Church* (Falls Church, VA: BWA, 2003).

17. *Conversations around the World: The Report of the International Conversations between the Anglican Communion and the Baptist World Alliance* (Falls Church, VA: BWA, 2005)

18. General Council, 1996, p. 82.

19. *BWA Yearbook,* 2001, p. 96.

20. Cupit, ed., *Baptist Faith & Witness, Book 2: The Papers of the Study and Research Division of the Baptist World Alliance 1995-2000* (McLean, VA: BWA, 1999).

21. From the conference was published a collection of prayers from around the world, *Hallowed Be Your Name,* and a selection of papers, *Baptists in Worship* (McLean, VA: BWA, 1998).

22. The conference papers were published: Daniel Carro and Robert F. Wilson, eds., *Contemporary Gospel Accents, Doing Theology in Africa, Asia, Southeast Asia, and Latin America* (Macon, GA: Mercer University Press, 1997).

23. *BWA News,* June 1997, p. 3.

24. *Baptist World,* January–March 1998, p. 8. For a fascinating collection of stories about contemporary Baptists, including Leena Lavanya, see Cupit, *Stars Lighting up the Sky: Stories of Contemporary Christian Heroes* (Falls Church, VA: BWA, 2003).

25. See the detailed progress report of the committee in *BWA Yearbook,* 2004, pp. 81–83.

26. *BWA Yearbook,* 2003, pp. 80–81; 2004, p. 79. The BWA Constitution (Art. IV, 2 and 3) and Bylaws (I, 7 and 8), were amended to create two new categories of membership: "Associate" and "Personal." Any Baptist church or organized Baptist body (college, seminary, mission society, state, regional, or associational divisions, etc.) would qualify for Associate Membership. Individual persons may join by paying an annual membership fee.

27. The relevant documents of the controversy are contained in an in-house publication, *BWA–SBC Concerns: Documents, Media Reports, Correspondence* (Falls Church, VA: BWA, 2004).

28. *BWA Yearbook,* 2004, p. 87.

29. *BWA Congress,* 2000, p. 9.

30. *Baptist World,* January–March 2000, p. 14.

AFTERWORD
Denton Lotz

An ancient tradition of the church holds that the Apostle Peter fled from Rome in the face of Nero's brutal persecution. While he was walking along the Appian Way, the road out of town, Jesus suddenly appeared to him. Peter recognized his Lord and asked in Latin, "*Quo vadis domine?* (Where are you going, Lord?)" Jesus replied, "I am going to Rome to be crucified again." Peter then repented of his faintheartedness and returned to the city to face martyrdom.

To ask the same question of the Baptist World Alliance (BWA) (*Quo vadis?*) in the twenty-first century—"Where are we going"—it is necessary to first ask, "Where have we been?" We are grateful to Richard Pierard, general editor, Eljee Bentley and Gerald Borchert, associate editors, and the authors of the various chapters for providing a succinct history of the past hundred years of this movement of people called Baptists who united together in the BWA.

On the occasion of the centennial or "centenary" in British English, it is proper that Baptists worldwide celebrate a century of unity. And where better than in England, the country where the BWA was founded in 1905? Baptists, of course, have a longer history than that. In 2009, they will commemorate in Amsterdam, the Netherlands, the 400th anniversary of the founding of the modern Baptist movement under the leadership of Thomas Helwys and John Smyth. But the BWA centennial is significant because for one hundred years this organization has given shape, form, identity, and unity to the many Baptist conventions and unions around the globe.

Where Have We Been?
These past one hundred years have been filled with much joy and sorrow. Certainly we should be interested in the growth of the church and thus about statistics. After all, there is a book of Numbers in the Old Testament. The Book of Acts is concerned about numbers, and the Apostle Paul repeatedly speaks of the growth of congregations. The expansion of the BWA and its member bodies has been the collective work of all Baptists,

from the individual believer to the local congregation; to state, provincial, and national bodies; and then to the whole world of Baptists. Let us rejoice at what God has done in and through our churches!

1. *Growth of the BWA:* In 1905, when Baptists came to London for the first World Congress and formed the BWA, there were around seven million baptized believers worldwide. As our centennial neared, the number of baptized people in just our constituent bodies had risen to forty-eight million.[1] Baptists count only baptized believers as members. If we were to include infants and children—as do such paedobaptists as Methodists, Presbyterians, Episcopalians, Lutherans, and others—the Baptist community would be much larger. One can speak of a worldwide Baptist community of more than one hundred and ten million worshippers, and this does not count the many independent Baptist groups who are not members of the BWA. If we were to include in our statistics those Christian believers who intentionally call themselves Baptists but do not belong to the BWA, the global Baptist community would probably number more than one hundred and fifty million.[2]

We continue to be amazed at the number of groups applying for membership in the BWA. Many are indigenous movements that started from believers reading the New Testament. As of 2004, 211 Baptist conventions and unions belong to the BWA.

2. *Internationalization—BWA Congresses, Conferences, and Councils:* Although many countries from Africa, Asia, and Latin America were represented in London in 1905, the BWA leadership was mainly European and North American. Not until 1960 was a President chosen who was neither English nor North American. Since then, however, BWA Presidents have come from Brazil, Liberia, Hong Kong, Australia, Denmark, and Korea. After World War II broke out, the BWA office moved from London to Washington, D.C., and the staff changed from mainly British to North American. Since the 1980s the staff has become internationalized, with executive staffpersons from Australia, England, Germany, Liberia, and Trinidad; and the various Regional Secretaries have been given executive staff status. Regional headquarters are now located in Africa, Asia, the Caribbean, Europe, and Latin America.

Internationalization included not only staff and officers, but also our agenda and venues for meetings. After holding a Congress in the southern hemisphere (Brazil) for the first time in 1960, we have since convened in Argentina and Australia, as well as in Japan and Korea. Although the BWA Congress reflects the culture of the country in which we meet, until 1960 that culture was always either European or North American.

As Brazil was the first developing country in which a Congress was held, it was a watershed experience for Baptists there, as well as for the BWA. Edgar Hallock, who was involved in the Rio de Janeiro Congress's logistics, told me that Brazilian Baptists speak of "after the Congress" as the time when they began to grow rapidly. He related how, through a series of "miracles," the final session with Billy Graham preaching was televised around the country, giving Baptists a national profile that they previously did not have. Today, Brazilian Baptists number one million baptized believers, with a community of more than two million.

Whereas the BWA Congress is held every five years, the General Council meets annually. To ensure that delegates have an opportunity at least once every quinquennium to participate in a Council meeting, the General Council meets every year on a different continent. This change of venues allows delegates from each particular region to instruct the Council on their joys, growth, problems, and special characteristics. Since 1980 the BWA Council has met in such diverse locations as Kenya (1982), Singapore (1986), Jordan (1987), the Bahamas (1988), Yugoslavia (1989), Jamaica (1992), Zimbabwe (1993), Hong Kong (1996), South Africa (1998), Cuba (2000), Spain (2002), Brazil (2003), and Korea (2004). Indeed, in every one of these countries, the BWA General Council members learned to appreciate the context in which Baptists, often a minority, must minister. Our resolutions became intentional and specific, dealing with economic injustice, racial prejudice, religious intolerance, or secularism. Such opportunities give members of the BWA the chance to learn firsthand what mission is all about. Prayer teams have been organized and Baptists worldwide continue to pray for one another in a more informed way.

3. *Regionalization:* To further internationalize and also to enable better mutual understanding and cooperation between neighboring countries and Baptist unions, the BWA Long Range Planning Committee of 1975-80 recommended the establishment of six regions. Bylaw VIII.1. (1)states that "the Regional Fellowship . . . shall reflect the objectives of the Alliance in their geographical regions and as such shall primarily be expressions of the Alliance." The European Baptist Federation, which began as a region of the BWA in 1949 with an associate secretary who also served as the BWA Regional Secretary, was the model for the other five regions: the All-Africa Baptist Fellowship, Asian Baptist Federation, Caribbean Baptist Fellowship, Union of Baptists in Latin America, and North American Baptist Fellowship.

Good stewardship, as well as good mission policy, dictated the need for regions. Baptists in a region had more in common, and their concerns for evangelism and mission were similar. They could learn from one another. Also, travel would be less expensive and cooperation greater. And what was anticipated is exactly what has happened: All of the regions are now actively engaging their members in evangelism and mission.

When the constitutional changes authorized regions, relations between them and the parent body were not clearly spelled out. Annual meetings of the Regional Secretaries and the BWA staff have helped them cooperate with one another. Member bodies relate directly to the BWA, not through the region. Bylaw VIII.1. (2) affirms this dual membership: "The respective member bodies may have direct membership in both the Alliance and the Region. Membership in a region does not in any way limit the direct relationship with the Alliance." This pattern represents Baptist polity at work. For example, the BWA does not ask the Asian Baptist Federation if it can relate to the Baptists in Japan, since Baptists in Japan are directly members of the BWA. But it is understood that leadership must be courteous to one another. Thus, if a BWA staffperson were to visit Tokyo, he or she would first inform the region.

The regions play a significant role in extending the loving care of the world BWA family into the local churches. This includes evangelism, mission, conferences, resolution of religious freedom issues, and the relief and development program of Baptist World Aid.

4. *Freedom and Justice:* Since the beginning of the BWA, the defense of religious freedom has been a major emphasis. In the 1920s and into the 1930s, General Secretary Rushbrooke visited with Romanian officials and impressed upon them the BWA concern for freedom. Of course, the BWA was also involved in defending the rights of believers in communist countries. In addition, Roman Catholicism was not as enlightened then as today. Often, Baptist churches in Catholic countries were burned to the ground or government restrictions prevented free assembly.

Although the BWA met in Hitler's Germany in 1934, the BWA issued a prophetic appeal against "racialism" that was clearly a challenge to Nazism. During the darkest days of white rule in South Africa, the BWA called for an end to apartheid and to the restrictions placed upon Baptist churches. Before the fall of communism in Russia, there was only one Baptist Church in Moscow; fifteen years later the number had risen to fifty-two. Other countries that were once under communist oppression have experienced the same type of growth: In Ukraine the number of churches increased from one thousand in 1990 to almost three thousand today.

We live in a world marked by a "clash of civilizations," and that implies a clash of religions as well. During the NATO air attacks upon Serbia in the 1990s, Baptist churches often were painted with swastikas. The tragic conflict between Christians and Muslims has continued in Nigeria, where in 2001 the Baptist seminary in Kaduna was burned down, five students hacked to death with machetes, and eighteen churches destroyed. A similar story was repeated in Indonesia, where a thousand believers from various Christian traditions were killed. What appear to be old-style KGB (secret police) leaders have taken over some of the former Soviet republics in Central Asia, and ruling with an iron hand, they refuse to grant religious freedom. Another concern is the hundred thousand refugees from Myanmar who live inside the Thai border, locked in with no visas and no passports.

The BWA's Freedom and Justice Commission has become a voice for the voiceless. Through our representations to governments, the United Nations (U.N.), and other international organizations, the BWA has made the cause of religious freedom a priority. Since the BWA has been recognized as an nongovernmental organization (NGO) at the U.N., it is able to make its voice heard at the highest levels. The General Secretary makes direct appeals to governments and international organizations on behalf of our suffering brothers and sisters. Still, given the volatile world situation and the increase of nationalism and hostility to other religions, more needs to be done to defend religious freedom. Therefore, the General Secretary recently recommended the creation of a permanent Division of Freedom and Justice, staffed by professionals whose main responsibilities would be to protest injustices and to work for religious freedom for all people everywhere.

5. *Study Commissions:* Bylaw Article VII.3. (3)authorizes the General Secretary to establish study commissions "to bring about the exchange of ideas on topics relating to Christian experience and mission; to encourage creative new solutions to problems of Christian mission in today's world." At present there are six of these. They are not esoteric committees where theologians exercise their erudition, but rather practical working groups that seek to serve the Baptist churches around the world as they carry out Christian mission. To determine what hinders the mission of the church means confronting the vital issues of the day, including HIV/AIDS, abortion, human sexuality, poverty, racism, human rights, religious freedom, injustice, and corruption in government, just to mention some of the more obvious. All are studied in the light of the Bible's meaning and message for our churches today.

The objects of study change from time to time to meet current needs and concerns. For example, because so-called "worship wars" were tearing at the fabric of many congregations, in 1990 the BWA established the Commission on Baptist Worship and Spirituality to deal with the problems regarding "proper forms" of worship. This commission examines the various forms of worship and encourages Baptists to consider the variety of expressions now existing and to learn from one another. It even sponsored a Conference on Worship in 1998 in Berlin and several regional meetings on worship elsewhere. Because of the increasing decline of emphasis on Baptist distinctiveness in many parts of the world, a restructuring of the Commission on Baptist Heritage in 2000 resulted in the addition of "Identity" to its title and purview.

The study commissions have been for many the highlight of the General Council meetings. Hundreds of pastors and laity attend these sessions. As an old hymn says, "New occasions teach new duties." Thus, every five years the BWA reviews the effectiveness of the study commissions and decides whether a need exists to delete any old ones or create new ones.

6. *Baptist Identity:* One of the challenges in a rapidly changing world is identity. This is true for nations as well as for churches. For areas in which phenomenal growth is occurring, the question of Baptist identity is particularly challenging. What does it mean to be a Baptist? What is the proper ecclesiology? What is the role of the pastor and the laity? What does our history have to teach us about structure and change? Such questions are relevant for the time in which we live. Whereas many European and North American Baptist churches have lost or downplayed their identity, this is not true of churches in the Two-thirds World. African, Asian, Latin American, and Caribbean Baptists are proud to be Baptist. They do not write Baptist with a lower case *b* but want to belong to our large historic family, one founded on the truths of the Bible.

The BWA contributes to Baptist identity through frequent visits by our staff. The President in particular strengthens the Baptist fellowship by appearing at the meetings of the various conventions and unions around the world. Much like the Olympic runners who pass on the torch from one country to another, the officers and BWA staff encourage Baptist identity.

Emphasizing Baptist distinctives contributes to developing a sense of identity. We were first called Baptists because we rejected the infant baptism of the state churches and insisted on believer's baptism as we read in Scripture. Over the years our distinctives came to include not only believer's baptism, but also separation of church and state; religious freedom and toleration for all; freedom of the individual conscience (soul liberty); the church as a redemptive community of born-again individuals; the evangelistic and missionary nature of the New Testament understanding of the church; the church as a prophetic voice in society against the sins of the state and society; and the Bible rather than imposed creeds as our sole source of authority in matters of faith. We join with other Christian groups in affirming these doctrines, but Baptist identity is characterized by the unique combination of all these facets into the blessed community that Baptists regard as the body of Christ. Therefore, when Baptists from around the globe gather, we encourage one another by reminding ourselves who we are and what we believe. The perspectives gained at these meetings enable us to return home as better followers of Christ and more effective evangelists and missionaries.

7. *The BWA as a Forum for Critical Conversation About the Future of Mission:* The statistics cited above demonstrate the tremendous growth of the Baptist movement during the past one hundred years. We have grown from a humble group accused of being a sect to one of the major Christian world communions. As stated above, we grew because mission is a central Baptist distinctive. Where there is no mission, there is no church. When the English Baptist shoemaker William Carey sailed for India in 1792, he set in motion a chain reaction. Before long, every Protestant church recognized the validity of his call to worldwide evangelization. As a result many call Carey "the father of modern missions." Of course, significant missionary work occurred before Carey, but it was his vision that carried the day and touched off the explosion of activity known as the modern missionary movement.

The BWA has encouraged missionary endeavor among its member bodies. Not only do the secretaries of Baptist mission agencies meet regularly, but also the BWA sponsors conferences enabling nationals to share their vision of where we need to go, such as the Baptist Summit on World Mission in Swanwick, England, in May 2003. It was made clear at this meeting that the missional church now exists throughout the world. The missionary challenge is not only for those in the western countries but also for every believer and every national convention/union.

Because nationals who have been cradled by the missionary movement are now adults, they will obviously have strong things to say about their identity, family, and mission upbringing, as well as about their future hopes and fears. Thus at BWA meetings it is not uncommon to hear criticism expressed against a certain mission policy or agency. Such criticisms are not necessarily the view of the BWA or its leadership. We are a forum of freedom, a platform where Two-thirds World delegates, as well as those from the First World, may voice their concerns and visions of the future. This type of dialogue is part of the prophetic witness that the BWA facilitates. We firmly believe that through the interchange among equal brothers and sisters we all grow in faith and together discern God's will for the future of the church.

While recognizing the courage, sacrifice, and love of the missionaries and their achievements in founding new Baptist conventions and churches, national leaders do not suspend critical judgment or view their history passively. We in Europe and North America must listen to their voices. By this means we learn and advance toward spiritual maturity.

We rejoice in the tremendous witness that indigenous Baptists have brought to what missiologists call the 10/40 window, or World A. In responding to the movement of the Spirit and efforts of indigenous workers, the BWA occasionally assists in founding Baptist conventions or unions. An example of this was the formation of the Nepal Baptist Church Council in 1994. In one decade it grew from five churches of two hundred and fifty to more than eighty churches, with three hundred mission points, a baptized membership of fourteen thousand, and a larger community of almost forty thousand people.

Where in the World Are We Going in the Twenty-first Century?

This centennial history gives sufficient reason to thank God for the progress that has occurred in the growth and maturing of the Baptist world fellowship since its inauguration in 1905. However, we must always look to the future. To be sure, there is a connectedness to human history, and many of the problems confronting Baptists in the twenty-first century will be the same as those faced in the past. Still, it is obvious that times and situations do change, and new ways of looking at reality (i.e., paradigm shifts) emerge that challenge all of us to ask what the appropriate response of the church must be. The BWA must continue to serve as a guardian of the faith "once delivered to the saints." Through its conferences, commissions, and World Congresses, it encourages Baptist conventions, unions, and individuals from every tribe, nation, and culture to affirm their biblical and orthodox Christian roots.

1. *Theological Affirmations and Basic Doctrines:* Too often when confronted by change, societies, nations, individuals, and even churches throw off their history and beliefs completely and adopt a new culture. Such revolutionary change, which fails to learn from the past, leads to repeating the same mistakes as made before. The church as the body of Christ is a divine institution, but it is also a temporal institution subject to the vicissitudes of human history. To use the classic phrase of the sixteenth century, there is a constant need for the church to be reformed and reforming (*reformata reformanda*).

Although as Baptists we have no creeds, still there are essentials of faith that we would acknowledge, core doctrines that must be confessed. As we enter a new century of life together, there are theological principles that Baptists, like all Christians, must uncompromisingly affirm in our multicultural and multireligious world:

a.) *Trinitarian Faith:* The doctrine of the Trinity affirms that in the person of Jesus Christ we meet God through the Holy Spirit. In Jesus Christ we do not meet only a part of God, but all of God! This doctrine must be restated for every new generation. It is a mystery that we cannot completely comprehend, but with the New Testament and the early church we confess that in Jesus Christ we have met God. It is an axiom of Christian history that wherever the Trinity is denied, the next generation denies Christ. A trinitarian faith is basic for witness in the twenty-first century.

b.) *Christology:* Following on the doctrine of the Trinity, we must acknowledge the divinity and humanity of our Savior, Jesus Christ. Like those in the early church we affirm that Jesus is "truly God and truly man." The incarnation means that God became a human being in Jesus of Nazareth (John 1:14). Therefore, although Jesus was a great teacher and socially compassionate, he is more. We confess Jesus Christ as God incarnate, Savior, and Lord. From Christ derives our understanding of God and from Christ we receive our commission to make known the Good News of new life and love in him.

c.) *Mission and Evangelism:* Because we affirm God's revelation of himself in Jesus Christ and because Christ calls us to make known this good news, Baptists have always been a missionary people. To follow Christ is to participate in mission and evangelism. When engaged in mission, the church grows. When mission is denied, the church falters and dies. The practice of believer's baptism is a constant reminder to us that the call of Christ is both one of decision and that of placing all of one's life under his control.

d.) *The Church:* Following Christ in baptism means following Christ in the church, both local and universal. Membership in the local church is not an option for the Christian. It is the command of Christ to fellowship with other believers who form his body. Therefore, as Baptists we summon men and women of every nation to follow Christ in baptism and church membership. In the cradle of the church one grows spiritually and matures as a faithful disciple of Christ. The church is God's instrument for announcing his coming kingdom and making that kingdom a reality in today's world.

e.) *The Bible and Ethical Demands:* The church does not have the freedom to change the message. Our message is Jesus Christ, and that is portrayed for all humanity in the Bible. The Bible is God's textbook for humanity and the church. Therefore, Bible study is of prime importance for the believer and the church. We must constantly test doctrine and action in light of what the Scriptures say. Following Christ is not only in the spiritual realm but in the physical one as well. Christ makes ethical demands of his followers. The implications of these demands are a great challenge to the church in the twenty-first century as it deals with the urgent personal and social problems of our day. The theological education of pastors and laity must always be grounded in biblical faith.

f.) *Relationship to Culture and Society:* Having this great treasure of faith in Christ, the church and individual believer must relate to the society in which they live. We are not to conduct our Christian lives in abstraction but in the concrete reality of the country, culture, and society of which we are a part. We relate to our governments and societies in various ways. For one thing, Baptists have found that separation of church and state is the best guarantee for the church to be the church and to be a prophetic witness against the sins of society and government. In pursuit of our goals, we do not reject governments as such. Rather we hold that Christians should be salt and light in a secular and hostile world, bringing their deeply held faith to bear on what it means to be human. We call upon the rulers to treat individuals with dignity and honor. As a result, Baptists are involved in the struggle for religious freedom for all people, opposing racism, poverty, and injustice. Like all Christians, Baptists should be involved in working for a more peaceful world, protecting the environment, and being good guardians of God's gift of life on this planet called Earth.

Exemplary Baptists of the twentieth century—such as Jimmy Carter, Billy Graham, and Martin Luther King, Jr., along with a host of unnamed saints and faithful followers of Christ—have all emphasized the unchanging demands of the gospel. As we enter our new century, we pray that God will raise up men and women to proclaim in a prophetic way the message of Jesus Christ for the new day in which we must live and witness.

2. *Challenges That Force Us to Change to Be Better Witnesses to God's Truth in Christ:* The poet said it well: "Once to every man and nation comes the moment to decide, in the strife of truth with falsehood, for the good or evil side; Some great cause, some great decision, offering each the bloom or blight, and the choice goes by forever 'twixt that darkness and that light."[3]

We hold the unchanging principles of our faith but must admit that change is all about us. In our desire to make Christ known, we Baptists must change those things that need changing so that we may be more faithful to the God who changes not. Let us consider some issues that may be divisive but certainly will not go away. We should regard them as challenges that will make us more effective witnesses for Jesus Christ in the coming years:

a.) *Unity Among Baptists and Other Christians:* From the very first page, the Old Testament is concerned with unity, beginning with the unity of God and man in the Garden of Eden and then the cursed fall of humanity that shattered this unity. From Adam and Eve's fall and the first murder—Cain killing his brother, Abel—the sorry story of disunity runs throughout the Scriptures. The Old Testament clearly shows that the consequence of the disunity of Adam and Eve with God was the alienation and disunity of all of humankind.

Any reader of the New Testament recognizes that unity was a dominant theme of the Apostle Paul. From the time those first churches began, there was conflict, and Paul upheld the principle of unity. For him the decisive question was I Corinthians 1:13: "Is Christ divided?" Paul's letters are a constant call to unity: "Make my joy complete: be of the same mind, having the same love, being in full accord and of one mind" (Phil. 2:2). The BWA theme has always been the Pauline formula of unity in Ephesians 4:5: "One Lord, one faith, one baptism."

The high priestly prayer of Jesus in John 17 is essentially a missionary prayer: "That they may all be one . . . so that the world may believe" (John 17:21). Jesus prayed that his followers might be united because unity was needed for the continuance of his mission. Church history bears witness that where disunity existed there was also a lack of evangelism. Disunity detracts from the essential mission of the church.

The preamble of our constitution stresses that our organization exists for unity: "The Baptist World Alliance, extending over every part of the world, exists as an expression of the essential oneness of Baptist people in the Lord Jesus Christ." The BWA recognizes unity in diversity. It does not demand uniformity because it recognizes the traditional autonomy of the conventions and unions. At the same time, the preamble underscores "the interdependence of Baptist churches and member bodies." During the recent discussions with Southern Baptist leaders, I emphasized that "we belong together because we belong to Christ." In other words, any schism in the worldwide Baptist community means that our witness will be less effective.

As we progress into the twenty-first century, the BWA will be confronted more and more with disunity and the desire of some to force uniformity on other Baptist bodies. We do not have an episcopal form of authority, as that goes against our Baptist principle of autonomy. On the other hand, this commitment to autonomy does not mean that unity with other Baptist groups and other Christians is not important. One objective of the BWA is "to promote understanding and cooperation among Baptist bodies and with other Christian groups, in keeping with our unity in Christ" (Constitution, Article II. 3). For that reason, the BWA has sponsored conversations with other Christian World Communions, including the Lutheran World Federation, World Alliance of Reformed Churches, Mennonite World Conference, (Roman Catholic) Pontifical Council for Promoting Church Unity, Anglican Consultative Council, and Eastern Orthodox Ecumenical Patriarchate. Conversations with other Christians have led to better understanding and have promoted the cause of religious freedom. The question of unity among Baptists and other Christian groups will be a challenge for the BWA in the coming years. It is a biblical challenge and one that Baptists must not shirk.

b.) *Youth and the Laity:* When the first BWA World Youth Conference took place in 1931 in Prague, Czechoslovakia, we were acknowledging the need to produce leaders for the future. Since that time we have created a vigorous Youth Department, which has held fourteen major youth world conferences, the last one in Hong Kong in August 2004.

But we must do more. If we are to stem the tide of young people being swept away into secularism and rejecting the historic Christian faith, there must be a new dynamic for involving youth and laity in our churches. The youth of today will be the leaders of tomorrow. This point was well-illustrated by the anecdote in an earlier chapter about the teenage Duke McCall who attended the 1931 Youth Conference in Prague and fifty years later became President of the BWA. It is essential that we involve youth in the work, and they need to be serving on our commissions and committees. David Coffey, who will serve as President beginning in 2005, has already indicated his intention to hold a series of conferences for young Baptist leaders.

Related to the involvement of youth is that of the laity. Too often BWA commissions and committees are dominated by pastors. We need all the people of God to participate in the work of the BWA. The Women's Department has done an excellent job in mobilizing women worldwide, but the Men's Department has not been as successful in its efforts to rally lay support. To be sure, this situation reflects a problem afflicting the church worldwide. Men's movements have suffered while women's movements have prospered. Perhaps the main explanation for this is that men already dominate the church. The larger issue of involving laity in the life of the church remains unresolved and is a major challenge for the twenty-first century.

c.) *The Charismatic Movement:* The gift of the Holy Spirit is freely promised to all believers who confess Jesus Christ as Lord. Yet, throughout the history of the church, leaders have tried to control the Holy Spirit either by placing control of the Spirit in the hands of the bishops at confirmation or by excluding renewal movements that emphasize the gifts of the Spirit. Because of what they perceive as excesses in the modern

Pentecostal movement—such as speaking in tongues and other forms of ecstatic behavior in worship services—many Baptists are wary of speaking at all about the Holy Spirit.

What a mistake! A renewed understanding of worship and a rediscovery of the gifts given to each believer are positive contributions of the modern charismatic movement. Our member bodies can learn from the charismatics. Since the BWA has had conversations with various churches of the Reformation, Roman Catholics, and the Eastern Orthodox, should we not also have similar talks with brothers and sisters in Christ who are part of the Pentecostal tradition? Such discussions will help us to deal with the manifestations of the charismatic movement that have caused divisions in our churches and often brought in practices that are not acceptable to large numbers of our people.

d.) *Gender and Ordination:* It will be a surprise to some that not every Baptist union or convention ordains its ministerial personnel. For some groups a simple service of installing a new individual as a pastor is sufficient; others have a very high view of ordination, requiring theological training, academic degrees, internships, and careful examination of the candidate. The position of pastor in most Baptist bodies was reserved for male clergy until the twentieth century, when some Baptists in North America, Britain, and Europe began to ordain women. The BWA does not prohibit or promote ordination of women. Ordination is an issue decided by Baptist bodies or local congregations. This will be a matter of ongoing debate in the twenty-first century. But one thing is clear, as secular society increasingly accepts women in leadership roles, pressures to do likewise in the church will mount.

The BWA is grateful to the Women's Department for working so compassionately and aggressively to ensure that women are given their rightful place in the church. Discrimination against women is contrary to Scripture, which clearly affirms that in Christ "there is no longer male and female" (Gal. 3:28).

e.) *Conflict Resolution:* Often the very practical matter of property that mission agencies left to national conventions becomes a cause for division. In India, for example, disagreements over power, control, finances, leadership, and education have contributed to divisions. Again and again the BWA mediates differences that arise in conventions/unions. Conflict resolution will undoubtedly continue to be an important BWA ministry in the coming century.

With the end of apartheid in South Africa, the BWA assisted in bringing together the Baptist Union and the Baptist Convention and eventually the other bodies to form the South African Baptist Alliance, which is committed to racial harmony in the country. In India, the BWA helped to bring unity to the Bengal Baptist Union and currently is engaged in mediating differences within the Samevesam Telugu Baptist Churches. In the former Soviet Union the BWA has been working to bring peace between the Autonomous Brotherhood and the All-Union Council, and in Ukraine the Brotherhood is now a member of the Alliance. The conflict within the Southern Baptist Convention led to the formation of the Cooperative Baptist Fellowship, but reconciliation between these two bodies has not yet occurred.

f.) *Political Involvement:* Baptists have been very firm in their understanding of the necessity for the separation of church and state, or of religion from the government. Historically, both Catholicism and Orthodoxy have been friendly towards the state and have encouraged the governments to carry out their religious programs. In countries where they were the majority faith, the Anglican, Lutheran, and Reformed traditions have also looked to the state to enforce their doctrines. It is precisely for the reason that these "state churches" used the secular power to restrict the freedom of others that Baptists espoused the concepts of religious freedom for all and a strict separation of the church from the state. Since Baptists were a minority, these principles were vital to their survival. However, in the United States—as well as in Nigeria, Brazil, and a few other countries where today Baptists make up a substantial proportion of the population—an unhealthy alliance between government and the church has begun to develop.

Several Baptist politicians—such as presidents William Tolbert of Liberia, Olusegun Obasanjo of Nigeria, and Jimmy Carter of the United States—have served ably as secular leaders. As more and more Baptists become involved in political activities, they will face the temptation of being "co-opted" by the system. The task of the congregations that nurture the new political figures is to ensure that they take a prophetic stance on public issues, one that is in harmony with the teachings of Christ and their Baptist heritage.

g.) *Racism and Ethnic Conflict:* The twentieth century was marred by racial and ethnic conflicts, and in this new century they are taking new and even more dangerous forms. The Baptist pastor and civil-rights leader, Martin Luther King, Jr., led a generation of African-Americans to confront the white power structures in the United States. His prophetic witness launched a revolution of freedom for all people of color that did not end with his assassination in 1968. The fight continued in South Africa until the apartheid system there collapsed in the early 1990s.

The Atlanta Covenant, which was drawn up at the 1999 International

Summit of Baptists Against Racism and Ethnic Conflict convened by the BWA, called for a continuing struggle against racism and ethnic conflict in all its forms and recommended that 2000–10 be declared "A Decade to Promote Racial Justice." Following the end of communism, tensions between ethnic groups that had been held down by military force erupted into open wars. Thousands were killed in the former Yugoslavia, as Croats, Serbs, Bosnians, and Albanians fought one another. In Africa tribalism brought genocidal terror to new heights with the deaths of a million people in the conflict between the Hutus and Tutsis in Rwanda. A special conference that met in Melbourne prior to the 2000 World Congress expressed support for the many people in the world who were suffering from racism and ethnic discrimination.

In the twenty-first century, the BWA will continue to strive to educate our people about the importance of working for racial justice and ethnic harmony in the compassionate and mighty name of Christ, in whom there is no east or west, north or south, red or yellow, black or white.

h.) *Power, Authority, and Ecclesiological Structures:* Structural and internal governance questions will increasingly confront Baptists in the twenty-first century. Our emphasis on autonomy is both a boon and a bane. Freedom and democracy are among the greatest contributions that Baptists have brought to the table of church structure. However, these traits have fueled bitter conflicts, and every major Baptist denomination has struggled with issues of power and authority. We claim that only Jesus is king of our congregations, but in reality, how does one control the hunger for power in Baptist church structures? I believe that as soon as possible, the BWA must convene a major conference to consider the entire question of Baptist polity, structure, power, and authority. There must be some agreement as to the proper relationship between discipline and freedom. In other words, we desperately need an ecclesiology for the twenty-first century.

i.) *Theological and Academic Education:* An ongoing concern of the BWA has been theological education. Throughout their history, Baptist conventions and unions started schools to train pastors and Christian workers. One of the first projects William Carey undertook in India was the theological education of nationals. Two centuries later, when communism ended in Eastern Europe, theological seminaries and Bible schools sprang up everywhere. In the twenty-first century Baptist bodies will increasingly confront situations where congregations cannot support a full-time pastor and a bivocational person will be needed. Is the present structure of theological education prepared for this shift to bivocational ministry?

Another question is what type of training should be provided? We will need to distinguish between propaganda and proclamation. *Propaganda* is the doctrinaire, authoritarian approach that requires individuals to become like the person teaching or preaching before they are permitted to hear the gospel. *Proclamation* is the preaching of the Word in the freedom of the Spirit, allowing the individual to become what God wants him or her to become. In this age of ideologically based cultural wars, the BWA can help show the way in theological education so that our future leaders are trained to be servants of the Word and not of society's conception of multiculturalism, which at times becomes a subtle attack upon the Christian faith itself.

j.) *Personal Versus Social Morality:* No greater conflict exists today in the churches than that between social and personal morality. A careful reading of the Old Testament prophets and the ethical teachings of Christ and the New Testament letters reveals that no conflict exists. Sadly, in many areas of Baptist life the struggle between those who preach social morality and those who preach personal morality has reached an impasse. The concerns of social morality are the large issues of poverty, hunger, justice, human rights, war and peace, and protecting the environment. Personal morality focuses on such questions as abortion, homosexuality, stem-cell research, marriage, personal ethical behavior, honesty, purity, and pornography.

It is strange that Christians try to separate issues of personal and social morality. The BWA must lead Baptists to recognize that both personal and social moral issues are biblical concerns. How do we proclaim the new life in Christ? What are the kingdom ethics for this "in-between" time in which we now live—the period between Christ's incarnation and ascension and his second coming? Is it not a question of life in the light of God's love in Christ? Concerns about abortion are concerns about life. Concerns about war are concerns about life. Can the BWA lead Baptists in bringing these issues into one unified and prophetic message? That is the challenge for the twenty-first century.

k.) *Faith for Our Children:* Since the 1780s Baptists have been instrumental in founding Sunday Schools, whose chief aim was to educate children with the Bible as their textbook. Whatever name we may give these institutions today, we must reach children if they are to have faith in the twenty-first century. In 1980 the BWA instituted a Christian Education and Literature Workgroup to help Baptist churches educate children as well as adults. If there is no strong Sunday School or other form of Christian education in the churches, instruction of our children in the faith is often left to parachurch groups, such as Youth for Christ, Youth with a Mission, Campus Crusade, or Young Life. Their outreach to the youth is praiseworthy, but Baptist churches must assume responsibility. An educational program should be integrated into the life of the church. If we do not take up the challenge, then we should not be surprised when secular education ends up negating a superficial religious training that has little biblical content.

These are the challenges confronting the BWA and our Baptist churches as we enter the twenty-first century. The list is long, and one could add others: conversations with world religions, the clash of civilizations, multiculturalism, terrorism, and the environment. Suffice it to say, individual Baptists cannot deal with these challenges alone. We need one another. Just a listing of these problems is motivation enough for Baptists to work together.

Quo Vadis *BWA in the Twenty-first Century?*

We have briefly reviewed where we have been in the past century. We have listed challenges that await us. Now, we conclude with some thoughts as to what the BWA can and must do. Where must we go?

1. *The Twenty-first Century Committee:* To deal with the concerns and challenges mentioned above, the Twenty-first Century Committee was formed. Its task is to study the whole structure and movement of the BWA and to make recommendations to increase its effectiveness for challenging and uniting Baptists worldwide as they witness for Christ in the twenty-first century.

The committee has done an excellent job. Its 2004 progress report to the General Council stated that the BWA must have a clear emphasis for its programs and work if it is to speak significantly for and to Baptists worldwide in the twenty-first century. The document identified and spelled out three "clusters of commitment."

> The BWA, at the dawn of the twenty-first century, builds fellowship and community, promotes vibrant Baptist identities, networks resources, and serves as a global voice. It equips and empowers Baptists:
> I. To nurture mission and evangelism
>   A. Discover and disseminate effective strategies throughout the world
>   B. Provide training and resources for a more effective global Christian witness
>   C. Facilitate research, dialogue, and publications that strengthen Baptist practices and identities
> II. To defend religious liberty and human rights
>   A. Gather and disseminate qualitative and quantitative data regarding human rights and religious freedom around the world
>   B. Support and advocate for human rights and religious freedom with and for member bodies around the world

C. Represent the global Baptist family as a United Nations non-governmental organization
III. To respond through relief and sustainable community development
   A. Fund relief and development projects of member bodies
   B. Build capacity of member bodies to access a broad array of relief and development resources locally, nationally, and internationally
   C. Respond to disasters through effective partnerships and collaborations with money, goods, and services.[4]

The challenge for the Baptist World Alliance in the twenty-first century is not only to implement the above recommendation but also to create structures with adequate funding to respond appropriately. The challenges of the next hundred years for the BWA are great. But God's grace is even greater. We believe that He who began a good work in us will complete it to the glory of Christ and His kingdom.[5]

The officers and staff are confident that if we keep our eyes on Christ, we will remain united and thereby be able to expect great things from God and to attempt great things for God. To God be the glory!

---

1. These figures are based on 2004 statistics that include the sixteen million members of the Southern Baptist Convention (SBC), a founding body of the Baptist World Alliance (BWA), in 1905. The SBC as a national organization withdrew from the BWA after these numbers had been compiled, but several state conventions, local associations, and churches decided to continue as members.

2. It is a remarkable achievement of modern church history that today so many denominations practice believer's baptism, when in 1905 many state churches still considered Baptists a sectarian movement. Alexander Maclaren had the assembled delegates at the first BWA Congress in 1905 stand and quote the Apostle's Creed in order to show that Baptists were not sectarian but orthodox, trinitarian believers in Jesus Christ and part of the historic church that existed from New Testament times until today.

3. James Russell Lowell, from the hymn, "Once to Every Man and Nation."

4. *BWA Yearbook*, 2004, pp. 83–85.

5. We are of course saddened that the Southern Baptist Convention in 2004 decided to leave the BWA, but we are encouraged that millions of individual Southern Baptists have continued to support the Alliance. The General Council, recognizing the changes that might occur, prepared for this eventuality by opening BWA membership to individuals, churches, and organized Baptist bodies. We are confident that the members in these groups will more than make up the funding deficit created by the SBC withdrawal.

APPENDIX I

Baptist World Congresses

Date	Place	Theme
1905	London, England (U.K.)	
1911	Philadelphia, Pennsylvania (U.S.)	The Christianization of the World
1923	Stockholm, Sweden	
1928	Toronto, Canada	Baptist Life in the World's Life
1934	Berlin, German	One Lord, One Faith, One Baptism: One God and Father of All
1939	Atlanta, Georgia (U.S.)	
1947	Copenhagen, Denmark	Unity in Christ
1950	Cleveland, Ohio (U.S.)	And the Light Shineth in the Darkness
1955	London, England (U.K.)	Jesus Christ, the Same Yesterday, and Today, and Forever
1960	Rio de Janeiro, Brazil	Jesus Is Lord
1965	Miami Beach, Florida (U.S.)	Jesus Christ in a Changing World
1970	Tokyo, Japan	Reconciliation Through Christ
1975	Stockholm, Sweden	New People for a New World—Through Christ
1980	Toronto, Canada	Celebrating Christ's Presence through the Spirit
1985	Los Angeles, California (U.S.)	Out of Darkness into the Light of Christ
1990	Seoul, South Korea	Together in Christ
1995	Buenos Aires, Argentina	Celebrate Christ: The Hope of the World
2000	Melbourne, Australia	Jesus Christ, Forever. Yes!
2005	Birmingham, England (U.K.)	Jesus Christ Living Water

Baptist World Youth Conferences

Date	Place
1931	Prague, Czechoslovakia
1937	Zurich, Switzerland
1949	Stockholm, Sweden
1953	Rio de Janeiro, Brazil
1958	Toronto, Canada
1963	Beirut, Lebanon
1968	Berne, Switzerland
1974	Portland, Oregon (U.S.)
1978	Manila, the Philippines
1984	Buenos Aires, Argentina
1988	Glasgow, Scotland (U.K.)
1993	Harare, Zimbabwe
1998	Houston, Texas (U.S.)
2004	Hong Kong, China

World Conferences for Baptist Men

Date	Place
1974	Hong Kong (British crown colony)
1978	Indianapolis, Indiana (U.S.)
1980	Nairobi, Kenya
1987	Cardiff, Wales (U.K.)
1993	Nashville, Tennessee (U.S.)

APPENDIX II

Officers of the Baptist World Alliance

Presidents	Dates Served
John Clifford, United Kingdom	1905–11
Robert Stuart MacArthur, United States	1911–23
Edgar Young Mullins, United States	1923–28
John McNeill, Canada	1928–34
George W. Truett, United States	1934–39
James Henry Rushbrooke, United Kingdom	1939–47*
C. Oscar Johnson, United States	1947–50
F. Townley Lord, United Kingdom	1950–55
Theodore F. Adams, United States	1955–60
João Filson Soren, Brazil	1960–65
William R. Tolbert, Jr., Liberia	1965–70
V. Carney Hargroves, United States	1970–75
David Y. K. Wong, Hong Kong	1975–80
Duke K. McCall, United States	1980–85
G. Noel Vose, Australia	1985–90
Knud Wümpelmann, Denmark	1990–95
Nilson do Amaral Fanini, Brazil	1995–2000
Billy Jang Hwan Kim, Korea	2000–05
David Coffey, United Kingdom	2005–

* After Rushbrooke's death in February 1947, the Executive Committee appointed two Vice Presidents, Elmer A. Fridell and C. J. Tinsley, as interim Presidents, to serve until after the Congress that summer. Tinsley presided at the Congress.

Vice-Presidents

Elected for the first time in 1905

K.O. Broady, Sweden	1905–11
J. V. Cova, Cuba	1905–11
Harry H. Driver, New Zealand	1905–11
T. Burnham King, South Africa	1905–11
Marius Larsen, Denmark	1905–11
Johann G. Lehmann, Germany	1905–11
Pastor Liu, China	1905–11
H. P. McCormick, Puerto Rico	1905–11
Joseph McLeod, Canada	1905–11
H. Novotny, Austria–Hungary	1905–11
D. Nursiah, India	1905–11
Jacob A. Ohrn, Norway	1905–11, 23–28
E. Paschetto, Italy	1905–11
B. Roeles, Netherlands	1905–11
Rueben Saillens, France	1905–11
A. Sims, Congo	1905–11
W. G. Stephens, Australia	1905–11
Augustus H. Strong, United States	1905–11
Z. C. Taylor, Brazil	1905–11
A. Trevino, Mexico	1905–11
Waldemar Uixkiull, Estonia (then a part of Russia)	1905–11
S. J. Washington, Jamaica	1905–11
George White, United Kingdom	1905–11
H. Yoshikawa, Japan	1905–11

Vice-Presidents　　　　　　　　　　　　　　　　　　　　　　**Dates Served**

Elected for first time in 1911

R. Cleghorn, British Honduras	1911–23
High Dixson, Australia	1911–23
Alfred North, New Zealand	1911–23
C. Palmer, Australia	1911–23
Ivan S. Prokhanoff, Russia	1911–28
H. S. Ramford, Australia	1911–23
A. R. Robinson, United States	1911–23
B. Werts, Germany	1911–23
Mornay Williams, Bahamas	1911–23
P. Williams, Jamaica	1911–23

Elected for first time in 1923

C. E. Benander, Sweden	1923–28
F. M. Edwards, Brazil	1923–28
Joel Waiz Lall, India	1923–28

Elected for first time in 1928

Clarence A. Barbour, United States	1928–34
Tsih Ching Bau, China	1928–34, 39–47
A. H. King, South Africa	1928–34
Friedrich Wilhelm Simoleit, Germany	1928–39
Stow Smith, Australia	1928–34
J. C. Varetto, Argentina	1928–34
Lacey Kirk Williams, United States	1928–43

Elected for first time in 1934

A.W. Beaven, United States	1934–39
B. A. Nag, India	1934–39
N. J. Nordstrom, Sweden	1934–47
J. A. Packer, Australia	1934–39
Manoel Avelino de Souza, Brazil	1934–39

Elected for first time in 1939

Elmer A. Fridell, United States	1939–47
Hans Luckey, Germany	1939–47
Lee R. Scarborough, United States	1939–45
C. J. Tinsley, Australia	1939–47

Elected for first time in 1947

Theodore F. Adams, United States	1947–50
Herbert Henry Bingham, Canada	1947–50
Henry Lin, China	1947–50
F. Townley Lord, United Kingdom	1947–50
Johannes Norgaard, Denmark	1947–50
G.L. Prince, United States	1947–50
Henry Prochazka, Czechoslovakia	1947–50

Elected in 1950

W. L. Jarvis, Australia	1950–55
D. V. Jemison, United States	1950–54
Sadamoto Kawano, Japan	1950–55
Louie D. Newton, United States	1950–55
Manfredi Ronchi, Italy	1950–55
William C. Smalley, Canada	1950–55
Per Gunnar Westin, Sweden	1950–55

Vice-Presidents **Dates Served**

Elected for first time in 1955

J. T. Ayorinde, Nigeria	1955–60, 70–75
Marion (Mrs. J. Edgar) Bates, Canada	1955–60
Honorio Espinoza, Chile	1955–59
Lam Chi Fung, Hong Kong	1955–65
Jakob Meister, West Germany	1955–60
Lawrence A. North, New Zealand	1955–60
Benjamin Pradhan, India	1955–60
P. S. Wilkinson, United States	1955–60
Yakov I. Zhidkov, Russia	1955–65

Elected for first time in 1960

V. Carney Hargroves, United States	1960–65
Joseph H. Jackson, United States	1960–65
Alfonso Olmedo, Argentina	1960–65
Louise Paw, Burma	1960–65
Alan C. Prior, Australia	1960–65
William R. Tolbert, Jr., Liberia	1960–65
Henri Vincent, France	1960–65

Elected in 1965

Herschel H. Hobbs, United States	1965–70
Aleksander Kircun, Poland	1965–70
Marie Wiley (Mrs. R. L.) Mathis, United States	1965–70
Shuichi Matsamura, Japan	1965–70
Paul Mbende, Cameroon	1965–70
Ernest A. Payne, United Kingdom	1965–70
Roberto Porras Maynes, Mexico	1965–70
Lawrence Silcock, New Zealand	1965–70
John W. Williams, United States	1965–70

Elected for first time in 1970

L. Venchael Booth, United States	1970–75
Daniel Y. K. Cheung, Hong Kong	1970–75
Isamu Chiba, Japan	1970–75
Owen Cooper, United States	1970–75
Alma Hunt, United States	1970–75
Janos Laczkovszki, Hungary	1970–75
Rubens Lopes, Brazil	1970–75
Agustin E. Masa, Philippines	1970–75
Thomas B. McDormand, Canada	1970–75
B. R. Moses, India	1970–75
Rudolf Thaut, West Germany	1970–75

Elected in 1975

Geoffrey H. Blackburn, Australia	1975–80
Robert C. Campbell, United States	1975–80
Nilson do Amaral Fanini, Brazil	1975–80
Advertus A. Hoff, Liberia	1975–80
Arthur Kinyanjui, Kenya	1975–80
David Lagergren, Sweden	1975–80
Akiko Matsumura, Japan	1975–80
Azariah McKenzie, Jamaica	1975–80
James L. Sullivan, United States	1975–80
Thelea Wesseler, United States	1975–80
M. L. Wilson, United States	1975–80
Michael Zhidkov, Soviet Union	1975–80

Vice-Presidents **Dates Served**

Elected in 1980

K. Imotemjen Aier, India	1980–85
Roy D. Bell, Canada	1980–85
A. S. Clement, United Kingdom	1980–85
Ethel Codrington, South Africa	1980–85
Rolf Dammann, East Germany	1980–85
Edward A. Freeman, United States	1980–85
Chester J. Jump, United States	1980–85
Mandole Molima Koli, Zaire	1980–85
Victor San Lone, Burma	1980–85
Jose dos Reis Pereira, Brazil	1980–85
Librado Ramos–Luzano, Mexico	1980–85
Fannie Thompson, United States	1980–85

Elected in 1985

Atinuke Bamijoko, Nigeria	1985–90
Samson H. Chowdhury, Bangladesh	1985–90
Ruferse S. Escoe, Costa Rica	1985–90
Peter Fehr, United States	1985–90
Roger Fredrikson, United States	1985–90
Christine Burton Gregory, United States	1985–90
Josip Horak, Yugoslavia	1985–90
Theodore J. Jemison, United States	1985–90
Birgit Karlsson, Sweden	1985–90
Billy Jang Hwan Kim, Korea	1985–90
Lorenzo Klink, Argentina	1985–90
João Makondekwa, Angola	1985–90

Elected in 1990

Harold C. Bennett, United States	1990–95
Shirley Bentall, Canada	1990–95
Jachin Y. Chang, Hong Kong	1990–95
Irmgard Claas, Germany	1990–95
Edna Lee de Gutiérrez, Mexico	1990–95
Eudora Mary Kalil, El Salvador	1990–95
Warren R. Magnuson, United States	1990–95
Joseph Mans, Sierra Leone	1990–95
John O. Peterson, United States	1990–95
Charles Smith, Bahamas	1990–95
Cora Sparrowk, United States	1990–95
Janos Viczian, Hungary	1990–95

Elected in 1995

John Binder, United States	1995–2000
Paul H. Eustache, Venezuela	1995–2000
Saw Mar Gay Gyi, Myanmar	1995–2000
C. B. Hogue, United States	1995–2000
Osadolor Imasogie, Nigeria	1995–2000
Emmett Johnson, United States	1995–2000
Mona Khauli, Lebanon	1995–2000
Gregory Komendant, Ukraine	1995–2000
Beatrice Nokuri, Cameroon	1995–2000
Mercy Jeyaraja Rao, India	1995–2000
Cynthia Perry Ray, United States	1995–2000
C. Sam Reid, Jamaica	1995–2000

Officers of the Baptist World Alliance

Vice-Presidents   **Dates Served**

Elected in 2000

Neville G. Callam, Jamaica	2000–05
Young Shim Chang, Korea	2000–05
Morris H. Chapman, United States	2000–04
David Coffey, United Kingdom	2000–05
Branko Lovrec, Croatia	2000–05
Ken R. Manley, Australia	2000–05
Amparo de Medina, Colombia	2000–05
Bruce Milne, Canada	2000–05
Zac Patnaik, India	2000–05
Robert S. Ricker, United States	2000–05
Raoul Scialabba, Argentina	2000–05
Dorothy Selebano, South Africa	2000–05
G. Elaine Smith, United States	2000–05
John A. Sundquist, United States	2000–05
Nathaniel Tyler-Lord, United States	2000–02*
Douglas W. Waruta, Kenya	2000–05

* Upon the death of Nathaniel Tyler-Lord, his widow Portia completed his term.

Elected in 2005

Fawaz Ameish, Jordan	2005–
Theo Angelov, Bulgaria	2005–
Andre Bokundoa bo-Likabe, Congo	2005–
Ian M. Chapman, United States	2005–
Chamunorwa Chiromo, Zimbabwe	2005–
Jason Das, Bangladesh	2005–
David Hahn, Korea	2005–
Clifford Jones, United States	2005–
Emmanuel McCall, United States	2005–
Gary Nelson, Canada	2005–
Delanna O'Brien, United States	2005–
Gustavo Parajon, Nicaragua	2005–
Jorge Pastor, Spain	2005–
Terry Rae, South Africa	2005–
Wallace Charles Smith, United States	2005–
Billy Taranger, Norway	2005–
William Thompson, Bahamas	2005–
Vincent Wood, Barbados	2005–
Fausto Vasconcelos, Brazil	2005–

Eastern or European Secretaries

John Howard Shakespeare, United Kingdom	1905–24
James Henry Rushbrooke, United Kingdom	1925–28

Western or American Secretaries

John Newton Prestridge, United States	1905–13
Robert Healy Pitt, United States	1913–23
Clifton Daggett Gray, United States	1923–28

General Secretaries

James Henry Rushbrooke, United Kingdom	1928–39
Walter O. Lewis, United States	1939–48
Arnold T. Ohrn, Norway	1948–60
Josef Nordenhaug, Norway	1960–69
Robert S. Denny, United States	1969–80
Gerhard Claas, Germany	1980–88
Denton Lotz, United States	1988–

Treasurers	**Dates Served**
Henry Kirke Porter, United States	1905–11*
Fred B. Rhodes, United States	1975–85**
John Rucker Jones, United States	1990–95
Clement Gimbert, United States	1995–2005

* Office of Treasurer was split 1911–1975; see below.
** The General Secretary served as Treasurer 1985–90.

Eastern or European Treasurer
Herbert Marnham, United Kingdom	1911–39
C.T. LeQuesne, United Kingdom	1939–54
Donald Finnemore, United Kingdom	1955–70
George Polson, United Kingdom	1970–75

Western or American Treasurer
Ezekiel M. Sipprell, Canada	1911–23
Albert Matthews, Canada	1923–50
George B. Frazer, United States	1950–53
Edward B. Willingham, United States	1955–56
Carl W. Tiller, United States	1956–72
Fred B. Rhodes, United States	1972–75

Staff of the Baptist World Alliance

Associate Secretaries	**Dates Served**
Clifton Daggett Gray, United States (unpaid)	1928–47
Louie D. Newton, United States (unpaid)	1939–47
Walter O. Lewis, United States (for Europe)	1948–55
Henry Cook (Acting), United Kingdom (for Europe)	1955–59
Robert S. Denny, United States (for Youth)	1956–69
Erik Rudén, Sweden (for Europe)	1959–65
C.Ronald Goulding, United Kingdom	1965–80

(for Europe 1965–76; for Relief and Development and for Evangelism and Education from 1976)

Frank H. Woyke, United States	1968–72

(for Relief, Study Commissions, and the North American Baptist Fellowship [NABF])

Cyril E. Bryant, United States	1971–80

(for Communications; served as Director of Publications from 1957)

Theo Patnaik, India (for Youth)	1971–75
Carl W. Tiller, United States	1972–78

(for Relief, Study Commissions, NABF; other responsibilities added)

Alan C. Prior, Australia (unpaid) (for Asia)	1975–80
Gerhard Claas, Germany (for Europe)	1976–80
Charles F. Wills, United States	1978–80

(for Study and Research and for NABF)

Reinhold J. Kerstan, United States	1980–85

(for Communications and for Study and Research)

Denton Lotz, United States	1980–85

(for Relief and Development 1980–81, for Evangelism and Education, and for Youth 1980–85)

Archibald R. (Archie) Goldie, Canada	1981–85

(for Relief and Development)

Division Directors
Reinhold Kerstan, United States	1985–88

(for Study and Research, for Promotion and Development)

Denton Lotz, United States	1985–88

(for Evangelism and Education; also Director of the Youth Department)

Archibald (Archie) R. Goldie, Canada	1985–90

(for Baptist World Aid)

Division Directors (continued)   **Dates Served**
John M. Wilkes, United States (for Communications)   1985–88
J. Ralph McIntyre, United States (interim)   1988–90
   (for Study and Research and for Evangelism and Education)
Wendy Ryan, Trinidad and Tobago (for Communications)   1988–2005
Paul Montacute, United Kingdom   1990–
   (for BWAid; also Director of Youth Department 1990–94)
L. A. (Tony) Cupit, Australia   1990–2005
   (for Study and Research and for Evangelism and Education)
Douglas Inglis, Scotland (for Promotion and Development)   1995–2000
Ellen Sims Teague, United States   2001–
   (for Finance and Administration; on staff from 1991, Director of Finance from 1994)
Alan Stanford, United States   2001–04
   (for Promotion and Development)
Ian M. Chapman, United States (acting)   2004–
   (for Promotion and Development)

Regional Secretaries
Edwin I. Lopez, Philippines (Asia)   1980–97
Knud Wümpelmann, Germany (Europe)   1980–89
Azariah McKenzie, Jamaica (Caribbean)   1982–97
Samuel T. Ola Akande, Nigeria (Africa)   1982–92
José Missena, Paraguay (Latin America)   1983–95
Karl Heinz Walter, Germany (Europe)   1989–98
Carolyn Weatherford Crumpler, United States (North America*)   1990–92
Eleazar Ziherambere, Rwanda (Africa)   1992–97
Daniel Carro, Argentina (Latin America)   1995–2001
Frank Adams, Ghana (Africa)   1997–
Bonny Resu, India (Asia)   1997–
Peter Pinder, Bahamas (Asia)   1997–
Theo Angelov, Bulgaria (Europe)   1998–2004
Alberto Prokopchuk, Argentina (Latin America)   2001–
Tony Peck, United Kingdom (Europe)   2004–

* With the exception of this interlude, a member of the BWA office staff has had responsibility for the North American Baptist Fellowship.

Other Elected or Appointed Staff
James Henry Rushbrooke, United Kingdom (Commissioner for Europe)   1920–28
Joel Sorenson, Sweden (Youth Secretary)   1950–55
Adolph Klaupiks, (Relief Coordinator) (on staff from 1947)   1961–68
Betty Lee Smith, United States   1976–81
   (Assistant Secretary for Youth and Conferences) (on staff from 1966)
Cyril E. Bryant, United States   1980–82
   (Administrative Assistant to the General Secretary)
Erna Redlich, Canada (Assistant Secretary for Relief)   1980–83
Samson S. K. Mathangani, Kenya (Associate Youth Director)   1982–88
Regina Claas, Germany (Associate Youth Director)   1990–94
Ruby J. Burke, Executive Assistant (on staff 1978–87)   1990–

Department Director
June Totten, United States (Women)   1982–86
Emmett Dunn, Liberia (Youth)   1994–
Elizabeth Hayward MacClaren, United States (Women)   1987–95
W.C. (Doc) Isbell, United States (Men)   1988–94
Willene Pierce, United States (Women)   1995–97
Doyle Pennington, United States (Men)   1994–96, 2003–
Patsy Davis, United States (Women)   1998–
Jerry Gash, United States (acting, Men)   1996–98

ABBREVIATIONS AS USED IN BOOK

AABF	All Africa Baptist Fellowship
ABC	American Baptist Convention
	(Later American Baptist Churches, USA)
ABF	Asian Baptist Federation
ABFMS	American Baptist Foreign Mission Society's
ABHMS	American Baptist Home Mission Society
ABMU	American Baptist Missionary Union
ACC	Anglican Consultative Council
AUCECB	All–Union Council of Evangelical Christians–Baptists
BGC	Baptist General Conference
BICTE	Baptist International Conference on Theological Education
BMS	Baptist Missionary Society
BR–E	Baptist Response–Europe
BU	Baptist Union
BWA	Baptist World Alliance
BWAid	Baptist World Aid
CARE	Cooperative for American Remittances to Europe
CBF	Cooperative Baptist Fellowship
CCORR	Church Committee on Overseas Relief and Reconstruction
CRALOG	Council of Relief Agencies Licensed for Operations in Germany
CWC	Christian World Communions
DP	Displaced person
EA	Evangelical Alliance
EBF	European Baptist Federation
FMB	Foreign Mission Board
IBTS	International Baptist Theological Seminary
IMS	International Mission Secretaries
IMSC	International Mission Secretaries Conference
NABC	North American Baptist Conference
NABF	North American Baptist Fellowship
NBC	Northern Baptist Convention
NGO	Nongovernmental organization
PRM	Passive Resistance Movement
SBC	Southern Baptist Convention
TAG	Theological Assistance Group
UBLA	Union of Baptists in Latin America
U.K.	United Kingdom
U.N.	United Nations
UNRRA	United Nations Relief and Rehabilitation Administration
U.S.	United States
WCC	World Council of Churches

BIBLIOGRAPHY

The literary output of the Baptist World Alliance (BWA) and its associated agencies is enormous Both the archival holdings and published works of the BWA are a treasure trove of source materials for students of Baptist history in the twentieth century. Space limitations preclude an exhaustive listing, but this bibliography will provide guidance for those interested in further pursuit of topics addressed in the book.

I. Archival and Unpublished Materials

The archives of the BWA are housed in the American Baptist Archive Center in Valley Forge, Pennsylvania, and contain materials into the 1980s. Among these are the papers of the General Secretaries; administrative and office files; minutes and correspondence of the Executive Committee, Administrative Committee, and General Council; the study commission papers; minutes and files of the Relief Committee and Baptist World Aid; and the papers of Carl W. Tiller. The guide is Susan M. Eltscher, *Records of the Baptist World Alliance*, RG #503 (Rochester, NY: American Baptist Historical Society, 1982). The more recent papers are held in the BWA office in Falls Church, Virginia.

The Angus Library, Regent's Park College, Oxford, U.K., holds some correspondence files from the late 1930s and on refugee and relief work, 1946–55; scrapbooks; a ledger with minutes of the preparatory meetings for the 1905 World Congress and of the BWA Executive Committee, 1908–11; papers of individuals involved in BWA life, including J. H. Rushbrooke, M. E. Aubrey, Ernest A. Payne, and David S. Russell, as well as many items relating to Europe and the European Baptist Federation.

The Treasure Room in the Library of the International Baptist Theological Seminary in Prague, Czech Republic, holds the archives of the European Baptist Federation (EBF); a file of BWA documents donated by Walter O. Lewis; the European Baptist Women's Union archive; and extensive materials on the German Baptists. Sue Mills of the Angus Library prepared a guide to the archival contents in 2003, and it is available at the library and at Regent's Park College, Oxford.

The American Baptist–Samuel Colgate Historical Library in Rochester, New York, has materials relating to the Baptist Congresses and early Northern Baptist support for the BWA, as well as some papers from the tenure of General Secretary Walter O. Lewis and Presidents C. Oscar Johnson, V. Carney Hargroves, and David Y. K. Wong. It also holds microfilm copies of the minutes of the various BWA committees from the earliest days and most of the study commission papers.

The Southern Baptist Historical Library and Archives in Nashville, Tennessee, has a large collection of materials pertaining to the BWA, including programs, study commission papers, brochures, and clippings. This collection also includes a microfilm copy of the EBF documents kept in Prague. There is BWA material in the papers of Herschel Hobbs, John David Hughey, Adolf J. Klaupiks, and Fred B. Rhodes, and in the files and minutes of the Southern Baptist Convention Executive Committee.

The James P. Boyce Centennial Library at Southern Baptist Theological Seminary, Louisville, Kentucky, holds the papers of E. Y. Mullins and A. T. Robertson, miscellaneous minutes and literature of the BWA, and a number of dissertations that touch upon BWA history and personalities. The A. Webb Roberts Library at Southwestern Baptist Theological Seminary, Fort Worth, Texas, has the papers of George W. Truett and a variety of recorded speeches and interviews by BWA personalities.

The Baylor University (Waco, Texas) Oral History Program has interviews with Robert S. Denny, Gerhard Class, G. Noel Vose, and Knud Wümpelmann. The Virginia Baptist Historical Society, Richmond, has papers of R. H. Pitt. The Oncken Archive at the German Baptist Seminary in Elstal bei Berlin holds the German documents relating to the 1934 Congress.

The Canadian Baptist Archives at McMaster Divinity College, Hamilton, Ontario, has a modest collection of BWA documents, including study commission papers, papers relating to the 1980 World Congress in Toronto, and correspondence from Archie Goldie. The archives at Acadia Divinity School in Wolfville, Nova Scotia, contain a small amount of published BWA materials.

II. Publications of the Baptist World Alliance and Its Bodies
A. Serials
Baptist World. 1954–. (Organ of the BWA.)
Baptist World Alliance Directory. 1926, 1927, 1928, 1935.
Baptist World Congress. Official Report. 1905–(Published by the BWA after each World Congress.) Perhaps the best starting point for anyone undertaking research on the Alliance.
BWA News, 1989–. (Now distributed online.)
Executive Committee. Minutes, 1934–1975. (Printed copies in Southern Baptist Theological Seminary and BWA Headquarters Office libraries. Those prior to 1934 are contained in the Minute Book [BWA IX], BWA Archives, held at the American Baptist Archives Center, with a microfilm copy at the Samuel Colgate–American Baptist Historical Library.)
General Council. Agenda Book. 1981–. (Complete set at the BWA Office Library.)
Official Report of the Baptist Youth World Conference, 1937–. (Complete set at the BWA Office Library.)
Together for the Whole World, 1962–. (Organ of the Women's Department; now distributed online.) From 1950–57, the Women's Department published *Quarterly Newsletter.*
Yearbook and Minutes of the General Council, 1975–. (Complete set at the BWA Office Library.)

B. Books and Other Works Published by and for the Baptist World Alliance
Allen, Catherine B. *Jesus Made Us Friends: The Story of the Women's Department of the Baptist World Alliance.* Falls Church, VA: BWA Women's Department, 2005.
Baptist World Alliance: First European Baptist Congress, held in Berlin, 1908 (August 29ᵗʰ to September 3ʳᵈ). London: Baptist Union Publication Department, 1908.
Baptist World Alliance. *BWA–SBC Concerns: Documents, Media Reports, Correspondence.* Falls Church, VA: BWA, 2004.
———. *Conversations Around the World: The Report of the International Conversations between the Anglican Communion and the Baptist World Alliance.* Falls Church, VA: BWA, 2005.
———. Division of Evangelism and Education. *Addresses and Papers: Baptist International Conference on Theological Education, Ridgecrest Baptist Conference Center, North Carolina, January 14–17, 1982.* Washington, D.C.: BWA, 1982.
———. Division of Study and Research. *Reports of Conversations between the Baptist World Alliance and the Following: World Alliance of Reformed Churches–1973; Lutheran World Federation–1990; Vatican Secretariat for Promoting Christian Unity–1988; Mennonite World Conference–1992.* McLean, VA: BWA, [c. 1993].
———. *From Darkened Minds into the Light of Truth.* McLean, VA: BWA, 1986.
———. *New People for a New World through Jesus Christ: Year of Commitment to Evangelism Around the World; Guidelines.* Washington, D.C.: BWA, 1978.
———. *Seoul Covenant, Derbyshire Declaration, Cyprus Guidelines.* McLean, VA: BWA, 1994.
———. Special Commission on Baptists Against Racism. *Report and Papers Presented at Harare, Zimbabwe, August 1993.* McLean, VA: BWA, 1993.
———. Women's Committee. *"Jesus Shall Reign": Highlights and Hopes of the Women United.* BWA. N.p.: North American Baptist Women's Union (1951).
Bentley, Eljee. *Manual for Developing a Baptist Archive.* McLean, VA: BWA Commission on Baptist Heritage, 1990.
Boney, William J. and Glenn A. Igleheart, eds. *Baptists and Ecumenism.* Valley Forge, PA: Judson Press, 1980.

Borchert, Gerald, Andrew D. MacRae, and Lewis A. Drummond. *From Darkened Minds into the Light of Truth*. McLean, VA: BWA Division of Education and Evangelism, 1986.

Brackney, William H., with Ruby J. Burke, eds. *Faith, Life, and Witness: The Papers of the Study and Research Divisions of the Baptist World Alliance*. Birmingham, AL: Samford University Press, 1990.

———, and L. A. (Tony) Cupit, eds. *Baptist Faith and Witness: The Papers of the Study and Research Division of the Baptist World Alliance 1990–1995*. Birmingham, AL: Samford University Press, 1995.

Brooks, Charles A. and J. H. Rushbrooke. *Baptist Work in Europe: Report of the Commissioners of the Baptist World Alliance, presented at the Conference in London, July 19, 1920*. London: Baptist Union Publication Department, 1920.

Carro, Daniel and Richard F. Wilson, eds. *Contemporary Gospel Accents: Doing Theology in Africa, Asia, Southeast Asia, and Latin America*. Macon: Mercer University Press, 1997.

Cupit, L. A. (Tony). *Biblical Models for Evangelism: 1st Century Strategies for the 21st Century Church*. McLean, VA: BWA Division of Evangelism and Education, 1997.

———. *Five till Midnight: Church Planting for A.D. 2000 and Beyond*. Atlanta: Home Mission Board, SBC, 1994.

———. *Peace I Leave with You: Bible Studies for Churches on the Subject of Peace*. Falls Church, VA: BWA, 2001.

———. *Stars Lighting up the Sky: Stories of Contemporary Heroes*. Falls Church, VA: BWA, 2003.

———, ed. *Baptist Faith and Witness, Book 2: The Papers of the Study and Research Division of the Baptist World Alliance 1995–2000*. McLean, VA: BWA, 1999.

———, ed. *Baptist Faith and Witness, Book 3: The Papers of the Study and Research Division of the Baptist World Alliance 2000–2005*. Falls Church, VA: BWA, 2005.

———, ed. *Baptist World Alliance Covenants and Declarations, 1990–2000*. McLean, VA: BWA, 1999.

———, ed. *Baptists in Worship*. Berlin, Germany, October 1998. McLean, VA: BWA, 1998.

———, ed. *Evangelism and the Peace Witness of the Church: Baptist World Alliance and Mennonite World Conference*, Philadelphia, Pennsylvania, U.S.A., January 10–12, 2002. Falls Church, VA: BWA, 1993.

———, ed. *Hallowed be Your Name: A Collection of Prayers from around the World*. McLean, VA: BWA, 1998.

Drummond, Lewis A. *The People of God in Ministry*. Washington, D.C.: BWA Commission on the Ministry of the Laity, 1985.

Edgemon, Roy T. and Arthur H. Cristoe. *A Biblical Model for Training Leaders*. Nashville: Convention Press, 1985.

Garrett, James Leo, Jr., ed. *Baptist Relations with Other Christians*. Valley Forge, PA: Judson Press, 1974.

———, ed. *We Baptists*. Franklin, TN: Providence House, for the BWA Study and Research Division, 1999.

Isbell, W. J., Jr. *Baptist Men's Manual*. McLean, VA: BWA Men's Department (1989).

Levy, Ferne. *God's Command– Our Response: A History of the Women's Department of the Baptist World Alliance*. McLean, VA: BWA, 1985.

Lorenzen, Thorwald. *Freedom of Religion as a Human Right*. McLean, VA: BWA Commission Human Rights 1999.

———. *The Rights of the Child*. McLean, VA: BWA Commission on Human Rights, 1999.

Lotz, Denton. *Spring Has Returned . . . Listening to the Church in China*. McLean, VA: BWA, 1986.

———, ed. *Baptists against Racism: Proceedings of the International Summit on Baptists against Racism and Ethnic Conflict*. Falls Church, VA: BWA, 1999.

———, ed. *Proceedings of the Summit on Baptist Mission in the 21st Century*. Falls Church, VA: BWA, 2003.

MacRae, Andrew D. *Building a Bible Teaching Ministry*. Washington, D.C.: BWA Division of Evangelism and Education, [c. 1985].

Manley, Ken. *The Baptist World Alliance and Inter–Church Relationships*, Falls Church, VA: BWA Commission on Baptist Heritage and Identity, 2003.

May, Lynn E., Jr., ed. *International Directory of Baptist Archives/Libraries*. McLean, VA: BWA Commission on Baptist Heritage, 1990.

Medina, Amparo. *Free from Violence in the Family.* Falls Church, VA: BWA Women's Department, 2003.

Monro, Harry, ed. *Witnesses Throughout the World: Seven Study Guides on Local and World Evangelism Based on the Seoul Covenant of the Baptist World Alliance.* Melbourne: Baptist Union of Australia, 1992.

Mullins, Edgar Young and J. H. Rushbrooke. *The Baptist World Alliance: Its Significance and Its Service.* London: Kingsgate Press, 1928.

Payne, Ernest A. *Baptists Speak to the World: A Description and Interpretation of the Sixth Baptist World Congress, Atlanta, 1939.* London: Carey Press, 1939.

———. *The Doctrine of Baptism: An Address, a Report, a Questionnaire, a Bibliography.* London and Washington, D.C.: BWA, 1951.

Prestridge, Fannie Clardy [Mrs. John N. Prestridge]. *The Baptist World Alliance: Its Beginning.* Nashville: Broadman Press, 1939.

Pusey, Yona. *European Baptist Women's Union: Our Story, 1948–1998.* Oakham, U.K.: European Baptist Women's Union, 1998.

Rushbrooke, James Henry. *The World Responsibility of Baptists.* London: Kingsgate Press, 1943; Philadelphia: Judson Press, 1944.

Sayers, Hilde. *The Transition from the Old to the New Europe.* Oakham, U.K.: European Baptist Women's Union, 1998.

Wood, James E., Jr. *Baptists and Human Rights.* McLean, VA: BWA Commission on Human Rights, 1997.

World Alliance of Reformed Churches. *Baptists and Reformed in Dialogue.* Geneva: WARC, 1983.

III. Works That Relate to the Baptist World Alliance
A. Books and Booklets

Baptists of the World 1950–1970: Recollections and Reflections by Josef Nordenhaug, J. D. Grey, Theodore F. Adams, Ernest F. Payne, V. Carney Hargroves, John W. Williams, Mrs. Edgar Bates, Robert S. Denny, Hershel H. Hobbs. Fort Worth: Southern Baptists' Radio and Television Commission, 1970.

Byrt, George W. *John Clifford: A Fighting Free Churchman.* London: Kingsgate Press, 1947.

Carlton, John W. *The World in His Heart: The Life and Legacy of Theodore F. Adams.* Nashville: Broadman Press, 1985.

Estep, William R., Jr. *Baptists and Christian Unity.* Nashville: Broadman Press, 1966.

Green, Bernard. *Crossing the Boundaries: A History of the European Baptist Federation.* Didcot, U.K.: Baptist Historical Society, 1999.

———. *Tomorrow's Man: A Biography of James Henry Rushbrooke.* Didcot, U.K.: Baptist Historical Society, 1997.

James, Powhatan W. *George W. Truett: A Biography.* New York: Macmillan, 1945 (rev. ed.).

Lord, Fred Townley. *Baptist World Fellowship: A Short History of the Baptist World Alliance.* Nashville: Broadman Press; London: Carey Kingsgate Press, 1955.

May, Lynn E., Jr. *Bibliography of Selected Histories of BWA Member Bodies in Countries other than U.S.A.* Nashville: Historical Commission, SBC, 1992.

[McCall, Duke K. and A. Ronald Tonks]. *Duke McCall: An Oral History.* Brentwood, TN: Baptist History and Heritage Society, 2001.

Payne, Earnest A. *James Henry Rushbrooke: 1870–1947.* A Baptist Greatheart. London: Carey Kingsgate Press, 1954.

Roberts–Thomson, Edward. *With Hands Outstretched: Baptists and the Ecumenical Movement.* London: Marshall, Morgan and Scott, 1962.

Rushbrooke, James Henry. *The Baptist Movement in the Continent of Europe.* 2nd ed., revised and rewritten. London: Kingsgate Press, 1923.

———. *Some Chapters in European Baptist History.* London: Carey Kingsgate Press, 1929.

Shepherd, Peter. *The Making of a Modern Denomination: John Howard Shakespeare and the English Baptists.* Carlisle, U.K.: Paternoster, 2001.

Shurden, Walter B., ed. *The Life of Baptists in the Life of the World: Eighty Years of the Baptist World Alliance.* Nashville: Broadman Press, 1985.

Tiller, Carl W. *The Twentieth Century Baptist: Chronicles of Baptists in the First Seventy–five Years of the Baptist World Alliance.* Valley Forge, PA: Judson Press, 1980.
Wardin, Albert W. *Baptists around the World.* Nashville: Broadman Press, 1995.
West, W. Morris S. *To Be a Pilgrim: A Memoir of Ernest A. Payne.* Guilford, U.K.: Lutterworth Press, 1983.

B. Articles, Book Chapters, and Dissertations

The periodicals of the several historical societies serving the churches in the BWA fellowship offer a rich mine of materials for the researcher. These are among the more important articles.

"Baptist World Alliance," *Encyclopedia of Southern Baptists,* by Louis DeVotie Newton, 1:127–134 (1958); by C. E. Bryant, 3:1601–1606 (1971); by C. E. Bryant, 4:2109–2115 (1982).
Bentley, Eljee. "Baptist Heritage and Identity Commission of the Baptist World Alliance," *American Baptist Quarterly* 32 (September 2003), 363–369.
Borchert, Gerald. "The Nature and Mission of the Church: A Baptist Perspective," *Perspectives in Religious Studies* 20 (Spring 1993), 19–41.
Briggs, John H. Y. "British Baptists and the Beginnings of the Baptist World Alliance," *Baptist Quarterly* 41 (January 2005), 2–24.
Clements, Keith W. "Baptists and the Outbreak of the First World War," *Baptist Quarterly* 26 (April 1975), 74–92.
———. "Towards the Common Expression of the Apostolic Faith Today: Baptist Reflections on This Faith and Order Project," *Baptist Quarterly* 33 (April 1989), 63–71.
Geldbach, Erich. "Die Dialoge des Baptistischen Weltbundes mit anderen Weltweiten Christlichen Gemeinschaften," *Zeitschrift für Theologie und Gemeinde* 9 (2004), 92–111.
———. "Gerechtigkeit in Berlin 1934? Ethische Fragen auf dem Fünften Kongress des Baptistischen Weltbundes," in Peter Dabrock, et. al., eds., *Kriterien der Gerechtigkeit. Begründungen – Anwendungen – Vermittlungen: Festschrift für Christofer Frey* (Gütersloh: Gütersloher Verlagshaus, 2003), 87–105.
———. "Katholiken und Baptisten im Gespräch," in Konrad Reiser and Dorothea Sattler, eds., *Oekumene vor neuen Zeiten: Festschrift für Theodor Schneider* (Freiburg: Herder Verlag, 2000), 411–424.
———. "The Petrine Ministry and the Unity of the Church: A Baptist Perspective," in James F. Puglisi, ed., *Petrine Ministry and the Unity of the Church: "Toward a Patient and Fraternal Dialogue"* (Collegeville, MN: The Liturgical Press, 1999), 153–169.
Hinson, E. Glenn. "The Baptist World Alliance: Its Identity and Ecumenical Involvement," *Ecumenical Review* 46 (October 1994), 406–412.
Lotz, Denton. "The Baptist Witness in Eastern Europe," *Baptist Quarterly* 38 (April 1979), 68–75.
Pierard, Richard V. "Baptist World Alliance Relief Efforts in Post–Second World War Europe," *Baptist History and Heritage* 36 (Winter/Spring 2001), 6–26.
Popov, Vladimir. "Vasilii Gurevich Pavlov and the Early Years of the Baptist World Alliance," *Baptist Quarterly* 36 (January 1995), 4–20.
Rushbrooke, J. H. [James Henry]. "The Baptist World Alliance: Origin, Constitution, Achievements, Objects," *The Chronicle: A Baptist Historical Quarterly* 1 (April 1938), 9–22.
Sherouse, Craig Alan. "The Social Teachings of the Baptist World Alliance 1905–1980," Ph.D. dissertation, Southern Baptist Theological Seminary, 1982.
Smith, Karen E. "British Women and the Baptist World Alliance: Honoured Partners and Fellow Workers?" *Baptist Quarterly* 41 (January 2005), 25–46.
Smith, Robin W. "Louie D. Newton and the Baptist World Alliance," *Baptist History and Heritage* 23 (October 1988), 14–27.
Thompson, David M. "Baptists and the World Fellowship of the Church," *Baptist Quarterly* 33 (Supplement in Honour of D. S. Russell, 1989), 54–63.
Woodfin, Carol. "Southern Baptist Relief Work in Germany, 1945–1950" *Baptist History and Heritage* 28 (April 1993), 34–47.

CONTRIBUTORS

Elna Jean "Eljee" Young Bentley, Ph.D. history, Emory University, taught at The University of Alabama. She was an editor and the founding archivist for the Woman's Missionary Union and author of numerous essays in Baptist history. Her church in Birmingham, Alabama, is affiliated with the Cooperative Baptist Fellowship, Alliance of Baptists, and Southern Baptist Convention.

Gerald L. Borchert, ordained Canadian Baptist minister, retired Coleman Professor of New Testament, Southern Baptist Theological Seminary, and Director of Doctoral Studies at Northern Baptist Theological Seminary. He holds membership in the American Baptist Churches U.S.A. and Southern Baptist Convention/Cooperative Baptist Fellowship. He is the author of sixteen books.

Faith Bowers, M.Phil. history, University of London, is subeditor of the *Baptist Quarterly*; author of numerous works on Baptist history and disability issues, including *A Bold Experiment: The Story of Bloomsbury Central Baptist Church, 1848–1999*; and a full–time layworker for Baptist bodies. She served on the Councils of the Baptist Union of Great Britain and the Baptist World Alliance.

John H. Y. Briggs edits the *Baptist Quarterly*. He is director of the Baptist History and Heritage Centre and senior research fellow in church history, Regent's Park College, Oxford. He was formerly Pro–Vice–Chancellor of the University of Birmingham, England. Author of *The English Baptists of the 19th Century*, he is a member of Highgate Baptist Church in Birmingham, England.

James Leo Garrett, Jr., is distinguished professor of theology, emeritus, Southwestern Baptist Theological Seminary, Fort Worth, Texas. He has taught at Southern Baptist Seminary, Baylor University, and Hong Kong Baptist Seminary. A specialist in systematic and historical theology, he has worked with the BWA since 1965. He belongs to Meadowridge Community Baptist Church in Fort Worth, Texas.

Erich Geldbach did his D.Theol. and Habilitation at the University of Marburg and served as a senior fellow at the Ecumenical Study and Research Center in Bensheim, Germany. From 1996 until his retirement in 2004, he was professor of ecumenical studies in the Theological Faculty of the Ruhr–University, Bochum, Germany. Author of many books, he is a theologian in the German Baptist Union.

Denton Lotz has been the General Secretary of the Baptist World Alliance since 1988. He joined the staff in 1980 as Director of Evangelism and Education and of the Youth Department. Prior to that he was professor of missions at the Baptist Seminary in Rüschlikon and a missionary to Eastern Europe under American Baptist of International Ministries. He belongs to Columbia Baptist Church in Falls Church, Virginia.

Ken R. Manley, formerly principal of Whitley College, University of Melbourne, is now distinguished professor of church history at the school. He is a member of Kew Baptist Church in Melbourne (Baptist Union of Australia) and served as a Vice President of the Baptist World Alliance from 2000 to 2005. He is author of *From Woolloomooloo to 'Eternity': A History of Baptists in Australia*.

W. Morgan Patterson was professor of church history at New Orleans Baptist Seminary and Southern Baptist Seminary. He then became dean of academic affairs at Golden Gate Baptist Seminary and from 1984 to 1991 was president of Georgetown College. He also served on various Baptist World Alliance commissions. He belongs to Tiburon Baptist Church (Southern Baptist Convention) Tiburon, California.

Richard V. Pierard, professor of history emeritus, Indiana State University, is now Stephen Phillips Professor of History, Gordon College. He was secretary–treasurer of the Conference on Faith and History and served on the American Baptist Historical Society's Board of Managers. He belongs to North Shore Community Baptist Church (BGC/ABC) in Beverly, Massachusetts.

Ian M. Randall is deputy principal and lecturer in church history and spirituality, Spurgeon's College in London, and a senior research fellow, International Baptist Theological Seminary in Prague. He is a minister in the Baptist Union of Great Britain and author of numerous works in Baptist and evangelical history, the most recent of which is *English Baptists of the 20th Century*.

Horace O. Russell, born in Jamaica, was president of the United Theological Seminary of the West Indies in Kingston. He later served as dean of chapel and professor of historical theology at Eastern Baptist Theological Seminary. A respected historian of West Indian Christianity, he is senior pastor of Saints Memorial Church (ABC, National Baptist Convention, USA, Inc.; Progressive National Baptist Convention, Inc.), Bryn Mawr, Pennsylvania

Albert W. Wardin, Jr., is professor of history emeritus, Belmont University. He has also taught at Western Conservative Baptist Seminary. He is author of *Evangelical Sectarianism in the Russian Empire and the Soviet Union* and editor of *Baptists Around the World*. A former president of the Southern Baptist Historical Society, he is a member of First Baptist Church in Nashville, Tennessee.

Robert S. Wilson is associate dean and professor of church history at Acadia Divinity College. He chairs the Acadia Center for Baptist and Anabaptist Studies administrative committee and the *Atlantic Baptist Heritage Series* publication committee. He is a member of Kentville (Nova Scotia) Baptist Church, which is affiliated with the Convention of Atlantic Baptist Churches and Canadian Baptist Ministries.

INDEX

A

AABF, *See All-Africa Baptist Fellowship.*
ABC, *See American Baptist Convention.*
ABF, *See Asian Baptist Federation.*
ABFMS, *See American Baptist Foreign Mission Society.*
ABHMS, *See American Baptist Home Mission Society.*
ABMU, *See American Baptist Missionary Union.*
Abraham, C. E., 121
ACC, *See Anglican Consultative Council.*
Adams, Charles G., 262
Adams, Earl F., 102
Adams, Frank, 276
Adams, Theodore F. 102, 104, 114, 121, 122, 123, 128, 129, 134, 155, 160, 170, 321, 322
Afghanistan, 223, 236, 237
Africa, 3, 4, 5, 12, 13, 22, 29, 56, 59, 67, 75, 123, 129, 139, 140, 143, 144, 145, 146, 156, 164, 170, 178, 179, 181, 186, 189, 194, 208, 212, 213, 214, 218, 223, 229, 235, 255, 264, 265, 266, 267, 268, 270, 275, 276, 277, 279, 280, 283, 284, 285, 286, 287, 288, 291, 292, 301, 302, 303, 305, 312, 313, 314
Africa Response Appeal, 229
African-American, 4, 8, 10, 56, 59, 66, 68, 90, 114, 180, 266, 271, 313
African Baptist Women's Union, 139
AIDS/HIV, 267, 268, 275, 284, 285, 292, 304
Aier, Wati, 256
Akande, Samuel T. Ola, 208, 214, 242, 327
Albania, 188, 236, 240, 314
Albaugh, Dana M., 101
Aldwinckle, Russell F., 142
All Africa Baptist Fellowship (AABF), 213, 214, 242, 276, 302
Allen, Catherine Bryant, 242
Allen, Clifton J., 146
All-Russian Union of Evangelical Christians, 62
All-Union Council of Evangelical Christians–Baptists (AUCECB), 118, 131, 161, 187, 224, 225, 236, 237
Alliance of Reformed Churches, 7 *See also World Alliance of Reformed Churches.*
American Baptist Churches, *See American Baptist Convention.*
American Baptist Congress, 10
American Baptist Convention (ABC) (later American Baptist Churches, USA), xvi, 130, 158, 160, 161, 175, 176, 216, 254, 258, 337
American Baptist Education Society, 7
American Baptist Foreign Mission Society (ABFMS), 7, 48, 51, 57, 93, 94, 104 *See also Triennial Convention.*
American Baptist Historical Society, xiii, 7, 338
American Baptist Home Mission Society (ABHMS), 7, 48, 148
American Baptist Missionary Union (ABMU), 12, 16 *See also Triennial Convention.*
American Baptist missions, 22
American Baptist Publication Society, 7, 11
American Council of Relief Agencies Licensed for Operations in Germany (CRALOG), 105
Andover Newton Theological School, 68, 75
Angelov, Theo, 277, 279, 325
Anglican, 6, 28, 53, 54, 76, 288, 313
Anglican Consultative Council (ACC), 288, 311
Angola,135, 144, 160, 170, 266, 282, 284
anti-Christian, 87
anti-ecumenical, 55
anti-God, 81
anti-Jewish, 78
anti-Semitism, 77, 78, 86, 109
Ao, Longri, 130
Arabs, 86
Argentina, 74, 129, 139, 145, 161, 188, 206, 207, 215, 225, 248, 261, 271, 276, 301
Armenia, 221, 279
Ashworth, R. A., 79
Asia, 3, 23, 59, 66, 75, 101, 123, 129, 137, 139, 145, 169, 170, 171, 178, 179, 182, 186, 189, 194, 195, 203, 208, 209, 212, 213, 214, 229, 235, 242, 250, 264, 267, 268, 270, 275, 276, 278, 283, 285, 287, 288, 292, 293, 296, 297, 301, 304, 305
Asian Baptist Federation (ABF), *See also Asian Baptist Fellowship,* 182, 189, 242, 254, 264, 276, 302, 303

Asian Baptist Fellowship, 145, 170, 182, 264
Asian Baptist Youth Conference, 139, 145
Asian Baptists, 66
Asian Youth Leadership Conference, 209
Associated Council of the Churches of the British and German Empires for Promoting Friendly Relations, 42
Atlanta Covenant, 279, 313
Aubrey, M. E., 91, 114
AUCECB, *See All-Union Council of Evangelical Christians–Baptists.*
Australia, 5, 6, 12, 13, 16, 21, 22, 27, 50, 52, 75, 78, 106, 118, 137, 141, 145, 148, 157, 158, 178, 182, 184, 197, 216, 217, 218, 222, 223, 224, 241, 253, 254, 255, 261, 262, 279, 280, 281, 292, 295, 296, 297, 301
Austria, 47, 52, 119, 145, 146
Austro-Hungarian, 49
Ayorinde, J. T., 147, 184, 323
Ayorinde, Mobola (Mrs. J. T.), 147
Azerbaijan, 279, 281
Azevedo, Irland Pereira de, 228

B

Ba, Thra San, 66
Backus, 4
Bahamas, 181, 215, 240, 255, 267, 276, 288, 302
Bakkevoll, Asbjorn, 209
Baleim Valley, 283
Balogh, L., 33
Bamijoko, Atinuke, 218, 261, 324
Bangladesh, 170, 181, 221, 230
Bangladesh Baptist Fellowship, 221
baptism, xv, 1, 11, 14, 34, 36, 59, 80, 92, 144, 158, 161, 180, 189, 262, 269, 289, 305, 308, 310
The Baptist Annual Register, 1, 2
Baptist Argus, 15, 17
Baptist Church House, 23, 50, 62, 100, 105
Baptist Commissioner for Europe, 52
Baptist Congress for the Discussion of Current Questions, 10
Baptist Convention of Ontario and Quebec, 65
Baptist Convention of Zambia, 286
Baptist Directory, 63
Baptist Doctrine and Interchurch Cooperation, 228, 290
Baptist General Conference of America (BGC), 103
Baptist Heritage Study Commission, xv, xvi, xvii, 7, 217, 290, 305
Baptist Identity and National Culture, 279, 287
Baptist Immanuelskyrkan, 56
Baptist International Conference on Establishing Churches, 263
Baptist International Conference on Theological Education (BICTE), 221, 264, 290, 291
The Baptist Magazine, 13
Baptist Mission of Zambia, 286
Baptist Missionary Society (BMS), 2, 3, 4, 11, 16, 17, 21, 30 77, 101, 103, 105, 119, 241, 246, 247
Baptist Peace Fellowship of North America, 224
Baptist persecution, 22
Baptist Preachers' School, 69
Baptist Quarterly, 63
Baptist Relief Train, 53
Baptist Response–Europe (BR–E), 240
Baptist South African and Colonial Missionary Society, 12
Baptist Times, 25, 64, 115
Baptist Union (BU), 5, 7, 12, 13, 19, 20, 21, 25, 32, 41, 50, 54, 55, 58, 62, 63, 76, 77, 79, 115, 116, 117, 119, 287, 312
Baptist Union, Latin America, *See Union of Baptists in Latin America.*
Baptist Union Council, 12, 18, 21
Baptist Union of Australia, 254
Baptist Union of Ceylon (Sri Lanka), 130
Baptist Union of Czechoslovakia, 238
Baptist Union of Denmark, 213
Baptist Union of Great Britain, 58, 103, 114, 130, 137, 170, 206, 209, 220, 225, 241
Baptist Union of Hungary, 155
Baptist Union of India, 131

Index   341

Baptist Union, Latin America, *See Union of Baptists in Latin America.*
Baptist Union of New Zealand, 137
Baptist Union of Norway, 116
Baptist Union of Scotland, 219
Baptist Union of South America 214
Baptist Union of Sweden, 123, 140, 181, 218
Baptist Union of Victoria, 241
Baptist Union of Wales, 142
Baptist Union of West Germany, 189, 216
Baptist unions, 61
Baptist unity, 7, 9, 35, 43, 51, 60
Baptist Women's Day of Prayer, 118
Baptist Women's League, 40, 57, 58
Baptist Women's Training College, 57
Baptist Women's Union of Latin America, 145
Baptist World, 15, 17, 119, 123, 138, 146, 163
Baptist World Aid (BWAid), 113, 162, 196, 212, 214, 228, 229, 230, 231, 240, 241, 242, 266, 267, 278, 284, 285, 303
Baptist World Alliance Sunday, 64
Baptist World Congresses, 8, 20, 25, 48, 53, 97, 105, 216, 224, 293
    First Congress 1905, 8, 24, 37
    Second Congress 1911, 35
    Third World Congress 1923, 56
    Fourth World Congress 1928, 64
    Fifth World Congress 1934, 80
    Sixth World Congress 1939, 90
    Seventh World Congress 1947, 106
    Eighth World Congress 1950, 113
    Ninth World Congress 1955, 119
    Tenth World Congress 1960, 128
    Eleventh World Congress 1965, 141
    Twelfth World Congress, 1970, 169
    Thirteenth World Congress, 1975, 180
    Fourteenth World Congress 1980, 194
    Fifteenth World Congress 1985, 217
    Sixteenth World Congress 1990, 243, 261
    Seventeenth World Congress 1995, 271, 275
    Eighteenth World Congress 2000, 296
Baptist World Council, 13
Baptist World Exhibition, 56
Baptist Young People's Union of America, 58, 150
Baptist youth ministries, 58
Baptist Youth World Conference in Prague, 211
Baptist International Youth Conference, 74
Baptist Zenana Mission, 40
Baptists of New York, 9
Barbour, Clarence A., 67, 322
Barbour, J. Pius, 106
Bates College, 61, 68
Bates, Marion (Mrs. J. Edgar), 106, 323
Bau, T. C., 66, 322
Beasley-Murray, George R., 143
Beaumont, Rodney, 255
Belgium, 43, 48, 52, 280
Bell, Edwin A., 104, 105
Bell, Roy D., 262, 324
Benander, C. E., 54, 322
Bengal Baptist Peace and Unification Celebration in Calcutta, 286
Bengal Baptist Union, 313
Benin, 285
Bender, Carl, 43
Bentall, Shirley, 223, 224, 324
Bentley, Elna Jean, xvi, xvii, 300, 337
Berlin, 5, 32, 33, 34, 41, 48, 74, 76, 77, 78, 79, 80, 81, 82, 88, 90, 91, 92, 93, 107, 108, 116, 173, 214, 220, 224, 239, 255, 263, 279, 287, 290, 305
Bethell, Lauren, 280

BGC, *See Baptist General Conference.*
Bichkov, Alexei, 217, 224, 225, 226, 237
BICTE, *See Baptist International Conference on Theological Education.*
Billy Graham Evangelistic Association, 180
Black Baptist, 8, 10, 141, 146
Blacks, 4, 22, 59, 67
BMS, *See Baptist Missionary Society.*
Boer War, 12
Bolivia, 181, 283, 284
Boltniev, George, 258, 292
Bonell, Harold C., 158
Bonhoeffer, Dietrich, 82
Bonner, Carey, 59
Bosnia, 285, 314
Brackney, William H., 217
Brazilian Baptists, 52, 74, 128, 135, 144, 302
BR–E, *See Baptist Response–Europe.*
Britain, *See United Kingdom.*
British Baptist Union, *See Baptist Union of Great Britain.*
British Baptist Union Young People's Department, 58
British Baptist Women's League, 57
British Baptists, 4, 10, 11, 12, 23, 25, 43, 52, 54, 55, 63, 95, 117
British Empire, 5, 47, 51
British League of Nations, 50
British Sunday School Union, 115
Brooks, Charles, 48, 49, 50
Brooks-Randolph, Angie, 170
Brown, A. Douglas, 60
Brown, Charles, 65
Brown, Eva (Mrs. Ernest), 94
Bryant, Cyril E., 123, 174, 177, 212, 326, 327
BU *See Baptist Union.*
Bucharest, 49, 89
Buckingham, Michael J., 230
Buddhism, 30
Buenos Aires, General Council in, 270
Bulgaria, 40, 51, 52, 120, 188, 239, 277, 279
Bullard, George, 255
Bullock, C. S., 4
Burke, Ruby J., xvi, 212, 217, 242, 327
Burkina Faso, 285
Burma, *See Myanmar*
Burma Baptist Convention, 130
Burroughs, Nannie Helen, 21, 40, 117, 147
Burundi, 170, 183, 266, 280
The BWA News, 240, 289
BWAid *See Baptist World Aid.*
BWA Committee on Evangelism, 108, 109
BWA General Secretaries, 325
BWA Human Rights Award, 200, 265, 281
BWA International Summit Against Racism and Ethnic Conflict, 252, 279
BWA News Service, 123
BWA Officers, 321-326
BWA Presidents, 321
BWA Relief Committee, 101, 102, 103, 105, 107, 111, 112, 113, 119, 135, 136, 142, 163, 171
BWA Secretaries (Eastern and Western), 325
BWA Staff, 326-327
BWA Vice Presidents, 321-325
BWA World Emergency Relief Committee, 102, 103
BWA Youth News, 112
Byford, Charles T., 40, 41

C

Cade, Walter, 242
Calvinism, 2
Cambodia, 283, 285
Cameroon, 43, 50, 89, 145, 283, 292
Canada, 5, 8, 13, 18, 21, 35, 38, 40, 50, 56, 61, 89, 100, 106, 110, 113, 118, 129, 140, 141, 142, 148, 150, 151, 184, 192, 194, 200, 208, 219, 259, 262, 277, 285, 290, 293, 297
Canadian Baptist Federation, 223
Canadian Baptist Overseas Mission Board, 65
Cardiff Baptist College, 37
CARE. *See Cooperative for American Remittances to Europe.*
Carey, William xvi, 2, 3, 121, 131, 268, 306, 314
Caribbean, 3, 22, 123, 170, 178, 186, 271, 285, 288, 301
Caribbean Baptist Fellowship, 170, 178, 213, 242, 268, 276, 302
Carlisle, J. C., 57
Carlson, C. Emanuel, 136, 138
Carnegie, Andrew, 42
Carro, Daniel, 252, 276, 327
Carter, Jimmy, 200, 217, 223, 226, 236, 265, 266, 309, 313
Carver, William O., 29, 90
caste system, 86
Castro, Fidel, 135, 255, 277
catholic, 34, 36, 131
Caudill, R. Paul, 105, 119, 134
Cauthen, Baker James, 130
CBF, *See Cooperative Baptist Fellowship.*
CCORR ,*See Church Committee of Overseas Relief and Reconstruction.*
Ceausescu, Nicolae, 239
Central America, 22, 267
Ceylon, *See Sri Lanka.*
Chafin, Kenneth, 145
Chang, Young Shim, 255, 324, 325
Chapman, Ian M., 258, 291, 293, 325, 327
Chapman, Joseph I., 196
Charter of Freedom, 107
Cheung, Daniel Y. K., 169, 323
Chiba, Yuguro, 59
Chiminelli, P., 150
China, 3, 22, 29, 30, 56, 59, 66, 89, 90, 116, 120, 128, 148, 170, 182, 188, 226, 238, 268, 269, 277, 284
China Christian Council, 226, 269, 277
China's Cultural Revolution, 128
China, Republic of, *See Taiwan.*
Chow, Leon, 175
Christian Century, 80, 88
Christian education, 51, 54, 56, 87, 128, 176, 290, 214
Christian Endeavor, 6
Christian World Communions (CWC), 228, 288, 311
Christianization of Society, 38
Church Committee of Overseas Relief and Reconstruction (CCORR), 101, 102
Church, F. J., 184
Church of England, 28, 54 *See also Anglican.*
Church of the Brethren, 43
Church Peace Union, 42
Church World Service, 102, 113, 162 *See also Church Committee of Overseas Relief and Reconstruction.*
Civil War, 5, 7
Claas, Gerhard, 145, 182, 189, 204, 209, 211, 212, 215, 216, 219, 220, 221, 222, 225, 226, 228, 229, 230, 231, 235, 240, 325, 326
Claas, Regina, 241, 265
Clement, A. S., 197, 324
Clifford, John 7, 12, 15, 16, 20, 21, 23, 27, 28, 31, 32, 34, 36, 38, 39, 41, 42, 43, 44, 47, 50, 56, 61, 76, 321
Cochabamba, Bolivia, 284
Coffey, David, 276, 311, 321, 325
Colgate, Samuel, 11
collectivism, 91
Colombia, 145, 170, 229, 230, 283

colonialism, 59
Commission on Cooperative Christianity, 146, 176, 179
Commission on Human Rights, 223, 224
Commission on Religious Freedom, 107
Commission to Hungary, 32
Committee on Future Congresses, 31
Committee on Unoccupied Mission Fields, 41 *See also Continental Committee.*
Committee on Young People's Work, 66, 74
Continental Committee, 32, 41, 42, 47, 48, 52, 110
Communism, 47, 56, 57, 84, 109, 141, 220, 235, 238, 240, 266, 271, 279, 291, 303, 314
communist tyranny, 69
Conference on Post-War Needs, 50
Confessing Church, 82
confessional organizations, 3, 6, 75
Confucianism, 30
Congregationalists, 30, 76
Continental Commission, 53, 62
Continental Committee, 32, 41, 42, 47, 48, 52, 110
Convention of Baptist Social Unions, 10
Conwell, Russell H., 11, 35
Cook, Henry, 108, 119, 123, 326
Cooper, Owen, 144, 170, 293, 323
Cooperative Baptist Fellowship (CBF), 286, 295, 296
Cooperative for American Remittances to Europe (CARE), 105
Costa Rica, 230
Costello, Tim, 297
Cothen, Grady, 220
Council for Religious Affairs in the Soviet Union, 179, 221
Council of the BU, 16
CRALOG, *See American Council of Relief Agencies Licensed for Operations in Germany.*
Crandall, Lathan A., 148
Crane, Edith Campbell, 40
Cranford, Clarence, 130
Crawley, Winston, 197
creedal tests, 22
creedalism, 37
creed, xv, 27, 30, 34, 37, 38, 107, 130, 183, 287, 306, 307
Crozer Theological Seminary in Pennsylvania, 26
Crumpler, Carolyn Weatherford, 230, 242, 268, 327
Cuba, 135, 171, 175, 251, 255, 264, 267, 268, 277, 281, 283, 285, 286, 291, 302
Cupit, L. A. (Tony), xvi, 222, 241, 250, 255, 262, 263, 265, 281, 282, 283,284, 290, 291, 293, 327
CWC, *See Christian World Communions.*
Cyprus, 263
Czech Republic, 74, 211, 265, 277, 291
Czechoslovakia, 49, 51, 52, 74, 89, 120, 145, 146, 187, 211, 238, 270, 311

D
Dakin, Arthur, 58, 87
Dall, J. W., 59
Dammann, Rolf, 235, 324
Danish, 23, 106, 191
Danish Baptist Union, 104, 242, 259
Dargan, E. C., 63
Datta, Dennis Dilip, 221
Davis, Patsy, 293. 327
Dawson, Joseph M., 103, 108, 109
Decade of Evangelism, 222, 262, 272
Declaration on Universal Disarmament, 131
Dehoney, Wayne, 146
Deiros, Pablo, 261
Democratic Republic of Congo, 285
Denia, Spain, 290
Denmark, 52, 104, 106, 153, 208, 213, 242, 259, 268, 301
Denny, Robert S., 112, 121, 123, 159, 163, 174, 178, 179, 181, 183, 195, 199, 203, 212, 216, 325, 326

Diamond Jubilee Congress, 189
Dickerson, J.S., 148
Diefenbaker, John G., 140
Der Wahrheitszeuge, 78
Dilday, Russell, 216
Disciples of Christ, 11, 24
Displaced Person (DP), 104, 109, 113, 135
Dixon, Amzi C., 55, 60
Dobbins, Gaines S., 136
doctrinal purity, 55
Dodge, William F., 5
Down Grade Controversy, 12, 22
DP *See Displaced Person.*
Dunn, Emmett F., 241, 268, 283, 292, 293, 327
Dunn, James M., 216

E

EA, *See Evangelical Alliance.*
Eastern Orthodox Churches, 288
Eastern Secretary, 47, 61, 62
Eaton, T. T., 15
EBF, *See European Baptist Fellowship.*
ecclesiastical axiom, 27
Ecumenical Methodist Conference, 7
Ecumenical Missionary Conference, 4
ecumenical spirit, 91, 93, 108
ecumenism, 3, 55, 70, 93, 108, 128, 164, 180
Ecumenical Session, 12
Edinburgh, 3, 12, 13, 90, 93
Education Act of 1902, 28
Edwards, Jonathan, 2
Edwards of Cardiff, Principal, 24
El Salvador, 265, 266, 285
England, *See United Kingdom.*
Episcopal, Episcopalians, 6, 30, 301
Estonia, 23, 51, 151, 221, 267, 280
Ethiopia, 89, 170, 214, 229
Europe, 2, 3, 4, 6, 9, 13, 21, 22, 23, 28, 29, 32, 33, 34, 36, 40, 41, 47, 48, 50, 51, 52, 53, 56, 61, 62, 63, 64, 66, 69, 74, 76, 77, 88, 89, 94, 95, 100, 101, 103, 104, 105, 106, 110, 111, 113, 116, 118, 119, 122, 123, 128, 135, 137, 139, 140, 144, 145, 146, 154, 155, 163, 164, 170, 174, 175, 176, 178, 179, 182, 183, 186, 187, 188, 189, 194, 204, 208, 212, 213, 216, 220, 225, 229, 230, 235, 236, 237, 2238, 239, 240, 242, 259, 260, 261, 263, 264, 265, 266, 267, 268, 271, 276, 277, 280, 287, 288, 289, 291, 301, 302, 305, 307, 312, 314
European Baptist "intelligence agency", 34-35
European Baptist Committee on Cooperation, 110
European Baptist Congress, 25, 32, 64, 110
    First European Congress, Berlin, 33
    Second European Congress, Stockholm, 41
European Baptist Fellowship (EBF), 110, 139, 140, 179, 187, 188, 213, 220, 236, 237, 239, 240, 242, 264, 265, 267, 268, 276, 277, 287, 291
European Baptist Seminary, 34, 49
European Baptist Women's Union, 111. 117. 139, 144, 189
European Baptists, 25, 32, 33, 41, 47, 48, 54, 69, 94, 110, 178, 179, 230, 237, 259
European Commissioner, 40, 53, 61, 63
Evangelical Alliance (EA), 4, 5, 12
evangelism, xvi, 3, 6, 20, 21, 27, 31, 36, 39, 42, 54, 55, 57, 59, 60, 65, 66, 69, 74, 82, 87, 91, 94, 107, 109, 110, 111, 120, 122, 123, 129, 130, 131, 143, 144, 146, 164, 171, 173, 176, 179, 180, 182, 186, 189, 190, 211, 215, 219, 220, 221, 222, 224, 229, 231, 236, 237, 249, 259, 262, 263, 264, 266, 272, 277, 278, 282, 283, 284, 289, 290, 302, 303, 308, 310, 316
Evans, Charles, 53
Evans, Milton, 26
Ewing, J. W., 34, 42

F

Falklands, 225
Fanini, Nilson do Amaral, 145, 170, 214, 254, 255, 272, 276, 282, 288, 297, 321, 323
Farmer, J. H., 148
Fascism, 47
Fetzer, B., 150
Fiddes, Paul, 288
Finland, 22, 51, 52, 283
Flügge, Carl August, 83
FMB, *See Foreign Mission Board.*
Foreign Mission Board (FMB), 7, 48, 51, 74, 104, 105, 110, 130, 138, 133, 182, 240, 264, 265
Fortress Monroe Conference, 8
Fosdick, Harry Emerson, 54
France, 2, 12, 43, 48, 52, 95, 96, 115, 263
Franklin, James H., 48, 50
Franks, Jesse D., 105
Free Churchmen, 28
Free Will Baptists, 11
Freeman, J. D., 25
Fridell, Elmer A., 106, 321, 322
Fuente, Johnnie de la, 203
Fuller, Andrew, 2, 3, 17
Fuller, Ellis A., 114
fundamentalist-modernist controversies, 55

G

Gaddy, Welton, 217
Gambia, 285
gambling, 60, 86, 87
Gambrell, James. B., 50
Garrett, Jr., James Leo, xvi, 143, 146, 179, 288
General Baptist Union, 21
General Convention of the Baptists of North America, 8, 14, 35
General Secretaries, BWA, 325
George, David, 4
German Baptist Missionary Society, 77
German Baptist Union or Union of Evangelical Free Churches, 105, 263
German Baptists, 33, 49, 52, 77, 78, 79, 82, 83, 84, 88, 89, 91, 94, 100, 104, 112, 204, 236, 239, 253, 287
German Christians, 78, 82
Germans, Germany, 2, 21, 32, 33, 36, 42, 47, 49, 50, 52, 56, 74, 77, 78, 79, 80, 81, 82, 83, 85, 86, 88, 89, 91, 94, 95, 96, 100, 103, 104, 105, 106, 111, 112, 113, 116, 119, 135, 140, 145, 150, 163, 175, 178, 181, 182, 184, 189, 204, 212, 213, 216, 217, 220, 226, 227, 235, 238, 239, 241, 242, 253, 255, 258, 260, 276, 277, 287, 301, 302
German North American Baptist Conference, 112
Gezork, Herbert, 74
Gill, Athol, 224
Gill, Sr., Everett, 51
Global Vision, 20
Glover, Richard, 29
Goatley, David Emmanuel, 255
Goebbels, Joseph, 79
Golden Jubilee Congress, 119, 122
Golden Jubilee Declaration on Religious Liberty, 120
Goldie, Archibald (Archie), 208, 229, 241, 326
Goodchild, Frank, 39
Goodwill, 42
Goodwin, R. Dean, 135, 163
Gorbachev, Mikhail, 237
Goulding, C. Ronald, 140, 145, 146, 174, 181, 182, 189, 200, 326
Graham, Billy, xi, 122, 131, 134, 140, 142, 145, 157, 170, 180, 181, 187 194, 204, 217, 238, 278, 279, 302, 309
Grantham, Thomas 1
Gray, Clifton Daggett, 61, 66, 68, 75, 77, 78, 82, 88, 90, 94, 100, 325, 326
Great Britain, *See United Kingdom.*
Great Commission, xv, 2
Greece, 62

Green, Bernard, 52, 75, 206, 225, 237, 238
Gregory, Christine, 218, 324
Gregory, Joel, 262
Grellert, Manfred, 227
Guarna, Saverio, 224
Gutiérrez, Edna Lee de, 208, 218, 324
Guyana, 181
Gwei, Solomon 145

H

Habte, Berhanu, 229
Haiti, 142, 183
Hallock, Jr., Edgar F., 128, 302
Hamburg Agreement, 265
Han, Maung Maung, 158
Hancock, Gordon B., 90
Hanno, 4
Haranti, L., 155
Harare, Zimbabwe, 214, 266, 268, 292
Harare, General Council in, 270
Harare Declaration, 266
Harding, Warren G., 53
Hargroves, V. Carney, 123, 155, 174, 175, 176, 177, 178, 181, 199, 321, 325
Harnack, Adolf, 36
Harris, Floyd, 146, 208, 293
Havana General Council, 281
Hays, Brooks, 106,141
Hayward, E. E., 58, 150
Hayworth, Elizabeth, 293
Heck, Fannie E. S., 40
Helm, Clay, 160
Helm, Harry C., 160
Helwys, Thomas, xv, 300
Henderson, J. Raymond, 90
Herzegovina, 285
Hicks, Jr., H. Beecher, 297
Hill, Edward V., 180
Hill, Samuel S., 55
Hingson, Robert, 129, 136, 160
Hino, Ayako, 181
Hinton, John Howard, 5
Hitler, Adolf, 77, 78, 79, 82, 303
HIV/AIDS, 267, 268, 275, 284, 285, 292, 304
Hobbs, Herschel H., 141, 144, 174, 175, 177, 323
Hoff, Advertus A., 200, 323
Hoffmeister, Desmond, 287
Hoglund, Gunnar, 145
Holman, Charles, 38
Hong Kong, 143, 145, 163, 169, 171, 178, 180, 182, 197, 229, 250, 277, 280, 292, 301, 302, 311
Hoover, Charlotte, 270
Hoover, Herbert, 96
Hoover, Lawrence, 270
Horak, Josip, 225, 235, 324
Howard, Randolph A., 113
Hughes, Charles Evans, 53
Hughey, John David, 146
Hull, William E., 216
Human Rights Day, 280
Hungary, 32, 33, 51, 120, 145, 155, 183, 187, 220, 235, 237, 282
Hunt, Alma, 180, 323
Huntington, Samuel P., 275
Hussein, King (Jordan), 159
Hutus, , 183, 279, 286, 314
Hyderabad, India, 256, 290

I

Igleheart, Glenn, 227, 242
IMSC, *See International Mission Secretaries Conference.*
IMS, *See International Mission Secretaries.*
indecency in the motion picture industry, 60
India, 2, 3, 21, 22, 29, 56, 59, 67, 86, 89, 93, 170, 171, 176, 178, 182, 183, 286-339
India, Council of North East, 270
Indonesia, 181
industrial relations, 56, 57
Inglis, Douglas, 209
International Baptist Theological Seminary (IBTS), 291
International Christian Writers' Conference, 264
International Congregational Council, 7
International Council of Unitarian and Other Liberal Religious Thinkers and Workers, 7
International Court of Justice, 92
International Mission Secretaries Conference (IMSC), 178, 188 *See also International Mission Secretaries.*
International Mission Secretaries (IMS) *formerly IMSC,* 220, 221
International Missionary Council, 93
International Religious Liberty Association, 279
International Youth Leadership Training Conference, 268
Iraq, 275, 285
Ireland, 2, 9, 16, 22
Isbell, Jr., W. J. (Doc), 242, 327
Islam, 41, 220, 221, 222
Israeli-Arab War, 128
Istanbul, 289
Italy, 52, 89, 111, 150, 228

J

Jackson, Joseph H., 123, 142, 158, 323
Jackson, William Dodds, 130
Jakarta, 283
Jamaica, 4, 13, 141, 184, 213, 208, 230, 242, 244, 262, 302
Jamaican Baptists, 4
James, Isabel (Mrs. Russell), 40, 57
James, Minnie Kennedy (Mrs. W. B.), 57
James, Paul S., 161
Japan, Japanese, 22, 23, 29, 56, 59, 90, 100, 138, 144, 150, 163, 169, 170, 171,180, 229, 282, 301, 303
Japan Baptist Convention, 138, 163
Jarvis, W. L., 114, 322
Jayapura, 283
Jews, Jewish, 78, 79, 82, 86, 88, 107, 109
Johnson, C. Oscar, 91, 110, 111, 114, 120, 142, 154, 211, 321
Johnson, Emmett, 254, 324
Johnson, Lyndon B., 141
Johnson, Thomas A., 17, 19
Jones, J. Ithel, 142
Jones, Jr., John R., 242
Jordan, 159, 215, 222, 283, 302

K

Kalil, Eudora Mary, 265, 266, 324
Kangpopki Mission, 286
Karlsson, Birgit, 217, 218, 324
Kawtholei Baptist Bible School, 281
Keidann, Daltro, 189
Kenya, 181, 200, 205, 206, 207, 215, 252, 288, 302
Kelsey, George D., 130
Kerry, Marie C., 40
Kerstan, Reinhold J., 212, 213, 227, 241, 326
Kiev, Ukraine, 179, 290
Kilgore, Jr., Thomas, 181

Kim, Billy Jang Hwan, 217, 254, 255, 276, 277, 278, 283, 287, 294, 295, 297, 321, 324
King, Bernice, 271
King, Coretta Scott, 252, 279
King, Jr., Martin Luther, 131, 139, 140, 142, 146, 271, 309, 313
King, Sr., Martin Luther, 131
Kinyanjui, Arthur, 200, 323
Kirchenkampf (Church Struggle), 82
Klaupiks, Adolf, 112, 113, 135, 136, 146, 160, 163, 171, 327
Knott, Harold, 20, 148
Korea, 114, 116, 119, 170, 217, 221, 229, 243, 255, 261, 262, 269, 276, 277, 278, 281, 282, 285, 297, 301, 302
Kozynko, Alexander, 258, 291
Kralice Bible, 187
Kretzschmar, Louise, 255
Kukis, 279, 286

L

Laczkovski, Janos, 235
Lall, Joel W., 67, 322
Lambeth Appeal, 54
Landmarkism, 13, 14, 22
      Landmark, 14, 16, 171
      Landmark belief, 14
      Landmarkers, Southern, 11
Landrum, William Warren, 13, 15, 17
Latin America, 40, 137, 139, 145, 164, 178, 194, 201, 207, 208, 214, 225, 227
Latin American Baptist Convention, 74
Latin American Baptist Youth Conference, 145
Latourette, Kenneth Scott, xiii, 140
Latvia, 51, 56, 64, 113, 135, 221
Lausanne Conference of the Faith and Order Group, 63
Lavanya, Leena, 257, 292
Lawoyin, S. A., 130
Laws, Curtis Lee, 60
Laws, Gilbert, 120
Lawson, William A., 139
LeQuesne, Charles T., 94
League of Nations, 50, 52, 85, 89, 92
Leavell, Frank H. Leavell, 112, 150
Lebanon, 139, 159, 229, 277, 280, 283
Lehmann, Gottfried Wilhelm, 33
Lehmann, Johann G., 33, 321
Leicester, 12, 21
Leon, Othelo D. de, 145
Leonard, Bill Leonard, 9
Lewis, J. Lee, 150
Lewis, Walter O., 51, 93, 94, 95, 96, 100, 102, 103, 104, 105, 106, 110, 113, 117, 118, 123, 154, 325, 326
liberalism, 55, 91, 122
Liberia, 136, 143, 146, 169, 170, 175, 183, 200, 241, 249, 255, 266, 268, 283, 301, 313
Libert, Samuel, 206
liberty of conscience, 41, 92, 228
Liele, George, 4
Litvinov, Maxim, 75
Lloyd George, David, 21, 28, 48, 57, 64
Logan, J. Moffat, 36, 37
London, 1, 2, 3, 4, 6, 7, 12, 15, 16, 20, 21, 22, 25, 28, 29, 32, 34, 35, 37, 38, 41, 47, 48, 50, 51, 53, 55, 57, 58, 59, 60, 61, 62, 63, 64, 65, 67, 68, 75, 76, 91, 94, 95, 100, 103, 105, 110, 114, 115, 117, 118, 119, 120, 121, 122, 123, 129, 130, 140, 146, 147, 148, 211, 216, 301
London Baptists, 21, 22
London Conference 1920, 48, 51, 53
Lorenzen, Thorwald, 216, 224, 281, 282
Lopez, Edwin I., 203, 208, 213, 242, 276, 281 327
Lord, Townley, 50, 89, 114, 115, 117, 118, 119, 120, 121, 122, 155, 321, 322
Lorenz, Wolfgang, 224
Lott Carey Baptist Foreign Mission Convention, 22, 184, 255

Lotz, Anne Graham, 297
Lotz, Denton, xiii, xvi, 177, 180, 207, 212, 215, 219, 221, 222, 225, 239, 240-242, 244, 249, 252, 255, 258, 259, 260, 262, 264, 265, 268, 269, 270, 279, 280-283, 287, 288, 293-296, 298, 300, 325, 326
Love, J. Franklin, 48, 50
Luckey, Hans, 91, 322
Lundquist, Carl H., 145
Luther, Hans, 78
Lutheran World Federation, 188, 227, 211
Lutherans, 30, 56, 106, 216, 228, 259, 288, 301, 313

M

MacArthur, Robert Stuart, 35, 41, 47, 50, 56, 321
MacClaren, Elizabeth Hayworth, 242, 293, 327
Mackey, Tomas, 207
Maclaren, Alexander, 12, 13, 16, 20, 21, 24, 38
MacNeill, John, 66, 67, 69, 74, 75, 81
MacLeish, Martha Hilliard (Mrs. Andrew), 37
MacRae, Andrew D., 219, 259, 260
Madagascar, South Africa, 285
Magnuson, Warren R., 184, 324
Malawi, 178, 181, 284
Malik, Charles, 139
Managua, Nicaragua, 290
Manchuria, 90
Manifesto on Religious Freedom, 107, 111
Manipur, India, 281, 286
Manipur Theological College, 286
Maring, Norman H., 179
Marnham, Herbert, 41, 61, 94, 326
Marshall, J. T., 26
Marshall, Newton H., 32, 33, 35, 40, 42
Martin, Olive Brinson (Mrs. George R.), 118
Masaryk, Thomas G., 49
Mathangani, Samson S. K., 207, 215, 252, 327
Mathews, Shailer, 11, 39
Matsamura, Shuichi, 163, 195, 323
Matthews, Albert, 61, 94, 326
Maxey Jarman Foundation, 129
Mays, Benjamin A., 114
McCall, Duke K., 134, 174, 175, 176, 190, 194, 203, 211, 213, 214, 217, 221, 225, 229, 230, 311, 321
McCrimmon, A. L., 8
McDormand, T. B., 184, 323
McGowan, F. B., 28
McIntyre, J. Ralph, 221, 241, 327
McKechnie, N.S., 150
McKenzie, Azariah, 184, 208, 213, 242, 323, 327
McLaurin, J. B., 81
McMaster University, 65, 66, 67, 142, 241
McNeil, Pearl L., 216
Mead, Silas, 12
Meeser, S. B., 148
Mennonites, xv, 2, 23, 24, 146, 228, 288
Mennonite Central Committee, 264
Mennonite World Conference, 227, 311
Methodists, 7, 30, 301
Mexico, 88, 139, 178, 208, 213, 218, 230, 279, 281
Mexico City, Mexico, 100, 144, 178
Meyer, F. B., 40
Meyer, Heinrich, 32
Miao, C. S., 59
Micah Challenge, 285
Midteide, Per, 224
Miller, Samuel H., 142
Milne, Bruce, 297, 325

Missena, José, 208, 214, 242, 327
Mission in Action groups, 297
missions, xvi, 2, 5, 6, 9, 14, 22, 29, 30, 40, 41, 47, 59, 60, 66, 68, 81, 85, 89, 91, 107, 116, 129, 131, 136, 138, 143, 146, 171, 172, 175, 176, 181, 221, 219, 282, 294, 306
Moehlman, Conrad Henry, 80
Monro, Harry, 254
Monrovia, Liberia, 146, 283
Montacute, Paul, 209, 219, 241, 242, 284, 293, 327
Montgomery, Helen Barrett, 57-58
moral axiom, 27
moral laxity, 56
morality, 77, 142, 183, 223, 315
Morehouse, H. L., 148
Morikawa, Audrey, 293
Morikawa, Jitsuo, 130
Morris, E. C., 21, 40, 60, 148
Moscow Theological Seminary, 266, 291
Mozambique, 181, 284
Mpanzu, Nlandu, 181
Mueller, William A., 91
Mukumbo, Edwin, 162
Müller, Reich Bishop Ludwig, 82, 83, 88
Mullins, Edgar Young, 26, 27, 28, 50, 60, 61, 63, 64, 65, 321
Myanmar (formerly Burma), 66, 89, 130, 150, 158, 171, 189, 213, 221, 230, 245, 257, 265, 281, 283, 285, 288, 304

N

NABC, *See North American Baptist Conference.*
NABF, *See North American Baptist Fellowship.*
Nagas, 279, 280, 286
Nallinger, Otto, 112
Nanjing Seminary, 269
National Baptist Convention, 10, 21, 40, 59, 65, 90, 103, 117, 123, 137, 142, 146, 147, 148, 158, 242
National Committee on Food for the Small Democracies, 96
National Socialist German Workers Party, 77
Nazi, 77, 78, 79, 80, 82, 83, 84, 85, 86, 88, 89, 91, 100, 106, 116, 236, 259, 303
National Training School for Women and Girls, 40
NBC, *See Northern Baptist Convention.*
Near East Relief, 62
Nelson, Ron, 142
Nepal, 230, 258, 263, 282, 283, 285, 307
Netherlands, 2, 52, 140, 146, 300
new "modernist" theology, 22
New York, 3, 4, 5, 9, 10, 35, 39, 41, 54, 75, 77, 79, 90, 95, 96, 101, 102, 114, 122, 260, 275, 280
New Zealand, 5, 6, 12, 22, 40, 60, 75, 83, 120, 137, 145, 178, 227, 297
Newman, Albert H., 33
Newton, Louie D., 91, 94, 95, 100, 106, 322, 326
NGO, *See nongovernmental organization.*
Nicaragua, 230
Niemöller, Martin, 82
Nikolaev, Sergei, 261
nongovernmental organization (NGO), 179, 223, 265, 304
Nordenhaug, Josef, 120, 132, 135, 136, 137, 138, 140, 141, 145, 146, 158, 163, 174, 325
Nordstrom, N. J., 90, 322
Norquist, Kenneth, 112
North America, 1, 3, 4, 5, 6, 8, 14, 22, 35, 53, 56, 59, 62, 63, 66, 69, 75, 96, 128, 132, 144, 146, 163, 164, 170, 175, 177, 178, 190, 194, 212, 214, 217, 224, 225, 264, 270, 271, 276, 286, 287, 288, 291, 294, 301, 305, 307, 312
North American Baptist Conference (NABC), 103, 113, 136, 213
North American Baptist Fellowship (NABF), 140, 145, 163, 174, 175, 176, 178, 189, 215, 242, 268, 302
North American Baptist Women's Union, 144
North Atlantic Treaty Organization (NATO), 116
North, J. J. (John James), 60
Northamptonshire Association, 2
Northern Baptist Convention (NBC), 9, 11, 35, 57, 68, 136, 163, 174
Norway, 52, 116, 132, 133, 136, 150, 209

Norwegian Baptist Theological Seminary, 105
Norwegian Sunday School Union, 116
Nova Scotia, 4, 177, 288

O

Obasanjo, Olusegun 313
Oddestad, Erling, 181
Officers, BWA, 321-325
Oh, Kwan Suk, 261
Ohm, Sven, 197, 221
Ohrn, Arnold T., 105, 110, 116, 117, 119, 123, 129, 130, 132, 135, 148, 150, 325
Okwakol, Michael, 255
Olaniyan, Samson, 293
Olmedo, Alfonso, 130, 161, 323
Oncken, Johann Gerhard, 33, 80, 83, 220
Operation Brother's Keeper, 129

P

Pakistan, 115, 170, 280
Palestine, 86, 89
Palme, Olof, 180
Pan American Union of Baptist Men, 171
pan-Anglican Conference, 6, *See also confessional organizations.*
Pan-Baptist Conference, 13, 15, 16, 25
Pan-Baptist Council, 13
Papua New Guinea, 158, 241, 244, 264, 297
Paraguay, 208, 242
Parajon, Gustavo, 136, 325
Parrish, C. H., 59, 68
Passive Resistance Movement (PRM), 28, 32
Patnaik, Theo, 178, 182, 326
Patterson, W. Morgan, 100, 179
Pavlov, Gospodin, 23
Paw, Louise, 130, 158, 323
Payne, Ernest A., 81, 91, 118, 130, 137, 155, 163, 323
Peabody, Lucy (Mrs. Norman Mather Waterbury), 21, 58
Peace and Reconciliation Commission, 277
Peck, George W., 216
Peck, Tony, 277, 327
Pennington, Doyle, 242, 293, 327
Pentateuch, 26
Pentecostal, 23, 24, 36, 312
Pereira, Jose da Reis, 184, 324
Peru, 170, 283
Peterson, John O., 266, 324
Philippines, 139, 145, 217, 203, 208, 230, 242, 276, 283, 297
Phillips, Harold Cooke, 106
Phillips, Thomas, 37, 38
Piasecki, Adam, 226
Pierard, Richard V., 100, 235, 300
Pierce, Willene, 293, 327
Pinder, Peter, 276, 327
Pitt, Robert Healy, 13, 14, 15, 16, 17, 41, 47, 61, 325
Pitt-Landrum vision, 15
Plymouth Brethren, 23
Poland, 2, 23, 51, 52, 53, 95, 111, 120, 145, 180, 187, 188, 220, 226, 229, 237, 264
Polish Baptists, 51, 237
Pope John Paul II, 228
Porter, Henry Kirke, 31, 326
Portugal, 52, 96, 135
Poteat, Edwin McNeill, 114
Potter, Philip, 180
Preachers' Institute, 32

Presbyterian alliance, 13
Presbyterians, 30, 301
Presidents, BWA, 321
Prestridge, John Newton, 15, 16, 17, 25, 31, 41, 148, 325
Principles of Comity, 8
Prior, Alan C., 141, 157, 182, 323, 326
PRM, *See Passive Resistance Movement*
Proctor, Samuel D., 145
Progressive National Baptist Convention, Inc., 262
Prokopchuk, Alberto, 276, 327
pro-Nazi "German Christians", 78, 82
Protestant, 2, 9, 25, 26, 29, 30, 49, 77, 79, 82, 84, 88, 89, 102, 105, 117, 130, 137, 180, 238, 279, 306
Pruden, Edward H., 106
Puerto Rico, 203, 213

Q
Quarterly Bulletin, 63
Queen Elizabeth II, 119

R
race relations, racism, 47, 56, 66, 70, 109, 120, 130, 169, 217, 223, 265, 266, 271, 278, 279, 304, 309, 314
radicalism, 57
Radstock, Third Baron, 23
Rae, Terry, 287, 325
Rao, Mercy Jeyaraja, 261, 293, 324
Rauschenbusch, Walter, 9, 11, 39, 57
Raws, John G., 27
Ray, T. Bronson, 74
Reagan, Ronald, 236
Redlich, Erna, 213, 215, 327
Reencontro, 276
Reeves, Marjorie, 106
Reformed churches, 7, 155, 188, 227, 288, 311
Reich Church, 83, 91
Reichert, Lutz, 255
Reichskirche, 77, 79, 82, 83
Reichsbischof, 82, 83
Reichstag, 83
Reiling, Jannes, 146
religious freedom, xv, 12, 20, 23, 47, 60, 64, 65, 95, 104, 107, 108, 111, 117, 120, 138, 156, 179, 183, 222, 237, 260, 263, 271, 278, 279, 280, 303, 304, 305, 309, 311, 313, 316
Religious Herald, 4, 13, 14, 16, 18
religious liberty, xv, xvi, 1, 5, 20, 34, 40, 49, 52, 54, 56, 60, 63, 64, 69, 75, 81, 91, 92, 95, 103, 104, 109, 110, 111, 114, 115, 123, 129, 131, 132, 133, 138, 143, 164, 173, 176, 179, 183, 187, 190, 217, 263, 265, 281, 289, 316
religious persecution, 9, 52, 75, 117, 138
Resu, Bonny, 250, 276, 283, 327
Review and Expositor, 17
Reynolds, William Jensen, 128
Rhodesia, *See Zimbabwe.*
Richard, Timothy, 30, 148
Richardson, H. F., 148
Rippon, John, 1, 2, 16, 24
Rivas, Rosalio Ramirez, 256
Roberts, J. E., 38, 60
Robertson, A. T., 15, 17, 19, 26, 148
Robinson, Henry Wheeler, 90
Rockford Seminary, 37
Rockschies, Friedrich, 91
Roman Catholic, 9, 28, 40, 105, 117, 134, 137, 164, 171, 179, 180, 188, 216, 227, 228, 277, 288, 298, 303, 311, 312, 313
Romania, 23, 49, 51, 52, 53, 65, 67, 69, 75, 89, 93, 95, 111, 120, 145, 183, 188, 213, 238, 239, 267, 280, 303
Romanian Baptists, 49, 65, 129
Romanian Orthodox Church, 49, 93

Roosevelt, Franklin D., 75, 76, 91
Rowland, A. J., 11
Rudén, Erik, 123, 140, 184, 326
Rudén, Kerstin (Mrs. Erik), 216, 218
Rushbrooke, 17, 26, 32, 48, 49, 50, 52, 53, 54, 55, 61, 62, 63, 64, 65, 66, 69, 74, 75, 76, 77, 78, 79, 80, 82, 83, 84, 87, 88, 89, 93-96, 100, 101, 102, 103-106, 108, 153, 211, 303, 321, 325, 327
Russell, Davis Syne, 170, 175, 184, 220, 224, 225
Russia (Soviet Union), 2, 12, 23, 33, 35, 36, 40, 43, 47, 48, 49, 51, 53, 56, 62, 69, 74, 75, 76, 80, 81, 90, 118, 120, 123, 149, 150, 188, 220, 224, 226, 237, 263, 264, 267, 280, 283, 285, 291, 303
Russian Baptist Union, 291
Russian Baptists, 23, 43, 67, 89, 120, 123, 129, 220, 258
Russian Empire, 23, 35
Russian Stundists, 12, 23
Russian-Ukranian Baptists, 258
Russian-Ukranian Evangelical Baptist Union, U.S.A., 292
Russian union, 33, 80
Rust, E. C., 106
Rutenber, Culbert G., 143
Ruthenia, 51
Rwanda, 142, 183, 230, 242, 266, 267, 276, 279, 280, 284, 285, 286, 314
Ryan, Wendy, 241, 255, 264, 283, 289, 292, 293, 327

S

Sabbath desecration, 60
Sadler, George W., 101
Saillens, Reuben, 12, 321
Saito, S., 150
Sam-Peel, Emile D. E., 249, 255
SBC, *See Southern Baptist Convention.*
SBC Brotherhood Commission, 144
SBC Foreign Mission Board, 48, 51, 74, 138
SBC Sunday School Board, 54, 63
SBC Woman's Missionary Union, 40, 218, 242, 296
Scarborough, Lee R., 60, 322
Schaff, Philip, 5
Schatz, Fred C., 113
Schmidt, Paul, 78, 84, 91
Schröder, Eberhard, 106
Schroeder, George W., 144
Scialabba, Raoul, 207, 325
Scotland, 2, 22, 40, 78, 209, 210, 219, 241, 293
Second Vatican Council, 128, 137, 138, 141, 171
Secretaries, BWA Eastern and Western, 325
Secretaries, BWA General, 325
Senior, W. C., 148
Shakespeare, Geoffrey, 48
Shakespeare, John Howard, 16, 17, 20, 21, 24, 25, 30, 31, 32, 33, 35, 36, 41, 42, 47, 50, 53, 54, 55, 56, 58, 61, 63, 148
Sharpe, Dores R., 106, 115
Shepherd, Peter, 54
Sherouse, Craig, 7, 10, 14, 92, 99
Shields, T. T., 65
Shurden, Walter, xv
Siberia, 23, 138
Simoleit, Friedrich Wilhelm, 52, 77, 78, 79, 322
Simpson, John, 255
Singapore, 178, 181, 209, 214, 222, 264, 302
Sipprell, E. M., 41, 61, 326
Six-Day Israeli-Arab War, 128
Skoglund, John E, 136
Slavery, Slave, Slaves, 3, 4, 5, 7, 17, 41, 57, 59, 100
Slovakia, 263
Slovenia, 285
Smith, Betty Lee, 189, 212, 327
Smyth, John, xv, 300

Socialism, Christian, 57
Social issues, 9, 10, 27, 28, 55, 57, 60, 69
Söderblom, Archbishop Nathan, 56
Somalia, 266
Soren, João Filson, 121, 132, 134, 140, 141, 157, 170, 321
Sorenson, Joel, 111, 112, 121, 327
soul liberty, 23, 24, 305
South Africa, 5, 12, 13, 22, 59, 75, 83, 144, 213, 223, 264, 265, 268, 277, 280, 283, 284, 285, 286, 287, 302, 303, 312, 313
South African Baptist Alliance, 287, 313
South America, 56, 77, 118, 146, 172, 212, 214, 272
Southeast Asian Baptist Women's Union, 139
Southern Baptist Convention (SBC), 8, 14, 15, 16, 40, 48, 50, 51, 54, 61, 63, 65, 72, 74, 140, 141, 146, 179, 184, 194, 223, 242, 264, 295-296
Southern Baptist Education Commission, 14
Southern Baptist Foreign Mission Board (FMB), *See Foreign Mission Board.*
Southern Baptist Home Mission Board, 8
Southern Baptist Seminary, 17, 29, 90
Southern Baptist Theological Seminary, 14, 15, 26, 61, 94, 111, 114, 132, 134, 174, 194
Southwestern Baptist Theological Seminary, 60, 217, 276
Soviet Union, 69, 75, 93, 104, 118, 128, 131, 138, 145, 146, 155, 161, 175, 178, 179, 182, 183, 187, 203, 213, 217, 220, 221, 224, 225, 226, 235, 236, 237, 238, 261, 270, 291, 313, *See also Russia.*
Spain, 52, 89, 96, 111, 171, 183, 277, 290, 291, 302
Sparrowk, Cora, 216, 228, 324
Special Commission of Baptists Against Racism and Ethnic Conflict, 266
Speer, Robert E., 91
Spurgeon, Charles H., 23, 55, 77, 80
Spurr, Mrs. F. C., 58
Sri Lanka, 130, 229, 280, 283
St. Amant, C. Penrose, 143, 180
Staff, BWA, 326-327
Stalin, 69
Stalinist, 80, 239, 291
The Standard, 68
Stanley, Ken, 254
Stassen, Harold E., 142, 161, 175
Stephens, E. W., 8, 148
stewardship, 60, 194, 302
Stewart, Bathsheba, 255
Stockholm, 14, 41, 48, 52, 53, 54, 56, 62, 63, 65, 66, 69, 111, 112, 150, 178, 180, 181, 183, 184, 185, 198, 236
Stockholm Statement, 63
Strong, Augustus H., 8, 24, 26, 37, 321
Strong, Josiah, 5
Stuber, Stanley I., 107
Student Volunteer Movement for Foreign Missions, 6
Study Commissions, xv, 84, 176, 186, 304
  Commission One, 84
  Commission Two, 85
  Commissions Three and Four, 86
  Commission Five, 87
  Commission Six, 217
Sudan, 230, 285
Sullivan, James L., 184, 323
Summer Institute of Theological Education, 264
Sunday School, 24, 28, 40, 54, 57, 59, 63, 114, 117, 120, 237, 315
Sunday School Board, 112, 174, 221
Sutcliff, John, 2
Sutton, Beverly, 207
Sweden, 33, 41, 50, 51, 52, 54, 56, 180, 181, 183, 184
Swedish Baptists, 41, 51, 80, 290
Swedish Baptist Young People's Union, 111
Swiss Baptists, 78
Switzerland, 2, 48, 52, 96, 110, 132, 133, 139, 144, 145, 178, 180, 213, 216, 291
Swoboda, Jörg, 238, 239
Szorbo´, Dr., 155

T

TAG, *See Theological Assistance Group.*
Taiwan (Republic of China), 175, 176, 229
Tanzania, 181, 217, 284
Taoism, 30
Taylor, Bob, 206
Taylor, Burchell, 262
Taylor, Gardner, 114, 142
Taylor, Harry L., 105
Teague, Ellen, 293, 327
temperance, 14, 28, 41, 60, 77, 86
Thailand, 169, 229, 230, 263, 281, 282, 286, 293
Than, U Kyaw, 169
Thaut, Rudolf, 146, 323
The Standard, 68
Theological Assistance Group (TAG), 264
theological axiom, 27
theological liberalism, 55
Thomas, John, 26
Thompson, R. J., 227
Tiller, Carl W., 173. 178, 189, 197, 223, 224, 227, 242, 265, 280, 326
Timoshenko, M.D., 150
Tinsley, C. J., 106, 321, 322
Together, 118, 267
Togo, 170, 283
Tolbert, Jr., William R., 142, 143, 145, 147, 169, 175, 313, 321, 323
Torbet, Robert G., 55, 60
Toronto, Toronto congresses, 16, 17, 25, 61, 62, 64, 65, 67, 69, 72, 74, 94, 121, 151, 178, 188, 189, 194, 200, 201, 202, 212, 222, 223, 224
totalitarianism, 91
Totten, June, 216, 327
Tournier, Paul, 145
Triennial Convention, 5, 7, 140
Truett, George W., 8, 50, 65, 67, 74, 81, 82, 87, 88, 89, 90, 91, 321
Truman, Harry S., 106, 114
Tura, 263, 282
Turkey, 62
Tutsis, 183, 279, 286, 314
Tutu, Archbishop Desmond, 277
Twenty-First (21st) Century Fund, 270
Tyrtova, Claudia, 120, 155

U

UBLA, *See Union of Baptists in Latin America.*
Uixkiull, Baron Waldemar, 23, 148, 321
Ukraine, 51, 52, 225, 264, 282, 283, 290, 291, 303, 313
U.N. Charter on Human Rights, 104
Underwood, Joseph B., 172, 182
Union of Baptists in Latin America (UBLA), 214, 242, 256, 268, 276, 302
Union of Evangelical Free Churches, 105 *See also German Baptist Union.*
United Bible Societies, 221
United Kingdom (U.K.), 1, 2, 4, 5, 12, 13, 15, 21, 22, 25, 26, 28, 32, 33, 35, 36, 40, 42, 47, 48, 53, 54, 55, 58, 60, 61, 67, 71, 94, 95, 97, 106, 118, 131, 143, 148, 150, 155, 178, 181, 188, 197, 225, 276, 277
United Nations (U.N.), 102, 103, 104, 107, 108, 109, 117, 131, 133, 139, 142, 170, 173, 178, 179, 183, 188, 217, 222, 223, 224, 242, 266, 275, 280, 285, 304, 317
United Nations Relief and Rehabilitation Administration (UNRRA), 102
United States (U.S.), 4, 5, 8, 9, 11, 12, 13, 15, 16, 21, 22, 23, 24, 26, 31, 35, 47, 50, 51, 53, 55, 59, 65, 75, 77, 79, 89, 91, 94, 95, 96, 100, 102, 103, 105, 106, 110, 112, 113, 116, 118, 119, 123, 128, 129, 131, 133, 134, 135, 136, 137, 138, 139, 141, 142, 143, 146, 149, 163, 164, 170, 171, 179, 184, 187, 196, 206, 214, 217, 218, 223, 224, 226, 236, 237, 241, 252, 258, 260, 262, 265, 266, 267, 270, 279, 280, 285, 286, 291, 292, 293, 297, 313
unity, 1, 2, 4, 7, 9, 11, 20, 33, 34, 35, 38, 43, 47, 51, 54, 60, 90, 92, 93, 109, 120, 130, 138, 141, 145, 174, 176, 178, 182, 187, 225, 240, 266, 278, 285, 286, 287, 289, 295, 296, 297, 300, 310, 311, 313
Union of Baptists in Latin America, 283
UNRRA, *See United Nations Relief and Rehabilitation Administration.*

Uppsala Cathedral, 56
Uruguay, 74
Uzbekistan, 279

V
Van Ness, I. J., 54, 59
Venezuela, 283, 293
Vice Presidents, BWA, 321-325
Vietnam War, 128, 146, 223
Vins, Georgi P., 187, 224, 225, 226
Vision 2000, 222
von Berge, Hermann, 81
von Hindenburg, Paul, 80, 82, 83
von Zinzendorf, Count Nicholas, 3
Vose, G. Noel, 215, 216, 217, 218, 219, 223, 227, 228, 230, 254, 259, 261, 262, 321
Vose, Heather, 223

W
Wagner, Günter, 227
Wales, 2, 22
Walesa, Lech, 237
Walter, Karl Heinz, 183, 242, 276, 280, 291, 327
Warlpiri people, 297
Waruta, Douglas W., 217, 229, 325
Washington, Booker T. Washington, 40
Washington, D.C., 40, 75, 77, 78, 91, 96, 100, 103, 104, 110, 113, 114, 121, 123, 130, 135, 138, 144, 184, 186, 189, 211, 212, 219, 269, 301
Watchman-Examiner, 17
Waterbury, Mrs. Norman Mather, *See Lucy Peabody.*
Watson, Ruth, 280
Wayland, Francis, 4
WCC, *See World Council of Churches.*
WCC Ecumenical Refugee Division, 113
Weatherford, Carolyn, *See Carolyn Crumpler.*
Weber, Dorothea, 32
Weiss, Daniel E., 222
Welsh Revival, 24
Western Recorder, 15
Westin, Per Gunnar, 106, 150, 322
White, George, 28, 321
White, James Asa, 58, 150
Whitley, William T., 16, 20, 50, 63, 65, 67, 68, 148
Whitsitt, William H., 14, 15, 61
Whitsitt controversy, 14, 61
Wickramasinghe, Willie, 130
Wilkes, John, 215, 241, 327
Willard, Conrad R., 141
Williams, Charles, 12
Williams, J. D., 197
Williams, John W., 146, 169, 174, 323
Williams, Lacey Kirk, 65, 68, 90, 322
Willebrands, Monsignor J. G. M., 137
Willis, Judge William, 23, 28
Wills, Charles F., 189, 212, 326
Wilson, E. Arlington, 60
Wilson, M. L., 184, 323
Woman's American Baptist Foreign Mission Society, 7
Woman's American Baptist Home Mission Society, 7
Woman's Baptist Foreign Missionary Society, 22
Woman's Baptist Foreign Missionary Society of the East, 22
Woman's Baptist Foreign Missionary Society of the West, 37
Woman's Home Missionary Society from the United States, 22
Woman's Missionary Union, 40, 57, 180, 218, 242, 296

Women's Auxiliary of the National Baptist Convention, 2, 1171
Women's Committee, 40, 58, 66, 94, 117, 118
Wong, David Yue Kwong, 171, 181, 182, 184, 197, 321
Wood, Jr., James E., 224, 281
World Alliance for Promoting International Friendship through the Churches, 42, 53
World Alliance of Reformed Churches, 188, 227, 311
World Baptist Young People's Committee, 59
World Baptist Young People's Union, 59, 66, 150
World Conference of Baptist Men, 178, 206, 219
World Council of Churches (WCC), 93, 108, 113, 115, 137, 146, 163, 180
World Emergency Relief Committee, 102, 103
World Evangelical Alliance, 5
World Evangelization Strategy Work Group, 220
World Methodist Council, 7
world peace, 40, 56, 87, 123, 129, 131, 133, 142, 143, 146, 164, 172, 173, 222, 224, 236
World Praise, 269
World War I (Great War), 40, 41, 43, 66, 67, 87, 101, 104, 115, 229
World War II, 68, 74, 76, 94, 95, 100, 111, 134, 135, 147, 179, 218, 236, 259, 277, 301
Woyke, Frank H., 136, 163, 174, 178, 196, 326
Wümpelmann, Knud, 179, 204, 208, 213, 235, 242, 254, 259, 265, 266, 269, 321, 327

Y

Yeahgar, S. Augustine, 249
Young Men's Christian Association, 6
Young Women's Christian Association, 6
Younger, George, 242, 280
youth, 58, 66, 74, 81, 82, 85, 89, 91, 107, 108, 111, 112, 116, 117, 121, 122, 128, 129, 131, 132, 139, 143, 145, 150, 159, 164, 170, 171, 173, 174, 178, 182, 183, 185, 189, 206, 207, 209, 210, 211, 215, 216, 219, 225, 237, 238, 240, 241, 261, 267, 268, 272, 278, 283, 292, 293, 311, 315
Yugoslavia, xiv, 51, 52, 144, 145, 180, 215, 222, 225, 235, 239, 264, 270, 284, 302, 314

Z

Zaire, 181, 213
Zambia, 162, 284, 285
Zhao, Han Wen, 226
Zhidkov, Michael, 161, 203, 235, 323
Zhidkov, Yakov I., 120, 131, 155, 161, 235, 323
Ziherambere, Eleazar, 242, 267, 276, 327
Zimbabwe *(formerly Rhodesia)*, 181, 214, 266, 268, 284, 286, 292, 302